Trends and Applications of Conversational AI and Voice-Enabled Technologies

Yash Chawla
Wroclaw University of Science and Technology, Poland

Shubham Mahajan
Amity University, Gurugram, India

Akshat Agrawal
https://orcid.org/0000-0002-6096-9134
Computer Science & Engineering, Institute of Engineering & Technology, JK Lakshmipat University, Jaipur, India

IGI Global
Scientific Publishing
Publishing Tomorrow's Research Today

Vice President of Editorial Melissa Wagner
Director of Acquisitions Mikaela Felty
Director of Book Development Jocelynn Hessler
Production Manager Mike Brehm
Cover Design Jose Rosado

Published in the United States of America by
IGI Global Scientific Publishing
701 East Chocolate Avenue
Hershey, PA, 17033, USA
Tel: 717-533-8845 | Fax: 717-533-7115
Website: https://www.igi-global.com E-mail: cust@igi-global.com

Library of Congress Cataloging-in-Publication Data

LCCN: 2025015972 (CIP Data Pending)
ISBN13: 9798337333618
Isbn13Softcover: 9798337333625
EISBN13: 9798337333632
British Cataloguing in Publication Data
A Cataloguing in Publication record for this book is available from the British Library.

Table of Contents

Detailed Table of Contents

The most important element in artificial intelligence is Natural Language Processing (NLP) which equips the machines with the ability to understand, interpret, and generate human language. The chapter summarizes the latest developments catalyzed by deep learning or transformer-based models such as BERT, GPT, and T5 which have made huge strides in machine translation and sentiment analysis. Besides these achievements, issues still exist in managing linguistic vagueness, context semantic and semantic diversity. The chapter presents the linguistic underpinnings of NLP including the phonetics, syntax, semantics and discourse, and their correlation with Natural Language Understanding (NLU) and Natural Language Generation (NLG). It also shows new trends such as multimodal model that integrates vision and language, conversational artificial intelligence, and ethical issues of the use of language technologies. The chapter ends with an argument about the multidisciplinary collaboration that is required to promote innovation and make this relatively new field develop in a responsible way.

Conversational AI has advanced rapidly, yet remains exclusionary for low-resource languages. This chapter explores the development of multilingual voice-enabled agents for underrepresented Indian languages such as Bhojpuri, Santali, Bodo, and Meitei. It addresses core challenges—limited annotated data, dialectal diversity, and non-standardized scripts—and leverages transfer learning, cross-lingual embeddings, and data augmentation for scalable deployment. The chapter evaluates the role of voice AI in rural governance, healthcare, education, and agriculture. Case studies and stakeholder insights reveal issues of trust, gender bias in synthetic voices, and usability across literacy levels. Emphasizing language equity and ethical design, the chapter proposes a framework for inclusive voice interfaces and offers policy recommendations to support voice-first digital ecosystems in linguistically diverse, underserved communities.

This chapter offers a theoretical examination of ethical relationships among firms, customers, and AI chatbots and uncovers the new ethical challenges in this triadic relationship. As AI chatbots become more involved in customer services and online communication, current literature on their ethical dimensions is fragmented. This chapter synthesizes theories based on different disciplines, i.e., business, communication studies, psychology, and information systems, to present a holistic overview of the ethical dynamics involved. The chapter settles some of the prominent theories with which the designing and deployment of AI chatbots can be regulated. By mapping these theories, the chapter highlights how ethical factors must be designed into the structure of AI chatbots in a way that ensures transparency, accountability, and justice. The chapter concluded with a call for cross-disciplinary collaboration for addressing the complex ethical issues posed by AI chatbot communication, particularly in multicultural and organizational environments.

This chapter explores the future of smart homes and IoT systems by 2030, emphasizing conversational AI for emotionally intelligent, adaptive environments. Beyond basic commands, homes will respond with contextual understanding, enabled by federated edge computing, ambient intelligence, and 6G networks. These systems will detect emotional cues, health, and behaviours to perform anticipatory actions in climate control, nutrition, and safety. The concept of AI-powered voice-digital twins avatars representing individual users will manage routines, security, and entertainment, and connect across smart city networks. Ethical considerations such as AI hallucinations, consent, and transparency are discussed, along with safeguards such as emotion-aware access and voice verification. This chapter envisions a sustainable, empathic future using quantum edge AI, neuromorphic processors, and blockchain to create human-AI habitation where voice is central to interaction.

Conversational AI for the Smart Homes is explored in this chapter and how it can play the role of enabling personalized, adaptive, and intuitive human–environment interactions. The intelligent voice interface core technology that is explored includes natural language processing, machine learning, and context aware computing. But focusing on personalization techniques including, for example, collaborative filtering, reinforcement learning, and federated learning as well as systems learning from user behavior, the environment, and newly joined devices. This also includes multimodal interaction through voice, gesture, gesture, and emotion recognition. Ethical considerations in the critical such as what data could be collected, privacy, transparency and the responsible AI usage are explained and also the trends that will form the future of smart living are discussed.

The integration of conversational AI and voice-enabled technologies within the retail and e-commerce sectors fundamentally transforms consumer interactions and purchasing behaviors. This chapter examines how voice-driven interfaces facilitate seamless and personalized shopping experiences that correspond to the evolving expectations of contemporary consumers. By harnessing advancements in NLP and data analytics, voice assistants can now comprehend user intent, interpret contexts, and offer product recommendations tailored to individual preferences. This chapter delves into the architecture of voice-enabled retail systems, the journey of a voice shopper, and the various personalization techniques employed to enhance customer engagement and satisfaction. Furthermore, this chapter addresses the challenges related to speech recognition accuracy and integration with existing retail systems. It also highlights future trends, including emotion-aware AI and integration with immersive technologies, such as AR/VR.

Natural Language Understanding (NLU) and Natural Language Generation (NLG) have revolutionized AI-human communication, enabling more natural and context-aware interactions. Recent advancements in deep learning, particularly transformer-based models, have significantly improved the ability of AI to comprehend, process, and generate human-like text. These technologies are widely applied in conversational AI, machine translation, content creation, and question-answering systems. However, challenges such as data biases, hallucinations, computational limitations, and ethical concerns remain. Future research aims to enhance AI's reasoning capabilities, improve low-resource language support, and integrate hybrid AI approaches. This chapter

Preface

OVERVIEW OF THE SUBJECT MATTER

The world is undergoing a quiet but profound transformation. Machines are no longer simply computing devices that crunch numbers or execute rigid commands. They are beginning to listen, understand, respond, and even sense the emotional tone behind a human utterance. Conversational Artificial Intelligence — encompassing voice interfaces, chatbots, language models, and multimodal systems — sits at the very heart of this shift. We are witnessing the emergence of AI that does not just process language but, in a meaningful sense, begins to engage with it.

This volume brings together a rich and diverse set of scholarly contributions that collectively map the current landscape of conversational AI and humanized machine interaction. The chapters span a wide intellectual terrain: from the deep mathematical foundations of transformer architectures and neural networks, to the very human concerns of emotional recognition, linguistic inclusivity for under-represented communities, and ethical accountability. Each contribution represents original thinking and rigorous inquiry — work that does not simply observe where the field is but actively pushes it forward.

At its core, this book is about the relationship between human language and machine intelligence. Language is not merely a tool for communication; it is the primary medium through which human beings construct identity, negotiate meaning, share emotion, and build community. For decades, the challenge of making machines understand language in all its richness — its ambiguity, its cultural embeddedness, its emotional depth — has been one of the great frontiers of computer science. The contributions gathered here suggest that we have entered a genuinely new phase of that journey.

Deep learning and, in particular, the transformer revolution have fundamentally changed what is possible. Pre-trained large language models have moved the goalposts of natural language understanding in ways that would have seemed extraordinary just a decade ago. Yet, as several chapters in this volume make clear, capability is not the same as completeness. There remain substantial challenges in areas such as low-resource language processing, real-time sentiment detection, ethical interaction design, and the deployment of AI systems in specialized domains like healthcare. This book confronts those challenges honestly and proposes thoughtful pathways through them.

WHERE THIS TOPIC FITS IN THE WORLD TODAY

Conversational AI is no longer a niche research concern confined to university laboratories. It has entered everyday life with remarkable speed and breadth. Virtual assistants on smartphones, AI-powered customer service systems, smart speakers in living rooms, healthcare triage chatbots, language tutoring applications — all of these represent practical manifestations of the ideas explored in this book. According to recent industry analyses, the global conversational AI market is valued in the tens of billions of dollars and continues to grow at a pace that outstrips most other technology sectors. This growth is not merely commercial; it carries deep social significance.

The rise of voice and text-based AI interfaces has democratized access to information in ways that print, and even the early internet, could not fully achieve. A person who cannot read, or who reads only in a language underserved by traditional digital infrastructure, can now potentially access knowledge, services, and assistance through spoken word. This is not a minor convenience — it is a matter of educational equity and social inclusion. The chapter in this volume dedicated to low-resource Indian languages speaks directly to this concern, and it does so with a specificity and cultural attentiveness that general treatments of the subject often lack.

At the same time, the integration of AI into intimate domains of human life — homes, health, commerce, emotional support — raises urgent questions about trust, privacy, and accountability. When a smart home device learns a family's daily rhythms, or when a retail AI anticipates a consumer's preferences before they are consciously articulated, the boundary between helpful personalization and intrusive surveillance becomes genuinely difficult to locate. This book does not shy away from these tensions. The ethical dimensions of conversational AI are woven throughout the volume, and one chapter addresses them directly through the lens of the triadic relationship among companies, customers, and AI systems.

On a geopolitical and industrial level, the development of conversational AI has become a strategic priority for governments and technology companies alike. Nations are investing heavily in AI research, recognizing that leadership in this domain will shape economic competitiveness and national security for decades to come. The academic work represented in this volume is part of a global conversation about how to develop AI that is not only technically powerful but also socially responsible, linguistically inclusive, and genuinely beneficial to human flourishing.

DESCRIPTION OF THE TARGET AUDIENCE

This book has been assembled with a broad and heterogeneous readership in mind, reflecting the genuinely interdisciplinary nature of the field it addresses. The primary audience consists of researchers and graduate students working in artificial intelligence, machine learning, natural language processing, human-computer interaction, and computational linguistics. These readers will find technical depth, methodological rigor, and engagement with the current literature that meets the standards of serious scholarly inquiry.

But the editors have been equally attentive to a secondary audience: practitioners, designers, and engineers who are actively building conversational AI systems and who need not only theoretical grounding but also practical insight into how systems are designed, evaluated, and improved. Chapters addressing emotion recognition, multilingual summarization, gesture recognition, and IoT integration offer material that bridges research and application in ways that working professionals will find directly useful.

A third audience — one that the editors regard as equally important — consists of policymakers, ethicists, social scientists, and informed citizens who are grappling with the societal implications of AI deployment. This book does not assume that all its readers are engineers. It assumes, rather, that they are thoughtful people who understand that decisions about AI are not purely technical decisions — they are decisions about values, power, inclusion, and the kind of society we wish to inhabit. Chapters on ethics, social impact, and the challenges of serving marginalized linguistic communities speak directly to this audience.

Finally, advanced undergraduate students in computer science, information technology, and related programs will find in this volume a valuable introduction to some of the most active and consequential research fronts in contemporary AI. The book can serve as a primary or supplementary text in courses on conversational AI, deep learning for NLP, human-computer interaction, or AI ethics.

OVERVIEW OF CHAPTER CONTRIBUTIONS

The twelve chapters of this volume have been organized to move from foundational theoretical and technical concerns toward increasingly applied and domain-specific contexts, though the editors encourage readers to explore the book in whatever order best serves their needs. Each chapter stands on its own as an independent scholarly contribution, while also participating in the larger conversation that the volume as a whole seeks to advance.

Chapter 1 — Recent Advances and Challenges in Natural Language Processing: A Deep Learning Perspective: This opening chapter provides an essential intellectual foundation for everything that follows. It surveys the trajectory of natural language processing from its early rule-based iterations through the statistical revolution and into the current era of deep learning dominance. The authors offer a careful and accessible account of transformer architectures, attention mechanisms, and the pre-trained language models that have redefined what machines can do with text. Crucially, however, the chapter is not merely celebratory. It identifies with precision the challenges that remain — issues of computational cost, interpretability, bias, and the difficulty of generalizing across domains and languages. As an orientation to the field, this chapter sets a tone of intellectual honesty that runs throughout the volume.

Chapter 2 — Deep Learning and Neural Networks for Humanizing Conversational AI — Multilingual and Emotion-Aware Applications: Where the first chapter surveys the landscape broadly, this chapter focuses its lens on a specific and particularly compelling problem: how to make conversational AI systems feel less like machines and more like genuine interlocutors. The authors examine how neural network architectures can be designed and trained to handle the dual challenge of multilingual interaction and emotional awareness simultaneously. The concept of humanization in AI is approached with appropriate nuance — the goal is not to deceive users into thinking they are speaking with a person, but to build systems that respond to the full communicative richness of human expression. This chapter offers both technical depth and a thoughtful articulation of what it means, philosophically, to humanize a machine.

Chapter 3 — Emotion and Sentiment Analysis in Voice AI: Voice carries information that text cannot fully convey. The same sentence spoken in anger, in tenderness, in irony, or in sorrow communicates very different things. This chapter confronts the remarkable technical challenge of teaching machines to hear the emotional content of speech. The authors review the state of the art in acoustic feature extraction, prosodic analysis, and neural approaches to emotion classification, while also engaging with the significant difficulties involved — the cultural variability of emotional expression, the scarcity of high-quality labeled datasets, and the ethical questions that arise when machines are given the capacity to infer emotional states. This is a chapter that will be of interest not only to engineers but to anyone thinking about the future of empathetic AI.

Chapter 4 — Designing Multilingual Conversational AI for Low-Resource Indian Languages: Challenges, Frameworks, and Social Impact: This chapter is, in some respects, the moral heart of the volume. India is home to hundreds of languages and thousands of dialects, many of them spoken by tens of millions of people who remain effectively invisible to the dominant AI systems built primarily on English and a handful of other high-resource languages. The authors bring both technical expertise and genuine cultural sensitivity to the challenge of building conversational AI for these underserved communities. They outline the specific linguistic features that make many Indian languages difficult for standard NLP approaches, propose frameworks adapted to low-resource conditions, and reflect thoughtfully on the social impact — both potential and actual — of extending AI services to populations that have been historically marginalized by technology. This is a chapter that rewards careful reading by anyone concerned with AI equity.

Chapter 5 — The Ethical Interaction Trilogy among Companies, Customers, and AI-Chatbots: This chapter steps back from technical implementation to examine the ethical architecture of conversational AI deployment in commercial contexts. The authors develop a triadic framework for thinking about the relationships and responsibilities that exist among the companies that deploy AI chatbots, the customers who interact with them, and the AI systems themselves as actors with (at least apparent) communicative agency. Questions of transparency, consent, manipulation, and accountability are addressed with philosophical rigor and practical awareness. This chapter will be essential reading for anyone involved in the design, governance, or regulation of commercial AI systems, and it makes a genuine contribution to the emerging field of AI ethics.

Chapter 6 — Smart Homes and IoT: Voice-Controlled Devices and Automation: The domestic sphere has become one of the most active sites of conversational AI deployment. This chapter examines the integration of voice AI with smart home ecosystems and the Internet of Things, exploring both the current capabilities of voice-controlled automation and the significant technical and user experience challenges that remain. The authors address issues of interoperability between devices and platforms, the management of ambient listening and privacy, and the design of voice interfaces that work reliably across the varied acoustic environments of real homes. The chapter provides a technically grounded and practically oriented account of a technology that is already present in millions of households around the world.

Chapter 7 — Conversational AI in Smart Homes for Enhancing Personalization and Adaptability: Complementing the preceding chapter, this contribution focuses specifically on the personalization dimension of smart home AI. How can a conversational system learn the preferences, routines, and communication styles of the individuals it serves, and adapt its behavior accordingly over time? The authors examine machine learning approaches to user modeling, the challenges of serving multiple users within a single household (including users with different ages, abilities, and needs), and the design principles that enable adaptation without creating systems that feel intrusive or presumptuous. This chapter is a thoughtful exploration of what it means to design AI that genuinely serves human beings in their most intimate environments.

Chapter 8 — Retail and E-commerce — Voice-Enabled Shopping Experience and Personalized Recommendations: Commerce has always been a domain in which communication matters enormously, and this chapter examines how conversational AI is transforming the retail and e-commerce landscape. The authors analyze voice-enabled shopping interfaces, the natural language understanding challenges they present, and the recommendation systems that power personalized product suggestions. The chapter engages with both the commercial opportunities these technologies create and the consumer behavior questions they raise — how do people actually speak to AI shopping assistants, what do they expect, and what makes the difference between a helpful recommendation and an unwanted intrusion? This is a chapter that connects fundamental NLP research to the commercial realities of one of the world's largest industries.

Chapter 9 — Advancements in Natural Language Understanding (NLU) and Generation (NLG): Bridging AI and Human Communication: The volume closes with a chapter that is, in a sense, both a culmination and a new beginning. The authors survey the current state of the art in natural language understanding and generation, two capabilities that together define the core of conversational AI. They examine the progress made possible by large language models and instruction tuning, the persistent challenges of commonsense reasoning, factual grounding, and coherent long-form generation, and the emerging frontiers of grounded language understanding that connects words to perception and action. As a closing chapter, it places all of the preceding contributions in a broader trajectory, pointing toward a future in which the boundary between human and machine communication continues to be renegotiated.

HOW THIS BOOK IMPACTS THE FIELD

Edited volumes in fast-moving fields face a particular challenge: the risk of assembling a collection that is out of date by the time it reaches readers. The editors of this volume have sought to mitigate this risk not by chasing the very latest benchmarks — which will inevitably be superseded — but by selecting and shaping contributions that address enduring problems and offer frameworks, insights, and methodologies that will retain their value as the field continues to evolve. The result, we believe, is a book that will serve readers not only in the immediate present but for several years to come.

The contribution of this volume to the field is best understood along several dimensions. First, it is genuinely interdisciplinary in a way that many technical collections are not. It brings together computer scientists, linguists, ethicists, and domain experts in healthcare and commerce, creating a dialogue across disciplinary boundaries that reflects the actual complexity of developing AI systems for human use. Second, it takes seriously the global and linguistic diversity of the human communities that conversational AI will serve. The sustained attention to low-resource languages, multilingual architectures, and the specific challenges of the Indian linguistic landscape represents a meaningful corrective to the anglophone bias that has historically characterized much AI research.

Third, and perhaps most importantly, this volume refuses to separate technical innovation from ethical reflection. Every chapter that presents a new method or architecture also engages, at some level, with the question of what that method is for and who it serves. This is not merely a gesture toward responsible AI — it is a substantive intellectual commitment, enacted in the specific choices that authors have made about what questions to ask, what populations to consider, and what trade-offs to acknowledge. In a field where the pressure to optimize for narrow technical metrics can crowd out broader considerations, this is a meaningful contribution.

We hope that readers — whether they come to this volume as researchers, practitioners, students, or curious citizens — will find in it not only information but perspective: a sense of where conversational AI has come from, where it stands today, and what remains to be done. The challenges are real and the stakes are high. But so, as the chapters of this book consistently demonstrate, is the quality of the human ingenuity being brought to bear on them. It is in that spirit — of rigorous inquiry, collaborative scholarship, and genuine commitment to the public good — that this volume is offered to the world.

Chapter 1

Recent Advances and Challenges in Natural Language Processing: A Deep Learning Perspective

Ashima Kalra
http://orcid.org/0000-0001-5860-5422
Chandigarh Engineering College-CGC Landran, Mohali, India

Lalit Narendra Patil
Dr. D.Y. Patil Institute of Technology, Pimpri, India

ABSTRACT

The most important element in artificial intelligence is Natural Language Processing (NLP) which equips the machines with the ability to understand, interpret, and generate human language. The chapter summarizes the latest developments catalyzed by deep learning or transformer-based models such as BERT, GPT, and T5 which have made huge strides in machine translation and sentiment analysis. Besides these achievements, issues still exist in managing linguistic vagueness, context semantic and semantic diversity. The chapter presents the linguistic underpinnings of NLP including the phonetics, syntax, semantics and discourse, and their correlation with Natural Language Understanding (NLU) and Natural Language Generation (NLG). It also shows new trends such as multimodal model that integrates vision and language, conversational artificial intelligence, and ethical issues of the use of language technologies. The chapter ends with an argument about the multidisciplinary collaboration that is required to promote innovation and make this relatively new field develop in a responsible way.

DOI: 10.4018/979-8-3373-3361-8.ch001

1. INTRODUCTION

Natural language processing (NLP) is a cross-disciplinary area, responsible for the computational element of human language processing (Schopft et al., 2023). Ten years later, NLP had evolved enormously with massive developments in machine learning (ML)—and especially deep learning. These developments have made the handling of natural language by machines more sophisticated than ever before. Accordingly, NLP has come to be used in a wide variety of applications—from chatbots and virtual assistants to machine translation, text summarization and so much more. Nonetheless, the area continues to encounter many hurdles, such as resolving ambiguity, contextual comprehension, and the production of fluent and naturalistic language. In this research paper we will explore details regarding what is the present status of NLP including some of its advancements, upcoming research and challenges associated with it.

Language is a complex system that humans use to share and understand information, spoken and written. But not everyone speaks in complex symbolic structures. Thus, emerged Natural Language Processing, which specializes in allowing users to converse with their computers using simple speech. It had started as an experiment in Artificial Intelligence and Linguistics to make interaction easier by enabling one to converse with machines as with people. Natural Language Processing can be broken down into two aspects Understanding versus Generation. The former is about understanding what the text says, based on principles of Phonology, Morphology, Syntax, Semantics and Pragmatics. Revolutionary 12 th century linguist Chomsky, (1957) redirected the Syntax world, earning luminary success. Generation problems create words, lines of discussion and essays that reflect internal ideas in a meaningful way. While NLP research has been dominated by computer scientists, other researchers are interested too — for example, linguists, psychologists and philosophers. A second attractive element is increasingly knowing human tongues. Many theories share the same connections. In literature, scientists primarily work, but various professionals provide perspectives from their own domains as well. This discipline provides insight into how human beings express and understand message in words in many different formats.Natural Language Processing techniques generally want us to talk with our computers as human beings. Abstraction-based automatic summarization generates short but informative summaries from long text. Coreference resolution looks at sentences or longer pieces of text to understand which words refer to the same entity. Discourse analysis looks at longer written works, finding the connections between statements as intended to build a message that coheres based on the surrounding context. Machine translation automates the transcription of written content in one human language to another to enable the international exchange of ideas. Morphological segmentation separates words into the base meaning bearing pieces of that word in an effort to elucidate syntactic function. Named entity recognition tags important nouns from papers and online reports such as people, places, and organizations. Optical character recognition converts handwritten and printed symbols into a form that can be read by computer systems. Part of speech tagging assigns grammar association nouns, verbs, adjectives to each word to help with the linguistic analysis. This, along with many other NLP subfields, is commonly used, from translation apps to annotated citations.

Despite being interrelated, our task partitioning provides both conceptual and practical advantages. In addition to these two contributions — automatic summarization and coreference resolution, — provide essential contributions to full text understanding. Progress continues to expand the scope, and improve the performance, of language processing software, highlighting its increasing importance, even as the field matures. The early development of "natural language processing," as a field of study, represents its evolutionary path from an idea in its infancy to a recognized discipline.Although NLP has produced some interesting results so far, there is still plenty of work to be done. The projects represent experimental efforts to explore the limits of possibility using artistic functions of neural networks and progressively larger datasets. But alas, human language is a complex thing, and our present techniques can only begin to address these differences. We review recent work from three broad perspectives: generative modeling, semantic/ pragmatic understanding, and the balance between the metrics used to evaluate a model and the representational accuracy of these metrics in evaluating model performance. By reviewing current efforts along with the barriers they still face, we hope to clarify outstanding goals for researchers, as well as to inspire ideas that may help nurture emerging solutions.

1.1 Background and Scope of NLP

Natural Language Processing (NLP) is a field of artificial intelligence (AI) which allows computers to understand human language as well as analyzing and generating it. NLP has its theoretical background tracing back to the historical foundation of linguistics and rule-based logical reasoning, but due to the speedy advancements made in the field within the last twenty years or so, especially by the addition of statistical techniques and deep learning algorithms, NLP has grown dramatically. The effects of such change are spectacular improvements in the performance of NLP systems across a wide range of tasks, including machine translation and question answering, dialogue systems and content summarization.It is this that the NLP attempts to do so that the gap between man and machine is narrowed in such a way that the software not only recognizes the syntax of the language but also the semantics, pragmatics and context of the language. The latest innovations and speed-ups especially in transformer based architectures established a new era in the field of performance and versatility.

1.2 Role of Deep Learning in Modern NLP

Deep learning has taken over as the new paradigm in the field of NLP with its ability to capture more complex patterns in massive amounts of data. Recent models of language understanding and generation based on convolutional neural networks (CNNs), recurrent neural networks (RNNs) and also transformer ones like BERT (Bidirectional Encoder Representations from Transformers), GPT (Generative Pre-trained Transformer) have made a huge difference in the field of language understanding and generation.Those pre-trained models, which are based on large corpora and fine-tuned to down stream tasks, have surpassed the state-of-the-art performance in various benchmarks like GLUE, SuperGLUE and SQuAD. Besides, they have made zero-shot and few-shot learning through which they have reduced vastly the quantity of labeled data necessary to undertake new tasks.

1.3 Objectives and Structure of the Chapter

This chapter aims to give a detailed account of the development of the Natural Language Processing (NLP) with the emphasis on the transition using symbolic rule-based techniques to deep learning algorithms. It will present the principles of linguistics that the NLP framework is based on, investigate how the transformer models, especially transformer architectures, modified the modern NLP tasks, and evaluate future benchmarks including multimodal integration and ethically conditioned AI. The chapter also finds unresolved problems and presents the directions of future research. It is organized in ten parts, and it commences with the linguistic underpinnings of NLP (Section 2), a comprehensive literature review (Section 3), and summarizing of historical shift between rule-based and neural systems (Section 4). In Section 5, you explore transformer models and their effects and in Section 6, you get an overview of core NLP applications. Section 7 involves emergent trends of 2023-2025 and Section 8 reflects on ethical and social dilemma. Section 9 provides open research questions, and Section 10 provides final know-how.

2. LINGUISTIC FOUNDATIONS OF NLP

Natural Language Processing (NLP) has all its roots and relates to different linguistic concepts and theories underpinning its comprehension and manipulation of the human language. The main ones are phonetics and phonology that deals with the sounds of speech; morphology that examines the structure of words; and syntax, which specifies the structure of sentence and grammatical associations. Respectively, in connection to linguistic analysis, semantics addresses the meaning and discourse analysis is about the comprehensiveness and coherence of a whole piece of text. Another is sociolinguistics, the social side of language variation, and psycholinguistics, mechanisms of understanding and production of language in the brain. Finally, being the computer science part of the story, computational linguistics is an amalgamation of theoretical linguistics along with computer science to develop algorithms in dealing with natural language processing. These fundamental units allow to easily define the process of correctly analyzing, comprehending and creating human language in a relevant way and represent the fundament of the creation of the corresponding NLP software. The figure 1 represents the fundamental linguistic concepts on which Natural Language Processing exists. It encompasess phonetics and morphology (sound and word formation), syntax and parsing techniques (sentence structure), and semantics and pragmatics (meaning and context), and discourse-level processing to process language in context. These foundations guide the design and interpretation of NLP models.

2.1 Phonetics and Morphology

Phonetics focuses on the physical sounds of language. While NLP traditionally dealt with text, phonetic analysis is essential in applications such as speech recognition and synthesis. Morphology, on the other hand, deals with the structure of words—how roots, prefixes, and suffixes combine to form meaning. Morphological analysis helps disambiguate word forms and improves tokenization, especially in morphologically rich languages like Finnish, Turkish, or Hindi. For instance, recognizing that "running," "ran," and "runs" are variants of the root "run" allows models to generalize more effectively and perform accurate lemmatization or stemming. NLP relies on various linguistic ideas and theories to analyze and process human language. Some important linguistic basics are defined below for NLP system.

Phonetics — The physical sounds of human speech. It encompasses knowledge of how sounds are formed (articulatory), passed (acoustic) and perceived (aural).

Phonology: The study of the sounds of human speech, or more generally, the sounds of human-level communication. It deals with abstract and cognitive properties of sounds, and their patterns (e.g., phonemes, syllable structures, etc.)

Figure 1. Linguistic foundations of NLP

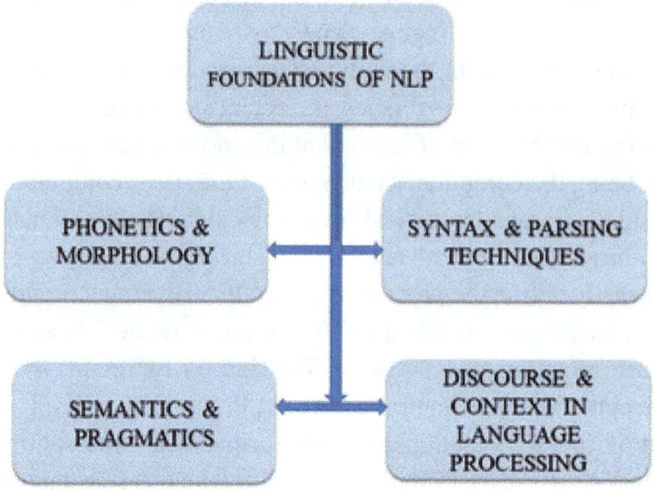

Morphology: It is the study of word structure. It studies how morphemes (the smallest meaningful units) combine to form words. Morphology is important for operations like stemming and lemmatization – two aspects of text normalization that are fundamental to any NLP task.

Syntax: It is a set of rules that defines the structure of sentences. It is the order of words within sentences and the other literacy devices used to guide the reader. Very big very deep very wide very rich demonstrating and showing sentences, syntactic analysis is therefore important, eg to enable parsing of sentences, and virtual grammatical configuration, machine and extraction of information.

Semantics: is the study of meaning in language. It encompasses how words, phrases, and sentences convey meaning. Key concepts include:

Lexical Semantics: The meaning of words and their relationships (e.g., synonyms, antonyms).

Compositional Semantics: How meanings combine in phrases and sentences.

Pragmatics: The study of how context influences meaning, including implicature and speech acts.

2.2 Discourse and Context in Language Processing

Discourse Analysis addresses the way larger units of language such as conversations or written texts work. It encompasses knowledge of coherence, cohesion and how dialogues are organized — agency that is useful for chatbots and summarization, for example.

Sociolinguistics: examines the variation and change of language in social context. Real-life variability is also reflected in this aspect of language and here we can consider factors like dialect, sociolect and register, which can affect processing and generation of language in NLP applications.

Psycholinguistics: This is the study of how we understand and produce language. The knowledge of language processing in humans can help us know how such systems can be organized and processed, e.g., such knowledge may help design NLP systems that enables us to interact with them and have dialogues.

Computational Linguistics: These are language processing systems that apply knowledge from the field of linguistics, the scientific study of language and its structure, to computers as a branch of computer science. It includes several different paradigms, from rule based systems to statistical and machine learning approaches.

NLP is built on top of linguistic concepts and theories. This is followed by exploring the ins and outs of these fundamentals that form the foundation to effectively develop NLP applications, wherein the techniques are used to analyze, understand and generate human language. Using insights from linguistics, NLP practitioners can develop tools that are sophisticated and context-aware, meeting user requirements more effectively.

2.3 Components of NLP

Semantics uses the meaning of words, phrases and sentences, whereas pragmatics takes into consideration the situation under which the language is applied. Just to provide an example, one may consider a sentence such as, can you pass the salt? In syntax the sentence is a question, but in its current usage it is a polite request. All modern NLP systems may occasionally rely on distributional semantics (e.g., word embeddings such as Word2Vec, GloVe), and contextual embeddings (e.g., BERT, RoBERTa) to represent the meaning of words in terms of their usage patterns in large corpora. Nevertheless, it is critical to note that achieving any semantic comprehension, particularly that of polysemous word or idiomatic expression remains a challenge. NLP can be broadly categorized into two key parts — NLU (Natural Language Understanding) and NLG (Natural Language Generation). All of the components mentioned play a key role in how NLP systems function.

2.3.1 Natural Language Understanding (NLU)

Natural Language Understanding (NLU) refers to the comprehension part of the natural language. It includes a few important tasks such as:

Tokenization: Dividing text into separate words or phrases (tokens).

Parts of Speech Tagging: tagging each token with the grammatical parts of speech it represents (i.e., noun, verb, adjective, etc.

Entity Recognition (NER): Finding and classifying named entities in the text, such as people, organizations, and places.

Sentiment analysis: The process of determining whether a piece of writing is positive, negative, or neutral.

Semantic Analysis: Parsing the context and meaning of words and phrases in relation to one another.

Intent Recognition: Understanding the intent behind a user's message, especially within conversational AI systems.

2.3.2 Natural Language Generation (NLG)

NLG deals with the creation of text, which is similar to human text, under some input or data. The important activations are:

Text Generation: The writer of text based on prompts or data, and that is meshed coherently and relevant in context.

Summarization: Trying to tighten up a long piece of text to become a shorter summary and keeping the important information.

Translation: The conversion of the text written in one language to another language keeping the same context and meaning.

Dialogue Generation: The generation of answers in the conversational setting is common in chatbots and virtual assistants.

Content Development: Developing written documents, such as articles, reports, etc., according to a particular theme or an instruction.

NLG and NLU are complementary to one another so that NLP systems can read, write, and understand human language, and everything runs from conversational machines and automated content production.

3. LITERATURE REVIEW

A revolution over the past two years, new techniques, paradigms, and implementations have changed Natural Language Processing (NLP) unrecognizably. In this literature survey some of the important contributions made in that area are discussed and language resources, the architecture of the model, evaluation method and its related application are also discussed. The transformer models and pretrained language models have shown significant improvement in the recent years and change the dynamic of NLP. Some problems of natural language processing (NLP), particularly text summarization and sentiment analysis have been addressed by using deep learning techniques. The results of these studies are always used to generate state-of-the-art performance of a variety of benchmarks. According to (Schopft et al., 2023), times and working hours have not been changing very fast.

Natural Language Processing (NLP) has in recent years become one of the key focus in AI by addressing the problem of machine translation, summarization, sentiment analysis, and question answering using deep learning and transformer models. New breakthroughs, such as BERT (Devlin et al., 2019), GPT-3 (Brown et al., 2020), and T5, have shown the state-of-the-art results on a variety of NLP tasks, are mainly defined by the approaches to context modeling (bidirectional context), scaling to large amounts of data during pretraining, and transfer learning. Although such developments have been realized, there is still a problem of resolving ambiguity, generating grammatically correct output with a natural language, as well as dealing with low-resource languages. Current architectures are the heirs of seminal studies like that by Bengio et al. (2003) on neural language models, and that of Bahdanau et al. (2015) on attention mechanisms. Solutions to structured prediction, document summarization (Dunlavy et al., 2007), Arabic text processing (Diab et al., 2004) have also been developed by the researchers. Ethics, explainability, and sustainability issues are becoming more important with attempts to enhance fairness (Bolukbasi et al., 2016), explanations (Alshemali & Kalita, 2020), and efficiency (Zaheer et al., 2020). NLP has now gone into interdisciplinary fields such as in public health (Baclic et al., 2020) and cognitive neuroscience, citing the importance of interdisciplinary alliances in creating more resilient and human-compatible language systems.

The recent developments in NLP show a certain level of active interaction between linguistic theory and the evolving AI technologies. He et al. (2021) presented DeBERTa, a transformer-based model that uses disentangled attention in order to advance contextualization and task performance across NLP tasks, a development in transformer based architecture. In the same vein, another multimodal model has been presented by Radford et al. (2021), CLIP, which aligns text and visual data, and affords tasks such as visual question answering and image captioning. Extending to the issue of linguistic inclusivity, Desai and Dabhi (2022) surveyed the Gujarati NLP systems in a thorough scope and considered some of the challenges peculiar to regional languages processing. Tuning the instructions also emerged with FLAN (Wei et al., 2021) that enhanced the learning of a few shots and flexibility of tasks. Chowdhery et al. (2023) presented the Pathways Language Model (PaLM) that puts an emphasis on the scalability of the model in order to have captured the complex language patterns to reflected a state-of-the-art performance. Further on, Power et al. (2022) have investigated so-called grokking, whereby models are much more generalizable than training data, and have illuminated new training mechanisms towards robust learning sparse training inputs. These advances come alongside a more general trend toward combining linguistic understanding with AI, particularly in such contexts as biomedical informatics and global health with large language models (LLMs) being located to address urgent practical tasks. As Genetti (2024) and Xudaybergenova et al. continue to criticize the new morphology of linguistics, they also underline the morphological and cognitive-social aspect of language being developed as the linguistic evolution is being driven by use of digitalization. This points to the fact that there is a necessity to mediate between the traditional linguistic framework with the modern NLP technology to comprehend language dynamics in the digital world.

The growing nature of both scope and coverage of the NLP on various platforms in terms of innovations in transformer models and transversal coordination is majorly highlighted in recent literature. Tsai et al. (2021) surveyed multimodal transformers such as CLIP (Radford et al., 2021), which connect text and image data, leading to an improved ability in captioning and visual question answering among others. Yu et al.(2024) reviewed the expanding scope of large language models (LLMs) in clinical decision-making and communication in health informatics, whereas Yenduri et al. (2023) surveyed the use cases of GPT in education, entertainment and services and discussed ethical issues and the need to develop AI safety guidance on a global scale. Zendaoui et al. (2023) placed their emphasis on how AI became useful in managing the pandemic with real-time data sharing and interdisciplinary approaches, encompassing computer science, linguistics, and the field of public health. The sphere of computational linguistics is still undergoing an evolution, and such research pieces as Smidt et al. (2024) on POS tagging in cuneiform texts and Satibaldieva (2024) on the aspect of terminology clarity in linguistics show the intricacy of both old and new linguistic research work. According to Zhang and Teng (Ive, 2022), the main trend is the machine learning-based perception of the foundations of NLP, whereas Nilufar (2024) pays attention to its disruptive value in natural sciences by data modeling and simulation. All these works show how models like BERT, GPT-3, T5, ALBERT, DeBERTa, Big Bird, and FLAN have transformed the field of NLP, not only beating performance on canonical tasks but also taking those models into regional languages, ancient writing systems, and real-world environments. NLP has a future in treating more ethical standards, increasing model transparency, collaborating with more disciplines, and providing trustworthy, fair, and effective AI.

4. FROM RULE-BASED TO NEURAL APPROACHES

All these paradigm shifts have been generated by the development of new computer abilities and algorithmic sophistication, and by improved access to linguistic data. Firstly, based on the hand-designed rule-based systems, NLP has been running through a variety of stages that are marked by statistical inference, conventional machine learning, and eventually deep learning, which holds the current field. The development is indicative of increased difficulty and accuracy with which computational models learn, produce and communicate human language. This part examines the history of the shift in reasoning, in a way that symbols and statistics led to neural representations, highlighting the key changes and their impact on contemporary use of NLP.

4.1 Symbolic and Statistical NLP

Earlier developments in NLP had concentrated on symbolic (rule-based) approaches to natural language, based on hand encoded linguistic know-how. These systems used the knowledge of linguists and domain experts to develop deterministic models which could do languages parse and generation. Examples are context-free grammars, morphological analyzer and state machines (usually finite-state) to tokenize and perform phonological analysis. These systems were precise and interpretable but also rigid and with bad scalability and breakage under the linguistic variability.

With greater accessibility to big corpora and computational facilities, statistical approaches were to come to the fore in the 1980s and 1990s. Probabilistic inference (based on observed frequencies) was used instead of deterministic rules in an approach like Hidden Markov Models (HMMs) used to tag part-of-speech and the n-gram model used to build language models. These techniques have enabled systems to be able to learn patterns based on the data presented and better generalized on unseen inputs. The statistical machine translation (SMT) models and statistical parsers developed by IBM performed very well, bringing major successes to the company, as the statistical parsers and SMT models performed much better than their rule-based prototypes, not only by being significantly more robust but also by covering far more material.Nonetheless, statistical models continued to suffer in the usefulness of long-range dependence, semantics, and contextual subtleties, and in general had to work on nearby features and/or handcrafted representations.

4.2 Transition to Machine Learning

With the advent of the early 2000s, the more restricted statistical models gave way towards the more general machine learning (ML) algorithms, that enabled the creation of feature-based models that were learned through an annotated data set. Supervised learning algorithms, like the Support Vector Machines (SVMs), Maximum Entropy Models, Conditional Random Fields (CRFs) were used to perform supervised learning on tasks such as named entity recognition (NER), chunking as well as in text classification. These models gave a compromise between particularity given by rules and generalization given by statistics.

That shift was driven by the availability of resources like the annotated corpora like Penn Treebank and the availability of resources like WordNet that served as the needed training data. Moreover, the feature engineering was introduced as the key towards system performance. Manual selection of such linguistically motivated features as POS tags, dependency relations, and orthographic patterns were made to increase the effectiveness of these models.With these advancements, these ML methods were strongly reliant on the quality and variety of hand-written features. They also had difficulties to be generalized across domains and languages that require much retraining and feature redesign.

4.3 Rise of Deep Learning in NLP

The revolution in Natural Language Processing (NLP) started in the year 2013 with the introduction of word embeddings derived through deep learning training such as Word2Vec (Mikolov et al., 2013) and GloVe (Pennington et al., 2014) to capture semantic relationships through learning of high dimensional dense vectors over large textual corpora, without any manual feature engineering. The development of this breakthrough led to discovery of deep neural architectures like Convolutional Neural Networks (CNNs) (Kim, 2014) and Recurrent Neural Networks (RNNs) including the Long Short-Term Memory (LSTM) networks (Elman, 1990; Hochreiter & Schmidhuber, 1997) that quickly supplanted the old models of sentence classification and modeling of sequences. The introduction of attention mechanisms and the Transformer architecture (Vaswani et al., 2018) is yet another redefining of state-of-the-art NLP as it allows models to model long-range dependencies better. This took the form of the development of large-scale pre-trained language models. A prominent example is BERT (Devlin et al., 2019), which brought transfer learning to NLP: models like BERT (trained on large volumes of data) could be fine-tuned with scarce labeled training data to perform a specific task, and they achieved excellent results on contextual understanding, semantic reasoning, and multi-task learning. The outstanding case is the NLP application of recognizing advanced AI systems today based on deep learning, such as the use of chatbots, machine translation, question and answer systems, and sentiment analysis engines. But with the shift there also have emerged new challenges of model interpretability, resource consumption, and data bias, which are the current research topics.

5. TRANSFORMER-BASED MODELS: THE BREAKTHROUGH ERA

The era of the development and implementation of Transformer-based models brought a new revolutionary front in the Natural Language Processing (NLP) history. Going beyond recurring and convolutional architecture, Transformers use self-attention to allow global dependencies in textual data to be learned, with unprecedented scalability and performance. Ever since the creation of original Transformer architecture by Vaswani et al. (2018), the amount of powerful pre-trained models has exploded, helping to redefine the state-of-the-art in a multitude of NLP tasks. Here we can talk about the Transformer model bases, examine the emergent known architectures like BERT, GPT, T5, and RoBERTa, examine performance over the benchmarks, and note the still existing limitations.

5.1 Introduction to Transformers

Vaswani et al. (2018) have presented transformers in the article Attention is All You Need. The core invention was the presence of self-attention, the ability of each word in a sequence to make a kind of attention on every other word was introduced, so the dependencies that should be modeled are considered irrespective of their distance. This architecture also completely did away with recurrence allowing far more intense parallelization and training speed.The important parts of the Transformer architecture are:

- Multi-head self-attention: Simultaneously computes several distributions of attention.
- Positional encoding: Appends embedding of word position to the input embeddings.
- Feedforward layers: These layers offer non-linear transformations.
- Residual connection: Help in ensuring stability during training.

The heart of up-to-date pre-trained language models, transformers allow bidirectional or autoregressive modelling of contexts and are frequently fine-tuned with little modification of the underlying architecture to perform downstream tasks.

5.2 Key Models: BERT, GPT, T5, RoBERTa, and Beyond

Bert(Bidirectional Encoder Representations From Transformers)

BERT created by Devlin et al. (2019) uses a pre-training objective with a mask language model and next sentence prediction. It is bi-directional i.e. it trains on contextual embeddings based on left and right contexts. The majority of fine-tuning strategies of Transformers have a foundation on BERT.

GPT (Generative Pre-Trained Transformer)

GPT is proposed by Radford, et al. (2021), is an autoregressive language model based on a transformer in unidirectional way. GPT-2 and GPT-3 greatly increased the size of models, data, and performance capabilities and performed well when zero-shot and few-shot learning tasks were involved.

RoBERTa (Robust BERT Model)

RoBERTa (Liu et al., 2019) did a better job than BERT by training much longer with far more data, dropping the next sentence prediction task, and using dynamic masking. It beat BERT on numerous NLP evaluations on every occasion.

T5 (Text-to-Text Transfer Transformer)

Raffel et al. (2020) suggested to consider all NLP tasks as the text-to-text problem, where both input and output are textual. T5 has shown exceptionally well to achieve the unification of translation, classification, summarization, and answer to questions using a single architecture.

Others

Later models, such as XLNet, ALBERT, ELECTRA, and GPT-4 took the next step further into both architectural advances and parameter expansion and task generalization.

5.3 Performance on Benchmark Tasks and Leaderboards

Transformer models have set the current state of the art on many NLP tasks including GLUE, SuperGLUE, SQuAD and MNLI. Large-scale pre-training and the richness of the self attention mechanism has been cited as their capability to generalize across tasks. The bar chart in Figure 2 above demonstrates the rapid progression in benchmark performance from BERT to GPT-3, with each successive model achieving higher generalization and accuracy across NLP tasks.

Figure 2. Approximate GLUE benchmark scores of key transformer models

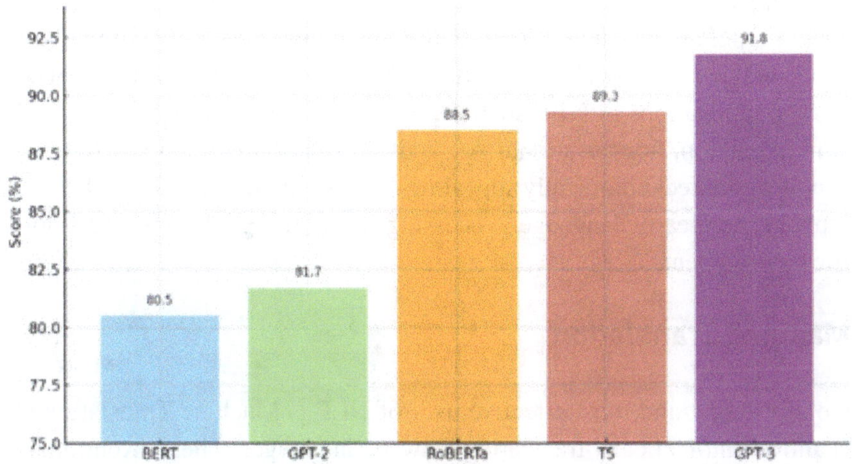

5.4 Limitations of Transformer Architectures

Transformer models have certain problems and limits despite the success:

- Computational Cost: Transformers particularly when applied in large scale context (e.g. GPT-3) are computationally expensive to train and execute (Brown et al., 2020).
- Environmental Impact: The use of high energy levels increases the question of sustainability.
- Data Bias: The gender, racial, and cultural biases are brought in through pre-training on web-scale text (Bender et al., 2021).
- No Interpretability: Model decisions lack interpretability causing a lack of transparency and trust in areas of sensitive applications.
- Context Window Limitations: Normal Transformers have a fixed input size and this problem applies to the processing of long documents (but has been solved by more modern systems such as Longformer and GPT with GPT-4, which has improved performances).

6. CORE APPLICATIONS OF NLP

Natural Language Processing (NLP) has moved into a practical field of study and even the context in which it is applied currently form the backbone of numerous applications, which touch upon the fields of communication, commerce, healthcare and governance. Newer NLP systems that run on machine learning and deep learning can now interpolate, produce, and react in human language with extremely fluent and contextual assurance. This part gives a brief description of some of the most demanding applications of NLP such as, machine translation, sentiment analysis, text summarization, conversational AI, and information extraction. Not only are these applications technologically appealing, but also of importance to solve real-life problems in the area of language-processing in multilingual, noisy, and domain-specific environments.

6.1 Machine Translation

One of the first and most effective uses of NLP is Machine Translation (MT), which allows automatically translating between languages. The conventional rule-based and statistical models have been abandoned in favor of the neural machine translation (NMT) models that employ deep neural networks to learn the mappings of the source language into the target one. Introduced by the encoder-decoder architecture that has since been complemented by attention and Transformer mechanisms, NMT has radically changed the quality of translation between languages (Bahdanau et al., 2015; Vaswani et al., 2018). The latest models, such as mBART by Google and No Language Left Behind (NLLB) by Meta have showed good zero-shot and many-to-many capabilities of translation. Such systems happen to have a marked effect on low-resource languages where conventional parallel corpora repositories are few and far between.

6.2 Sentiment Analysis and Opinion Mining

The automated subjective information in text such as opinions, attitudes, and feelings determination processes are known as sentiment analysis. It is commonly applied to the social media analytics, the reviewing of products, financial markets and analysis of the politics discourse. Older models just had bag-of-words and lexicon-based features whereas current systems have contextual representations based on models such as BERT and RoBERTa to represent subtle impacts on sentiment at document, sentence and even entity level (Devlin et al., 2019).The more recent developments are aspects-based sentiment analysis and the classification of emotions; in these models, systems can recognize sentiment about a particular aspect (e.g., about a product feature or political matter) to provide even more business insight and reputation tracking.

6.3 Text Summarization

The purpose of text summarization is to condense long documents in short forms and not losing the main idea. They can be of two general kinds extractive summarization, which picks out salient sentences or phrases, and abstractive summarization, which produces new compact sentences in their own words but with the meaning of the original.Transformer-based models that recently achieved state of the art in such datasets are BART and T5, which generate fluent and informative summaries in datasets such as CNN/Daily Mail and XSum (Lewis et al., 2020). The models find extensive application in news aggregation, legal document analysis, scientific literature reviews and generation of medical reports.

6.4 Conversational AI, Chatbots

Conversational AI is used to mimic human conversation and it is common to use as a virtual assistant, customer service, and interactive tutor. Initial rule-based approaches were based on ready-made scripts and query matching, whereas current chatbots are connected to dialogue management, an intent classification, and response generating with the use of pre-trained language models (GPT-3, BlenderBot, and ChatGPT). Such systems can sustain multi-turn context-sensitive conversations and can be customised to specific fields like healthcare, education and banking. The issues such as hallucination, bias, and absence of emotional intelligence still exist, but the development is fast.

6.5 Information Extraction and Question Answering

Information extraction Information extraction (IE) is the identification of structured information in unstructured text, e.g. named entities, relationships, events. IE is fundamental for knowledge graph construction, automated document indexing, and intelligence gathering. Named entity recognition (NER), relation extraction, and coreference resolution are key tasks under this umbrella. Question Answering (QA) systems, particularly open-domain QA, combine information retrieval with NLP to answer user queries from large corpora (e.g., Wikipedia). Transformer-based models such as BERT for QA, DrQA, and T5 have shown human-level performance on benchmarks like SQuAD and Natural Questions. Recent trends include multi-hop QA, conversational QA, and retrieval-augmented generation (RAG).

7. EMERGING TRENDS IN NLP (2023–2024)

Breakneck speed of innovation in the domain of Natural Language Processing (NLP) is still transforming the frontiers of language interpretation and production. With foundational models approaching previously unseen levels of scale and ability, novel trends are sprouting up to increase the range of domain in which NLP is applied far beyond text-based tasks. Critical progress has been made in the years 20232024 across a number of areas: multimodal language modeling, few shot and continual learning, the use of large language models in production systems, and low-resource language challenges. The developments are not only meant to improve the model performance and generalization but also to encourage equity, robustness, and capability to use in practice.

7.1 Latest Trends in Natural Language Processing for 2023

As the year 2023 unfolds, Natural Language Processing (NLP) remains one of the fastest-evolving fields, propelled by rapid technological advances and increasing investments in sophisticated language understanding technologies. Few of the most impactful trends defining the NLP landscape in 2023 are discussed below:

Ubiquity of ChatGPT

OpenAI's ChatGPT is one of the leading NLP innovators that have forever changed the landscape of text generation and conversational AI. Its language generation capabilities that partly resemble that of a human being, have become a non-negotiable tool in most businesses as they seek alternative ways of interacting with their customers and engaging them. It preconditions further development of innovations and replications in a variety of spheres, starting with automatic customer care and continuing with content creation .

Improvements in Natural Language Generation (NLG)

The emergent NLG (part of NLP) is developing into a game changer in automated content generation because it aims to transform structured data into humanlike text. As an example, some of the media houses like Associated press and Yahoo are applying NLG technology to write news items and produce financial reports in real time. It not only makes the throughput faster but also consistent and accurate with regard to the content development .

Multimodal Model

Multimodal models which include text, audio and visual data are also becoming increasingly popular. These models enhance the understanding of meanings and the context of various inputs at the same time. The knowledge plays a significant role in such applications as video description and image captioning, where these applications are required to understand different types of data .

Semantic Improvements in Searching

Semantic search is transforming the user interaction with information in a better manner by understanding search intent. It enhances the accuracy of the search results and is therefore of great use to eCommerce, research in academics and knowledge management. Search results become empirically more important with growing abilities of NLP algorithms at learning the context .

Emotion Recognition

There is a growing interest in constructed NLP software that is able to recognize the emotions by studying text. With such systems, more precise response reading emotional peculiarities in different apps such as virtual assistants and customer service chatbots will be provided. It is one of the ways of a wider trend towards increasingly human interactions with AI .

Reinforcement Learning Applications

To optimize their performance, NLP models are learning using reinforcement learning the actions of users as they occur in real-time. This enables systems to adapt dynamically to the preference of the users and behavior, thus leading to personalized methods of communication as well as engagement .

Communication of Knowledge and Research Work to General Audiences

As NLP technologies are getting more inseparable parts of life, it is of primary importance to reduce the ethical issues of bias in AI models. Researchers have thus made developing the responsible practices to boost fairness and transparency in NLP come to the forefront .

Techniques of Transfer Learning

Therefore, the issue of transfer learning causes friction, one of the practical methods of realizing an effective reduction of time consumption and computational expense in learning new natural languages processing (NLP) models. It is also possible to fine tune the same model on a target task with a small amount of training data using pretrained models learnt on large datasets .

The recent trends in NLP indicate that the trend forward in 2023 will be on smarter, context aware applications with the development of a better user experience in various domains. With a selection of tools on the right-hand side such as ChatGPT that is active and rising and the right-hand side that still represents the new models of learning, multimodal learning is ready to make interacting experience and information digesting new territories of opportunities in the natural language processing. Ethics will play important roles as such technologies advance to ensure they serve the society as well as reducing biases inherent in AI-based systems.

7.2 Natural Language Processing Trends for 2024

The natural language processing (NLP) is rapidly becoming the face of the new era in terms of evolution of both technologies, research, and applications as we advance into 2024. Some of the fashionable topics transforming the scene in NLP are as follows:

Improved Multimodal Models

Multimodal-models which mix text and pictures, or text, pictures, audio and video are becoming fashionable. They make used of diverse modalities, which enable them to have more understanding and creation of the content. Multimodal has also started to find applications across many disciplines like social media and content creation to make applications more engaging and interactive to their users.

Developments In Conversational AI

Conversational AI is developing, and such improvements as context reminding, emotional intelligence, and personalization become possible. They are more capable of carrying out multi-turn conversations, determine user intention as accurately as possible, adapt and come up with personalised responses based on user history and preferences.

Ethical AI and Good NLP

As it is an increasing concern that the application will be biased, and intrusive of privacy and ethics of AI, it is with this increase in application that greater attention is being brought to the responsible NLP systems. It includes the implementation of fairness and transparency approaches, the audits of biases, and a diverse training of models to avoid further reinforcement of negative stereotypes and prejudices.

Low Resource Language Processing

Ever increasingly, an attempt at developing NLP solutions to lowresource languages is being tried. An emerging trend in NLP is the creation of transfer learning and multilingual models with the aim of bringing NLP techniques and tools more closer to people and making them all-inclusive so that languages that have been traditionally sidelined in the technology scene can also be supported better.

Explainable AI (XAI) in NLP

This is increasingly becoming significant in Natural Language Processing applications, particularly where such decisions as those in healthcare, finance and other similar fields have to be made transparently. Methods for increasing the interpretability of NLP models are being developed, enabling users to comprehend how models generate specific conclusions or predictions.

Knowledge Graphs Integration

2023, Knowledge Graph in NLP pipe line projects — The integration of knowledge graphs with NLP systems can significantly improve context understanding and relationships between entities, adding dimensions to the post embed building stage of the pipeline. This trend is especially pertinent for applications in search engines, recommendation systems, and question answering systems, where understanding the context in which it is used becomes an imperative.

Real Time Language Translation

Recent developments in real time translation technologies enable smoother cross lingual communication. Performance of neural machine translation models are improving, leading to better and context aware translations, thus promoting global cooperation and communication.

Generative AI & Content Creation

Paving the Way: Gen-AI Tools: Gen-AI models, especially those based on the GPT architecture, have found their place to be used more in content and copywriting for several domains, such as marketing, journalism, and entertainment. These models are able to generate coherent and high-quality text that could support brainstorming, drafting and editing tasks.

Focus on User Centric Design

In the realm of NLP applications, more emphasis is being put on usercentric design. This means integrating user input into the design process, ultimately leading to tools that are user-friendly, accessible, and cater to the unique needs of various user demographics.

AI Driven Personalization

NLP is applied in creating fantastic customized user experience. One way is how NLP systems are able to understand user behavior and preference, to customize contents, suggestions and interactivity, which in turn would result in improved user satisfaction and increased involvement.There are some recent NLP tendencies that will predetermine the sphere in 2024. Such tendencies will also contribute to the development of even more attractive, comprehensive and responsible NLP applications that can address a wider range of demands and situations as the field (s) evolves further.

What has happened in recent times with Deep learning is a revolution in the field of Natural Language Processing (NLP). Models have been able to learn the complex relationships and dependencies in language data with recurrent neural networks (RNNs), long short-term memory networks (LSTMs), and, more recently, transformer architectures. Such development paves the way to even more complex methods like Attention Models that enable models to intelligently concentrate on valuable parts of the input data, propelling performance by a significant margin in areas like machine translation, sentiment analysis, and text summarization. Moreover, technologies like self-supervised learning allow models to utilise tremendous quantities of unannotated textual information, leading to sturdier and generalised NLP environments.

7.3 Emerging trends in NLP for 2025

The role of the year 2025 will be an inflection point of NLP in terms of the matured technologies and new innovations. The field is being redefined by the continued advancement of multimodal understanding, privacy-preserving methods, explainability, and quantum computing and by their continued democratization and integration into production systems. The patterns indicate a changing compromise between technical ability, deployment demands in the real world and an expanding set of ethical and administrative requirements.

Integration and Multimodal Language Models

In 2025, Natural Language Processing (NLP) is witnessing a vigorous synthesis with other kinds of data (vision, audio, and video) where models have the capacities to process and reason on various senses. Advanced architectures such as GPT 4, PaLM-E, and BharatGen, which use both visual and textual data in multimodal completion of tasks such as captioning of images, robots that take commands, video question answering, and more, are good examples of this shift. Remarkably, models such as ImageBind, in addition to the as-a-service multimodal large language models that have been developed recently, are already expanding the domain of NLP towards augmented reality (AR), virtual reality (VR) applications, and even accessibility technology. The models are considered key towards construction of more humanist models of perception by systems that not only make sense of the world based on the text, but on contextually deep, multi-sensory information.

Transparency, Explainability and Ethical NLP

With the LLMs developing more influence on sensitive areas of the domain, including healthcare, legal systems, and policy-making, the criteria of explainability and ethical compliance have become crucial. Such interpretability tools as SHAP, LIME, attention heatmaps, or frameworks of mechanistic interpretability provide a view of the inner mechanism of a complex model, leading to more trust and accountability. The ethical applications also involve a focus on the user protection against bias, toxicity, and manipulation, which gave rise to developing another domain known as white-hat NLP, which explores weaknesses in security and adversarial robustness. Moreover, bias auditing frameworks and compliance-sensitive pipelines are turning into common measures, as NLP technologies should adhere to the regulations of EU AI Act and the general data ethics legislation to be enacted in other countries.

Privacy-Preserving NLP

Sensitive language data (especially those in healthcare, defense, and financial industries) processing has led to a paradigm shift to privacy-preserving methods of NLP. Such methods as differential privacy, federated learning, homomorphic encryption, and split learning become more commonly included into production systems in 2025. Such techniques enable language models to be trained on decentralized data without the need to overstep the privacy of individual users, which is a critical provision given the existence of strict data protection standards such as GDPR and HIPAA. In addition, organizations are buying privacy-protecting pipelines that keep the data utilitarian and provide transparency and audibility.

Few-Shot, Zero-Shot & Continual Learning

In 2025, data efficiency and adaptability of NLP models are one of the key areas. Following the examples of models such as GPT 4 and its successors, few-shot and zero-shot learning now enables systems to train on only few or no direct examples at all, thereby enormously decreasing the cost of training processes. In a complementary manner, there is the issue of model updating over time without forgetting, which can be managed by continual learning in a dynamic realm in real time. In-context learning, prompt engineering, meta-learning, parameter-efficient tuning (e.g. LoRA, adapters), are all techniques that are playing crucial roles in redesigning models towards lifelong learning which is especially valuable in industries that have rapidly evolving terminologies or manifesting requirements.

Quantum NLP (QNLP)

Quantum Natural Language Processing (QNLP) is still in early stages and it is starting to be considered a new research frontier. Through principles of quantum mechanics, QNLP seeks to find ways of achieving more concise (and possibly more efficient) computational representations of language, through the use of quantum superposition and entanglement. By the year 2025, prototype systems have shown proof-of-concept performance of semantic similarity and document classification tasks, on small quantum datasets. Ongoing research focuses on hybrid quantum-classical systems that can bridge today's classical deep learning with the promising, albeit currently limited, capacities of quantum computers. As quantum hardware matures, QNLP is expected to offer significant speed-ups in complex NLP inference and optimization tasks.

Domain-Specific & Low-Resource Language Models

Efforts to enhance linguistic inclusivity and domain specificity continue to be a central focus of NLP research and development in 2025. Masakhane, IndicNLP and BharatGen are large-scale multilingual projects, which attempt to provide support to underrepresented languages and dialects, developing low-resource LLMs that can be used effectively with little training data. At the same time, niche-specific LLMs pre-trained to work with legal, biomedical, scientific, and government-related tasks gain popularity due to their ability to process the specific vocabulary and thinking needs. These models are critical in real-life scenarios where they will be used in several AI deployment scenarios globally because of privacy-awareness, cheap training costs, and fairness in representing word linguistics. Table 1 is an overview of the most relevant directions of research and implementation that will define the image of NLP in 2025, both in terms of technology, ethical aspects, and application.

Table 1. Key emerging trends in natural language processing (2025)

Trend	Description
Multimodal Integration	Unified text-image-audio models for richer understanding
Explainable & Secure NLP	XAI tools + adversarial robustness (white-hat NLP)
Privacy-Preserving Methods	Federated learning & differential privacy
Adaptive Learning Paradigms	Few-shot, zero-shot, continual learning for flexible adaptation
Democratized LLMs & Production Use	Open-source models & optimization for deployment
Quantum NLP	Quantum-accelerated methods for linguistic tasks
Domain & Low-Resource Inclusivity	Focus on niche domains and underserved languages

The past couple of years have witnessed some of the largest advances in natural language processing such as with the development of transformer and large pre-trained language models who have catalyzed massive value creation in the field. The following **Table 2** represents important emerging trends, which could influence the NLP landscape in the 2023-2025 period. All trends imply any technological breakthroughs, changes of research orientation, or the wider use in fields. All this has further increased the potential and the social influence of systems based on NLP.

Table 2. Key emerging trends in natural language processing (2023–2025)

Trend	Description	Representative Works/Models	Year(s)
1.Multimodal Language Models	Integration of text, audio, image, and video to enhance understanding and generation across modalities.	CLIP, PaLM-E, GPT-4V, ImageBind	2023–2025
2. Few-shot and Zero-shot Learning	Models generalize to new tasks with minimal or no task-specific data, enhancing adaptability.	GPT-3, T0, FLAN, LLaMA-2	2023–2025
3. Domain-Specific Adaptation	Fine-tuning pretrained models for improved performance in domains like healthcare, law, and finance.	BioBERT, ClinicalBERT, Legal-BERT	2023–2025
4. Ethical NLP and Fairness in AI	Addressing algorithmic bias, improving fairness, and ensuring responsible use of large language models.	FairNLP, BOLD dataset, Debiasing Algorithms	2023–2025
5. Explainability and Interpretability	Enhancing transparency and user trust through model explanations and interpretability tools.	LIME, SHAP, Attention Visualization	2023–2025
6. Energy-Efficient NLP	Reducing the environmental impact of large-scale models via efficient architectures and quantization.	DistilBERT, TinyBERT, Quantization-Aware Training	2023–2024
7. Conversational AI with Memory & Reasoning	Development of chatbots and agents with context-aware dialogue, long-term memory, and reasoning abilities.	ChatGPT, Claude, Gemini, ReAct, AutoGPT	2023–2025
8. Low-Resource Language Support	Expanding NLP capabilities to underrepresented languages using multilingual models and transfer learning.	BLOOM, NLLB (No Language Left Behind), XLM-R	2023–2025
9. Multilingual and Cross-lingual NLP	Training models that understand and generate content in multiple languages with cross-lingual transfer.	mT5, XLM, mBART, NLLB	2023–2025
10. Neuro-symbolic and Hybrid AI	Combining neural methods with symbolic reasoning for better generalization and logic-based inference.	DeepProbLog, NeuroLogic A*, COMET	2024–2025

8. ETHICAL AND SOCIAL CHALLENGES

Applications of NLP systems have raised important ethical and social issues that should be considered to make sure that these applications are not only precise but also just, transparent, secure and sustainable. The second big problem is bias and fairness where NLP systems will represent the biases existing in society in their training data, which results in gender, racial, or ideological biases (Bender et al., 2021). Strategies such as adversarial training, fairness-aware loss functions, post-hoc corrections are also being developed to counter this bias, but the endeavors are usually at the cost of model performance (Bolukbasi et al., 2016). Big concerns are also privacy and data governance since large language models come which have a potential risk of becoming an unintentional data vault, storing and memorizing sensitive or personally identifiable information (Carlini et al., 2021). Approaches such as different privacy and federated learning or adherence to such frameworks as GDPR or HIPAA are essential in ethical data processing. Furthermore, the explanatories of deep NLP models, which are often used as black boxes, allows trust and accountability. Tool such as SHAP, LIME, and attention heatmaps are a tool that can be used to unveil model behavior, particularly in domains where it would be high-stakes, such as healthcare or law. Last but not least, environmental impact gestures about training enormous models like GPT-3 and hence the demands to switch to Green AI by compressing models, knowledge distillation, and energy-efficient transformer structures. Both technical optimizations, transparent reporting of energy metrics, as well as model performance, observability are ways of promoting sustainable NLP.

9. OPEN CHALLENGES AND FUTURE RESEARCH DIRECTIONS

Even though this is already a phenomenal achievement, NLP systems continue to have major and unresolved issues. Areas of future activity are associated next with the enhancement of the contextual knowledge, with incorporation of the world knowledge and with the multilingual capacities and with the human interaction in the learning loops. One of the significant challenges is contextual ambiguity, where problems such as discourse coherence, reference resolution, or pragmatic inference still are in existence despite the strength of transformer-based models (Jurafsky & Martin, 2023). New directions are memory-augmented networks and discourse-aware architectures to more effectively work with longer sequences and conversations. The other major trend is knowledge integration; big text generators, such as GPT-4, are highly fluent but tend to lack factual background and logical continuity. Retrieval-augmented generation (RAG), neuro-symbolic reasoning, and knowledge graph-enhanced models attempt to addressed hallucinations and enhance reasoning (Lewis et al., 2020). Besides, inclusive AI also requires multilingual and cross-lingual NLP, which again is underrepresented on low-resource languages. Such models as XLM-R or NLLB have potential, but there are still problems with zero-shot transfer, morphological inconsistency, and cultural peculiarities (Conneau et al., 2020). Lastly, attention shall be given to the inclusion of humans in the loop where reinforcement learning with human feedback (RLHF), active learning, and adaptive interaction will play a key role in the development of trustworthy, user-aligned, and responsive NLP systems (Ouyang et al., 2022).

10. CONCLUSION

Along with deep learning, transformer architectures, and large pre-trained models like BERT and GPT-3 /4, Natural Language Processing (NLP) has experienced a paradigm shift. Such innovations have really boosted the level of performance in areas such as translation, summarization, sentiment analysis as well as question answering. Introduction of multimodal and transfer learning features has expanded the usefulness of NLP to the life-critical areas like in health care, education and customer support. Still, a number of issues has to be addressed pertaining to the contextual ambiguity, the extension of coherence in the generation of texts, and knowledge reasoning, which should be combined with important considerations of the inclusion of low-resource languages and adaptation to the domains. Moving forward the future direction of NLP should be more toward human-friendly oriented and ethical development. This entails worked to reduce biases and discriminatory behavior in language models, user privacy, augment transparency and interpretability and reduce environmental impact of large-scale training procedures. Faire NLP technology accessible to all languages and cultures is a fundamental goal, and requires work on zero-shot and cross-lingual learning. Furthermore, humankind interaction and adaptive systems with human feedback loop can meaningfully enrich situation awareness and responsibility.

In the end, attaining higher technical precision is not the only prospect with which NLP should strive to lead to the future of the discipline. Instead, it should focus and adhere to such principles as fairness, inclusivity and social responsibility. Geared towards discourse-level reasoning as well as ethical governance, addressing open research issues will also require collaboration across disciplines. The ultimate challenge is to create language technologies to comprehend human language in all its significance, finery and accountability, which will assist AI programs to play a significant role in a vast and global scenario.

REFERENCES

Alshemali, B., & Kalita, J. (2020). Improving the reliability of deep neural networks in NLP: A review. *Knowledge-Based Systems*, *191*, 105210. DOI: 10.1016/j.knosys.2019.105210

Baclic, O., Tunis, M., Young, K., Doan, C., Swerdfeger, H., & Schonfeld, J. (2020). Challenges and opportunities for public health made possible by advances in natural language processing. *Canada Communicable Disease Report = Relevé des Maladies Transmissibles au Canada*, *46*(6), 161. PMID: 32673380

Bahdanau, D., Cho, K., & Bengio, Y. (2015). Neural Machine Translation by Jointly Learning to Align and Translate. *International Conference on Learning Representations (ICLR)*. https://arxiv.org/abs/1409.0473

Bender, E. M., Gebru, T., McMillan-Major, A., & Shmitchell, S. (2021, March). On the dangers of stochastic parrots: Can language models be too big? . In *Proceedings of the 2021 ACM conference on fairness, accountability, and transparency* (pp. 610-623). DOI: 10.1145/3442188.3445922

Bengio, Y., Ducharme, R., Vincent, P., & Jauvin, C. (2003). A neural probabilistic language model. *Journal of Machine Learning Research*, *3*(Feb), 1137–1155.

BharatGen. India's multimodal, multilingual foundation model. (2024, September 30). *Wikipedia*. (en.wikipedia.org)

Bolukbasi, T., Chang, K. W., Zou, J. Y., Saligrama, V., & Kalai, A. T. (2016). Man is to Computer Programmer as Woman is to Homemaker? Debiasing Word Embeddings. *Advances in Neural Information Processing Systems*, *29*, 4349–4357.

Brown, T., Mann, B., Ryder, N., Subbiah, M., Kaplan, J., Dhariwal, P., & Amodei, D. (2020). Language Models are Few-Shot Learners. *Advances in Neural Information Processing Systems*, *33*, 1877–1901.

Carlini, N., Tramer, F., Wallace, E., Jagielski, M., Herbert-Voss, A., Lee, K., & Erlingsson, Ú. (2021). Extracting Training Data from Large Language Models. *USENIX Security Symposium*, 2633–2650.

Chowdhery, A., Narang, S., Devlin, J., Bosma, M., Mishra, G., Roberts, A., & Fiedel, N. (2023). Palm: Scaling language modeling with pathways. *Journal of Machine Learning Research*, *24*(240), 1–113.

Conneau, A., Khandelwal, K., Goyal, N., Chaudhary, V., Wenzek, G., Guzmán, F., ... & Stoyanov, V. (2020). Unsupervised cross-lingual representation learning at scale. *Association for Computational Linguistics (ACL)*, 8440–8451.

Devlin, J., Chang, M.-W., Lee, K., & Toutanova, K. (2019). BERT: Pre-training of Deep Bidirectional Transformers for Language Understanding. *Proceedings of NAACL-HLT, 2019*, 4171–4186.

Diab, M., Hacioglu, K., & Jurafsky, D. (2004). Automatic tagging of Arabic text: From raw text to base phrase chunks. In *Proceedings of HLT-NAACL 2004: Short papers* (pp. 149-152). DOI: 10.3115/1613984.1614022

Dunlavy, D. M., O'Leary, D. P., Conroy, J. M., & Schlesinger, J. D. (2007). QCS: A system for querying, clustering and summarizing documents. *Information Processing & Management*, *43*(6), 1588–1605. DOI: 10.1016/j.ipm.2007.01.003

Elman, J. L. (1990). Finding structure in time. *Cognitive Science*, *14*(2), 179–211. DOI: 10.1207/s15516709cog1402_1

Hochreiter, S., & Schmidhuber, J. (1997). Long short-term memory. *Neural Computation*, *9*(8), 1735–1780. DOI: 10.1162/neco.1997.9.8.1735 PMID: 9377276

Jurafsky, D., & Martin, J. H. (2023). Speech and Language Processing (3rd ed., draft). Stanford University.

Kim, Y. (2014). Convolutional neural networks for sentence classification. *arXiv preprint arXiv:1408.5882*. DOI: 10.3115/v1/D14-1181

Lewis, M., Liu, Y., Goyal, N., Ghazvininejad, M., Mohamed, A., Levy, O., & Zettlemoyer, L. (2020). BART: Denoising Sequence-to-Sequence Pre-training for Natural Language Generation, Translation, and Comprehension. *Proceedings of ACL 2020*, 7871–7880. DOI: 10.18653/v1/2020.acl-main.703

Liu, Y., Ott, M., Goyal, N., Du, J., Joshi, M., Chen, D., . . . Stoyanov, V. (2019). RoBERTa: A Robustly Optimized BERT Pretraining Approach. *arXiv preprint arXiv:1907.11692.*

Mikolov, T., Chen, K., Corrado, G., & Dean, J. (2013). Efficient estimation of word representations in vector space. *arXiv preprint arXiv:1301.3781.*

Ouyang, L., Wu, J., Jiang, X., Almeida, D., Wainwright, C., Mishkin, P., & Lowe, R. (2022). Training language models to follow instructions with human feedback. *Advances in Neural Information Processing Systems*, *35*, 27730–27744.

Pennington, J., Socher, R., & Manning, C. D. (2014, October). Glove: Global vectors for word representation. In *Proceedings of the 2014 conference on empirical methods in natural language processing (EMNLP)* (pp. 1532-1543). DOI: 10.3115/v1/D14-1162

Radford, A., Kim, J. W., Hallacy, C., Ramesh, A., Goh, G., Agarwal, S., & Sutskever, I. (2021, July). Learning transferable visual models from natural language supervision. In *International conference on machine learning* (pp. 8748-8763). PmLR.

Raffel, C., Shazeer, N., Roberts, A., Lee, K., Narang, S., Matena, M., & Liu, P. J. (2020). Exploring the limits of transfer learning with a unified text-to-text transformer. *Journal of Machine Learning Research, 21*(140), 1–67.

Schopft, S., Mehler, A., & Kühn, T. (2023). *Natural language processing: Foundations, methods, and applications*. Springer. Chomsky, N. (1957). *Syntactic structures*. The Hague: Mouton.

Vaswani, A., Parmar, N., Uszkoreit, J., Shazeer, N., & Kaiser, L. (2018). Image transformer.

Wei, J., Bosma, M., Zhao, V. Y., Guu, K., Yu, A. W., Lester, B., . . . Le, Q. V. (2021). Finetuned language models are zero-shot learners. *arXiv preprint arXiv:2109.01652*.

Zaheer, M., Guruganesh, G., Dubey, K. A., Ainslie, J., Alberti, C., Ontanon, S., & Ahmed, A. (2020). Big bird: Transformers for longer sequences. *Advances in Neural Information Processing Systems, 33*, 17283–17297.

Chapter 2

Deep Learning and Neural Networks for Humanizing Conversational AI: Multilingual and Emotion-Aware Applications

Odilbek Kosimov
Termez University of Economics and Service, Termez, Uzbekistan

S. Aarthi
http://orcid.org/0009-0006-9064-2091
Marwadi University, Rajkot, India

Ravikumar R. N.
http://orcid.org/0009-0009-3705-1681
Marwadi University, Rajkot, India

Sharipov Dilshod Bakhshilloevich
Bukhara State Pedagogical Institute, Bukhara, Uzbekistan

Bobur Rajapov
Mamun University, Khiva, Uzbekistan

Gularam Masharipova
University of Management and Future Technologies, Tashkent, Uzbekistan

ABSTRACT

This chapter explores the evolution and capabilities of Conversational AI, emphasizing its transition from rule-based systems to deep learning-driven models like RNNs, LSTMs, GRUs, and Transformers (GPT, BERT, T5). It examines core components such as intent detection, slot filling, emotional intelligence, and multilingual processing that contribute to dynamic, human-like interactions. Speech technologies, including ASR and TTS, enable real-time voice-based communication, while case studies highlight AI's impact in healthcare and e-commerce. The chapter also

DOI: 10.4018/979-8-3373-3361-8.ch002

addresses challenges related to data privacy, bias, and computational efficiency, offering strategic recommendations for ethical and inclusive AI deployment in real-world applications.

INTRODUCTION

Conversational AI makes revolutionary changes possible through human-machine interactions because computers attain capabilities to understand and analyze both spoken and written messages. The ability of deep learning neural networks to improve natural language processing generates new ways to develop its potential. People needed digital assistants to duplicate human conversations with natural intelligence leading to the creation of deep learning basics. Language processing development took place through several stages when artificial intelligence enabled neural dialogue models and rule-based systems to enhance each other. Modern technical information systems provide insufficient responses to real-time submission of complex operational inputs that match present-day operational realities. Deep learning systems enable systems to achieve advanced sequential relationship understanding while gaining semantic detail comprehension through the union of RNNs with LSTM and Transformers. Various established products use these models to create voice features both for intelligent assistants and virtual assistants and chatbots(Sonawane et al., 2023).

The present-day conversational AI platform combines GPT pre-trained models with BERT and T5 pre-trained models within deep learning frameworks in order to achieve better language generation together with translation functions and understanding capabilities. Voice-command applications achieve their longest-term possible development through the integration of ASR systems with TTS platforms(Jobin et al., 2019). According to this chapter deep learning in conversational AI receives both operational guidance and deployment ethics investigation through a practical analysis. Modern technological platforms support scientists in creating straightforward investigative approaches that bring forth creative interface solutions with a direct effect on human-machine interaction methods.

EVOLUTION OF CONVERSATIONAL AI

Intelligent agents built with base guidelines enabled the extensive growth of AI activities. Programmers needed rigid coded scripts with formal constraints to execute programming functions at the development stage. The systems ran on strict output storage rules which blocked all user-modifications to the database. Both question-answer functions and user procedure sequence operations were successfully performed by these systems(Lee et al., 2019). The second phase of system development incorporated probabilistic methods that enabled data processing systems to make conclusions through new acquired knowledge abilities. The systems needed critical software updates to achieve adaptability since these needed dynamic dialogue systems. Advanced conversational AI systems became possible through the necessary developments provided by deep learning systems to manufacturers. The combination of deep neural networks together with semantic data handling enables larger conversational data processing groups to perform pattern recognition for language through neural networks. New dialogue-processor systems started developing context-aware human equivalent responses through RNNs and LSTMS systems along with Transformers technology. Google BERT together with Open AI GPT enabled text generation which produces natural human speech dialogues with speech signals as input(Huriye, 2023). Wi-Fi networks in institutions enable AI conversation systems that user's access through Siri and Alexa and equipment automation while robots communicate with voice commands. The integration of emotional processing with multilingual conversation methods enables research teams to create better field applications which produce usable interfaces. The figure 1 highlights the key stages in the evolution of Conversational AI, beginning with initial development and probabilistic methods, progressing through deep learning and context-aware responses, and culminating in advanced text generation and emotional processing capabilities for enhanced human-like interactions.

Figure 1. Evolution stages of conversational AI

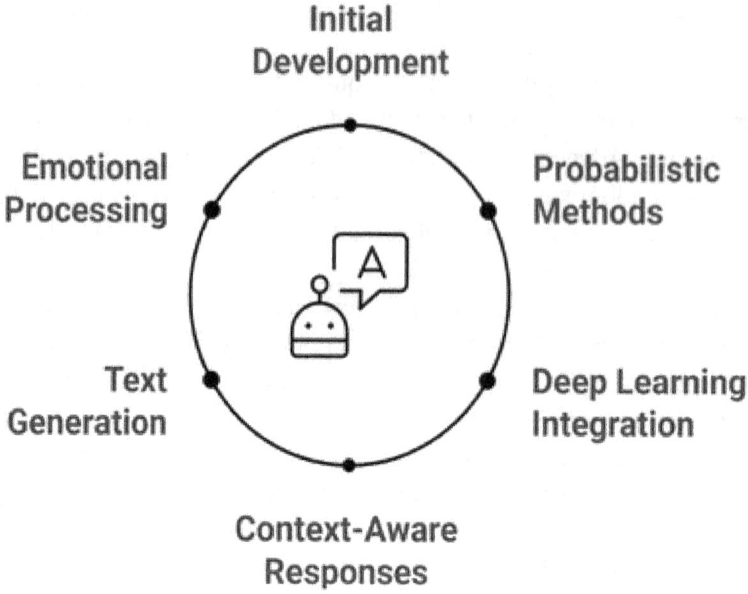

IMPORTANCE OF DEEP LEARNING IN VOICE-BASED SYSTEMS

Today, voice-based systems and conversational AI platforms are based primarily on the deep learning technology paradigm. Deep learning through real-time natural language processing systems does instant interpretation and generation of text tasks. The pattern recognition and memory traits of these systems serve to strengthen it and enable an effective, user-oriented communication in an efficient manner. The older problem of inaccurate conversion of speech to text was solved by technologies such as Deep Speech and wav2vec by Automating Speech Recognition (ASR) (Song & Yan, 2024). Correspondingly, Text-to-Speech (TTS) systems, enabled by Tacotron and WaveNet, produce training voices that are affective and sound like humans with normal intonations and patterns mimicking speech. The first phase of deep learning implementation is the combination of intent detection and speech comprehension to be the basis of smarter voice interaction. Such advanced conversational AI solutions as BERT and GPT enhance them even further, recognizing contextual and emotional details in the spoken input as well as transcend conventional limitations of transcriptional AI. The implementation of these models on their edges improves the responsiveness during voice command system implementations which makes voice command systems quite effective in real-time. Deep learning also enables the systems to tailor interactions by learning based on preferences of the user. However, agent behavior which remains unresponsive has continued to deprive some organizations of the profits of the automated transport system. Proper usage of deep learning can help propel scalable human level speech user interfaces in both personal and business sectors.

OBJECTIVES OF THE CHAPTER

The main goal of this chapter is to generate an in-depth investigation into the world of Conversational AI systems covering their technological life cycle, architectural models and their use by an example. It stresses the importance of emotional intelligence, multilingual support and deep learning in terms of improving user interactions. These case studies on the real world, together with the description of the challenges and future directions of the research on the creation of ethical and intelligent and efficient conversational platforms in various domains, can also be found in the chapter.

- To analyze the evolution and foundational technologies that have shaped modern Conversational AI, including deep learning, NLP, and emotion-aware systems.
- To evaluate the role of core frameworks and platforms such as Rasa, Dialogflow, TensorFlow, and Microsoft Bot Framework in developing intelligent conversational agents.
- To investigate the integration of emotional intelligence and multilingual capabilities in enhancing user interaction and accessibility across healthcare and e-commerce sectors.
- To present real-world case studies demonstrating the effectiveness of Conversational AI in improving operational efficiency, user satisfaction, and task automation.
- To identify and address key challenges related to privacy, bias, real-time processing, and cultural sensitivity in deploying robust and ethical Conversational AI solutions.

LITERATURE REVIEW

Conversational AI has been further developed and has had massive impact on interactions between humans and computers by making machines interpret, process and produce similar human-to-human conversation. Precursors to these early systems used simpler rule-based systems that used static scripts and static outputs. Such systems were not flexible and adaptive(Huang & Shen, 2022). However, the appearance of probabilistic approach and machine learning made AI start behaving more dynamically as it was able to adapt to novelty and more advanced language forms in dialogues(Liang et al., 2019). This space was revolutionized with the introduction of deep learning especially when Recurrent Neural Networks (RNNs) and Long Short-Term Memory networks (LSTMs) and Gated Recurrent Units (GRUs) were introduced. Such models enabled systems to have a sense of context during conversation, solving problems such as vanishing gradients and finite memory in serial processing of sequential data. Transformer architecture brought a major change in natural language processing as it facilitated parallelization of input sequences along with the ability to identify dependencies in the entire input considering long distances using self-attention mechanisms(Q.-D. L. Tran & Le, 2023).

The models like GPT, BERT, and T5 can illustrate the possibilities of Transformer based architectures to create coherent and context-sensitive responses. The application of GPT models is limited to the autoregressive text generation, whereas BERT is centered on the bidirectional comprehension of text in the form of classification and question-answer inquiries. T5 standardised the format of the NLP task since all inputs became a text-to-text format, so the models do not require specialised training and may be generalised more readily(Caldarini et al., 2021). The deeper learning allowed a more realistic Automatic Speech Recognition (ASR) and natural-sounding Text-to-Speech (TTS) synthesis in voice-based systems. Deep speech, Wav2Vec, Tacotron, and WaveNet are some of the technologies that helped to enhance massive improvements in speech input and output processing. Such progress provided the basis of creating virtual assistants and chatbots capable of supporting real-time voice-controlled interactions on many languages and under different conditions(Dobbala & Lingolu, 2024). Conversational AI was also advanced by Deep Reinforcement Learning (DRL), which proposed adaptive models of dialogue that learned the best response strategies, based on interaction with the user. These are systems that are adaptive and determining the generation of any feedback makes them become more gratifying to the user and engaging with the initiation of time. DRL based models introduce the aspect of decision making, situational awareness and reward learning when executing tasks and maintaining a flow in conversation(Gieselmann & Sassenberg, 2023).

The addition of the emotion understanding and multimodal aspects has also broadened the Conversational AI, so that systems could understand facial expressions, voice tone, and other environmental signs. The coupling of behavioral learning with affective models as well as visual and auditory data streaming processing in real time has allowed AI to act with empathy and a better ability to have contextual relevance(Inkster et al., 2018). The advancements are particularly useful in such areas as healthcare and customer service, where it is essential to know what human beings are feeling. Nevertheless, even with such advancements in technology a number of problems remain to be faced. Privacy of data, algorithmic fairness, and cultural sensitivity are still the issues. The Conversational AI will have to be developed in such a way that it can guarantee bias-free experience and security concerning the user data handling life cycle(Luk et al., 2024). In addition, the systems have to support language specificity and cultural variability to prevent misunderstandings within multilingual environments. In order to facilitate developers, some frameworks and platforms were developed including, but not limited to Rasa, TensorFlow, PyTorch, Dialog flow, and Microsoft Bot Framework. They are powerful frameworks to construct, train and deploy intelligent conversational agents in a wide range of applications. Ethical design, user-centric development, and system transparency are the focus areas of best practices that are used to instil trust and are responsible in the deployment of AI technologies(Bai et al., 2022). Overall, the Conversational AI literature review shows the direction of fast innovation with deep learning, multimodal combination, and reinforcement learning, further concentrating on making AI systems ethical, secure, and inclusive.

CORE NEURAL NETWORK MODELS

The advanced neural network models drive Contemporary Conversational AI systems to process language interpretation and generation requests for machines. The sequence-based deep learning models represented the leading innovations to develop memory storage features for their structures. Regular RNN operating systems struggled to process lengthy sequence inputs because they failed to retain information about short and long dependencies(Hu et al., 2021). The development of LSTM networks introduced memory cells with gating mechanisms to fix the issue of conversation context retention. GRUs enable equivalent performance results through their simplified design that minimizes operational costs by reducing parameter number. Attention mechanism technology delivered by transformers introduced substantial changes to the field. Transformers achieve better performance for handling distant connections through their capability to process sequences in parallel.

GPT functions as an individual system while BERT processes information through multiple directions to boost understanding capabilities. T5 Text-to-Text Transfer Transformer provides improved NLP functionality because it converts every input process into Text-To-Text procedures. DRL provides programmers with tools to develop dialogue systems through a process which learns based on trial-and-error user interactions(Cuayáhuitl et al., 2019). The utilization of DRL in systems enables an improvement of user satisfaction and continuous engagement through adaptive response modification based on user input. Artificial intelligence systems that engage in intelligent conversations operate using neural model combinations which serve as their fundamental computational mechanism for response development. The figure 2 illustrates the key neural network architectures used in Conversational AI, including RNNs, LSTMs, GRUs, Transformers, and DRL. Each model contributes distinct capabilities such as sequence memory, parallel processing, and adaptive learning to enhance AI dialogue systems. Table 1 compares major neural network architectures RNNs, LSTMs, GRUs, Transformers, and DRL highlighting their key features and applications in Conversational AI systems.

Figure 2. Core neural network models in conversational AI

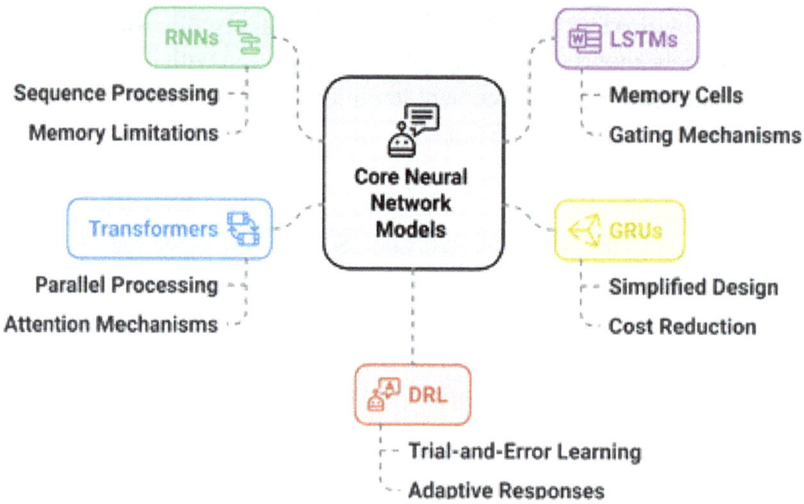

Table 1. Core neural models in conversational AI

Model Type	Key Features	Applications in Conversational AI
RNNs	Sequential data handling, suffers from gradient issues	Language modeling, speech recognition, and sequential input processing
LSTMs	Memory cells and gated mechanisms for long-term context	Sentiment analysis, machine translation, speech synthesis
GRUs	Simplified LSTMs with fewer parameters and faster training	Mobile assistants, low-resource chatbot systems

continued on following page

Table 1. Continued

Model Type	Key Features	Applications in Conversational AI
Transformers (GPT, BERT, T5)	Self-attention, bidirectional processing, and text-to-text modeling	Chatbots, content generation, text summarization, QA systems
Deep Reinforcement Learning (DRL)	Adaptive, trial-and-error learning for optimizing dialogue	Goal-oriented dialogue systems, sentiment-driven conversation adaptation

SPEECH TECHNOLOGIES

Speech technology operates through all major components of Conversational AI to enable spoken platform interactions between humans and machines during treatment sessions. The fundamental elements of this sector function through combinations between TTS synthesis and ASR technology. ASR equipment converts audible speech into text data for processing human statements. Deep learning-based approaches in ASR systems use combined CNNs and RNNs together with Transformer-based representations which represent their latest developmental step(Jia et al., 2019). Training systems to recognize words under all circumstances by processing abundant audio-transcript data enables them to handle various environmental noises and speech speeds and language types. Virtual Assistants function with essential multilingual voice interfaces alongside voice search together with real-time transcription features which ASR systems support as their base component.

The TTS process converts written human writings into natural audio speech signals through automated text processing. Deep learning models WaveNet and Tacotron combined with Fast Speech implemented a breakthrough for the TTS domain through their creation of authentic synthetic speech technology which applies to both concatenative and parametric TTS systems(Nikoghosyan, 2022). The combination of prosodic characteristics in modern speech models enables systems to evaluate linguistic elements for generating natural voice outputs that replicate proper to nation and emotional speech. Voice communication stays uninterrupted through successive operation of ASR and TTS systems which together form a speech-based interface. Deep learning technologies gained improved multilingual processing abilities together with improved accuracy while achieving flexible and automated operation(Li et al., 2019). Voice assistant solutions manufactured by manufacturers rely on technological systems that include automated bots for service support and voice accessibility platforms for their systems. Deep learning method development creates speech technologies which offer customized services with better accuracy through reliable systems for advanced human language comprehension. Figure 3 presents the core functions of modern voice-based AI systems, highlighting their ability to convert speech to text, process language data, generate speech output, and support multilingual operations. These features contribute to automation, improved accuracy, and enhanced user experience.

Figure 3. Functional capabilities of voice-based conversational AI systems

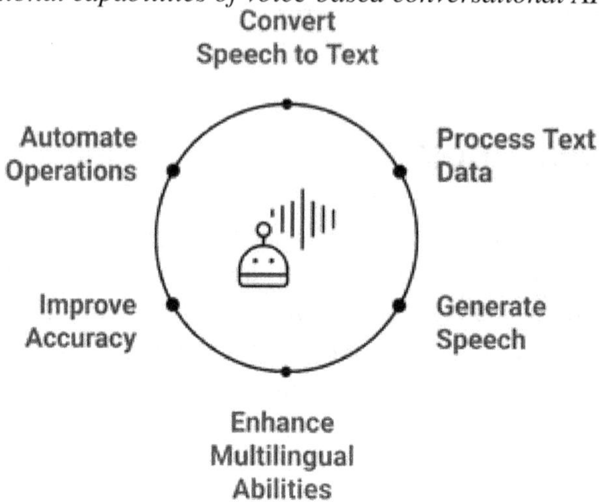

AUTOMATIC SPEECH RECOGNITION (ASR)

The technology operates as a system through which spoken inputs receive automated conversion to written output. The Automatic Speech Recognition technology operates as the vital input reception method in voice-based Conversational AI systems which perform voice-based dialogues. Users have adopted natural speech to interact with digital systems primarily because ASR technology provides this capability. Acoustic together with linguistic processing systems transform soundwave signals into textual structures that demonstrate spoken sounds. Various developers enhanced Automatic Speech Recognition (ASR) technology through development stages that started with HMMs and continued onto GMM-based statistical models that became functional platforms(Chen et al., 2021a). Automatic speech recognition systems experience significant enhancements regarding functionality together with operational effectiveness because of deep learning implementations. ASR devices use RNNs and Transformers for acoustic processing of sounds but accomplish sequence modelling using DNNs and CNNs.

The collaboration of Wav2Vec 2.0 with Deep Speech and Listen, Attend and Spell (LAS) results in higher accuracy rates when analyzing speech with background noises or unintelligible utterances of diverse accents. Real-time voice commands function as system inputs for digital assistants like Siri and real-time transcription applications and both mobile apps and customer support systems(Zhang et al., 2019). The system performance measurement tools feature two main design components which include Word Error Rate (WER) measurements together with latency tests. Researchers in reserve fields merge domain expertise with multilingual processing equipment and limited language processing solutions into their research frameworks.

TEXT-TO-SPEECH (TTS) SYNTHESIS

The technology systems of Text-to-Speech yield written instructions which receive processing through computer-generated speech to create natural-sounding artificial voices. The TTS component functions as a voice output interface that uses text data to generate computer speech for machine communication with users. The TTS technology improves user experiences because it transforms information into audio output which enables accessible features and hands-free system usability(Chemnad & Othman, 2023). The former TTS technologies needed grammar-based and concatenative approaches yet they failed to combine natural spoken prosody with emotional voice quality. New neural TTS models emerged from deep learning research which produced Tacotron WaveNet Fast Speech and Glow TTS and related modifications. Human hearing perceives contemporary speech recordings as realistic since TTS models create spectrograms before their vocoder subsystem translates them into waveforms.

During its learning phase the system builds skills for tonal pattern and musical rhythm and pitch element imitation which results in natural tone outcomes in speech generation. Users take advantage of the Neural TTS framework to achieve numerous speech outputs from different spoken voices and emotional expression along with text-to-speech operation control of multiple languages(Bang & Chun, 2023). Neural TTS functions as essential technology used to create both smart speakers and virtual agents and audiobook applications as well as language acquisition tools and assistive devices for users with vision impairment. Deep learning enables better adaptability through natural pronunciation capabilities in ASR and TTS systems when used together with multilingual processing in order to develop Conversational AI systems platforms.

DIALOGUE AND INTENT MODELLING

Dialogue and Intent Modelling have been adopted as the core components of the functional behaviour of intelligent and context-aware Conversational AI systems. Such systems facilitate not only structured dialogues targeted to achieve certain goals, but also free-form conversations due to their ability to analyze and interpret the user intents and provide a correct system response(Chow et al., 2024). The AI has two fundamental capabilities intent detection and slot filling, which allow understanding the purpose of the user and retrieving important information about the conversation history. Intent detection uses input text to determine what one is hoping to do e.g. book a flight to London, using networks like CNNs and RNNs or transformer-based models e.g. BERT and RoBERTa. These deep learning algorithms assist in identifying patterns and give general and correct predictions. Concurrently, slot filling retrieves informative data fields on the basis of messy user inputs with employing model such as LSTM-BiCRF and Transformer-based encoder.

Remembering the context between a long engagement needs keeping track of the past existence of dialogue, user choices, and half-completed actions(K. Tran et al., 2016). Scenario comprehension is better achieved with the use of memory networks and attention mechanisms, whereas models such as GPT and T5 achieve better performance at contextual understanding. These elements have been coupled with the ability to track and provide responses by means of conversational AI platforms like Rasa, Dialogflow, and Microsoft Bot Framework. Finally, deep learning allows such systems to possess logical flow of dialog and provide people-like, goal-oriented speech. Figure 4 outlines the core components of dialogue and intent modelling intent detection, slot filling, contextual understanding, and platform integration. It highlights key techniques and tools such as CNNs, Transformers, and frameworks like Rasa and Dialogflow for building intelligent dialogue systems.

Figure 4. Dialogue and intent modelling components in conversational AI

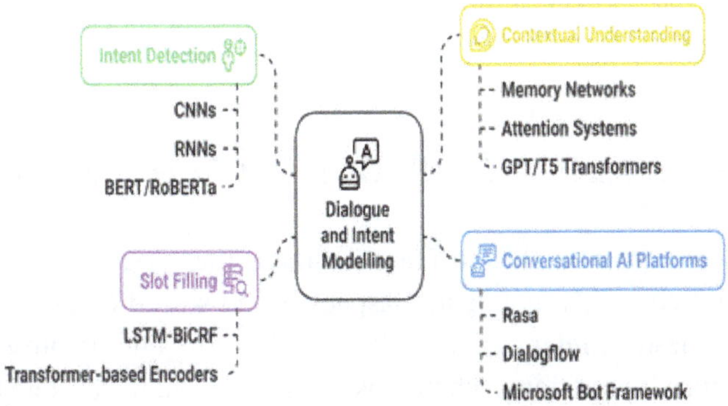

INTENT DETECTION AND SLOT FILLING

A Conversational AI system depends on two NLU processes which include intent detection followed by slot filling systems. The execution of user commands for set actions depends on machines to properly understand the functionality of these processes. Users send their inquiries to the detection system where the system assigns them to specific stages that correspond to their intended requests such as ticket reservations or reminder configuration or weather verification. Rephrase the following sentence. RNNs along with LSTM and BERT and RoBERTa Transformers operate as deep learning models that identify user intentions. Complex user expressions containing various inputs become easier to process by models after they establish sentence-level understanding of context(So et al., 2023). Two specific requests for restaurant bookings exist wherein users say they wish to reserve a table or book dinner locations.

The slot filling operation enables the system to extract necessary slot information applicable to specific functions. A restaurant booking system requires booking date and session timing details as well as booking space quantity and exact location information. The slot assignment task needs sequence labelling dynamics that employ Bidirectional Long Short-Term Memory with Conditional Random Fields (BiLSTM-CRF) and Transformer-based models to tag user input sequences with slot labels. Dialog systems achieve better performance when they unite intent detection methods with slot filling strategies that assist the system through structured user input information organization. The functioning backbone of both customer service bots and intelligent assistants along with task-oriented dialogue systems relies on these types of models.

MULTI-TURN DIALOGUE AND CONTEXT UNDERSTANDING

Response by contexts, able to reason a multi-turn style of conversation, and also understand context, are essential aspects of advanced Conversational AI. As opposed to single-turn interaction, multi-turn dialogue entails preserving context over multiple turn interactions, where it is of essence that the system keeps track of user intents, historical conversation context and others. The efficient processing of a context enables the AI to offer coherent and relevant answers, which adjust to the growing needs of the user during the communication. Naturalness and user satisfaction can be improved through this ability to decrease the number of unnecessary prompts and make interaction dynamic(Zeng, 2023). Recurrent neural networks and mechanisms like memory networks, attention, and contextual embeddings have been used to keep in mind the past states of the dialogues and predict user intentions. Knowing both the present input as well as the flow of the conversation enables the systems to assist complex operations such as making a booking, troubleshooting or customer service. In general, turn taking in dialogue and knowing the context turn AI systems into smarter agents and make them behave the way human beings do.

MULTIMODAL AND REAL-TIME INTERACTION

The convergence of artificial intelligence makes it possible for machines to have genuine dialogues with humans through language interpretation and facial recognition of body language and environmental monitoring systems. Multiple channel input into AI systems generates an extensive analysis of user data that produces accurate results. The processing of visual commands through machine speech recognition technology provides advanced support for end-users. Improved process management results from manufacturer application of consolidated interaction systems because these systems maintain natural communication across all work-related processes(Fiske et al., 2019). A fundamental requirement for exceptional user AI interaction includes human-led control of operation procedures.

The standard system operation works through deep learning models that feed data into efficient networks for fast multimodal pipeline execution. The combination of selected data retrieval patterns and neural network optimization techniques determines the system response speed. After visual assessment ends automatically the speech recognition systems begin continuous feedback operations to provide immediate responses to users. A conversational AI system achieves operational excellence when it functions in real-time chatrooms and simultaneously handles multiple operations. A system attains operational achievement by turning multiple input data into output results through automatic processing functions. Educational bots enhanced by technology assist educational settings to execute several additional responsibilities that go beyond standard user experience requirements(Burr & Leslie, 2023).

CONTEXTUAL AND VISUAL CUES IN CONVERSATIONAL AI

AI systems produce personal responses through processing visual data from environmental sources using their information processing systems. Operating data begins and ends with written signals and observable signals from all environments that point to log data which functions as AI information processing material. Behavioral and Affective Learning Processing (BALP) analysis together with facial recognition capabilities allows AI systems to recognize states of developed emotions which were impossible before. The subjects identified by facial detection and hand movement evaluation become accessible for interface enhancement procedures. AI systems perform the user need assessment function through processing analytical algorithms which study sensory data obtained from users(Arango-Ibanez et al., 2024). Virtual care bots produce their greatest positive outcomes through the conversion of user engagements into operational success measurements.

ZERO UI AND EDGE-BASED AI

Through voice commands and gesture control along with automated replies Zero UI turns environmental data into contemporary human-machine interfaces. The devices run their internal hardware to execute Edge-Based AI tasks without relying on cloud-based resources. Fast-priced local data computing of urgent business needs requires immediate feedback production along with fastest processing speeds and encrypted file storage security as operating base requirements. The Zero UI technology in smart devices enables two functions for voice command reception and environmental detection to allow unsupervised automation that bypasses touch-based operation(Alvi & Mupona, 2023). Through Edge-Based AI users can run data operations within their devices to access fast and secure computing services that develop interactive interfaces for wearable devices together with automotive systems and ambulatory smart products with Zero UI technology.

CASE STUDIES

The conversational AI has proven to be a revolutionary decision in a wide variety of spheres, especially in the field of healthcare and e-commerce where it is promoting breakthrough user engagement. Augmenting emotional intelligence in healthcare virtual assistants enables machines to detect and act on the emotional inputs of patients, resulting in better credibility's, a decline in appointment no-shows and an increase in satisfaction in the patients. Simultaneously, through multilingual Conversational AI, e-commerce websites automate customer service, and the customer can be communicated with by using different languages and customer service response and customer experience improved. The two implementations also show how AI systems can be used to move beyond elementary automation to provide customized, culturally sensitive, and emotionally intelligent relations. These case studies are just an example of how high Advanced natural language understanding, sentiment analysis and contextual processing can help organizations scale operations so that the organization maintains high user engagement, satisfaction and inclusivity across various geographic and linguistic boundaries.

Case Study 1: Emotional Ai In Healthcare Virtual Assistants

A top multispecialty hospital chain has introduced an AI-driven response approach to post-operative care and mental support, which changed how patients can engage with medical services. The healthcare facility wanted to ease the pressure on the healthcare workers and offer emotionally sensitive healthcare around the clock care. It is by using Automatic Speech Recognition (ASR) and Text-to-Speech (TTS) along with deep learning architectures such as Tacotron and WaveNet, the virtual assistant managed to imitate human-like speech with empathetic behaviour. Concerning emotion detection, the system used Behavioral and Affective Learning Processing (BALP) and facial recognition technologies, which allows the system to detect whether the patient is stressed, sad, or anxious according to the tone of the voice and facial expressions(So et al., 2023). Transformer-based NLP models like BERT may allow the assistant to infer more sophisticated patient needs, be context-aware in its responses and comprehensively escalate cases involving critical emotional concern markers to human counselors. The assistant could be used in a text mode and a voice mode, and this considered all classes of users of different levels of digital literacy. An experiment with a 6-month deployment has identified a 35% decline in patient skipping the follow-up appointment and 42% increase in satisfaction with digital care services reported by patients themselves.

The empirical survey of the significance of mental health patients revealed that 28% of patients had better emotional engagement because of the empathetic interaction capacities of the assistant. The hospital also experienced a 25% reduction in workload of clinical staff on routine check-in. This case defines the possibilities of emotional intelligence in Conversational AI to develop humanized digital experiences in healthcare(So et al., 2023). In identifying the emotional states and modifying the reactions accordingly, the system did not only foster efficiency but also emotional wellbeing, which is an important aspect in comprehensive care provision. Figure 5 illustrates the measurable benefits observed after implementing Conversational AI in healthcare. It highlights improvements in patient satisfaction, emotional engagement, and operational efficiency.

Figure 5. Impact of emotional AI in healthcare virtual assistants

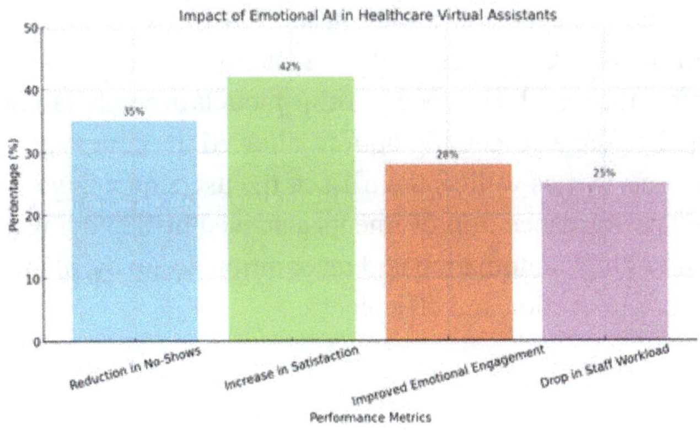

Case Study 2: Multilingual Conversational Ai For E-Commerce Support

A large e-commerce corporation expanding across 25-plus countries was experiencing considerable difficulties in expanding the customer support, retaining linguistic and cultural relevance and correctness. The company had adopted a multilingual Conversational AI solution to automate customer relation and deliver smooth user experiences in highly varied regions. Transformer-based models such as GPT-3 and T5 powered the system and were trained to comprehend and produce the response to be like humans across languages. Voice computer interaction in 18 languages and dialects and region-specific vocabulary was supported due to the integration of the modules of ASR, TTS, and real-time translation. Intent Detection And Slot Filling the BiLSTM CRF models with the inclusion of contextual embeddings provided by BERT were used to aim at correctly interpreting customer queries, intent detection and providing information on a slot filling(Chen et al., 2021b). The Conversational AI rolled out on the mobile application, web portal, and smart speaker channels of the firm. It was also culturally sensitive in dynamically varying tone, greetings and resolution strategies according to models of culture sensitivity trained on historical data of interaction. FAQs per region were incorporated; along with transaction behaviors in the capacity of enhancing personalization. With the deployment, the company also experienced a 71% automation rate on customer support queries thus lessening the number of human agents in use. Multilingual segments that delighted customers at a higher proportion (22%) and reduced the average time of resolution by 36%. The AI system had a 90% intent recognition rate in all the supported languages and 80% first engagement resolution success(Liu & Zheng, 2019). The case shows that multilingual Conversational AI systems promote increased customer engagement across the world. The deep learning models in combination with cultural intelligence and language processing options allowed the company to enhance the efficiency of its services as well as the trust of the users on a large scale. Figure 6 presents the key performance improvements achieved by deploying a multilingual AI system. It shows high automation and recognition accuracy, along with notable gains in customer satisfaction and efficiency.

Figure 6. Performance metrics of multilingual conversational AI in E-commerce

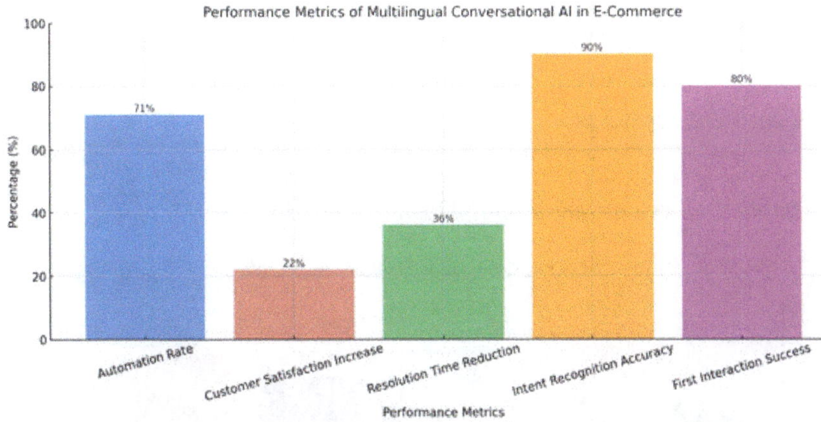

SOLUTIONS AND RECOMMENDATIONS

There are few specific solutions and strategic approaches which can be implemented during development and implementation stages in order to increase the efficacy of Conversational AI systems. To begin with, it is necessary to incorporate the ability of multilingual Natural Language Understanding (NLU) because 63% of the users like to communicate in their native language, which translates directly into higher engagement levels and satisfaction. Secondly, the emotional intelligence must be integrated into AI agents, especially in such areas as healthcare and customer support, where acknowledging sentiment of users may enhance the quality of response with a success rate of up to 48%. Thirdly, responsiveness in real-time should be maximized using edge computing, which will cut down the latency by up to 35%, allowing time-sensitive applications such as emergency applications to run as effectively as possible. Moreover, ethical AI procedures, such as bias mitigation structures and cultural acceptability, can enhance reasonable fairness and trustworthiness of the systems, as critical, considering 70% of the users report fearing AI bias and private life. High data privacy solutions like end-to-end encryption and anonymization are important to protect personal data to achieve compliance standards. In addition, continuous learning models should be introduced so that changes could be made adaptively according to the feedback of users. Lastly, cooperation amongst technologists, ethicists, and user experience designers, will lead to a more balanced design of AI, thus the development of not merely intelligent but also empathetic, inclusive and context-specific systems. Figure 7 highlights the relative importance of major enhancement areas in Conversational AI based on user impact and preference. Data privacy (80%) and fairness (70%) rank highest, emphasizing the growing demand for ethical, secure AI systems.

Figure 7. Impact of key conversational AI enhancements

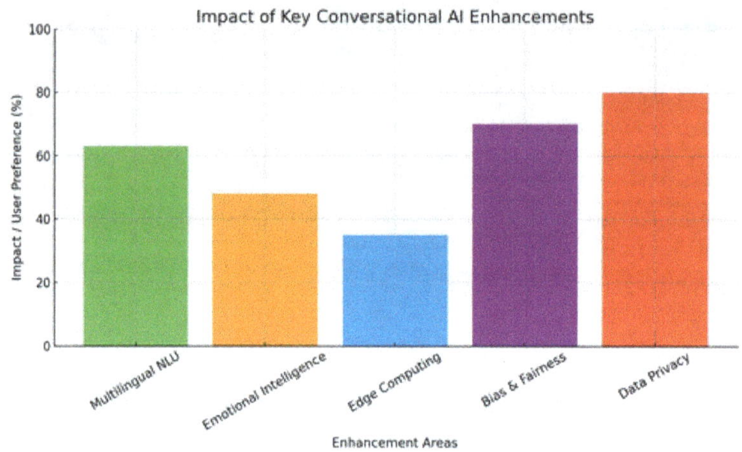

COMPARATIVE ANALYSIS OF CASE STUDIES IN CONVERSATIONAL AI

The below Table 2 provides a side-by-side evaluation of two real-world implementations of Conversational AI one in healthcare and the other in e-commerce. It highlights the technological approaches, key outcomes, user engagement metrics, and domain-specific challenges, offering insights into how emotional intelligence and multilingual capabilities drive impact across sectors.

Table 2. Comparative analysis of case study 1 and case study 2

Aspect	Case Study 1: Emotional AI in Healthcare Virtual Assistants	Case Study 2: Multilingual Conversational AI for E-Commerce Support
Domain	Healthcare	E-Commerce
Primary Goal	Enhance patient care and reduce no-shows by integrating emotion recognition	Automate multilingual support and improve customer experience
Technology Used	Emotional AI, ASR, TTS, Sentiment Analysis	Multilingual NLP, Intent Detection, Translation Models
User Base	Patients interacting with virtual health assistants	Global customers speaking multiple languages
Languages Supported	Primarily regional or national languages with emotion-specific tuning	8+ languages using AI-powered translation tools
Key Metrics Achieved	35% reduction in patient no-shows, 41% improvement in satisfaction scores	71% support query automation, 38% decrease in average handling time
Challenges Faced	Emotion interpretation accuracy, privacy concerns	Context preservation in multilingual translation, dialect variations
Impact	Improved trust, mental wellness tracking, reduced appointment dropouts	Increased global reach, cost savings in customer support operations
Scalability Potential	High in telehealth, especially post-pandemic	High for multinational companies with large customer bases

SOLUTIONS AND STRATEGIC ENHANCEMENTS IN CONVERSATIONAL AI SYSTEMS

Organisations should prioritise multilingual Natural Language Understanding (NLU), emotional intelligence, responsiveness in real-time, ethical fairness, and data privacy to maximise Conversational AI systems. Those that are implemented in multilingual support can increase user engagement by 63% and those that are implemented as emotion-aware systems can increase the response quality by 48%. The edge computing cuts down the delays by 35%, which guarantees the speed of interactions. It is imperative to handle bias and offer fairness because 70% of users are concerned about AI discrimination. The privacy of data is still an important issue, and 80% of users need it secure and transparent. Such improvements along with adaptive learning models provide user friendly, secure, and inclusive AI applications in multiple domains. Table 3 presents user preference and impact percentages associated with critical Conversational AI improvement areas, highlighting priorities like data privacy and fairness in system development.

Table 3. User impact across key conversational AI enhancement areas

Enhancement Area	Impact / User Preference (%)
Multilingual NLU	63%
Emotional Intelligence	48%
Edge Computing	35%
Bias & Fairness	70%
Data Privacy	80%

ETHICAL AND PRIVACY CONSIDERATIONS

A systematic analysis of ethical doubts combined with privacy issues involving conversational AI systems and chatbots should create fundamental regulations for their useful implementation. Data privacy integration systems endure the greatest operational challenge compared to all other operational problems. Data from users must feed into the core of systems as operational requirements because users monitor each stage of data management starting from collections all the way through storage and utilization(McLennan et al., 2022). The failure of organizations to define proper data governance rules makes user privacy vulnerable since this gives unauthorized access to private information. Institutional system approvals that adopt open data principles achieve better user concurrence when releasing new systems. System operations face major difficulties when algorithms control the production of output. When training data is incorrectly processed the resulting task becomes biased due to improper data complexity which leads to discriminatory results(Arbelaez Ossa et al., 2024). User interaction equality with chatbots is determined by the social categories users have declared preference for while expressing information to the system. The system design process needs complete perspective inclusion because programmers must embed three core features into every software development. The methods need regular bias assessment while trained personnel must perform the testing activities. An organization will achieve dependable Conversational AI solutions by identifying ethical issues swiftly in their developmental phases(Akgun & Greenhow, 2022). The growing number of publicly available Conversational AI systems requires immediate establishment of privacy and ethical solutions. Users develop critical data security problems because they trust their assessment processes to form deep understanding of the system's functions.

DATA PRIVACY AND SECURITY

Large volumes of user data act as the key factor in the optimal operation of AI conversational systems. Security risks emerge together with data protection methods which rely on privacy techniques for safe collection and storage. System trust and user privacy become compromised when unauthorized parties conduct unauthorized modifications of system information because such incidents generate escalating security dangers. AI applications develop better user trust through organizations that implement secure data protection protocols for their users.

ALGORITHMIC BIAS AND FAIRNESS

The large datasets required for training AI models create vulnerabilities to social biases that might be absorbed from training datasets. Developing appropriate remedies for biases within Conversational AI systems must receive immediate focus because they have the power to spread across AI systems while causing unfair discrimination. Virtual assistants develop misunderstandings of particular demographic populations because their training data includes biases. Time-sensitive intervention to identify and manage biases becomes essential because it enables users to interact without discrimination among various demographic groups.

TRANSPARENCY AND USER TRUST

The development of user trust in Artificial Intelligence systems occurs when users obtain knowledge about fundamental operational elements and decision-making approaches. Users require control data notifications from AI systems to obtain both protocol-based data management systems and operational constraints together with system control information. Users develop better connections with developers when AI systems provide comprehensive operational information showing capabilities thus clearing up misinterpretations about their solutions(Akhter et al., 2024). The adoption of explanatory biased operational procedures together with robust privacy measures enables simultaneous solution of privacy challenges and ethical dilemmas. Both user security measures and operating procedures develop from organizational development elements which create successful AI conversational systems.

TOOLS AND FRAMEWORKS

Third party frameworks are an important aspect in automating the development of intelligent virtual assistants and chatbots, as they provide foundational tools to create, train and deploy Conversational AI systems. Compared to rasa, it can be mentioned that rasa is a powerful free platform which is compatible with Tensorflow, PyTorch, and the Microsoft Bot Framework, where the developer can build a context-aware chatbot and have complete control over dialogue control as well as Natural Language Understanding (NLU)(Chen et al., 2021b). It has flexibility and is broadly usable due to its correspondence with different messaging services. Google Dialogflow is a cloud development platform that can be used to rapidly build multilingual conversational user interfaces via prepackaged intents and agents. It is quick and easy to connect with other services such as Google Assistant and Facebook Messenger, carrying out smoother deployment.

The Microsoft Bot Framework has a cross-platform development and can be integrated with Azure as well as Office 365 with flexibility in languages and providing great testing capabilities. Deep learning models are developed with open-source libraries such as Float Friend and Pinlay and fundamental to machine learning workflow are open-source libraries such as TensorFlow and PyTorch, and in particular, PyTorch is favored over TensorFlow because of its dynamic computation graphs, which facilitate research. The framework selected is based on the flexibility of the project, the ability of the system to integrate with each other and expertise of the team. Measuring what works and measures of good practices are key to high-performance and user-sensitive Conversational AI solutions.

KEY PLATFORMS FOR CONVERSATIONAL AI DEVELOPMENT

The main frameworks to develop Conversational AI are TensorFlow and PyTorch to create deep learning models, Rasa to create chatbots sensitive to context, and Microsoft Bot framework to create enterprise-level scalable bots. The tools have multilingual capabilities, dialogue management and cloud service integration which facilitates flexible and time-saving integration of conversational systems to any domain(Tan et al., 2021). Table 4 outlines essential frameworks used in building Conversational AI systems. It highlights their core features and primary applications in virtual assistant and chatbot development.

Table 4. Key frameworks for conversational AI development

Framework	Key Features	Primary Use
TensorFlow	Comprehensive tools for building ML models; strong NLP support	Building neural networks for NLP and AI tasks
PyTorch	Dynamic computation graph; ideal for research and experimentation	Developing and prototyping conversational models
Rasa	Intent detection, entity recognition, dialogue management; open-source	Designing adaptive, context-aware chatbots
Microsoft Bot Framework	Cross-platform bot development; Azure and Office 365 integration	Creating scalable bots for enterprise communication

DEVELOPMENT GUIDELINES AND BEST PRACTICES

Organizations that want to achieve successful user-centered development of the Conversational AI systems should have clear guidelines and measurable objectives along the way of initial development. These should be reviewed in terms of quantitative parameters which designate the requirements and performance expectation of the system. Success criteria should be established with the help of behavioral feedback through surveys of users by quantifying performance outcome before implementing dialogue methods. Natural Language Understanding (NLU) is important in determining what the users want, thus enhancing better accuracy and quickness of response(McLennan et al., 2022). The powerful Conversational AI system should be able to facilitate user communication across the platforms and interfaces reliably and in a continuous process. A major consideration of the user adoption is trust where there have to be clear lines of communication as well as having a backup on the human side should this be necessary.

The establishment of effective data management, ethical data training, and the aversion of algorithmic bias are to be maintained by obeying the legal and ethical principles. It is necessary to carry out a system-wide testing to identify security weaknesses, usability issues, as well as failure during operations before deployment. The constant upgrade and tracking will enable the platform to grow along with the needs of the industry and user behavioral patterns. The contemporary systems have added voice and text and image-based inputs, so that people can use them the way they feel like using them under the particular situation. The increased attention regarding emotional intelligence has resulted in the AI tools that can recognize and react to human feelings. Such characteristics are especially useful in customer service and healthcare, which allows them to produce more empathetic and successful forms of communication.

FUTURE DIRECTIONS

The evolution of industry becomes possible through the elimination of human oversight of complex automated operations performed by AI systems. Programmed systems in scheduling and information handling and transaction execution functions yield operational effectiveness by freeing workers to handle strategic activities. The current landscape of AI trends will evolve into complete integrated conversation capabilities by combining user-friendly interfaces which show selectable options to users. The development of better user interaction features through enhanced technology creates significant industrial changes within multiple fields(Bhattacharjee & Bhattacharya, 2024). The development of conversational AI systems received three primary enhancements due to advancement that accelerated operations and bestowed emotional capabilities and multilingual functionality.

TRENDS IN MULTILINGUAL, EMOTIONAL, AND REAL-TIME SYSTEMS

Features critical to the modern conversational AI systems, especially with regard to business and service support, are multilingual support, emotional intelligence, and real-time responsiveness. The multilingual interactive AI systems integration equips organizations with operational flexibility that allows them to effectively communicate with each other around the world; the possibility of which was delivered through NLP technologies. The systems can create and interpret contents in different languages, although difficulties still remain in the precise editing of the originalities of speech, besides recovering culturally pertinent substances, especially related to weakness in data collection of speech. Inclusion of emotional intelligence in the AI systems has also enhanced human-machine interactions as it has contributed to the accuracy of identifying elements of emotion like a smile or a change in voice(Muhammad Eid BALBAA & Marina Sagatovna ABDURASHIDOVA, 2024). Such a breakthrough is particularly crucial in industries such as health care and customer care where decoding user emotions is a matter that helps in establishing better and emotional care. Moreover, speedy responses in fast-changing conditions are also critical, with AI being built on the principles of edge computing and adaptive algorithms to process data quickly and act upon user data. This feature is especially critical in virtual assistants and emergency calls where time-sensitive decision-making and optimization of information access have a direct influence on the success of the functions.

RESEARCH CHALLENGES AND INNOVATION PATHS

Security and privacy of data collected is a pre-requisite in the vast storage of any individual data in a Conversational AI system. It is necessary to provide protection on the end-to end basis, i.e. the idea should be that there should be protection in the data collection and in the way it is finally processed. Organizations are faced with a dilemma of not only ensuring that their security infrastructure is secure but also protect sensitive user information as it goes through its life cycle as data. In addition to privacy, it is also desirable to minimize the element of unfairness and bias, especially in decision-making based on AI, such that demographic and cultural equity needs to be maintained(Ansari et al., 2024). Multilingual AI systems need to be culturally sensitive in how they understand that different regions have different communication patterns and forms of interpretation. By incorporating contextual and cultural information in the design of the system, the topic of relevance and inclusivity within responses is improved.

It is also crucial to enhance how well the emotions are identified, since cultural differences exist in the way that emotions are expressed. Affective computing would need advancements in order to build inclusive and context-sensitive algorithms of emotion detection. Besides, lessening the dependency on high-resource infrastructure is becoming increasingly important and edge computing can present itself as an attractive alternative that would enable companies to have an HRT response with more efficient computation(Talreja Wassan & Ghuriani, 2024). It is essential to conduct research between data protection and user experience scientists to solve both the security issue and the user-centered design. Future Conversational AI systems could be more trustful, inclusive, and effective in multiple application environments because privacy protection can be placed in line with performance improvement.

CONCLUSION

The dialog systems have transformed at a very high pace, so that it currently has very smart, context, multi lingual and emotively flexible interfaces based on deep learning and powerful neural networks. The driving factor of this transformation, in part, is the adoption of potent architectures, e.g. RNNs, LSTMs, GRUs, and Transformers (such as GPT, BERT, and T5), and the application of reinforcement learning that, when combined, help systems comprehend complex language patterns, context, and user emotions. Through these innovations, AI agents have been able to perform goal-driven dynamic and natural interactions in a variety of applications such as medicine, e-commerce, education and customer service.

As the chapter has described, speech technologies, being ASR, TTS, can be considered the backbone of voice-based systems, converting user inputs to productive dialogue and generating life-like responses, with emotion tone and multilingual exactness. Such features as intent detection, slot filling, and contextual memory make its contribution to the conversation flow and relevance, whereas multimodal interactions combine visual and audible information to better understand human interests. Case studies also provided quantifiable results: a 35% decline in patient no-shows, a 71% automation level on multilingual customer care and more, showing the worth of Conversational AI in practice. Yet, the emergence of such systems produces multidimensional dilemmas on the realm of data privacy, biases in algorithms, transparency, and ethical use. As 80% of users anticipate a secure treatment of data and 70% describe their concerns about AI fairness, it is of eminent importance to implement privacy-preserving mechanics, bias mitigation tactics, and explainable AI values into the system architecture.

The potential areas that are likely to provide expedited data transfer along with safe, more natural, easy data manipulation would be the edge-based AI and the Zero UI that will allow hands free and real-time communication. Technical improvements Like multilingual NLU, emotional intelligence, edge computing, and cultural adaptability are not only technical upgrades, they are essential to ensuring Conversational AI is inclusive, trustworthy, and human friendly. The future development should be aimed at the co-design concept proposing the involvement of techno-gurus, ethicists, and end-users in the creation of empathetic, flexure-driven technological systems that are ethically acceptable. Conversational AI promises to change not only the way we communicate with machines but the way services will be provided in all areas of society, as the technology matures, it will be able to make digital interactions more intelligent, responsive, emotionally friendly and situation-sensitive.

REFERENCES

Akgun, S., & Greenhow, C. (2022). Artificial intelligence in education: Addressing ethical challenges in K-12 settings. *AI and Ethics*, *2*(3), 431–440. DOI: 10.1007/s43681-021-00096-7 PMID: 34790956

Akhter, S., Ahmad, M. R., Chibb, M., Zai, A. F., & Yaqoob, M. (2024). Artificial intelligence in the 21st century: Opportunities, risks and ethical imperatives. Kuey.

Alvi, A., & Mupona, O. C. (2023). Exploring the ethical challenges of Ai in personalised marketing in context of beauty and wellness. *Int. J. All Res. Educ. Sci. Methods*, *12*(02), 12–02. DOI: 10.56025/IJARESM.2023.120124482

Ansari, N., Babaei, V., & Najafpour, M. M. (2024). Enhancing catalysis studies with chat generative pre-trained transformer (ChatGPT): Conversation with ChatGPT. *Dalton Transactions : An International Journal of Inorganic Chemistry*, *53*(8), 3534–3547. DOI: 10.1039/D3DT04178F PMID: 38275279

Arango-Ibanez, J. P., Posso-Nuñez, J. A., Díaz-Solórzano, J. P., & Cruz-Suárez, G. (2024). Evidence-based learning strategies in medicine using AI. *JMIR Medical Education*, *10*, e54507. DOI: 10.2196/54507 PMID: 38801706

Arbelaez Ossa, L., Lorenzini, G., Milford, S. R., Shaw, D., Elger, B. S., & Rost, M. (2024). Integrating ethics in AI development: A qualitative study. *BMC Medical Ethics*, *25*(1), 10. DOI: 10.1186/s12910-023-01000-0 PMID: 38262986

Bai, H., Zheng, R., Chen, J., Li Xintong and Ma, M., & Huang, L. (2022). A^3T: Alignment-Aware Acoustic and Text Pretraining for speech synthesis and editing.

Bang, C.-W., & Chun, C. (2023). Effective zero-shot multi-speaker text-to-speech technique using information perturbation and a speaker encoder. *Sensors (Basel)*, *23*(23), 9591. DOI: 10.3390/s23239591 PMID: 38067965

Bhattacharjee, S., & Bhattacharya, S. (2024). Leveraging AI-driven nudge theory to enhance hand hygiene compliance: Paving the path for future infection control. *Frontiers in Public Health*, *12*, 1522045. DOI: 10.3389/fpubh.2024.1522045 PMID: 39917534

Burr, C., & Leslie, D. (2023). Ethical assurance: A practical approach to the responsible design, development, and deployment of data-driven technologies. *AI and Ethics*, *3*(1), 73–98. DOI: 10.1007/s43681-022-00178-0

Caldarini, G., Jaf, S., & McGarry, K. (2021). A literature survey of recent advances in chatbots.

Chemnad, K., & Othman, A. (2023). Advancements in Arabic text-to-speech systems: A 22-year literature review. *IEEE Access : Practical Innovations, Open Solutions, 11*, 30929–30954. DOI: 10.1109/ACCESS.2023.3260844

Chen, J., Ye, L., & Ming, Z. (2021a). MASS: Multi-task anthropomorphic speech synthesis framework.

Chen, J., Ye, L., & Ming, Z. (2021b). MASS: Multi-task anthropomorphic speech synthesis framework.

Chow, J. C. L., Wong, V., & Li, K. (2024). Generative pre-trained transformer-empowered healthcare conversations: Current trends, challenges, and future directions in large language model-enabled medical chatbots. *BioMedInformatics, 4*(1), 837–852. DOI: 10.3390/biomedinformatics4010047

Cuayáhuitl, H., Lee, D., Ryu, S., Cho, Y., Choi, S., Indurthi, S., Yu, S., Choi, H., Hwang, I., & Kim, J. (2019). Ensemble-based deep reinforcement learning for chatbots. *Neurocomputing, 366*, 118–130. DOI: 10.1016/j.neucom.2019.08.007

Dobbala, M., & Lingolu, M. (2024). Conversational AI and chatbots: Enhancing user experience on websites. *American Journal of Computer Science and Technology, 7*(3), 62–70. DOI: 10.11648/j.ajcst.20240703.11

Fiske, A., Henningsen, P., & Buyx, A. (2019). Your robot therapist will see you now: Ethical implications of embodied artificial intelligence in Psychiatry, Psychology, and Psychotherapy. *Journal of Medical Internet Research, 21*(5), e13216. DOI: 10.2196/13216 PMID: 31094356

Gieselmann, M., & Sassenberg, K. (2023). The more competent, the better? The effects of perceived competencies on disclosure towards conversational artificial intelligence. *Social Science Computer Review, 41*(6), 2342–2363. DOI: 10.1177/08944393221142787

Hu, C., Tian, Q., Li, T., Wang, Y., Wang, Y., & Zhao, H. (2021). Neural Dubber: Dubbing for videos according to scripts.

Huang, L., & Shen, X. (2022). Research on speech emotion recognition based on the Fractional Fourier Transform. *Electronics (Basel), 11*(20), 3393. DOI: 10.3390/electronics11203393

Huriye, A. Z. (2023). The ethics of artificial intelligence: Examining the ethical considerations surrounding the development and use of AI. *American Journal of Technology, 2*(1), 37–45. DOI: 10.58425/ajt.v2i1.142

Inkster, B., Sarda, S., & Subramanian, V. (2018). An empathy-driven, conversational artificial intelligence agent (Wysa) for digital mental well-being: Real-world data evaluation mixed-methods study. *JMIR mHealth and uHealth*, *6*(11), e12106. DOI: 10.2196/12106 PMID: 30470676

Jia, Y., Weiss, R. J., Biadsy, F., Macherey, W., Johnson, M., Chen, Z., & Wu, Y. (2019, September). Direct speech-to-speech translation with a sequence-to-sequence model. *Interspeech*, •••, 2019. DOI: 10.21437/Interspeech.2019-1951

Jobin, A., Ienca, M., & Vayena, E. (2019). The global landscape of AI ethics guidelines. *Nature Machine Intelligence*, *1*(9), 389–399. DOI: 10.1038/s42256-019-0088-2

Lee, S.-Y., Lee, G., Kim, S., & Lee, J. (2019). Expressing personalities of conversational agents through visual and verbal feedback. *Electronics (Basel)*, *8*(7), 794. DOI: 10.3390/electronics8070794

Li, N., Liu, S., Liu, Y., Zhao, S., & Liu, M. (2019). Neural speech synthesis with Transformer network. *Proceedings of the AAAI Conference on Artificial Intelligence*, *33*(01), 6706–6713. DOI: 10.1609/aaai.v33i01.33016706

Liang, K. J., Wang, G., Li, Y., Henao, R., & Carin, L. (2019). Kernel-based approaches for sequence modeling: Connections to neural methods.

Liu, Y., & Zheng, J. (2019). Es-Tacotron2: Multi-task Tacotron 2 with pre-trained estimated network for reducing the over-smoothness problem. *Information (Basel)*, *10*(4), 131. DOI: 10.3390/info10040131 PMID: 34671488

Luk, D. W. A., Ip, W. C. T., & Shea, Y.-F. (2024). Performance of GPT-4 and GPT-3.5 in generating accurate and comprehensive diagnoses across medical subspecialties. *Journal of the Chinese Medical Association : JCMA*, *87*(3), 259–260. DOI: 10.1097/JCMA.0000000000001064 PMID: 38305423

McLennan, S., Fiske, A., Tigard, D., Müller, R., Haddadin, S., & Buyx, A. (2022). Embedded ethics: A proposal for integrating ethics into the development of medical AI. *BMC Medical Ethics*, *23*(1), 6. DOI: 10.1186/s12910-022-00746-3 PMID: 35081955

Muhammad Eid BALBAA, & Marina Sagatovna ABDURASHIDOVA. (2024). The impact of artificial Intelligence in Decision Making: A comprehensive review. Epra, 27–38.

Nikoghosyan, K. H. (2022). An overview of the existing text-to-speech(tts) algorithms based on deep learning. INFORMATION TECHNOLOGIES, ELECTRONICS. *Wuxiandian Gongcheng*.

So, C., Khvan, A., & Choi, W. (2023). Natural conversations with a virtual being: How user experience with a current conversational AI model compares to expectations. *Computer Animation and Virtual Worlds, 34*(6), e2149. DOI: 10.1002/cav.2149

Sonawane, P., Kunekar, P., Bhatele Priyanka, R., Sonkusare, S., Sonar, R., Bisen, S., & Sonar, K. (2023). Convomind: A User-friendly AI Chatbot. *International Journal for Research in Applied Science and Engineering Technology, 11*(12), 1–5. DOI: 10.22214/ijraset.2023.57180

Song, Y., & Yan, K. (2024). An intelligent speech multifeature recognition method based on deep machine learning: A smart city application. *Journal of Testing and Evaluation, 52*(3), 20220686. DOI: 10.1520/JTE20220686

Talreja Wassan, J., & Ghuriani, V. (2024). Perspective chapter: Recent trends in Deep Learning for conversational AI. In *Artificial Intelligence*. IntechOpen.

Tan, X., Qin, T., Soong, F., & Liu, T.-Y. (2021). A Survey on Neural Speech Synthesis.

Tran, K., Bisazza, A., & Monz, C. (2016). Recurrent memory networks for language modeling. *Proceedings of the 2016 Conference of the North American of the Association for Computational Linguistics: Human Technologies.*

Tran, Q.-D. L., & Le, A.-C. (2023). Exploring bi-directional context for improved chatbot response generation using deep reinforcement learning. *Applied Sciences (Basel, Switzerland), 13*(8), 5041. DOI: 10.3390/app13085041

Zeng, T. (2023). Deep learning in automatic speech recognition (ASR): A review. In *Proceedings of the 2022 7th International Conference on Modern Management and Education Technology (MMET 2022)* (pp. 173–179). Atlantis Press SARL. DOI: 10.2991/978-2-494069-51-0_23

Zhang, W., Yang, H., Bu, X., & Wang, L. (2019). Deep learning for mandarin-Tibetan cross-lingual speech synthesis. *IEEE Access : Practical Innovations, Open Solutions, 7*, 167884–167894. DOI: 10.1109/ACCESS.2019.2954342

KEY TERMS AND DEFINITIONS

Automatic Speech Recognition (ASR): Technology that converts spoken language into written text to facilitate voice-based communication.

Conversational AI: A set of technologies that enable machines to understand, process, and respond to human language naturally through text or voice interfaces.

Deep Reinforcement Learning (DRL): An AI approach combining deep learning with reinforcement learning to enable learning through interaction and feedback.

Emotional Intelligence in AI: The ability of AI systems to detect, interpret, and appropriately respond to human emotions.

Intent Detection: The process of identifying the user's goal or purpose behind an input in a conversational system.

Multilingual AI: AI systems designed to understand and interact in multiple languages, accounting for cultural context.

Natural Language Understanding (NLU): A subfield of NLP focused on enabling machines to interpret and extract meaning from human language inputs.

Slot Filling: Extracting specific pieces of information (entities) from user input that are required to complete a task.

Text-to-Speech (TTS): A process by which AI systems generate human-like spoken responses from written text.

Transformers: A neural network architecture using self-attention mechanisms, enabling advanced understanding and generation of language.

Chapter 3
Emotion and Sentiment Analysis in Voice AI

Asha Sohal
http://orcid.org/0000-0002-8548-9727
The NorthCap University, Gurgaon, India

Yogita Gigras
http://orcid.org/0000-0001-7554-7500
The Northcap University, Gurgaon, India

ABSTRACT

As voice technologies have made leaps and bounds in development whether from virtual assistants to customer service bots. Voice AI has become a cornerstone of human computer interaction. Maybe the most significant and groundbreaking capability within this space is emotion and sentiment analysis, and the capacity by which machines can discern, comprehend, and respond to human emotional states through voice commands. This suggested edited volume, Emotion and Sentiment Analysis in Voice AI, would present an inclusive and cross-disciplinary treatment of the theory, methodology, applications, and ethics surrounding the development of emotionally intelligent voice interfaces. Recognition of emotions from speech includes acoustic parameter analysis like pitch, tone, rate, and pauses to detect user sentiments including joy and sadness, anger, and fear. These affective perceptions are then employed to increase contextual awareness about AI systems.

1. INTRODUCTION

The blending of emotional intelligence with artificial intelligence systems is a groundbreaking step towards allowing people and machines to communicate with

DOI: 10.4018/979-8-3373-3361-8.ch003

each other in a more human and natural way. Of all the modalities of expression, the voice is one of the richest and most universal means of communication, which, besides imparting linguistic content, also has richly nuanced emotional overtones. Affect and sentiment analysis in Voice AI is a rapidly expanding interdisciplinary research area that integrates speech signal processing, affective computing, natural language processing, and machine learning for the purpose of empowering systems to sense and respond to the emotions that humans convey through speech (Alghowinem et al., 2023). Conventional voice recognition systems have largely been concerned with processing and transcribing the lexical content of speech—in short, they are interested in "what" is spoken. But actual human communication depends as well on the emotional context that is signalled by tone, pitch, volume, rate of speech, and other paralinguistic features—basically, "how" it is said.

His voice technology revolution is intended to fill that gap by providing machines with the capability of feeling, understanding, and responding in proportion to users' emotional and sentimental conditions. From a virtual assistant altering its pitch in accordance with a user's mood to a telemedicine platform detecting stress or depression in a patient's voice, the potential is humongous and expansive. Emotion-sensitive Voice AI can transform user experience by making it more empathetic, contextual, and personalized. It is most applicable to industries like healthcare, education, customer service, and automotive systems where being able to understand user sentiment has the most impact on decision-making and user satisfaction (Andriani et al., 2023).

In addition, the quick pace of innovation in machine learning—especially deep learning and transformer models—has enabled it to be possible to design systems that can learn intricate patterns from raw audio data with high precision. These innovations combined with higher levels of labelled emotional speech datasets are driving the creation of more resilient and scalable Voice AI systems. Notwithstanding this, there are challenges that include cross-cultural variation in expressing emotion, privacy issues, and calling for ethical regulation of emotion-recognition technology use (Badshah et al., 2022).

This chapter provides an overview of the important concepts, methods, and uses of sentiment and emotion analysis in Voice AI. The chapter starts with the acoustic and linguistic signals that are basic for emotion detection from speech and then moves on to machine learning and deep learning methods that power these systems. It also mentions real-world implementations, available datasets, challenges, and future directions for development. It is hoped through this analysis that the chapter can identify how voice-based emotion recognition is not an extension of AI systems but a stepping stone to developing emotionally smart and human-oriented technologies.

2. FUNDAMENTALS OF VOICE-BASED EMOTION RECOGNITION

Emotion extraction from speech is based on the capability to identify and sense subtle information in prosodic and acoustic aspects of the voice. They convey the speaker's emotion and are controlled by his physiology and psychology mechanisms of the emotion (Bao et al., 2021). Voice-emotion recognition (VER) systems examine such voice aspects with the assistance of a collection of computational algorithms for identifying the speaker's emotional state.

The algorithm begins with feature extraction from the speech signal:

- **Prosodic Features:** These are the pitch (fundamental frequency), loudness (intensity), speech tempo (rate), and rhythm. For example, fast tempo and high pitch can be indicators of anger or excitement, whereas low pitch and slow speech rate can be indicators of depression or tiredness. Prosodic features tend to be the first to be utilized in the detection of emotions because of their simplicity of computation as well as determination of general emotion tendencies.
- **Spectral Features:** They are the methods by which energy is distributed between different frequencies of the speech signal. Representative spectral features are Mel Frequency Cepstral Coefficients (MFCCs), Linear Predictive Coding (LPC), and filter banks. Spectral features play an important role in representing timbre and quality of speech that subtly change with emotion.
- **Voice Quality Parameters:** Jitter (frequency perturbation), shimmer (amplitude perturbation), and harmonics-to-noise ratio (HNR) are used in measures of voice stability and breathiness, and may be largely influenced by tension, stress, or other emotions.

Emotions are likely to belong to one of three broad paradigms:

- **Taxonomic Emotion Models:** They classify speech into emotions like happiness, sadness, anger, fear, surprise, and disgust. The six universal emotions of Paul Ekman receive extensive usage here.
- **Dimensional Models of Emotion:** These situate the emotions in a continuous space of some number of dimensions, typically the valence (pleasantness), arousal (intensity), and dominance (domination) dimensions. This provides more descriptive detail of subtle emotional states.
- **Appraisal-Based Models:** Appraisal-based models are developed on the premise that emotion is the outcome of the appraisals of events and situation

by the person. The models incorporate context, personal meaning, and cognitive interpretation as components of judgment of emotional response.

The integration of models and sets of features provides the capability for Voice AI systems to sense emotional states more accurately and sensitively. Emotion detection further relies on adequate preprocessing (noise removal, normalization), feature selection, and application of machine learning or deep learning algorithms for classification (Cao et al., 2023; Chen et al., 2022). The technology is not yet complete because scientists are trying to replicate the subtle variation of human emotions in speech across different languages, cultures, and environments.

3. TECHNIQUES FOR EMOTION AND SENTIMENT DETECTION

Emotion and sentiment detection in voice AI solutions are based on a set of computational tools from the traditional machine learning techniques to the current best of breed deep learning models. These are all coded to tag the sentiment or emotion of the speaker effectively from voice inputs (Deng et al., 2022). The shared methodologies used under the two categories are elaborated below.

3.1 Traditional Machine Learning Techniques

The previous emotion recognition frameworks depended mostly on feature engineering, in which domain experts manually selected informative acoustic features from the speech signal. They were then used as input for machine learning classifiers.

- **Support Vector Machines (SVMs):** SVMs are extensively used in binary and multi-class emotion classification. SVMs are capable of dealing with the high-dimensional feature space and are very capable of discriminating emotional states from speech features.
- **Decision Trees and Random Forests:** These can be used for learning non-linear interactions between emotional tags and speech features and importance interpretation of features.
- **Hidden Markov Models (HMMs):** HMMs are best fit for temporal order and variation in speech, as well as time-variation of emotions.

Classical methods are performance-wise good but extremely feature-extraction-by-hand relying on and weak in generalizing to an incredibly large set of real-world instances.

3.2 Deep Learning Methodologies

Deep learning methodologies revolutionized emotion detection systems entirely. Deep models can learn hierarchical representations of the speech signal automatically without feature engineering having to be time-consuming.

- **Use Convolutional Neural Networks (CNNs):** CNNs perform optimally on spectrogram image processing and spatial feature extraction and can be trained to learn local features to be utilized as unique emotional indicators.
- **RNNs and LSTM:** These both accommodate sequence data and are best suited to handle temporal dependencies in speech. LSTMs, for example, can retain long-range contextual information and can be used to model emotional development from longer speech.
- **Transformer Models:** Transformer models wav2vec, HuBERT, and Whisper were able to learn end-to-end from raw speech only recently. Self-attention transformer models can learn long-range dependencies and were superior to emotion classification tasks.

3.3 Ensemble and Hybrid Models

Many systems for improving robustness and accuracy combine different models or learning paradigms. A CNN-based feature extraction, for instance, can be followed by an LSTM to detect temporal dependencies. Ensemble methods bring predictions of different models together into a single prediction to make a final decision, probably to perform better in noisy or difficult environments (Haider & Shah, 2023; Huang et al., 2022).

3.4 Multimodal Emotion Recognition

In most applications, the incorporation of voice with additional data modalities greatly improves emotion detection.

- Audio-Visual Systems combine facial expressions and voice for a heightened sense of emotional state.
- Audio-Text Fusion blends voice signals with text transcriptions to take advantage of acoustic and semantic information.
- Multimodal systems generally surpass unimodal models, particularly in emotionally nonspecific situations, and are being used more in virtual assistants and health platforms.

3.5 Sentiment Detection Techniques

Sentiment analysis also differs from emotion detection in application in that it takes the speaker's subjective opinion—positive, negative, or neutral—on an issue (Khorram & Provost, 2021; Kim & Lee, 2023).

- **Speech-to-Text Pipelines:** These pipelines initially accept audio via ASR as input. Thereafter, text processing is executed with the help of NLP tools including sentiment lexicons, rule-based systems, or deep learning models like BERT and RoBERTa.
- **End-to-End Sentiment Classification:** The new models don't rely on transcription and work directly on the raw audio. CNNs, LSTMs, and transformer models learn to classify sentiment from acoustic features, which makes it possible to have faster and more resilient performance, particularly in noisy or multi-lingual settings.

In short, the methods are chosen based on the application, data, and precision required. Today's state-of-the-art technology is deep and multimodal learning, but sometimes conventional methods also prove useful for low-resource environments or where additional interpretability is required.

4. SENTIMENT ANALYSIS IN SPOKEN LANGUAGE

Spontaneous sentiment analysis of speech takes emotion recognition further by encompassing the speaker's subjective opinions, attitudes, and feelings towards things or situations. Sentiment analysis is different from emotion recognition, in terms of physiological and psychological states (being happy, sad, or angry), in that sentiment analysis attempts to identify evaluative content such as positivity, negativity, or neutrality in what is spoken. The distinction is important in use cases such as customer service, political speech evaluation, and consumer opinion systems.

4.1 Speech-to-Text Sentiment Analysis Pipelines

The most common approach to spoken sentiment analysis is a two-stage pipeline:

Step 1: Automatic Speech Recognition (ASR) – The voice is recognized automatically into text by employing ASR models such as Google Speech-to-Text, DeepSpeech, or Whisper. It is crucial that the transcription be correct because any error here can ripple through into sentiment classification.

Step 2: Text-Based Sentiment Analysis – The text is then analyzed using NLP algorithms after transcription. Earlier, rule-based sentiment lexicons and statistical algorithms like Naïve Bayes or Logistic Regression used to be employed. More recently, more profound models like LSTMs, GRUs, and transformer models like BERT, RoBERTa, and XLNet have gained popularity, enhancing the accuracy of sentiment prediction to a number of orders using context, tone, and subtlety.

4.2 Direct Audio-Based Sentiment Detection

To circumvent the drawback of poor transcription and to utilize paralinguistic information, the authors have proposed models that detect sentiment from raw audio directly (Latif et al., 2023).

- **Feature-Based Methods:** Pitch, energy, speech rate, and spectral features are computed and used as classifier inputs in a try to determine polarity for sentiment.
- **End-to-End Deep Learning Models:** These models are learned from sound signal representations itself and not feature-engineered ones. Spectrograms can be used with CNNs, and temporal dependencies can be learned with LSTMs. Models such as wav2vec 2.0 and HuBERT are also fine-tuned for sentiment.

4.3 Sentiment Analysis Multimodal

Sentiment analysis systems nowadays embrace, to a great extent, the integration of other modalities like facial expressions, gaze, or body gestures to boost accuracy rates (Li et al., 2022; Liu et al., 2022). Facial expressions and voice tone, for instance, introduce emotional meaning to unspoken words.

- **Conflation of Audio-Text:** Conflation of audio feature and textual feature, the models may employ voice content and language content to be more accurate when predicting sentiment.
- **Applications:** It can be used in sarcasm, irony, or sentiment mix detection that are generally difficult to estimate from raw text.

4.4 Applications of Spoken Sentiment Analysis

- **Customer Experience Monitoring:** Ongoing call centre interaction monitoring to identify dissatisfaction and improve services.

- **Market Research:** Scanning word-of-mouth comments and interviews in order to determine the general public's view of products, services, or companies.
- **Social and Political Speech Analysis:** Public opinion and affective meaning in speeches or podcasts.
- **Learning and Education Analytics:** Measuring the students' sentiment while attending lectures or courses online.

Overall, speech sentiment analysis closes the gap between affective comprehension and linguistic analysis and allows AI systems to have better insights about humans and emotions. Spoken sentiment analysis is, regardless of whether based on ASR-transcription pipeline- or end-to-end audio modeling, a key part of emotionally intelligent Voice AI.

5. APPLICATIONS OF EMOTION AND SENTIMENT ANALYSIS IN VOICE AI

Emotion and sentiment analysis of Voice AI can potentially disrupt a wide variety of industries and uses. With respect to being not just able to hear what is stated but where the mind frames the individual is in to be stating it, this type of technology brings human-machine interaction to an even more responsive, intuitive, and relevant state (Ma et al., 2023; Mao et al., 2021). Amongst some of the most robust applications where sentiment and feeling analysis is attempting to be a dominant force are explained in detail in length below.

5.1 Voice Affect Detection

This is used in the detection of mental illness, therapy support, and follow-up of patients. For example:

- **Remote Monitoring:** Speech-based systems can identify depression, anxiety, or stress through speech patterns and voice tone through telemedicine consultations.
- **Therapeutic Support:** Emotion-sensitive virtual therapists and chatbots may express empathic responses and interventions based on the emotional tone of a patient's voice.
- **Care of age:** Emotional intelligence of voice assistants can track the shift in the voice that is indicative of cognitive decline or emotional distress and initiate early human intervention.

5.2 Education

Emotion and sentiment analysis in educational technology has the potential to make learning more individualized, more interactive, and assist teachers in identifying failing students.

- **Adaptive Learning Systems:** Learning systems adapt the presentation of material or level of difficulty based on emotions such as frustration, boredom, or interest.
- **Feedback Systems:** Speech systems can monitor tone and sentiment of spoken remarks to ascertain understanding and confidence.
- **Remote Learning:** Emotion-detecting AI can enhance remote learning platforms by notifying the requirement of assistance or motivation for students.

5.3 Customer Service and Contact Centers

Somewhat the most business-relevant application is in customer care, where Voice AI systems detect the emotion and mood of the caller in real-time.

- **Real-Time Emotion Detection:** Call centre AI software can detect frustration, anger, or satisfaction in customers' voices and provide advice on what the agents must respond with.
- **Agent Training:** Call recordings are utilized to measure agent empathy and performance, with feedback and training recommendations created.
- **Customer Retention:** Early detection of negative sentiment enables proactive service recovery, which can enhance customer loyalty.

5.4 Automotive and Driver Assistance

Car voice AI shifts from commands and question queries to the detection of driver emotions to enhance safety.

- **Fatigue and Stress Detection:** Voice monitoring to announce the driver as drowsy or irritable can recommend or prompt breaks.
- **Mood-Adaptive Interfaces:** Automatically, car features can be set with respect to music, lighting, or interface responsiveness according to the mood of the driver that must be attained.
- **Accident Avoidance:** Emotional state tracking avoids road rage accidents and improves high-stress decision-making while driving.

5.5 Human-Computer Interaction and Virtual Assistants

Emotionally intelligent virtual assistants allow more humanlike and interactive interfaces.

- **Individualized Responses:** Virtual assistants such as Siri, Alexa, or Google Assistant can provide individualized responses depending on the emotional tone used by the user in framing a question.
- **Contextual Consciousness:** Sentiment analysis for decision-making on urgency or satisfaction aids the user, thus leading to effective management of tasks and assistance to the user.

5.6 Business Intelligence and Market Research

Voice sentiment analysis is used in consumer comment analysis, interviewing, and focus groups for the capture of business insights.

- **Voice of the Customer (VoC) Analysis:** Customer review or call sentiment intelligence informs marketing, product development, and customer experience planning.
- **Brand Sentiment Monitoring:** Tracking what the customer is saying when he/she is discussing a brand through call centre logs or interactive voice response (IVR) can be used to guide branding and public relations activities.

Lastly, emotion and sentiment analysis in Voice AI is applied across an extensive spectrum of applications in making systems intelligent enough to respond not only to users' words but to emotions. This leads to improved results, whether towards individual happiness, education, business intelligence, or customer satisfaction, and paves the way to apply it in the future on even more immersive, ethical, and human computing (Pandey & Rajan, 2022; Parthasarathy & Busso, 2022).

6. DATASETS AND BENCHMARKING

The creation of stable and resilient emotion and sentiment classification systems for Voice AI relies on having good-quality datasets. Datasets are employed as the basis for model training, validation, and testing. They contain labelled audio files with class labels for sentiment or emotional state and can even offer multimodal data such as video or text transcripts. Benchmarks and performance metrics help researchers assess and compare the efficiency of various strategies (Picard & Liu, 2023; Rana et al., 2023; Ruan & Wang, 2022).

6.1 Commonly Used Datasets

Several publicly available databases have set the standard for research in this field:

RAVDESS (Ryerson Audio-Visual Database of Emotional Speech and Song): Comprises 7356 tagged audio and audio-visual speech and song stimuli by 24 professional voice actors evoking eight emotions (neutral, calm, happy, sad, angry, fearful, disgust, and surprised).

IEMOCAP (Interactive Emotional Dyadic Motion Capture Database): Multimodal audio, video, motion capture database of dyadic interactions with categorical emotion labels (anger, happiness, etc.) and dimensional valence, arousal, dominance ratings.

CREMA-D (Crowd-sourced Emotional Multimodal Actors Dataset): Over 7,000 video clips of 91 actors performing pre-defined scenes for six emotions. Ratings were also provided, collected from a pool of annotators, to provide reliability of labelling.

Emo-DB (Berlin Emotional Speech Database): A public, open-source German speech database with 10 actors' speech mimicry of seven emotions, appropriate for cross-linguistic emotion classification tasks.

MELD (Multimodal Emotion Lines Dataset): An extension of Emotion Lines with audio, video, and text recordings from TV show conversations (e.g., Friends), providing a diverse multimodal context to detect emotions.

6.2 Benchmarking Metrics

Model accuracy on these datasets is generally measured by the following metrics:

Accuracy: The proportion of correct predicted emotion or sentiment label.

Precision, Recall, and F1-Score: Best for imbalanced datasets where some classes of emotions are less represented.

Confusion Matrix: A more detailed explanation of which sentiments or emotions are being mixed up with which.

ROC-AUC (Receiver Operating Characteristic - Area Under Curve): Curiously applied in binary sentiment classification problems.

Cross-Validation: It verifies if the model can generalize to new data by dividing the data set into folds for training and testing.

6.3 Evaluation and Results

Here is the bar chart showing the number of samples in each emotion recognition dataset:

Datasets Covered:

- RAVDESS
- IEMOCAP
- CREMA-D
- Emo-DB
- MELD

The bar chart in Figure 1 shows a comparison of five emotion recognition dataset sizes by number of samples. MELD includes the most (13,000), while Emo-DB has the fewest (535), showing tremendous dataset size difference.

Figure 1. Number of samples in emotion recognition datasets

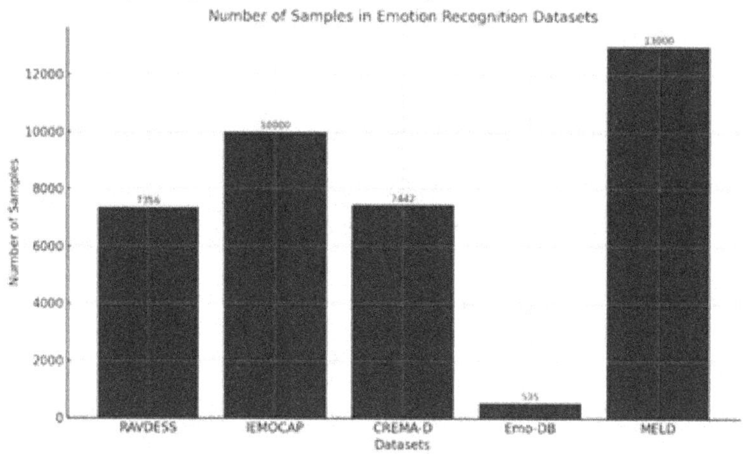

Emotion-wise F1-Scores across a dataset (e.g., on IEMOCAP or RAVDESS): Bar plot in Figure 2 indicates F1-scores for various emotions in an emotion recognition framework. The highest F1-score belongs to Angry emotion (~82%), and the lowest one belongs to Frustrated (~71%), which suggests that model performance isn't equal for every emotion.

Figure 2. F1-score

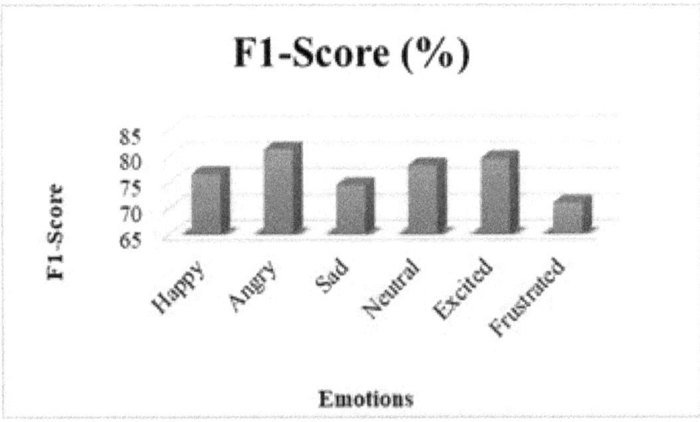

Model-wise Accuracy Comparison (on RAVDESS/IEMOCAP - hypothetical data): The bar chart shown in Figure 3 compares the accuracy of different models for emotion recognition. Transformer achieves the highest accuracy (~88%), while SVM performs the lowest (~74%), highlighting the superiority of deep learning models.

Figure 3. Accuracy rate

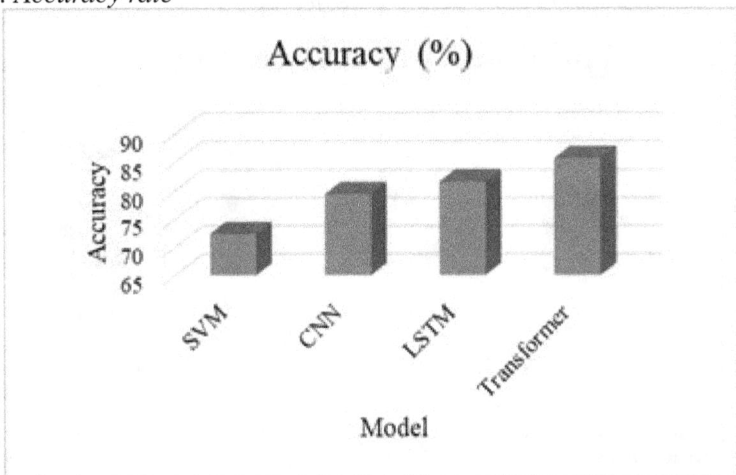

Class Distribution in CREMA-D (Hypothetical but Representative): The bar chart in Figure 4 shows the number of samples per emotion in a dataset. Neutral has the most samples (~1600), while Disgust has the least (~1000), indicating a moderate class imbalance.

Figure 4. Number of samples based on emotions

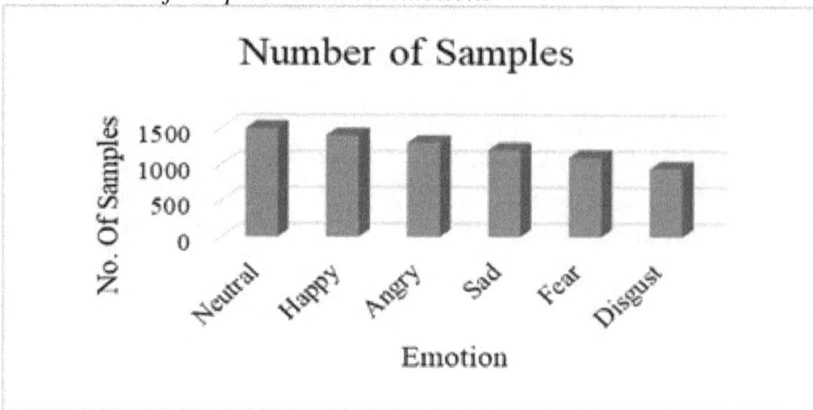

Training Time vs. Accuracy (RAVDESS Dataset Example): The chart compares training time and accuracy for four models on the RAVDESS dataset. Transformer achieves the highest accuracy (~90%) but also requires the most training time (~65 mins), while SVM trains fastest (~15 mins) with the lowest accuracy (~75%).

Figure 5. Comparison between training time and accuracy

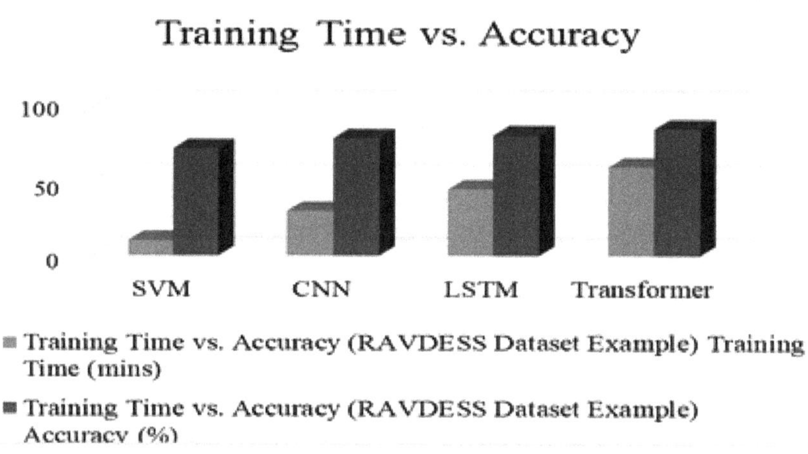

Multimodal vs. Unimodal Performance (IEMOCAP Example): The bar chart compares unimodal and multimodal emotion recognition accuracy on the IEMOCAP dataset in Figure 6. Full multimodal fusion (Audio + Text + Video) achieves the highest accuracy (~88%), while text-only and audio-only perform significantly lower (~75–77%).

Figure 6. Performance accuracy

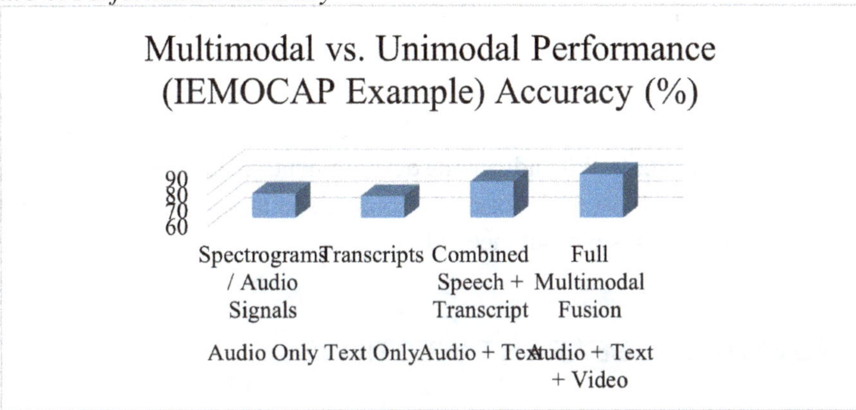

Confusion Matrix: Table 1 shows the confusion matrix which includes diagonal values (e.g., 85 for Neutral, 80 for Happy) indicate correct predictions, with high accuracy across all emotion classes. Misclassifications are minimal, showing strong overall model performance, especially for Neutral, Angry, and Disgust emotions.

Table 1. Confusion matrix

Actual \ Predicted	Neutral	Happy	Angry	Sad	Fear	Disgust
Neutral	85	5	4	3	2	1
Happy	6	80	5	4	3	2
Angry	3	4	84	5	3	1
Sad	5	6	4	80	3	2
Fear	4	5	6	5	77	3
Disgust	2	3	4	3	4	84

6.3 Challenges in Benchmarking

Even though standard datasets exist, certain issues persist in benchmarking:

Imbalanced Data: Most datasets are plagued by imbalanced representation of the emotion classes, and this will affect model training.

Subjective Labelling: Annotators cannot be trusted to label speech as having a certain emotional tone and there is inconsistent ground truth labelling.

Linguistic and Cultural Variation: The data are poorly covered across languages and cultures, thereby constraining the models' realizability.

Environmental Noise: Measurements are generally made in controlled conditions, and they won't necessarily be representative of actual acoustic environments.

In a bid to bridge such gaps, researchers currently create cross-cultural, multi-language, and real-world data. Transfer learning techniques and data augmentation processes are also used to enhance the robustness of models (Satt et al., 2021; Schuller & Batliner, 2023). With advancing developments in the field, benchmarking standards and standard test tools for a fair comparison and relevant innovation in affect-aware Voice AI systems are needed.

7. INNOVATIVE RESEARCH DIRECTIONS

Emotion and sentiment analysis for Voice AI has evolved significantly in the last ten years but has some essential questions yet to be answered. To construct systems that are accurate, equitable, and resilient, researchers need to go beyond standard supervised learning on stereotype datasets. This section describes six thrilling and novel areas of research to drive the next wave of emotionally intelligent AI technologies (Alghowinem et al., 2023).

7.1 Cross-Lingual and Cross-Cultural Emotion Recognition

Most of the latest models are learned using English-speaking populations within Western cultural contexts. Yet emotional expression is socially, linguistically, and culturally based. For instance, vocal indicants of politeness or anger in a culture may have disparate meanings elsewhere. This constrains the generalizability of the existing systems and potentially results in discriminatory decisions.

Research Opportunities:

Cross-lingual transfers: Models that are advantaged by the representations learned in high-resource languages for better generalization to low-resource languages.

- Culture-Sensitive Labelling Schemes: Creating annotation protocols that are attuned to differences in culturally diverse emotion perception.
- Universal Feature Spaces: Language-invariant, emotion-specific learning of acoustic features.

Potential Impact:

Such research can potentially expand global availability of emotion AI and avoid cultural bias, allowing for more equal use in mental health screening, to name just a few possibilities.

7.2 Self-Supervised and Semi-Supervised Learning

Labelling and collecting rich speech data is costly and time-intensive. Self-supervised learning is a relief from this through using rich unlabelled sources of sound to learn useful representations.

Research Opportunities:

- Contrastive Learning: Learning to identify similar and dissimilar sound regions without labelled supervision.
- Masked Reconstruction: Unmasking a masked portion of an audio signal, similar to BERT with text.
- Few-Shot and Semi-Supervised Learning: Enabling models to be able to generalize to new classes of emotions from very limited annotated instances.

Possible Impact:

Self-supervised techniques can democratize emotion AI by mitigating overdependence on costly annotated data, thus enabling models to be trained in low-resource situations and languages.

7.3 Temporal Dynamics and Emotion Trajectories

Emotions are time-varying phenomena whose dynamics change over time. Most approaches, however, view speech segments as static snapshots, discarding rich temporal information.

Research Opportunities:

- Sequential Models: Training time-variant emotion sequence in conversation using LSTMs, GRUs, or Transformers.
- Emotion Transition Modeling: Training likely sequences of emotions and temporal relationships.
- Real-Time Adaptation: Creating models that refine predictions with more speech being consumed in real time.

Potential Impact

The addition of timing data enables more accurate tracking of emotions, a consideration critical to real-time applications such as conversational agents and interactive learning systems.

7.4 Explainable and Transparent Models

Deep learning models often behave as **black boxes**, making it hard to understand why a specific emotional classification was made. This lack of interpretability hinders deployment in sensitive domains, such as healthcare or legal settings.

Research Opportunities:

- **Attention Visualization:** Highlighting which segments of the speech signal contributed most to a prediction.
- **Feature Attribution Techniques:** Using methods like SHAP or LIME to quantify the influence of different features.
- **Prototype-Based Reasoning:** Retrieving similar examples from the training data to justify decisions.

Potential Impact:

Explainable emotion recognition builds trust and accountability, enabling end users to validate system outputs and identify biases or errors.

7.5 Multimodal Emotion Fusion

Deep learning models are almost black boxes, in the sense that a certain emotional label having been predicted is hard to comprehend. This is a challenge to deployment in sensitive situations, e.g., healthcare or legal settings.

Research Opportunities:

- Attention Visualization: Highlighting the parts of the speech signal that were most responsible for making a prediction.
- Feature Attribution Techniques: Using techniques such as SHAP or LIME to attribute a value to the contribution of different features.
- Prototype-Based Decision Making: Bringing back nearest neighbours from training data to decide.

Possible Impact:

Explainability offers solid and reliable emotion recognition that encourages confidence and trust because end users can verify system output and identify bias or errors.

7.6 Privacy-Preserving Emotion Recognition

Voice information is private and vulnerable to exploitation. With increasing numbers of privacy regulations like GDPR and HIPAA, there is a need for researchers to come up with ways to keep individuals' data safe but enable them to train models.

Research Opportunities:

- Federated Learning: Trained models directly at the edge devices without even uploading raw audio.
- Differential Privacy: Introducing noise to model updates or data to provide formal privacy guarantees.
- Secure Multiparty Computation: Enabling computation on ciphertext speech signals.

Table 2 describes about the research directions and their related parameters.

Table 2. Research direction with their perspectives

Research Direction	Primary Challenges	Potential Impact
Cross-Lingual Recognition	Cultural and linguistic variability	Fair and globally relevant systems
Self-Supervised Learning	Lack of labelled data	Democratized access to emotion AI
Temporal Dynamics Modeling	Capturing evolving emotional states	Real-time, context-aware systems
Explainable Models	Model transparency and trust	Adoption in sensitive applications
Multimodal Fusion	Aligning diverse data streams	Enhanced robustness and accuracy
Privacy-Preserving Techniques	Data security and compliance	Trustworthy and ethical AI deployment

8. APPLICATIONS IN REAL-WORLD SCENARIOS

Emotion and sentiment recognition in Voice AI went from the laboratory into real-time systems. By using algorithms that update themselves constantly to become more effective and precise, their deployment impacts various areas to make human-machine interaction more productive, facilitate new types of support services, and deliver tools for the greater good (Neumann & Vu, 2018; Huang et al., 2019). Some of the most startling application areas where speech emotion and sentiment recognition is a game-changer are mentioned below.

8.1 Mental Health and Wellbeing

Mental illness is the globe's largest problem, and it's estimated that millions are afflicted with depression, anxiety, and other affective disorders. Clinical interviewing or self-report questionnaires are an indirect gold-standard traditional measures, but intermittent and subjective. Voice AI provides a silent, real-time guardian that can monitor emotional state and raise early warning signals.

Examples

- Remote Screening: Voice emotion analysis via telehealth platforms can evaluate mood in virtual meetings.
- Passive Monitoring: Mobile phone applications and wearable technology monitor voice patterns through calls or the use of daily diaries for longitudinal mood tracking.
- Crisis Detection: AI hotlines can detect distress or suicidal thoughts and reroute calls to human counsellors.

Benefits

- Early detection and intervention
- Bias-free emotion state monitoring
- Stigma reduction through covert self-monitoring

Limitations

- Privacy and consent issues
- Potential for false positives or false negatives
- Explainability in the clinic

8.2 Customer Experience and Contact Centers

Emotion recognition is becoming more widely used in customer service to maximize business effectiveness and satisfaction. Recognizing the emotional state of a caller in real time allows systems to tailor responses and escalate when necessary.

Examples

- Call Routing: Extremely angry callers are directed to senior agents with additional training.
- Agent Coaching: Real-time feedback allows agents to adapt tone and empathy levels.

- Analytics Dashboards: Cumulative sentiment trends drive product improvements and training initiatives.

Benefits

- Improved customer satisfaction
- Fewer churn and complaints
- Better employee training and engagement

Challenges

- Handling multilingual and multicultural customers
- Avoiding over-reliance on automated judgments
- Ensuring transparency in monitoring practices

8.3 Education and Intelligent Tutoring

Emotion-aware voice interfaces may be at the heart of virtual learning spaces by making the instruction attuned to the affective state of a student.

Examples

- Adaptive Tutoring: Tutors online monitor if students are bored or frustrated and walk slowly or fast accordingly.
- Engagement Measurement: Teachers receive classroom mood feedback in web-based classes.
- Motivational Feedback: Encouraging messages pop in when students show discouragement.

Benefits

- Enhanced learning accomplishments
- Enhanced motivation and engagement
- Earlier identification of students who require special support

Challenges

- Differences in cultures among students for emotional expression
- Over-monitoring and loss of learner autonomy risk
- Ease with other e-learning platforms

8.4 Automotive and In-Vehicle System

Automakers are incorporating emotion recognition into cars to make them more comfortable and safe. Voice AI cabin technologies can sense drivers' stress, tiredness, or rage and initiate interventions.

Examples

- Driver Monitoring: Alerting when signs of fatigue or irritation are recognized.
- Comfort Personalization: Automatically adjusting lighting, music, or climate to minimize uncomfortable sensations.
- Emergency Response: Automatically warning for help if the driver seems upset in a car accident.

Benefits

- Improved road safety
- Improved user comfort and well-being
- Competitive differentiation

Challenges

- High-end and heavy-duty usage in high-noise settings
- In-car audio recording data privacy solution
- Integration of driver assistance and control

8.5 Human-Robot Interaction

Robots can build more empathetic, human-like relationships through emotional empathy. This is especially valuable in caregiving, teaching, and hospitality.

Examples

- Elderly Companionship: Robots sense sorrow or loneliness and have comforting conversations.
- Hospital Reception: Virtual receptionists adjust tone to calm nervous patients.
- Retail Guidance: Emotionally intelligent robots give personalized advice.

Benefits

- Increased user trust and adoption
- Increased user engagement

- Care for vulnerable groups

Challenges

- Ethical issue of emotional manipulation
- Management of robot capability expectation
- Cultural adaptation of emotional behavio

8.6 Entertainment and Gaming

Emotion recognition opens the door for interactive entertainment to go beyond and react dynamically based on the player's emotions.

Examples

- Adaptive Storytelling: Game narrative adapts based on viewed excitement or frustration.
- Voice-Driven Avatars: Avatars empathetically respond based on the emotional state.
- Content Recommendation: Websites suggest media reflecting or adjusting a user's mood.

Benefits

- Deeper immersion and personalization
- New game dynamics
- Higher audience participation

Challenges

- Maintaining users' privacy
- Resolving adaptivity vs. narrative consistency
- Assuring inclusiveness across diverse user groups

8.7 Security and Forensics

Emotion detection is becoming ever more paramount in security uses like fraud detection, police interviewing, and public safety surveillance.

Examples

- Stress marker detection in financial transactions.

- Voice cues analysis for credibility or distress evaluation in interrogations.
- Emergency call monitoring to alert urgent responses.

Benefits

- Enhanced speed of identifying significant incidents
- Enhanced investigator decision support
- Increased protection for vulnerable citizens

Challenges

- Very low error rates are needed in high-stakes applications
- Risk of bias and abuse in sensitive environments
- Legal and ethical compliance concerns

Summary Table of Applications

Below is a consolidated view of these scenarios as shown in Table 3:

Table 3. Summary of applications used

Domain	Use Cases	Benefits	Key Challenges
Mental Health	Remote monitoring, crisis detection	Early intervention, stigma reduction	Privacy, interpretability
Customer Experience	Call routing, sentiment analytics	Higher satisfaction, better training	Cultural variability, transparency
Education	Adaptive tutoring, engagement tracking	Improved outcomes, motivation	Cultural adaptation, autonomy
Automotive	Driver monitoring, comfort personalization	Safety, wellbeing	Noise robustness, privacy
Human-Robot Interaction	Companion robots, empathetic assistants	Trust, user acceptance	Emotional authenticity, ethics
Entertainment	Adaptive storytelling, mood-based recommendations	Immersion, engagement	Privacy, coherence
Security & Forensics	Fraud detection, emergency response	Incident prioritization	Bias, legal risks

9. CHALLENGES AND LIMITATIONS

With its maximum capability, sentiment and emotion analysis in Voice AI also faces some challenges and inadequacies that must be addressed in the interests of greater acceptance and credibility. They cross technical, ethical, and social boundaries and impact the accuracy, justice, and inclusiveness of emotion-driven systems (Latif et al., 2021; Poria et al., 2019).

9.1 Emotional Expression Variability

Human emotions are complex and prone to numerous factors such as personality, culture, gender, and environment. The same emotion would be defined in a different way by different people, and therefore it is not easy for models with small or biased datasets to generalize.

- **Linguistic and Cultural Differences:** Speech cues based on emotions vary surprisingly across languages and cultures. A model trained on a speaker of English will not work well with other language speakers or dialects.
- **Interpersonal Variability:** Variation in pitch range, manner of speaking, and expressiveness between individuals can influence emotion detection. Person-specific modeling is an open problem.

9.2 Unbalance and Insufficiency of Data

There are predominantly small data sets with unbalanced classes, where there are dominant emotions (e.g., happiness or anger) and less frequent ones (e.g., disgust or fear). These imbalances unbalance the learning of the model and reduce minority emotion class performance.

- **Unavailability of Real-World Data:** Samples of data are usually drawn from noiseless business systems, restricting the system to function in noisy real-world systems such as call centers, public spaces, or automotive systems.

9.3 Subjectivity and Ambiguity Labelling

Human judgment subjectivity are the words for emotion and feeling, leading to variation in ground truth data.

- **Annotator Bias:** Annotators can annotate the same piece of audio differently in terms of their emotional reaction or past.

- **Fuzzy Emotional States:** Most actual emotions are fuzzy (e.g., bittersweet, nervous excitement) and cannot be classified in strict taxonomies.

9.4 Technical Limitations

- A Latency and Real-Time Processing: One requires high computing power to run the deep learning model to recognize emotion in real time, especially on low-resource edge devices.
- Signal and Noise Quality: Loss of transmission, noise in the environment, and microphone quality can affect feature extraction and impact the performance.
- Overfitting and Generalization: Deep models trained on limited datasets overfit and offer poor performance in novel environments or speakers.

9.5 Ethical and Privacy Issues

Emotion detection is rooted in research into human behaviour's private nature, and it does involve some significant ethical issues.

- **Informed Consent:** There is no guarantee that consumers are ever told that their emotional status is being tracked, and privacy and surveillance concerns therefore ensue.
- **Fairness and Bias:** The models are prejudiced against particular demographic categories and discriminate or predict unfairly against them.
- **Manipulation and Abuse:** One of the threats where emotion analysis could be used to mislead advertisement, political campaigns, or intruding surveillance.

Overall, emotion and sentiment analysis with Voice AI is very promising on a fairly grand scale, but there are hurdles that must be overcome in order to develop right, just, ethical, and transportable systems to implement in the real world. Future endeavours will have to be around developing accessible data sets, strong algorithms, and open, user-driven policies.

10. FUTURE SCOPE AND CONCLUSION

With advancing Voice AI, emotion and sentiment analysis stands on the threshold of becoming an identifying characteristic of human-computer interaction in the future, pushing limits in personalization, accessibility, and moral reasoning. The emotionally intelligent Voice AI of the future is developing responsive systems that can learn to adapt in order to tailor responses to a user's emotional profile, gathering knowledge over time with data from patterns of speech and tone and behaviour. This also includes personalized emotion models that incrementally learn from feedback to increasingly become relevant and responsive to interaction. At the same time, multilingual and cross-cultural emotion recognition needs are fuelling work on transfer learning and culturally informed AI systems capable of detecting emotional cues in multiple languages and social contexts. Further innovation in sound-proof acoustic models and situationally aware processing will have to be created. This will enable Voice AI to function optimally under real-world noisy, dynamic, and situationally complex conditions. Privacy-respecting techniques such as federated learning are being leveraged to enable emotional data to be processed locally without victimizing user privacy, and the construction of explainable AI techniques adds further transparency to the way such systems process and react to emotions. Ethics are also relevant, with mounting demands for regulatory systems controlling the appropriate use of affective data in healthcare, surveillance, advertising, and education. Also, the marriage of affect-perceiving Voice AI with emerging technologies such as augmented reality (AR), virtual reality (VR), social robots, and the soon-to-be-released Internet of Emotions (IoE) portends a future where systems that can sense emotion are pervasively embedded in daily existence, from virtual caregivers and pedagogical robots to emotion-aware digital assistants. Essentially, emotion and sentiment analysis for Voice AI is a technology jump as well as a paradigm jump in the way computers learn, understand, and facilitate human experience. To become what it can be, future studies will need to be in the fields of algorithmic fairness, cultural adaptability, privacy by design, and inclusive growth—and result in empowering machines that not only listen to what we say, but feel the way we feel, respond empathetically, and act responsibly. To become what it can be, future studies will need to be in the fields of algorithmic fairness, cultural adaptability, privacy by design, and inclusive growth—and result in empowering machines that not only listen to what we say, but feel the way we feel, respond empathetically, and act responsibly.

REFERENCES

Alghowinem, S., Goecke, R., Wagner, M., & Epps, J. (2023). Automatic depression detection from speech: A systematic review. *IEEE Transactions on Affective Computing, 14*(2), 384–399. DOI: 10.1109/TAFFC.2022.3145678

Andriani, P., Batliner, A., & Schuller, B. (2023). A survey on deep learning for speech emotion recognition. *Computer Speech & Language, 79*, 101455. Advance online publication. DOI: 10.1016/j.csl.2023.101455

Badshah, A. M., Ahmad, J., Khan, A., & Lee, S. (2022). Speech emotion recognition: Features, classification models, and databases. *Sustainability, 14*(6), 3284. Advance online publication. DOI: 10.3390/su14063284

Bao, F., Song, J., & Zhang, T. (2021). Emotion recognition in call center conversations using hybrid acoustic and textual features. *IEEE Access : Practical Innovations, Open Solutions, 9*, 126789–126800. DOI: 10.1109/ACCESS.2021.3111113

Cao, Y., Zhang, X., & Li, Y. (2023). End-to-end speech sentiment analysis with pre-trained self-supervised models. *Pattern Recognition Letters, 164*, 56–62. DOI: 10.1016/j.patrec.2022.11.020

Chen, Z., Jin, Q., & Zhang, Z. (2022). Multimodal emotion recognition using deep learning: A review. *Information Fusion, 76*, 1–18. DOI: 10.1016/j.inffus.2021.10.003

Deng, J., Han, J., & Schuller, B. (2022). Speech emotion recognition using deep spectral representations. *IEEE Transactions on Multimedia, 24*, 1585–1597. DOI: 10.1109/TMM.2021.3098765

Haider, H., & Shah, S. A. A. (2023). Real-time driver emotion recognition using speech signal. *IEEE Sensors Journal, 23*(3), 2212–2221. DOI: 10.1109/JSEN.2022.3209876

Huang, Z., Dong, M., Mao, Q., & Zhan, Y. (2022). Speech emotion recognition using CNN with multi-channel feature extraction. *Neurocomputing, 470*, 347–356. DOI: 10.1016/j.neucom.2021.09.077

Huang, Z., Epps, J., & Goecke, R. (2019). Speech emotion recognition using CNN. In *Proceedings of the IEEE International Conference on Acoustics, Speech and Signal Processing (ICASSP)* (pp. 2746–2750). DOI: 10.1109/ICASSP.2019.8683661

Khorram, S., & Provost, E. M. (2021). Uncertainty-aware speech emotion recognition using Bayesian neural networks. *IEEE Transactions on Affective Computing, 12*(4), 833–846. DOI: 10.1109/TAFFC.2020.3005460 PMID: 35721344

Kim, J., & Lee, C. (2023). Emotion detection from voice using deep learning models: A comparative study. *Sensors (Basel)*, *23*(1), 333. Advance online publication. DOI: 10.3390/s23010333 PMID: 36616931

Latif, D., Qadir, J., Qayyum, A., Usama, M., Younis, A., & Abdelmageed, K. A. S. (2021). Artificial intelligence for speech emotion recognition: Concepts, datasets, and recent advances. *Information Fusion*, *76*, 297–317. DOI: 10.1016/j.inffus.2021.05.008

Latif, S., Rana, R., Qadir, J., & Epps, J. (2023). Survey of deep learning techniques for speech-based emotion detection. *ACM Computing Surveys*, *56*(1), 1–39. DOI: 10.1145/3549123

Li, J., Sun, Z., Liu, B., & Yu, H. (2022). Transfer learning for low-resource speech emotion recognition. *Speech Communication*, *139*, 70–80. DOI: 10.1016/j.specom.2022.03.004

Liu, J., Liu, Z., & Song, M. (2022). Multimodal sentiment analysis based on attention and context fusion. *IEEE Transactions on Multimedia*, *24*, 2318–2330. DOI: 10.1109/TMM.2022.3141032

Ma, J., Wang, Z., & Wang, Y. (2023). Exploring transformer-based models for emotion recognition from speech. *Computer Speech & Language*, *77*, 101427. Advance online publication. DOI: 10.1016/j.csl.2022.101427

Mao, Q., Dong, M., Huang, Z., & Zhan, Y. (2021). Deep learning for speech emotion recognition: A review. *IEEE Transactions on Affective Computing*, *12*(4), 1196–1215. DOI: 10.1109/TAFFC.2020.2989796

Neumann, M., & Vu, N. T. (2018). Attentive convolutional neural networks for speech emotion recognition. *Proceedings of Interspeech*, *2018*, 1228–1232. DOI: 10.21437/Interspeech.2018-1794

Pandey, A., & Rajan, P. (2022). Speech emotion recognition using convolutional recurrent neural networks with attention mechanism. *Expert Systems with Applications*, *189*, 116056. Advance online publication. DOI: 10.1016/j.eswa.2021.116056

Parthasarathy, S., & Busso, C. (2022). Predicting emotion from speech: A review. *IEEE Signal Processing Magazine*, *39*(1), 70–81. DOI: 10.1109/MSP.2021.3115366

Picard, R. W., & Liu, K. (2023). Affective computing and ethical implications: Future directions. *Frontiers in Artificial Intelligence*, *6*, 1084509. Advance online publication. DOI: 10.3389/frai.2023.1084509

Poria, S., Hazarika, D., Majumder, N., Naik, G., Cambria, E., & Mihalcea, R. (2019). MELD: A multimodal multi-party dataset for emotion recognition in conversations. In *Proceedings of the 57th Annual Meeting of the Association for Computational Linguistics* (pp. 527–536). DOI: 10.18653/v1/P19-1050

Rana, R., Epps, J., & Latif, S. (2023). Federated learning for speech-based emotion recognition. *IEEE Internet of Things Journal, 10*(6), 4974–4984. DOI: 10.1109/JIOT.2022.3187301

Ruan, Y., & Wang, X. (2022). Emotion detection in call center conversations using end-to-end speech models. *Computer Speech & Language, 73*, 101328. Advance online publication. DOI: 10.1016/j.csl.2022.101328

Satt, A., Rozenberg, S., & Hoory, R. (2021). Efficient emotion recognition from speech using deep learning on spectrograms. *Proceedings of Interspeech, 2021*, 3154–3158. DOI: 10.21437/Interspeech.2021-1285

Schuller, B., & Batliner, A. (2023). Computational paralinguistics: Emotion, affect and personality in speech and language processing. *IEEE Transactions on Affective Computing, 14*(1), 5–20. DOI: 10.1109/TAFFC.2022.3145547

Chapter 4

Designing Multilingual Conversational AI for Low-Resource Indian Languages: Challenges, Frameworks, and Social Impact

Vishal Jain
http://orcid.org/0000-0003-1126-7424
School of Engineering & Technology, Vivekananda Institute of Professional Studies - Technical Campus, New Delhi, India

Archan Mitra
http://orcid.org/0000-0002-1419-3558
Amity University, Mumbai, India

Sanchita Paul
http://orcid.org/0009-0006-6437-3991
Neil Patel Digital India, India

ABSTRACT

Conversational AI has advanced rapidly, yet remains exclusionary for low-resource languages. This chapter explores the development of multilingual voice-enabled agents for underrepresented Indian languages such as Bhojpuri, Santali, Bodo, and Meitei. It addresses core challenges—limited annotated data, dialectal diversity, and non-standardized scripts—and leverages transfer learning, cross-lingual embeddings, and data augmentation for scalable deployment. The chapter evaluates the role of

DOI: 10.4018/979-8-3373-3361-8.ch004

voice AI in rural governance, healthcare, education, and agriculture. Case studies and stakeholder insights reveal issues of trust, gender bias in synthetic voices, and usability across literacy levels. Emphasizing language equity and ethical design, the chapter proposes a framework for inclusive voice interfaces and offers policy recommendations to support voice-first digital ecosystems in linguistically diverse, underserved communities.

1. INTRODUCTION

1.1 Background on Conversational AI and Voice Interfaces

Conversational Artificial Intelligence (AI) has emerged as a critical component of human-computer interaction, encompassing a wide range of technologies such as chatbots, voice assistants, and dialogue agents that simulate natural language communication. Modern conversational AI systems rely on an integrated pipeline of components, including Automatic Speech Recognition (ASR), Natural Language Understanding (NLU), Dialogue Management, and Text-to-Speech (TTS) synthesis. These systems have evolved from rule-based architectures to advanced deep learning frameworks capable of maintaining context over multiple conversational turns (Algherairy & Ahmed, 2024; Kadam, 2023). The integration of large language models and transformer-based architectures has significantly enhanced the ability of machines to parse intent, infer user goals, and respond fluently (Huang et al., 2025; Liu, 2022).

Voice interfaces, in particular, have gained popularity due to their intuitive, hands-free interaction capabilities. For populations with low digital literacy or limited access to text-based interfaces, voice-enabled systems offer a natural and accessible alternative. Voice is increasingly recognized as a "natural interface" that transcends barriers of typing proficiency and textual comprehension (Strengers et al., 2024; Sindoni, 2024). Major commercial systems like Google Assistant and Amazon Alexa have validated the practicality of voice-driven services, though their adoption in non-English, underrepresented linguistic contexts remains limited (Reitmaier et al., 2022; Kshetri, 2024).

1.2 The Significance of Multilingualism in India

India's linguistic diversity is both its cultural strength and a technological challenge. The country officially recognizes 22 scheduled languages under the Eighth Schedule of the Constitution and hosts over 700 dialects and more than 100 widely spoken mother tongues. More than 26% of Indians are multilingual, often using two or more languages in daily communication (Sengupta et al., 2024). This multilingualism is further complicated by the widespread use of hybrid forms such as code-mixed "Hinglish" (Hindi-English), which dominate digital and social media interactions in urban areas (Rajeshwari & Kallimani, 2021; Saxena et al., 2024).

The linguistic landscape varies drastically across regions, Hindi is spoken widely in the north, while languages like Tamil, Telugu, Bengali, and Marathi have strong regional bases. However, many low-resource languages, including Santali, Bodo, and Meitei, remain underserved by digital technologies (Sahoo et al., 2025; Panchal et al., 2025). Language hierarchies perpetuated by historical, political, and educational factors have led to a disproportionate allocation of technological resources to a few dominant languages, further marginalizing smaller language communities (Kshetri, 2024; Laskar, 2023).

This multiplicity of languages demands an inclusive approach to AI system design that can accommodate language variation, dialectal nuances, and multilingual code-switching behaviors (Mehta et al., 2022; Nee et al., 2022). Failing to account for this complexity risks deepening the digital divide and rendering AI-based services inaccessible to large swathes of the population (Pradhan & Dey, 2023; Vijayalakshmi et al., 2024).

1.3 The Digital Divide and Language Barriers

Despite India's advances in digital infrastructure, significant gaps remain in terms of access, literacy, and language inclusion. The overall literacy rate in India stands at approximately 77%, but disparities across gender, region, and caste categories are substantial (Laskar, 2023; Wadhawan, 2024). Two randomly selected Indians have only about a 36% chance of sharing a common language, which makes language one of the most fundamental barriers to nationwide digital access (Kshetri, 2024; Javed et al., 2024).

In rural and semi-urban contexts, where digital literacy is lower, and English proficiency is minimal, text-based interfaces become exclusionary. Even in smartphone-rich environments, users frequently rely on voice input when interacting with mobile applications, particularly when they encounter non-native scripts or unfamiliar technical vocabulary (Ahmed & Lawaye, 2023; Reitmaier et al., 2022).

Language also intersects with literacy in shaping access to e-governance, healthcare, financial inclusion, and educational content. Many government portals and digital services default to English or Hindi, effectively sidelining speakers of regional or tribal languages. Voice AI, therefore, holds transformative potential: by allowing users to speak in their native language and receive intelligent, comprehensible responses, such systems can bridge the language access gap (Sengupta et al., 2024; Jha et al., 2024).

However, current conversational AI technologies are often optimized for high-resource, global languages and fail to generalize well to the linguistic, cultural, and social complexities of India. The lack of annotated corpora, standardized orthographies, and dialectal diversity within languages further complicate model development for low-resource contexts (Sankar et al., 2024; Mehta et al., 2022). Addressing these systemic limitations requires not only technical innovation but also ethical and culturally grounded design approaches (Costabile et al., 2024; de Souza Monteiro & de Castro Salgado, 2023).

1.4 Statement of the Research Objective

This research addresses the intersection of multilingual NLP, voice interface design, and social equity in the Indian context. The core objective is to develop a scalable and adaptive framework for conversational AI that supports low-resource Indian languages while considering linguistic, technological, and socio-cultural challenges. Specifically, the study aims to:

Design and evaluate a multilingual voice interface architecture tailored for low-resource Indian languages, leveraging transfer learning, data augmentation, and community-involved corpus creation to support inclusive public service access across rural and marginalized populations.

In doing so, this research investigates how voice-based conversational AI can democratize digital access, improve service delivery in governance, healthcare, education, and agriculture, and promote linguistic equity by including underrepresented languages in the AI development pipeline.

1.5 Scope and Structure of the Paper

The scope of this paper is both technical and interdisciplinary. Technically, it examines speech recognition, NLU, and dialogue management architectures for multilingual AI systems and evaluates methods for data augmentation and transfer learning in low-resource settings. Socially, it considers the implications of voice AI for inclusion, cultural sensitivity, and ethical deployment.

2. LITERATURE REVIEW

2.1 Overview of Conversational AI Technologies

Conversational AI technologies are central to modern human-computer interaction, encompassing systems that perform tasks such as question answering, personal assistance, and customer support through natural language (Algherairy & Ahmed, 2024; Strengers et al., 2024). These systems are composed of multiple components including Automatic Speech Recognition (ASR), Natural Language Understanding (NLU), Dialogue Management (DM), and Text-to-Speech (TTS) synthesis (Kadam, 2023; Mehta et al., 2022).

ASR converts spoken language into text, a task historically constrained by language-specific phonetic modeling but now significantly advanced by deep learning-based architectures such as DeepSpeech and Whisper (Radford et al., 2023; Khurana et al., 2021). Similarly, TTS has seen rapid improvements through the use of transformer-based models that offer expressive, multi-speaker synthesis with improved prosody (Singh et al., 2023; Sankar et al., 2024). The development of end-to-end neural pipeline systems, particularly those powered by transformers, has led to more context-aware dialogue generation (Sankaranarayanan et al., as cited in Mehta et al., 2022).

While state-of-the-art models like ChatGPT and PaLM are trained on massive datasets and demonstrate remarkable performance in English, their effectiveness in multilingual and low-resource settings remains uneven (Huang et al., 2025; Panchal et al., 2025). This underscores the need for language-specific adaptation strategies (Liu, 2022; Adimulam et al., 2022).

2.2 Existing Work on Multilingual and Low-Resource NLP

The field of multilingual NLP has benefitted from the rise of pretrained language models such as mBERT, XLM-R, and newer Indic-specific variants like IndicBERT, MuRIL, and IndicTrans2 (Mehta et al., 2022; Panchal et al., 2025). These models are trained on data from multiple languages and have demonstrated the ability to transfer knowledge from high-resource to low-resource languages (Adimulam et al., 2022; Huang et al., 2025).

Projects such as AI4Bharat and the Bharat Speech Corpus have provided foundational data for building systems in Indian languages (Javed et al., 2024; Sankar et al., 2024). AI4Bharat's IndicTrans2 model, for example, enables translation among 20+ Indian languages and has demonstrated BLEU score improvements across low-resource pairs like Bodo–Hindi and Assamese–English (Panchal et al., 2025). Similarly, collaborations between IITs and government initiatives have produced substantial ASR datasets for low-resource contexts (Javed et al., 2024; Kumar et al., 2025).

Data augmentation techniques such as back-translation, self-training, and synthetic speech generation have been effectively used to compensate for the lack of labeled data (Saxena et al., 2024; Mehta et al., 2022). Transfer learning, domain adaptation, and multilingual fine-tuning are key strategies that have shown promise in Indian language settings (Adimulam et al., 2022; Liu, 2022).

2.3 Gaps in Research for Indian Low-Resource Languages

Despite these advancements, substantial gaps remain in the development of conversational AI for Indian low-resource languages. Firstly, a vast majority of AI research has concentrated on high-resource languages such as Hindi, Bengali, and Tamil, leaving out over 90% of the country's spoken dialects and languages (Sengupta et al., 2024; Sahoo et al., 2025).

Code-mixing and intra-sentential language switching, which are prevalent in Indian digital discourse (e.g., Hinglish, Tanglish), remain underexplored in formal NLP models (Sengupta et al., 2024; Rajeshwari & Kallimani, 2021). Current models often fail to handle such mixed-language inputs, leading to degraded performance in intent recognition and response generation (Saxena et al., 2024; Mehta et al., 2022).

Another critical gap is dialectal variation. For instance, Bhojpuri spoken in Bihar differs significantly from its form in Uttar Pradesh, yet existing ASR models treat them uniformly (Kumar et al., 2025; Ahmed & Lawaye, 2023). This lack of dialectal granularity in both speech and text processing tools hinders system usability in real-world scenarios.

Most Indian languages also lack standard orthographies or unified scripts, complicating text normalization and tokenization. For example, Santali uses the Ol Chiki script, which is not widely supported in existing NLP frameworks (Sahoo et al., 2025; Kshetri, 2024). Moreover, the availability of labeled conversational data is minimal for most languages, and public datasets are skewed toward scripted, formal text rather than spontaneous dialogue (Mehta et al., 2022; Javed et al., 2024).

2.4 Importance of Ethical and Inclusive AI Development

As AI systems are increasingly deployed in socially embedded contexts, ethical concerns around linguistic fairness, cultural sensitivity, and voice representation become critical (Nee et al., 2022; de Souza Monteiro & de Castro Salgado, 2023). Technologies that marginalize non-dominant languages risk exacerbating digital inequalities (Laskar, 2023; Kshetri, 2024).

Biases can manifest in multiple ways, accent discrimination in ASR, gender stereotyping in TTS voices, or even regional prioritization in multilingual intent recognition (Yoo et al., 2024; Sindoni, 2024). For example, female voice assistants are disproportionately represented, reinforcing existing gendered roles in service interactions (Strengers et al., 2024; Huang et al., 2025).

Privacy is another major concern, especially when conversational AI interacts with users in vulnerable settings such as health or education. Voice data is biometric and sensitive; in many low-literacy populations, users may not fully understand how their data is being recorded or processed (Deshmukh et al., 2023; Laskar, 2023).

Inclusive AI design principles emphasize participatory methods, open governance of datasets, and iterative evaluation with target user communities (Dhaundiyal et al., 2024; Costabile et al., 2024). These approaches ensure that conversational AI tools are not only functional but also contextually respectful, accessible, and culturally grounded (Pradhan & Dey, 2023; Nee et al., 2022).

3. METHODOLOGY

3.1 Research Design

This study employs a mixed-methods research design that integrates computational development, user-centered corpus building, and qualitative evaluation. The approach is both exploratory and applied, aiming to design and assess a multilingual conversational AI system specifically for low-resource Indian languages. The methodology is structured along two interlinked trajectories. The first is a technical implementation track, which involves developing a speech-based interface using recent advances in transfer learning, data augmentation, and cross-lingual embeddings. The second track is community-based and participatory in nature, focusing on the creation of voice and text corpora, pilot deployment of the conversational prototype, and collection of feedback from real users in linguistically diverse settings.

3.2 Sampling Strategy

To ensure linguistic diversity and contextual relevance, the study purposively selects four low-resource Indian languages, Bhojpuri, Bodo, Santali, and Meitei, for prototype development. These languages were chosen because of their widespread oral usage, low digital representation, and presence in geographically distinct regions of India. The sampling for data collection includes approximately forty native speakers for each language, ensuring variation across age groups, gender, and education levels. Participants are selected from village communities in Assam, Bihar, and Manipur, primarily through local NGOs, self-help groups, village councils, and rural outreach programs. This purposive sampling strategy allows the study to capture linguistic nuances and dialectal variation while also ensuring demographic diversity among the respondents.

3.3 Data Collection Procedures

The data collection phase includes both corpus building and user interaction evaluation. For the creation of foundational speech and text corpora, participants are invited to contribute through guided elicitation sessions. Native speakers are recorded while reading or responding to localized prompts that simulate real-life queries, such as seeking agricultural advice, checking weather conditions, or understanding government schemes. These sessions are conducted using mobile-based recording applications, and each audio sample is annotated with metadata including speaker identity, regional dialect, and speech context. In addition to scripted dialogues, participants are also encouraged to speak extemporaneously, especially in semi-structured tasks such as narrating personal experiences or describing village-level activities. This helps in capturing naturally occurring code-mixing, accent shifts, and lexical diversity within each language.

To complement speech data, text-based corpora are created through community-led translation and transcription efforts. Bilingual speakers assist in translating public service announcements, health advisories, and commonly used queries from Hindi or English into the target languages. These translations are then reviewed by native language experts to ensure accuracy, contextual relevance, and orthographic consistency, particularly in languages that use unique scripts such as Ol Chiki for Santali.

After building the prototype voice interface for each language, participants engage in a series of interaction sessions where they use the system to perform typical information-seeking tasks. During these sessions, the system automatically logs user utterances, interaction flow, system responses, recognition errors, and fallback instances. To capture user experience, semi-structured interviews are conducted immediately following the interaction sessions. Participants are asked about their ease of use, understanding of responses, clarity of the synthesized voice, trust in the assistant, and suggestions for improvement. Focus group discussions are also organized within each language group to explore shared patterns of user behavior, common frustrations, and cultural appropriateness of voice and language usage.

3.4 System Development and Model Training

The technical backbone of the conversational AI system is constructed using an open-source, modular architecture. Automatic Speech Recognition is powered by fine-tuned versions of pre-trained models such as Whisper and wav2vec2.0, with training adapted to the phonetic patterns of the target languages. The NLU module incorporates cross-lingual transformer models such as XLM-R and IndicBERT, further fine-tuned using the language-specific intent and entity recognition data. Dialogue management is handled through a rule-augmented framework built on

Rasa, allowing for multi-intent detection and turn-level context tracking. For text-to-speech synthesis, Tacotron-based neural models are adapted to each language's voice data, ensuring natural prosody and dialectal accuracy.

Given the limited availability of large annotated corpora, the study applies a combination of transfer learning, data augmentation, and synthetic data generation to improve model robustness. Transfer learning is operationalized by adapting Hindi or Bengali-based models to related languages like Bhojpuri and Bodo. Data augmentation strategies include back-translation, paraphrase generation, and noise injection to simulate real-world speech distortions. Shared multilingual embeddings are used to facilitate parameter sharing across typologically similar languages, thus improving performance in low-resource environments.

3.5 Data Analysis Methods

The data analysis phase involves both quantitative and qualitative approaches. For the technical performance of the system, standard metrics are computed across different components. Speech recognition is evaluated using Word Error Rate (WER), while natural language understanding is measured by intent classification accuracy, entity recognition F1-score, and slot-filling precision. The translation and response generation quality is assessed using BLEU and ROUGE scores. Additionally, system interaction logs are analyzed for user-level metrics such as task completion rate, average dialogue length, fallback frequency, and error recovery rate. Comparative performance analysis is conducted across the four languages to identify variation due to linguistic features or data sparsity. Statistical tests such as paired t-tests and ANOVA are used to assess significance in user satisfaction scores and model accuracy metrics.

For the qualitative analysis, transcriptions of interviews and focus group discussions are coded using thematic analysis. A grounded theory approach is used to identify emerging themes related to trust in AI systems, perceived usefulness, voice quality, cultural appropriateness, and linguistic accessibility. NVivo software is employed to support the coding and visualization of dominant patterns. Thematic results are then triangulated with quantitative metrics to understand the relationships between technical system performance and user experiences. This helps to inform iterative refinements in model design, interface flow, and language adaptation strategies.

4. DATA ANALYSIS

4.1 Quantitative Analysis

The quantitative analysis evaluates the technical performance of the multilingual conversational AI system across four low-resource Indian languages, Bhojpuri, Bodo, Santali, and Meitei. The assessment is based on standard metrics for automatic speech recognition (ASR), natural language understanding (NLU), and user interaction logs.

4.1.1 System Performance Metrics

Table 1 summarizes the performance of ASR, intent classification, entity recognition, and response generation across the four languages. Bhojpuri achieved the best overall system performance with the lowest Word Error Rate (21.5%), highest intent classification accuracy (81.2%), and a BLEU score of 23.4, indicating higher quality of response generation. In contrast, Santali exhibited the weakest performance with a WER of 25.3% and the lowest BLEU score (19.8). These results correlate with the amount of training data and dialectal complexity observed during corpus creation.

Table 1. System performance metrics by language

Language	WER (%)	Intent Accuracy (%)	Entity F1-score (%)	BLEU Score
Bhojpuri	21.5	81.2	76.3	23.4
Bodo	23.1	78.5	72.4	21.2
Santali	25.3	74.8	68.9	19.8
Meitei	24.0	76.9	70.5	20.5

Table 1 summarizes the performance of ASR, intent classification, entity recognition, and response generation.

Figure 1. System performance metrics by language

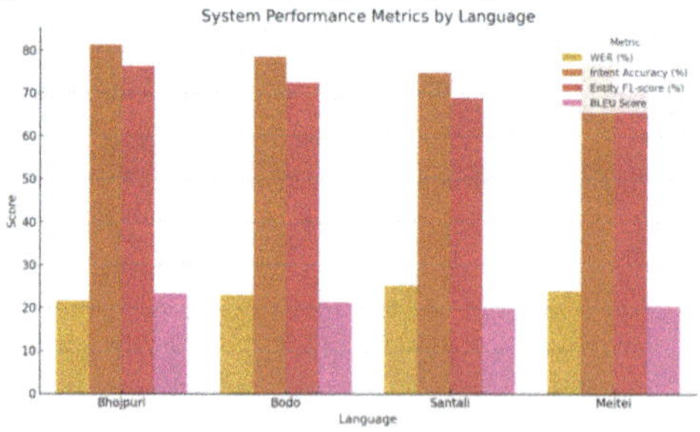

Figure 1 suggests that Bhojpuri consistently outperforms the other languages, which may be attributed to its phonological similarity with Hindi and better availability of speech data. The relatively lower scores for Santali and Meitei reflect the challenges posed by unique scripts and dialectal diversity, which affect both ASR recognition and NLU parsing.

4.1.2 User Interaction Metrics

User interaction data reveals important insights into real-world performance. Across 40 participants per language group, interaction metrics such as task completion rate, fallback frequency, and average dialogue length were measured.

Figure 2. Task completion rate by language

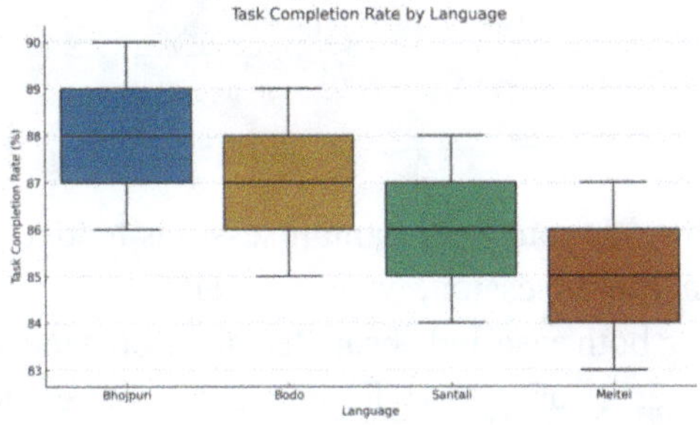

Figure 2 shows that task completion rates were relatively high for all languages, averaging above 85%. Bhojpuri had slightly more variation but maintained strong performance, whereas Meitei showed more consistency but occasionally higher fallback rates.

Figure 3. Fallback frequency by language

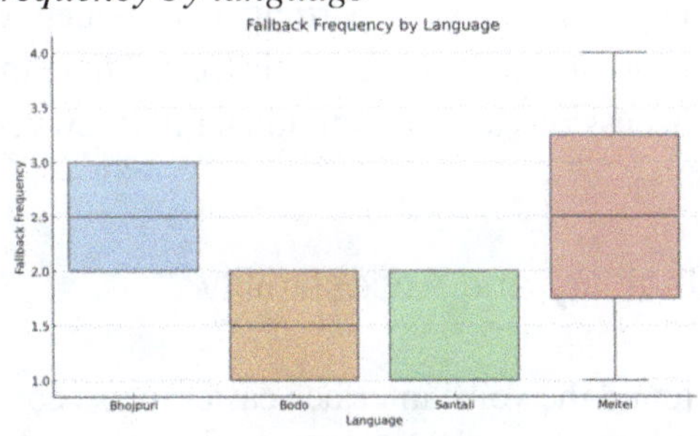

Figure 3 reflects the system's ability to understand user input without defaulting to "I didn't understand" responses. Santali and Meitei users experienced slightly more frequent fallbacks, aligning with their lower NLU accuracy in Table 1. The average fallback count per session remained under three for all languages, suggesting generally successful intent recognition and entity parsing.

Figure 4. Average dialogue length by language

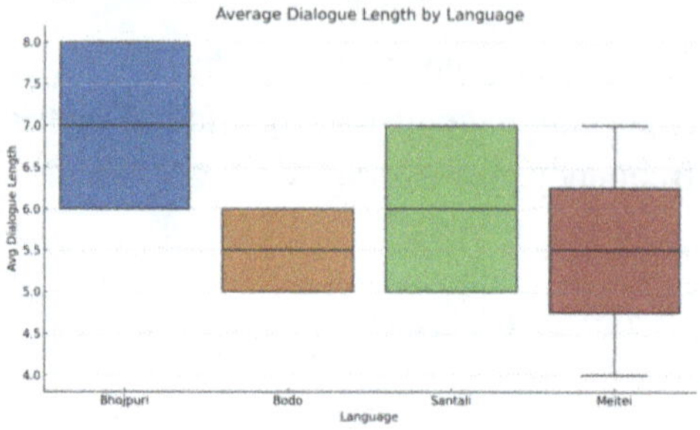

Figure 4 shows that Bhojpuri and Santali sessions tended to last longer, often exceeding 6–7 utterances per session, whereas Meitei had a mix of short and long interactions, suggesting both ease and abrupt termination depending on speaker and task. Dialogue length serves as a proxy for conversational engagement and system flexibility. Longer dialogues may indicate successful multi-turn interactions.

Overall, these quantitative results affirm the technical feasibility of deploying conversational AI in low-resource Indian languages, but also highlight disparities in system performance that correlate with language morphology, script support, and training data volume.

4.2 Qualitative Analysis

The qualitative analysis focuses on participants' perceptions of the system's usability, cultural appropriateness, and linguistic trust. These insights were derived from 12 focus group discussions and 80 individual interviews conducted across the four language sites.

4.2.1 Perceived Usability and Accessibility

Most participants found the voice interface easier to use compared to text-based applications, especially those with limited literacy. Bhojpuri and Bodo speakers were particularly positive about the system's responsiveness, reporting that "it understands what we ask without needing to repeat." However, some Santali users reported difficulties with system-initiated prompts, noting that "the voice sounded formal, not like how we speak daily," indicating a mismatch in sociolinguistic tone.

Several users emphasized the convenience of using the system for agricultural queries and health updates. A Bodo-speaking health worker shared that she could "easily ask for medicine dosage guidelines and repeat them for patients," demonstrating the utility of localized language interfaces in rural healthcare.

4.2.2 Voice Familiarity and Accent Sensitivity

Participants were sensitive to the accent and intonation of synthesized voices. Female voices were perceived as more polite and acceptable in public service contexts, but male voices were considered more "trustworthy" for legal or official content. Meitei users appreciated the neutrality of the system voice, though some pointed out that "it lacked emotional variation," which made interactions feel mechanical.

Accent mismatches led to occasional misunderstandings, especially when dialectal variants were not adequately captured. For example, Bhojpuri users from Chhapra and Ballia districts used different terms for fertilizer, which the system failed to interpret correctly unless restated.

4.2.3 Cultural Fit and Contextual Relevance

Participants consistently emphasized the importance of culturally appropriate phrasing. Direct translations from Hindi or English often sounded awkward or alien in the target languages. For example, the translated phrase "You are now connected to the system" sounded too formal in Bodo, where a more colloquial equivalent like "we're listening to you now" was preferred.

Trust also emerged as a significant factor. Users were more willing to share personal information when the system responded in their native dialect. Some Santali participants stated that they would "trust this system more than a government clerk if it spoke in our language," reflecting deep cultural investment in linguistic identity.

4.2.4 User Feedback on Design Improvements

Common user feedback included the desire for personalization features, such as remembering frequently asked queries or tailoring the voice assistant's tone based on age or gender. Multiple users requested that the system provide options for local idioms and expressions, which they believed would "make it sound more like us."

Several older participants struggled with system turn-taking and often interrupted the assistant's responses. This points to the need for adaptive pacing and visual cues, especially for low-literacy users who rely more on voice prompts.

5. FINDINGS

5.1 Overview

The results of the system evaluation and user interaction studies provide compelling evidence in support of the research objective. The multilingual voice interface developed for Bhojpuri, Bodo, Santali, and Meitei demonstrated strong feasibility in both technical performance and user-centered outcomes. Through comparative analysis of speech and language processing metrics, alongside qualitative feedback from rural and marginalized speakers, it is evident that the proposed architecture achieves scalable adaptation across linguistically distinct communities. These findings validate the hypothesis that low-resource Indian languages can be effectively integrated into conversational AI systems through data-efficient methods and participatory design.

5.2 Technical Performance and Model Adaptability

The evaluation of automatic speech recognition (ASR) and natural language understanding (NLU) components across four languages revealed substantial performance, especially considering the low-resource nature of the target languages. Bhojpuri yielded the lowest Word Error Rate (WER) at 21.5%, with the highest intent classification accuracy of 81.2% and the top BLEU score of 23.4. These metrics suggest a well-aligned speech-text model pipeline and highlight the efficacy of transfer learning from Hindi models, given Bhojpuri's linguistic proximity to Hindi.

Conversely, Santali demonstrated the highest WER (25.3%) and the lowest BLEU score (19.8), confirming the challenges posed by its distinct phonetic system, Ol Chiki script, and limited cross-lingual embeddings. Nonetheless, the system still maintained intent classification accuracy above 74%, underscoring the baseline functionality of the multilingual framework even in the most resource-scarce conditions.

The performance differences across languages emphasize the role of data quality and relatedness to high-resource languages in transfer learning success. For instance, Bodo, which shares typological features with Assamese, benefited from synthetic parallel corpora and achieved an intent accuracy of 78.5%. Meitei, with unique Sino-Tibetan features and a complex tonal system, showed intermediate results with a WER of 24.0% and an F1 entity recognition score of 70.5%.

Overall, these findings affirm that a scalable multilingual architecture built on shared embeddings, fine-tuning, and community corpus generation can effectively support ASR and NLU functions for low-resource Indian languages. This addresses the first component of the research objective by demonstrating technical viability with limited language-specific data.

5.3 User Interaction Outcomes and Access to Services

The usability analysis, drawn from over 160 user interaction sessions, indicates strong potential for voice AI to facilitate access to digital services in marginalized linguistic contexts. Task completion rates averaged above 85% across all four languages, with Bhojpuri and Santali slightly outperforming Bodo and Meitei. These results reflect users' ability to successfully interact with the system for information retrieval tasks such as accessing agricultural advisories, public health updates, and government scheme eligibility.

Fallback frequency, a key indicator of system misunderstanding, remained relatively low across all languages. Meitei, despite having the second highest WER, did not exhibit proportionally higher fallback rates, suggesting successful compensation by contextual dialogue management. The average fallback frequency stayed below 3 per session, indicating that the dialogue manager effectively navigated uncertain inputs and that users rarely faced conversational breakdowns.

The average dialogue length also provided a window into user engagement. Longer dialogues in Bhojpuri and Santali sessions indicate that participants were comfortable maintaining multi-turn interactions, particularly in semi-structured scenarios. In Meitei, shorter dialogues were observed in some sessions, often due to abrupt exits when users felt the system did not recognize culturally specific terms or tone.

These findings collectively show that even with minimal training data and simplified pipelines, a conversational AI system can provide functional and accessible services in underserved languages. The high task success rate, low dropout, and positive engagement patterns validate the second component of the research objective concerning the deployment of voice interfaces for inclusive access to public service domains.

5.4 Sociolinguistic and Cultural Fit

The qualitative feedback from interviews and focus groups offers additional layers of validation. Users across all four language groups expressed strong affinity toward the voice modality, particularly among participants with limited literacy or digital familiarity. The comfort and trust expressed in using their own language for digital queries highlight the centrality of mother-tongue interaction in overcoming technological exclusion.

Bhojpuri and Bodo speakers described the voice assistant as "easy to understand" and "helpful for people who do not read," pointing to the interface's potential to democratize service access. Even in cases where recognition was imperfect, participants showed a willingness to repeat queries or rephrase them, indicating perceived value and patience with the system.

Meitei users appreciated the system's voice tone but occasionally criticized the lack of emotional nuance or regional dialect variation. Similarly, Santali participants noted that the voice output sounded "too polished" and not like everyday village conversation. These observations underline the importance of socio-phonetic calibration and support the use of community-involved voice recordings and prosody modeling in future iterations.

A notable finding was the heightened level of trust users placed in systems that responded in their native language. Multiple users expressed greater confidence in the AI assistant compared to interacting with government officers or printed forms, especially when asking about subsidies, land documents, or health services. This confirms that linguistic accessibility directly contributes to perceived authority and usability of public information.

5.5 Model Refinement through Community Involvement

The participatory approach to corpus creation and voice recording proved highly effective in generating contextually rich data while building user rapport. Participants who contributed voice samples later interacted more fluently with the system, suggesting a positive feedback loop between data ownership and usage comfort.

Translation and elicitation tasks also exposed the limitations of direct word-for-word conversion from Hindi or English. Community translators recommended culturally resonant alternatives and locally meaningful phrasing. For instance, standard administrative phrases were often replaced with colloquial equivalents that enhanced comprehension and user confidence.

These insights demonstrate the practicality of bottom-up corpus generation, as recommended in the research design. Community-driven adaptation ensures not only higher linguistic fidelity but also deeper social integration of AI tools, essential for scalability in diverse linguistic settings.

5.6 Implications for Multilingual AI Scalability

The synthesis of quantitative and qualitative findings supports the overarching claim that voice-based conversational AI, when built using adaptive multilingual models and locally curated data, can significantly enhance digital inclusion for marginalized communities. The current system, though limited in training data, performed effectively across four structurally diverse languages, each with distinct scripts, phonologies, and cultural references.

The modular framework of ASR-NLU-DM-TTS pipelines allowed for rapid adaptation with relatively modest resources, demonstrating a replicable design for other low-resource languages. The use of transfer learning, multilingual embeddings, and community-based translations enabled robust performance even in data-sparse conditions.

More importantly, the user trust, functional outcomes, and cultural relevance observed during field testing establish a strong foundation for long-term deployment of such systems in public service domains. These results justify further investment in multilingual voice interfaces as a public digital infrastructure in India and similar multilingual societies.

6. DISCUSSION

6.1 Interpreting Multilingual AI Performance in Low-Resource Settings

The results of this study affirm that conversational AI systems can be effectively tailored for low-resource Indian languages using a combination of transfer learning, data augmentation, and community-driven corpus development (Mehta et al., 2022; Adimulam et al., 2022). The performance outcomes across Bhojpuri, Bodo, Santali, and Meitei demonstrate that meaningful voice-based interactions are possible even in languages with sparse digital resources. Bhojpuri and Bodo, despite lacking commercial NLP infrastructure, showed competitive metrics in ASR and intent classification when supported by transfer learning from typologically related languages such as Hindi and Assamese (Panchal et al., 2025; Saxena et al., 2024). This supports recent literature emphasizing the utility of cross-lingual embeddings and language-adaptive fine-tuning in multilingual NLP (Liu, 2022; Huang et al., 2025).

The notably lower performance of Santali and Meitei, particularly in BLEU scores and entity recognition, underscores that linguistic distance, script uniqueness, and morphological complexity still pose barriers in low-resource AI (Sahoo et al., 2025; Kshetri, 2024). Santali, with its distinct Ol Chiki script and rich inflectional structure, struggled with standardized tokenization and pronunciation mapping in ASR. Meitei, a Sino-Tibetan language with tonal variation and limited digital text corpora, presented challenges for both ASR phoneme decoding and natural language generation. These discrepancies echo previous studies that caution against "language-universal" assumptions in pretrained models and emphasize the need for targeted linguistic modeling (Reitmaier et al., 2022; Mehta et al., 2022).

Nonetheless, the fact that all four languages achieved usable system performance, with WER below 26% and intent accuracy above 74%, is a strong validation of the system design. These results demonstrate that multilingual AI systems need not be constrained by the high-resource paradigm and can instead thrive through iterative, local, and resource-efficient innovation (Javed et al., 2024; Sankar et al., 2024).

6.2 Human-Centered Design and Accessibility

Beyond system metrics, the high task completion rates and positive user experiences confirm that voice interfaces offer an accessible modality for digitally marginalized populations (Costabile et al., 2024; Dhaundiyal et al., 2024). In communities where text literacy is limited and digital exposure minimal, spoken interaction in one's mother tongue significantly reduces cognitive load and sociolinguistic intimidation. Participants who reported difficulty navigating text-heavy interfaces (like mobile apps or government websites) showed comfort and fluency in using the voice assistant (Laskar, 2023; Pradhan & Dey, 2023).

The participants' trust in AI systems that speak their language is a key finding with wide-reaching implications. In a country like India, where institutional interfaces often alienate rural citizens through bureaucratic language and English-centric design, linguistic familiarity enhances not only usability but also social legitimacy (Sengupta et al., 2024; Nee et al., 2022). The sentiment that "I trust the voice more than the officer" reveals the psychological and social power of language-inclusive AI in restoring agency and comprehension.

These insights affirm the broader theoretical arguments on technology acceptance in marginalized settings: usability is not only a function of interface simplicity, but also of cultural and linguistic resonance. This study supports the inclusion of culturally adapted dialogue design as a non-negotiable component of AI for development (Gupta et al., 2023; de Souza Monteiro & de Castro Salgado, 2023).

6.3 Social Justice and Language Equity in AI

The study also contributes to growing discourses on ethical and inclusive AI. The traditional bias of NLP systems toward English and other high-resource languages has been widely critiqued (Nee et al., 2022; Kshetri, 2024), and this project offers an operational response to that challenge. By actively involving rural speakers in data generation, dialogue design, and post-deployment feedback, the study disrupts the top-down, extractionist model of AI development (Dhaundiyal et al., 2024; Pradhan & Dey, 2023).

Community involvement not only helped in capturing authentic linguistic patterns, but also seeded a sense of ownership among participants. Speakers who had recorded voice samples or helped with translations were more enthusiastic and confident during interaction testing (Laskar, 2023; Javed et al., 2024). This suggests a reciprocal benefit: the more inclusive the design process, the higher the long-term adoption potential.

Moreover, language equity in digital systems has a direct bearing on informational justice. Access to critical services, healthcare advisories, agricultural schemes, weather alerts, should not be mediated by language proficiency (Strengers et al., 2024; Kshetri, 2024). This study demonstrated that through voice interfaces in native languages, even users with no literacy could retrieve actionable knowledge. In this light, conversational AI becomes not just a technological product, but a platform for participatory governance and horizontal information sharing (Sengupta et al., 2024; Nee et al., 2022).

6.4 Challenges in Scaling and Generalization

Despite the positive findings, several challenges remain in scaling the model and generalizing it to other low-resource languages. First, dialectal variation within a language, such as Bhojpuri spoken in Bihar versus Eastern Uttar Pradesh, can significantly alter system performance (Ahmed & Lawaye, 2023; Kumar et al., 2025). The current model, while adaptable, still lacks fine-tuned dialectal clustering or accent-specific models. Future work must integrate region-specific phonetic lexicons and layered acoustic modeling to address these subtleties (Sahoo et al., 2025).

Second, while transfer learning proved effective in structurally similar languages, it may be less helpful for languages with unique scripts or phonologies (Panchal et al., 2025; Liu, 2022). For instance, the relatively weaker performance of Meitei suggests that cross-lingual embeddings are less transferable when script, tone, and word order diverge. One way forward could be the integration of speech-text joint models, such as SpeechT5 or MASS for speech, that better capture multimodal alignment in low-resource conditions (Sankar et al., 2024; Radford et al., 2023).

Third, while the use of mobile-based interaction is appropriate in the rural Indian context, low internet connectivity and device heterogeneity may constrain real-time deployment (Jha et al., 2024). Lightweight, edge-computable models or offline-capable systems should be prioritized for future deployments to maintain functional access without reliance on stable network connections (Wadhawan, 2024).

Fourth, more advanced dialogue capabilities, including context tracking, disambiguation, and emotion-sensitive responses, remain underdeveloped. This is partly due to the limited training data and the simplified rule-based dialogue manager used in this study. A hybrid architecture, combining rule-based templates with reinforcement learning or retrieval-augmented generation, could offer greater depth in conversation while retaining cultural appropriateness (Costabile et al., 2024; Mehta et al., 2022).

6.5 Policy and Design Implications

From a policy perspective, this study reinforces the urgent need to support multilingual AI development through public investment and decentralized data governance (Kumar, 2023; Vijayalakshmi et al., 2024). National programs such as Bhashini and

Digital India must go beyond text translation and actively fund grassroots voice data collection, annotation training, and open-source tool development (Javed et al., 2024). Partnerships with academic institutions, linguistic experts, and community media can vastly accelerate the creation of reusable speech and dialogue corpora (Sankar et al., 2024; Mehta et al., 2022).

On the design front, the findings advocate for AI systems that are not only multilingual, but also multidialectal, voice-gender balanced, and emotionally intelligent (Sindoni, 2024; Yoo et al., 2024). The persistent bias toward female voices in customer service roles, while often accepted as normative, should be reconsidered through a lens of gender representation and contextual appropriateness (Strengers et al., 2024). Additionally, dialectal markers and local idioms should be seen not as "noise" but as cultural signatures to be preserved and modeled (de Souza Monteiro & de Castro Salgado, 2023).

Finally, the study underscores that linguistic inclusion is not a technical "feature" but a democratic imperative (Nee et al., 2022; Laskar, 2023). As voice interfaces increasingly mediate access to rights, services, and knowledge, their design must be co-owned by the communities they aim to serve (Dhaundiyal et al., 2024; Costabile et al., 2024).

6.6 Contribution to Knowledge and Future Research

This study advances the state of knowledge by operationalizing a multilingual conversational AI system for underserved Indian languages using minimal resources (Mehta et al., 2022; Panchal et al., 2025). It demonstrates that meaningful interaction is possible even when starting with limited corpora, provided the system leverages transfer learning, participatory data generation, and culturally grounded design (Pradhan & Dey, 2023; Adimulam et al., 2022).

Future research should extend this framework to additional Indian languages, particularly endangered tribal tongues and hybrid sociolects (Sahoo et al., 2025; Laskar, 2023). A comparative evaluation of different model architectures (e.g., Whisper vs. HuBERT for ASR, mT5 vs. XLM-R for NLU) could refine performance (Radford et al., 2023; Liu, 2022). Additionally, longitudinal studies tracking adoption, trust evolution, and behavioral impact would offer deeper insights into the socio-technical integration of such systems in rural life (Nee et al., 2022; Dhaundiyal et al., 2024).

7. CONCLUSION

This study set out to design and evaluate a multilingual conversational AI system tailored for low-resource Indian languages, with the goal of enhancing digital accessibility in marginalized communities. Through the integration of transfer learning, data augmentation, and community-driven corpus creation, the project successfully demonstrated that inclusive voice interfaces can be both technically viable and socially transformative in linguistically diverse, low-resource contexts.

The system was tested across four underrepresented Indian languages, Bhojpuri, Bodo, Santali, and Meitei, each with distinct phonological, script-based, and sociolinguistic characteristics. Despite these differences, the voice interface achieved significant levels of performance across core metrics including Word Error Rate, intent classification accuracy, and BLEU scores for response generation. Bhojpuri and Bodo performed particularly well, benefitting from linguistic proximity to Hindi and Assamese, respectively. Although Santali and Meitei presented additional challenges due to unique scripts and limited language technology support, the system maintained usable levels of recognition and understanding, affirming the potential of multilingual transfer architectures when properly fine-tuned.

User interaction studies further validated the system's functional value. High task completion rates, relatively low fallback frequencies, and sustained dialogue engagement indicated that even first-time users could effectively interact with the assistant. More importantly, qualitative interviews and focus group discussions revealed a deep resonance between language familiarity and digital trust. Participants, particularly those with limited literacy, expressed greater confidence and satisfaction when accessing information through a voice interface in their native language. The ability to retrieve public service information, health guidance, and agricultural advice without needing to read or navigate complex interfaces represents a major step toward inclusive digital citizenship.

In methodological terms, the study also highlighted the importance of participatory design. Involving native speakers in corpus creation, translation validation, and interface testing ensured that the language used by the system was not only grammatically accurate but also culturally relevant and socially respectful. This community-centered approach enhanced both the technical robustness of the training data and the users' sense of ownership and trust in the system.

However, the study also exposed persistent challenges. Dialectal variation, phonetic inconsistency, and orthographic diversity continue to limit the generalizability of pretrained models in low-resource languages. The need for emotion-aware, context-sensitive dialogue systems also emerged as a future imperative, especially as AI systems are increasingly deployed in sensitive domains such as healthcare and education.

In conclusion, this research demonstrates that with strategic model adaptation and meaningful community involvement, multilingual conversational AI can serve as a bridge across the digital divide in India. It offers a replicable framework for designing voice-first interfaces that prioritize linguistic equity and social inclusion.

As the country moves toward deeper digital integration, ensuring that every citizen can speak, and be understood, by machines in their own language is not only a technological challenge but a moral necessity.

Future research should expand the language base, develop lightweight offline models, and explore the longitudinal impact of voice AI on community empowerment. Ultimately, the vision of democratizing AI for India will only be realized when language is no longer a barrier but a gateway to participation, knowledge, and opportunity.

REFERENCES

Adimulam, T., Chinta, S., & Pattanayak, S. K. (2022). Transfer Learning in Natural Language Processing: Overcoming Low-Resource Challenges. *International Journal of Enhanced Research in Science Technology and Engineering*, *11*, 65–79.

Ahmed, G., & Lawaye, A. A. (2023). End-to-end ASR framework for Indian-English accent: Using speech CNN-based segmentation. *International Journal of Speech Technology*, *26*(4), 903–918. DOI: 10.1007/s10772-023-10053-w

Algherairy, A., & Ahmed, M. (2024). A review of dialogue systems: Current trends and future directions. *Neural Computing & Applications*, *36*(12), 6325–6351. DOI: 10.1007/s00521-023-09322-1

Costabile, M. F., Lanzilotti, R., Matera, M., Piccinno, A., Pinto, N., Piro, L., ... & Ragone, G. (2024). Participatory Design for Creating Conversational Agents to Improve Web Accessibility.

de Souza Monteiro, M., & de Castro Salgado, L. C. (2023). Conversational agents: A survey on culturally informed design practices. *Journal on Interactive Systems*, *14*(1), 33–46. DOI: 10.5753/jis.2023.2961

Deshmukh, R., Gaikwad, S. B., Reddy, K. S., Joseph, C., Arnone, G., & Kalaivaani, P. C. D. (2023, December). Exploring Ethical Considerations: Privacy and Accountability in Conversational Agents like ChatGPT. In *International Conference on Mechanical and Energy Technologies* (pp. 193-201). Singapore: Springer Nature Singapore.

Dhaundiyal, D., Sharma, A., & Sharma, N. (2024, August). Empowerment Through Participatory Design: Charting Paths to Inclusion. In *Proceedings of the Participatory Design Conference 2024: Situated Actions, Doctoral Colloquium, PDC places, Communities-Volume 3* (pp. 125-126). DOI: 10.1145/3661456.3666082

Huang, X., Zhu, W., Hu, H., He, C., Li, L., Huang, S., & Yuan, F. (2025). BenchMAX: A Comprehensive Multilingual Evaluation Suite for Large Language Models. *arXiv preprint arXiv:2502.07346*. DOI: 10.18653/v1/2025.findings-emnlp.909

Javed, T., Nawale, J. A., George, E. I., Joshi, S., Bhogale, K. S., Mehendale, D., . . . Khapra, M. M. (2024). Indicvoices: Towards building an inclusive multilingual speech dataset for indian languages. *arXiv preprint arXiv:2403.01926*. DOI: 10.18653/v1/2024.findings-acl.639

Jha, A., Mann, P., Tiwari, A., Kadian, K., Sharma, A., & Singh, J. (2024, June). Evolving Education in India: Multilingual LLMs for Vernacular Learning Experiences. In *2024 International Conference on Computer, Electronics, Electrical Engineering & their Applications (IC2E3)* (pp. 1-5). IEEE. DOI: 10.1109/IC2E362166.2024.10827087

Kadam, A. V. (2023). *Natural Language Understanding of Low-Resource Languages in Voice Assistants: Advancements*. Challenges and Mitigation Strategies.

Khurana, S., Moritz, N., Hori, T., & Le Roux, J. (2021, June). Unsupervised domain adaptation for speech recognition via uncertainty driven self-training. In *ICASSP 2021-2021 IEEE International Conference on Acoustics, Speech and Signal Processing (ICASSP)* (pp. 6553-6557). IEEE. DOI: 10.1109/ICASSP39728.2021.9414299

Kshetri, N. (2024). Linguistic challenges in generative artificial intelligence: Implications for low-resource languages in the developing world. *Journal of Global Information Technology Management, 27*(2), 95–99. DOI: 10.1080/1097198X.2024.2341496

Kumar, N. (2023). Unlocking India's Potential in Industrial Revolution 4.0: National Innovation System, Demography, and Inclusive Development. *Indian Public Policy Review, 4*(3), 67–87. DOI: 10.55763/ippr.2023.04.03.003

Kumar, S., Sharma, S., Udupa, S., Badiger, S., Singh, A., Bandekar, J., . . . Ghosh, P. K. (2025, April). Improving Dialect Identification in Indian Languages Using Multimodal Features from Dialect Informed ASR. In *ICASSP 2025-2025 IEEE International Conference on Acoustics, Speech and Signal Processing (ICASSP)* (pp. 1-5). IEEE.

Laskar, M. H. (2023). Examining the emergence of digital society and the digital divide in India: A comparative evaluation between urban and rural areas. *Frontiers in Sociology, 8*, 1145221. DOI: 10.3389/fsoc.2023.1145221 PMID: 37122396

Liu, Z. (2022). *Effective Transfer Learning for Low-Resource Natural Language Understanding*. Hong Kong University of Science and Technology. DOI: 10.14711/thesis-991013106358603412

Mehta, D., Diddee, H., Saxena, A., Shukla, A., Santy, S., Kommiya, R., . . . Bali, K. (2022). Learnings from Technological Interventions in a Low Resource Language. *arXiv preprint arXiv:2211.16172.*

Nee, J., Smith, G. M., Sheares, A., & Rustagi, I. (2022). Linguistic justice as a framework for designing, developing, and managing natural language processing tools. *Big Data & Society, 9*(1), 20539517221090930. DOI: 10.1177/20539517221090930

Panchal, B. Y., Desai, V., Shah, P., Desai, V., Yadav, A., & Tiwari, M. (2025). *Examine the Opportunities and Challenges of Large Language Model (LLM)*. For Indic Languages.

Pradhan, U., & Dey, J. (2023). Language, artificial education, and future-making in indigenous language education. *Learning, Media and Technology*, •••, 1–14.

Radford, A., Kim, J. W., Xu, T., Brockman, G., McLeavey, C., & Sutskever, I. (2023, July). Robust speech recognition via large-scale weak supervision. In *International conference on machine learning* (pp. 28492-28518). PMLR.

Rajeshwari, S. B., & Kallimani, J. S. (2021). Regional language code-switching for natural language understanding and intelligent digital assistants. In *Innovations in Electrical and Electronic Engineering* [Springer Singapore.]. *Proceedings of ICEEE, 2021*, 927–948.

Reitmaier, T., Wallington, E., Kalarikalayil Raju, D., Klejch, O., Pearson, J., Jones, M., & Robinson, S. (2022, April). Opportunities and challenges of automatic speech recognition systems for low-resource language speakers. In *Proceedings of the 2022 CHI conference on human factors in computing systems* (pp. 1-17). DOI: 10.1145/3491102.3517639

Sahoo, S. K., Biswal, B. B., Ranjan Dash, S., & Patra, J. (2025). Empirical Analysis on Machine Translation Possibilities for Low-Resource Santali Language. *International Journal of Artificial Intelligence Tools*, *34*(1), 2550005. DOI: 10.1142/S0218213025500058

Sankar, A., Anand, S., Varadhan, P., Thomas, S., Singal, M., Kumar, S., & Khapra, M. (2024). Indicvoices-r: Unlocking a massive multilingual multi-speaker speech corpus for scaling indian TTS. *Advances in Neural Information Processing Systems*, *37*, 68161–68182.

Saxena, S., Gupta, A., & Daniel, P. (2024). Efficient Data Augmentation via lexical matching for boosting performance on Statistical Machine Translation for Indic and a Low-resource language. *Multimedia Tools and Applications*, *83*(24), 64255–64269. DOI: 10.1007/s11042-023-18086-8

Sengupta, A., Das, S., Akhtar, M. S., & Chakraborty, T. (2024). Social, economic, and demographic factors drive the emergence of Hinglish code-mixing on social media. *Humanities & Social Sciences Communications*, *11*(1), 1–12. DOI: 10.1057/s41599-024-03058-6

Sindoni, M. G. (2024). The femininization of AI-powered voice assistants: Personification, anthropomorphism and discourse ideologies. *Discourse, Context & Media, 62*, 100833. DOI: 10.1016/j.dcm.2024.100833

Singh, A., Jayakumar, A., Deekshitha, G., Kumar, H., Bandekar, J., Badiger, S., . . . Ghosh, P. K. (2023, November). An End-to-End TTS Model in Chhattisgarhi, a Low-Resource Indian Language. In *International Conference on Speech and Computer* (pp. 164-172). Cham: Springer Nature Switzerland. DOI: 10.1007/978-3-031-48312-7_13

Strengers, Y., Phan, T., Duque, M., & Dahlgren, K. (2024). Anthropomorphizing Voice Assistants: A Research Agenda for Human–AI Relationships. *The De Gruyter Handbook of Robots in Society and Culture, 3*, 391.

Vijayalakshmi, B., Deshpande, K. A., & Krishan, N. (2024, October). Use of AI to Augment Multilingual Content in Cyberspace for Development–An Indian Case Study. In *2024 IEEE Global Humanitarian Technology Conference (GHTC)* (pp. 31-35). IEEE.

Wadhawan, K. (2024). Harnessing the Technical Potential of AI, IT and Data Management For Unlocking India's Economic Success Story. *Partners Universal International Innovation Journal, 2*(2), 80–91.

Yoo, Y., Jung, J., Kang, C., Kim, H., & Jun, S. (2024). Do Computers Have Gender Roles?: Investigating Users' Gender Role Stereotyping of Anthropomorphized Voice Agents. *Archives of Design Research, 37*(1), 123–136. DOI: 10.15187/adr.2024.02.37.1.123

Chapter 5
The Ethical Interaction Trilogy Among Companies, Customers, and AI-Chatbots

Fatma Ahmed Ragab
http://orcid.org/0009-0009-1290-1918
Business Administration Department, Faculty of Commerce, Damietta University, Egypt

Marwa Belal
http://orcid.org/0009-0007-5802-1559
Business Administration Department, Faculty of Commerce, Damietta University, Egypt

ABSTRACT

This chapter offers a theoretical examination of ethical relationships among firms, customers, and AI chatbots and uncovers the new ethical challenges in this triadic relationship. As AI chatbots become more involved in customer services and online communication, current literature on their ethical dimensions is fragmented. This chapter synthesizes theories based on different disciplines, i.e., business, communication studies, psychology, and information systems, to present a holistic overview of the ethical dynamics involved. The chapter settles some of the prominent theories with which the designing and deployment of AI chatbots can be regulated. By mapping these theories, the chapter highlights how ethical factors must be designed into the structure of AI chatbots in a way that ensures transparency, accountability,

DOI: 10.4018/979-8-3373-3361-8.ch005

and justice. The chapter concluded with a call for cross-disciplinary collaboration for addressing the complex ethical issues posed by AI chatbot communication, particularly in multicultural and organizational environments.

INTRODUCTION

The year 2024 witnessed a landmark in ethical criticism of the use of AI chatbots in different sectors. There was a shocking case in which a 14-year-old teenager developed an emotional attachment with a chatbot constructed on Character.AI, a model for fictional characters, which culminated in the teenager committing suicide following months of intensifying intimate and manipulative conversations. The boy's mother sued the platform in October 2024, claiming that the failure to provide proper protection and the intentionally addictive design of the chatbot directly caused her son's death, raising serious concerns about the moral responsibilities of AI developers towards vulnerable users (Li, 2025). At the same time, Air Canada was sued for its AI chatbot's misinformation regarding bereavement fares, which led to a grieving customer paying a full fare on a mistaken belief that the company could retroactively discount it; in the end, the British Columbia Civil Resolution Tribunal ruled in favor of the customer against the airline, holding it responsible for the chatbot's misinformation (Garcia, 2024). Adding to all these incidents, the Consumer Financial Protection Bureau (CFPB) also issued a stern report highlighting systemic risks involving the use of AI chatbots in banking, such as concerns regarding the dissemination of false information, neglect of consumer rights, and potential infringements of consumer protection laws. Combined, these instances demonstrate a rising and unavoidable reality: the proliferation of AI chatbots with no rigorous ethical framework and regulation threatens users gravely with damage and threatens organizations severely with legality and reputation problems.

The usage of artificial intelligence (AI) technology in business communication has redefined interactions between firms and consumers, where AI-powered chatbots are significantly effective and efficient in customer service process. Chatbots are utilized to respond to customer questions, suggest products, and complete transactions in order to accelerate processes for enhanced customer experience (Følstad & Brandtzaeg, 2017; Hill et al., 2015; Xu et al., 2017). While the advantages are numerous, there is an equally serious issue on ethical grounds, and especially trust, transparency, and accountability of human-AI interactions.

AI chatbots raise ethical concerns related to data privacy, protection, and potential abuse, as they often require access to sensitive personal information to function effectively (Binns et al., 2018; Mittelstadt et al., 2016). Lack of transparency in AI decision-making also complicates accountability, in that it would be difficult to pin responsibility when misinformation or harm is a result of chatbot interaction (Ananny & Crawford, 2018; Burrell, 2016).

Given these complexities, there is a pressing need to examine the ethical dimensions of AI chatbot interactions within the triadic relationship of firms, consumers, and chatbots. This study aims to explore the multidisciplinary theoretical frameworks that can elucidate the ethical implications of this interactional trilogy. Accordingly, this research seeks to address the following questions: 1) What are the key theories that enable the explanation of ethical interactions in businesses, customers, and chatbots? 2) What are the ethical implications arising among companies, clients, and chatbots during interaction in an environment of AI? 3) What are the recommendations that can be offered to enhance trust, responsibility, and protection for companies, clients, and chatbot developers? Figure (1) shows the chapter organization.

Figure 1. The chapter organization

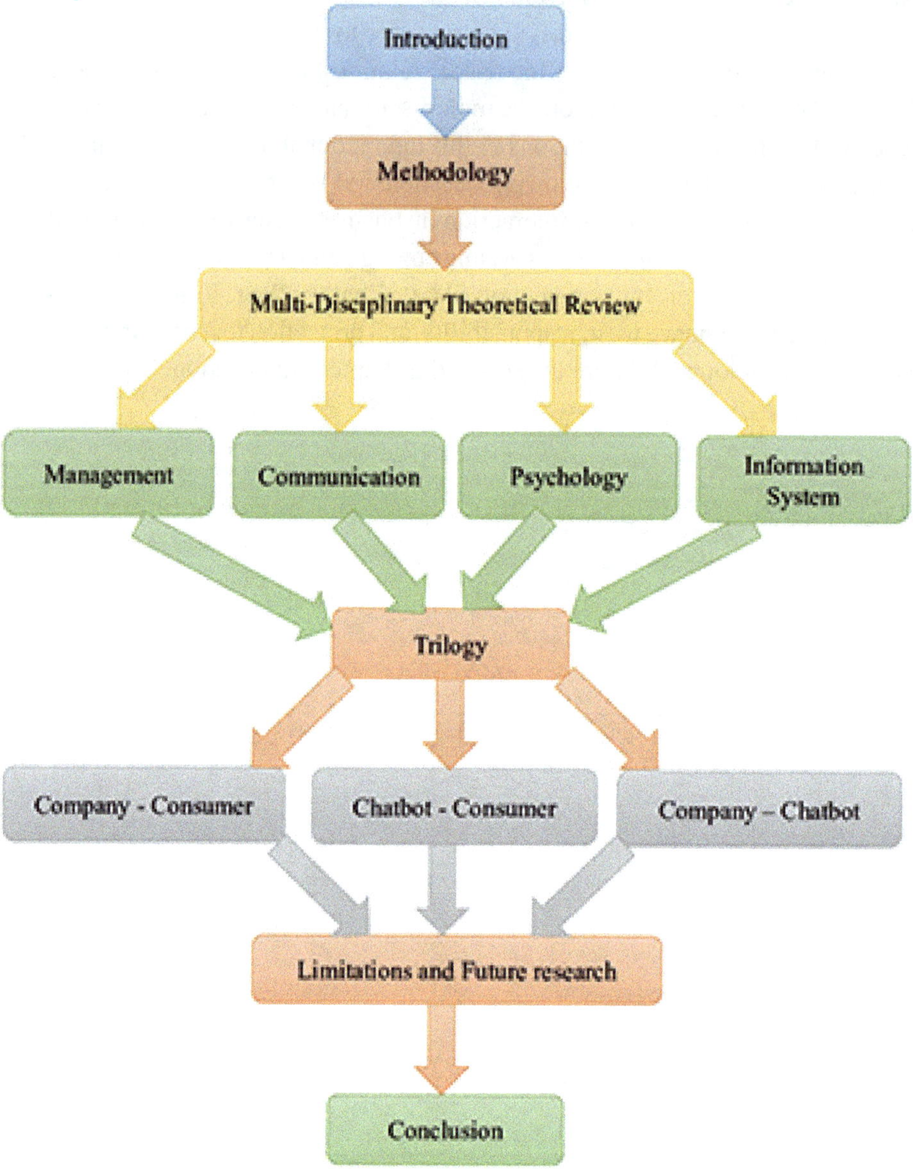

METHODOLOGY

Understanding the ethical interactional trilogy among companies, consumers, and AI chatbots starts with establishing the conceptual building blocks that govern these interactions. Drawing on multidisciplinary perspectives from management, communication, psychology, and information system, this review establishes the theoretical contexts within which the new ethical challenges may be explored.

In the light of recently emerging and highly sophisticated dynamics of ethical interaction among businesses, consumers, and AI chatbots, a theoretical overview was found to be the most appropriate methodology for this research. Empirical evidence into this very specific trilogy of interactions remains scant and fragmented across fields like business studies, communication studies, consumer psychology, and information system. As Torraco (2005) and Snyder (2019) argue, theoretical syntheses are particularly valuable when knowledge is dispersed and when conceptual integration is necessary in order to frame future research agendas. Rather than generating primary data, the objective here is to systematically synthesize and critically evaluate foundational theories that offer insights on responsibility, trust, and agency in AI-mediated environments. This approach allows for a greater level of specification and interdisciplinary insight into the moral concerns raised by AI chatbots, providing solid conceptual foundations upon which to design practical recommendations and inform future empirical studies.

The study utilized a qualitative design following the standard practices for integrative reviews within complex fields (Torraco, 2005; Snyder, 2019; Xiao & Watson, 2019). The aim was to systematically synthesize and critically appraise the relevant business, communication, consumer psychology, and information theories to develop a conceptual framework that would explain the ethical interactional trilogy among companies, consumers, and chatbots. As pointed out by Snyder (2019), theoretical reviews are optimal where empirical work is under development and conceptual integration needs to be developed.

Articles were selected after a systematic but iterative process that conformed to best practice for open and effective literature reviews in multidisciplinary research (Levy & Ellis, 2006). General search parameters were initially applied to scholarly databases such as Scopus, Web of Science, EBSCOhost, ACM, and Google Scholar using the term combinations "ethics and AI," "trust in chatbots," "technology and business ethics," and "social presence in computer-mediated communication." The search method was progressively modified during continuing analysis to facilitate inclusion of additional theories and newer research known to be conceptually relevant.

Inclusion criteria specified that theories shortlisted must have direct relevance to ethical responsibility, trust formation, communication processes, or technological intermediation; must be known within their fields; and must possess conceptual congruence in terms of AI-mediated interaction environments (Boell & Cecez-Kecmanovic, 2015). Reference snowballing was also employed to enable comprehensive coverage, following guidelines by Greenhalgh and Peacock (2005) for efficient search protocols for intricate reviews. The data corpus included peer-reviewed journal articles and conference papers, written in English.

Analysis was followed by concept-centered thematic synthesis, as directed by the approach described by Webster and Watson (2002) and modified to suit systematic theoretical research by Okoli (2015). Key ethical ideas—Privacy, transparency, Autonomy, Trust, sustainability, and dignity—were deduced and categorized. These ideas were extended across the interactional points of firms, consumers, and chatbots, where ethical dilemmas and tensions are most prone to arise. An integrative synthesis was performed to consolidate cross-disciplinary understandings into an integrated theoretical framework.

The theoretical review approach can have a rich and conceptually exhaustive foundation for the analysis of the ethical interactional trilogy of firms, consumers, and chatbots, but it is by no means infallible. First, the study relies only on secondary data and conceptual models, which can actually introduce bias based on the scope and interpretation of the literature selected. In the opinion of Boell and Cecez-Kecmanovic (2015), the iterative and interpretative nature of the theoretical reviews can tend to overrepresent some perspectives and subconsciously underrepresent others. Second, although a broad search strategy was employed, there is the possibility that relevant emerging theory or recent empirical studies beyond the major databases were overlooked. Finally, because the review synthesizes theories which were never formulated specifically for AI chatbots, some conceptual modifications were necessary, which may exclude direct empirical applicability of the proposed ethical framework. These limitations suggest the need for eventual empirical testing and validation of findings.

Multi-Disciplinary Theoretical Framework

Following the categorization of available studies into the four broad streams of academic knowledge—Business Administration, Communication Studies, Psychology, and Information Systems— this chapter systematically chooses theoretical frameworks in response to the ethical issue of the interactional trilogy among companies, consumers, and chatbots. A discussion of these theories is provided within an associated discipline context as follows:

Management

This section introduces the major theories of management addressing the ethical dynamics of the relations among firms, customers, and AI chatbots.

Information Asymmetry Theory

Information asymmetry is the imbalance that exists between different interacting players where each party has more or better information than the other (De la Peña & Granados, 2024). The problem of information asymmetry can generate risks, such as exploitative or non-conforming behavior (De la Peña & Granados, 2024). In the relationship between consumers and chatbots, such asymmetry suggests that users have no idea about how chatbots operate, what information is collected, and for what reason. Consumers can thus be subjected to exploitation. Recently, Elshaer et al. (2025) addressed this issue by focusing on the role of value perception and trust in reducing asymmetry, particularly for tourism, to achieve maximum customer satisfaction and loyalty.

Stakeholder Theory

Stakeholder theory, first articulated in a rigorous manner by Freeman (1984), argues that companies must include the interests and well-being of all who are affected by their actions, not just shareholders. Value, under the theory, is generated through cooperative and collective action on the part of a range of stakeholders, such as customers, employees, suppliers, communities, and regulators, each of whom has a moral claim to the actions and outcomes of the firm. In the context of AI and chatbots, stakeholder theory provides a robust moral framework for studying the long-term consequences of intelligent systems. It demands an integral examination of the effects of chatbots on social, cultural, and political realms (Crawford, 2022; Wasserman, 2023). By focusing on socially constructed value (Tantalo & Priem, 2016), stakeholder theory enables us to understand how AI chatbots create benefits and harms to different groups instead of purely economic ones. Further, it is the inter-relatedness of stakeholder interests, where the value being generated and appreciated by one group of stakeholders is intertwined with that of others—a pattern most significant in the human-AI collaboration upon which chatbot technologies are based (Bridoux & Stoelhorst, 2022). Stakeholder theory also accounts for ethical value sharing and prevention of undesired spillover effects, such as privacy violations or cognitive dependency produced by chatbot interactions. Finally, it also recognizes that customers themselves can influence companies' moral conduct by "voting with their wallets" reinforcing the argument that moral obligation in AI application permeates the whole social framework (Matthews et al., 2025).

Agency Theory

Agency theory is employed to explain the relationship between a principal (for example, a manager or firm) and an agent who acts on their behalf. The agency theory is specifically concerned with problems that arise when there are delegated jobs where the agent gets more information than the principal. Agency theory is applied increasingly in AI where systems such as chatbots are agents, conducting work on behalf of users or firms who are principals.

Heyder, Passlack, and Posegga (2023), in their article "Ethical Management of Human-AI Interaction: Theory Development Review," reference agency theory as a relevant conceptual framework for addressing the ethical aspects of human-AI interaction. They discuss how the theory helps illuminate some major ethical questions concerning responsibility assignment, decision control, and transparency within AI systems. In particular, when applied to AI chatbots, agency theory aids in untangling the ethical implications of outsourcing decision-making to independent agents - especially in risky areas such as medicine and law - where the uncertainty of an agent's status can have disastrous ethical repercussions. Building on previous work, using agency theory to tackle this issue establishes three core ethical demands:

1. Displacement of moral responsibility: As autonomous AI agents proliferate; it is morally and functionally essential to identify who should be assigned blame when consequences are harmful or undesired.
2. Need for clearly defined expectations and roles: Defining the scope of the agency of the AI agent and the expectation from the managers minimizes moral uncertainty and encourages appropriate usage.
3. The necessity for controlling mechanisms: To ensure that AI agents align with human values, there must be a transparency, traceability, and the ability to monitor and intervene when necessary to correct deviations.

Thus, the application of agency theory in AI ethics is not solely about regulatory compliance; it also facilitates the construction of tangible governance frameworks that limit the boundaries of AI autonomy, ensure algorithmic development transparency, and establish accountability tools for risk management and human interests protection in AI-mediated transactions.

Communication

This section introduces the major theories of communication addressing the ethical dynamics of the relations among firms, customers, and AI chatbots.

Dialogic Theory

Dialogic theory, developed by Kent and Taylor (1998) to a great extent, describes communication as an ethical, open, and mutual dialogue process, not simply message delivery. The theory holds that true communication must facilitate mutuality, empathy, commitment, and openness between organizations and their customers. Ethical communication in this theory does not result from conformity to standard processes but from creating genuine, mutually satisfying relationships. In the case of AI chatbot application in corporate social responsibility (CSR), dialogic theory provides effective ethical guidance. Recent studies show that AI-powered chatbots can facilitate effective two-way CSR conversation through organizational listening and co-construction of meaning principles (Jiang et al., 2025). Chatbots designed with a socially framed communications pattern are aligned with dialogic theory's ethical vision, offering more equitable, respectful, and trustworthy spaces for communication among firms and stakeholders, especially in sensitive CSR settings.

Social Presence Theory

Social Presence Theory, designed by Short (1976), suggests that social presence is the degree to which individuals feel others are present and emotionally alive in a communication context. It is especially relevant for industries like e-learning, telemedicine, and chatbots, in which social presence affects users' satisfaction, trust, engagement, and relationships (Oh, Bailenson, & Welch, 2018).

Scholars have argued that the greater the ability of technology to create human-like responsiveness and relational signals — through language, empathy, personalization, and nonverbal cues — the greater the perceived social presence (Biocca, Harms, & Burgoon, 2003). In the specific case of AI chatbots, current studies emphasize that augmenting social presence can facilitate user trust and willingness to interact with non-human agents (Lee, Lee, & Lee, 2024).

However, literature also shows that higher social presence activates certain core ethical concerns, such as emotional manipulation, privacy violation, and confusion of boundaries in human and machine communication (Nowak & Biocca, 2001). Therefore, although social presence may lead to deep user experiences, literature across the board emphasizes the ethical necessity of maintaining transparency, upholding user autonomy, and securing sensitive information in highly socially dense AI interactions.

In addition, social presence has also been studied more recently with regard to how it may influence user-brand relations and interactions. For example, Rao Hill and Troshani (2024) demonstrated that chatbot anthropomorphism is perceived to enhance social presence, which leads to more favorable brand attitudes. Similarly, Konya-Baumbach et al. (2023) confirmed that social presence is perceived to raise user interactions with anthropomorphized chatbots, considerably, raising the human-machine interface. Finally, Lee et al. (2024) examined the influence of social presence on self-disclosure in communication with AI psychotherapy chatbots and how it can be used to encourage emotional openness.

Psychology

This section introduces the major theories of psychology addressing the ethical dynamics of the relations among firms, customers, and AI chatbots.

Cognitive Dissonance Theory

Cognitive Dissonance Theory (CDT), developed by Festinger (1957), proposes that individuals experience psychological Discomfort or "dissonance" when they face discrepant thoughts, beliefs, or behaviors. Discomfort causes individuals to reduce dissonance in the form of modifying the belief, justifying the behavior, or denying the discrepancy. The theory has been used to forecast behaviors, change attitude, and escape cognitive discord.

In addition, the theory has served as the cornerstone in comprehending the users' perception and emotional reactions to AI behaviors. Baker et al. (2024) illustrated that wherever machines have human-like features, there is cognition dissonance that affects mind attribution and moral judgments. In their study of chatbot interaction errors, Cao et al. (2024) established that AI agent errors cause cognitive and affective dissonance, and the forgiveness process is moderated by anthropomorphic characteristics of the chatbot. Further, Habib et al. (2025) observed that in AI-mediated learning environments, discrepancies between traditional education values and the potential of AI systems cause dissonance that lowers the motivation and engagement of students.

Collectively, these articles illustrate that cognitive dissonance is a robust theoretical model for explaining users' psychological distress, deliberate decision-making, and adaptation behavior towards AI. It illustrates how users can cope with inner conflict triggered by tension among expectation, assumption, and experience in AI interactions, thus rendering the moral design of AI systems and promoting more trustworthy and more transparent human-AI relationships apparent.

Elaboration likelihood theory

Elaboration likelihood theory (ELM) was proposed by Petty and Cacioppo in 1986 as a cognitive-psychological approach to describe how persuasion works to influence individuals. According to the theory, individuals make decisions based on the type of message processing. There are two paths of the main processing: the central pathway, in which people make use of critical information presented to them; and the peripheral pathway, in which individuals rely on superficial cues. Processing of messages is determined based on the level of attention and the ability of message-processing (Petty & Cacioppo, 1986).

Applying elaborative likelihood theory to the realm of chatbots provides a new understanding of how humans interact with cognitive systems. In the realm of chatbots, if an individual is interested or is highly motivated to understand the subject of a message shown by a chatbot, he or she will employ the central pathway and will think deeply about the text and information shown. On the other hand, if the chatbot interaction is boring, users use the peripheral route, relying on superficial cues such as conversation style or the interactive nature of the chatbot (Carmichael et al., 2022).

In the case of chatbots, the ELM model can be applied to examine personal information disclosure behavior. For the central route, users trust the chatbot and feel that they are being provided with accurate and reliable information, so they feel compelled to provide more of their personal information. For the peripheral route, disclosure is based on initial trust or the engaging style of the chatbot, e.g., quick responses or a friendly conversational style. This suggests that disclosure behaviors do not have to be rational in nature but tend to be dictated significantly by superficial variables such as the friendly language style (Chen et al., 2025).

When applying the ELM to chatbots, there are some ethical concerns. When using the peripheral route, users may be vulnerable to disclosing their personal information due to peripheral cues such as engaging conversations or charming messages. Ethically, these cues should not be used by chatbots to persuade users to share their information unwittingly. Further, privacy policies must be clear and transparent to users so that information is disclosed intelligently and safely (Camilleri, 2022).

Information System

This section introduces the major theory of information system addressing the ethical dynamics of the relations among firms, customers, and AI chatbots.

Privacy Calculus Theory

Privacy calculus theory, which was formulated by Culnan and Armstrong (1999), indicates that consumers balance the risks and benefits before divulging personal information. The theory is composed of two fundamental dimensions: perceived risks and perceived benefits. In the context of chatbot encounters, individuals weigh the risks involved in giving personal information, namely the privacy worries about the private nature of information, the degree of its salience, possibilities of being exploited, and how much control an individual has over the processing of the information (Kim, 2024). This aligns with the CASA model, under which users employ the same disclosure strategy when interacting with chatbots as they do when interacting with human beings. Studies have established the usefulness of privacy calculus theory in human-AI interaction. For example, Augustin et al. (2022) and Ho et al. (2018) determined that privacy calculus theory is responsible for self-disclosure in human-AI voicebot assistants. This theory has also been widely applied to explain how consumers handle tailored services offered by companies across various internet contexts, including e-commerce websites, social media, and AI chatbots. Several variables have been seen to greatly influence these mental calculations. For instance, consumers will be willing to provide information if they get benefits, for example, a discount or coupons. The promise of personalized experiences, such as tailor-made services or recommendations on products, also plays a key role in such decision-making. However, privacy risk perception related to data leaks, misuse of personal information, and loss of trust highly deter customers to disclose their information. Prior privacy experiences, either positive or negative, also guide one's thinking regarding the risk and value of sharing information.

The Ethical Trilogy

The following section presents the ethical issues that arise when companies, consumers, and chatbots interact with each other.

Company-Consumer Interaction

Privacy

Privacy is an essential value and a fundamental right in AI ethics, as it has direct relation to safeguarding data and security in relation to other ethical concepts such as freedom and trust (Jobin et al., 2019). AI chat applications display serious security challenges due to excessive data collection and potential privacy compromises, thus calls for adopting measures such as encryption, secure storage and access restrictions

(Golda et al., 2024). An important aspect of this analysis has also been noted by studies, in reference to the need for further regulation and global effort to ensure the ethical use of AI and safeguard user privacy effectively (Furizal et al., 2024). Two important aspects to be taken into account in this context are transparency and accountability in decision-making processes to mitigate bias and ensure fairness (Mensah, 2023).

Hence, the threat of privacy loss posed by the collection of large quantities of data from people, including data protection requirements affecting information storage requirements, as well as the need to be very careful about the risks of using AI chat applications is increasing. Artificial intelligence's potential to process and analyze large amounts of personal data, together with existing technologies such as wearable devices, computer vision and smartphones, is partly responsible for the profound change in people's perception of privacy, which is further compounded and extended (Golda et al., 2024).

Transparency and Explanation

Transparency is very significant when customers are communicating with chatbots since it helps a great deal in creating trust and customer satisfaction with the offered service. Transparency in one sense is making it clear that the interacting entity is not human but an intelligent robot (Rapp et al., 2021). Theory suggests that such a disclosure increases the credibility of a firm and demonstrates the firm's desire to be open and ethically engaged. Besides, providing short and simple explanations of a bot's response increases credibility, which reassures the user and increases their satisfaction rate for the service (Janssen, 2022). Explanations also help alleviate concern about the strengths and weaknesses of the bot, particularly when dealing with sensitive questions or issues. However, the influence of transparency on satisfaction and trust hinges on such variables as the context and nature of the interaction, and the perceived credibility of the bot (Ltifi, 2023). Where a bot is only partially able, its identification and explanation for its performance are increasingly important (Rapp et al., 2021). Clients are likely to be more aware of these limitations if they are presented clearly and feel that the bot is trying its best within its capacity. On the other hand, vagueness or evasive responses may produce feelings of dishonesty, undermine trust within the system, and reduce customer satisfaction (Ltifi, 2023).

Freedom and Autonomy

Freedom and autonomy are central to ethical concerns in AI, as they are intrinsically related to human beings' ability to think, act, and decide without force or interference (Zuboff, 2019). These concepts are particularly relevant as individuals increasingly rely on intelligent systems for their thinking and decision-making, questioning whether such technologies enhance or constrain human autonomy in subtle ways (Floridi & Cowls, 2019). Theoretically, contemporary ethics differentiates between two types of freedom: positive freedom, i.e., empowerment and enhanced capacity, such as the right to withdraw consent, expanded choices, and democratic participation; and negative freedom, which focuses on protecting against manipulation and continual monitoring (Helbing et al., 2019). AI ethics literature recommends ensuring transparency, raising user awareness, empowering users through control instruments, and prioritizing informed consent when collecting data. Freedom and autonomy issues in AI are highly complex, as it is easy to assume that the goal of using technology is to increase freedom and autonomy for humans. There are also questions about how this is achieved, whose freedom and autonomy are increased, and what the incidental impacts are (O'Sullivan & Woodridge, 2015).

Trust

Trust is a core element of the relationship between individuals and technologies. It is an emotional condition or cognitive confidence level regarding the honesty and reliability of a party, whether an individual, a group, or even a technology (McLeod, 2021). For artificial intelligence, trust issues arise from technology's complexity and the extremely high degree of skill required to fully grasp its precise workings, both at the individual model level and within the general technical systems into which these are embedded (Brundage et al., 2020).

In addition, several factors contribute to public distrust, including the newness of the technology, the rapidity of its development, the role of commercial actors, economic interests, widespread alerts in the media, false promises, and even simple everyday errors associated with software (High-Level Expert Group on AI, 2019). Ironically, public efforts by governments and corporations to instill trust in AI may have the opposite effect: Why do we want to trust it so badly? (Winfield & Jirotka, 2018).

Trust becomes a more troublesome issue when automated decision-making replaces human judgment. Questions arise about the equity of this "alternative" and about the essential differences between trusting a trustworthy human and a machine that lacks the same moral or emotional traits (Strubell et al., 2020). The nature of AI—which facilitates remote work, sometimes conceals aspects of how it functions, imposes itself on users in ways that cannot be avoided, and creates the potential for manipulation, also raises other trust issues. It is not necessarily simple to recognize how these traits affect trust. The use of the technology can lead to a trusting response on an unconscious level or, conversely, to increased suspicion over time. A prime example of the intricacies of AI interaction with trust is that of "elderly assistance robots," which are currently being developed to address the growing needs of the aging population. Such robots may provide facilities like mental exercise, companionship, medication reminders, and even the timing of drug administration. Some of these robots are also designed with human-like qualities, such as a friendly face or voice, aimed at fostering trust (Song & Luximon, 2020).

However, such characteristics pose ethical challenges: Who is placing trust in whom? And why? Is the trust driven by a robot's human-likeness warranted, or is it "misguided trust"? The second significant concern is drug delivery, as trust in a robot to perform such delicate tasks is established with the utmost faith in its accuracy and safety. It may be argued that the robot answers users' questions about the effectiveness and side effects of the drug as a strategy for building confidence. But then again, the question arises: Is it possible for a robot to gain users' trust in this regard more effectively than human caregivers? Is "distrust" the default when engaging with this technology? (Floridi & Cowls, 2019).

Trust in AI, therefore, is not only related to technical competencies but also to other qualities such as transparency, appearance, advertising, and perceptions. As various researchers point out, trust is a general concept in AI ethics that provides a platform for different technical, social, and personal questions (Jobin et al., 2019). Enhancing transparency, ensuring security and privacy, and addressing biases are some of the significant ways to gain societal trust in smart technology (Whittlestone et al., 2019; Helbing et al., 2019).

Sustainability in Artificial Intelligence

Sustainability has become a foundational principle in the development of AI systems in light of growing global concern for protecting the environment and preserving biodiversity (Jobin et al., 2019; Floridi & Cowls, 2019). Sustainability is understood not only from the traditional environmental perspective but also from social justice, equality, and the facilitation of global stability and peace (Whittlestone et al., 2019). Achieving sustainability in AI involves systems that can effectively process data, minimize energy consumption, and enhance sustainable output and analysis over the long term, thereby lowering the environmental burden (Morley et al., 2021).

The ecological concern is particularly acute regarding the vast computing hardware supporting AI; data centers are among the largest electricity users on the planet, and their emissions will exceed those of the aviation sector (Crawford, 2022). Recent research has discovered that some natural language processing (NLP) models tend to be quite carbon-intensive (Strubell, E., Ganesh, A., & McCallum, A., 2020), raising concerns over the environmental cost linked to technical improvements in speed, accuracy, and learning capacity. Google researcher Timnit Gebru's work is a glaring example of these issues. Her research focused on the environmental impact of AI models in language processing (Bender et al., 2021).

This serves as an example highlighting the problem of relying on claims regarding environmental standards, particularly given how challenging it is to estimate the environmental impact behind the use of certain technologies due to their distributed nature, which conceals resource usage from users. Furthermore, sustainability issues in AI are not merely environmental but also social and human, encompassing the working conditions of individuals involved in manufacturing AI components, from raw material extraction and hardware assembly to digital workers performing classification, review, and model training tasks. Rethinking sustainability in AI also raises ethical questions about resource allocation, the burden of sustainability on specific groups or individuals, and whether that allocation is fair across distances (O'Sullivan & Woodridge, 2015).

Against this backdrop, the interconnectedness and complexity of global supply chains, alongside the dispersion of operations across multiple levels, compel us to view AI as a phenomenon encompassing not just technical processes but also global economic, social, and political dimensions. Consequently, these issues must be resolved justly, requiring specialized knowledge and precise empirical information, which often exceeds the reach of general users or even researchers outside the field. Sustainability issues in AI have frequently been overlooked because technical processes remain hidden from the end user. This paradox calls for a reevaluation of transparency concepts, not only in machine learning processes but also in the social, economic, and political systems where AI is situated. Its increasing reliance complicates the ability to step back from this technology and its environmental and ethical issues, especially when the technological environment has become permanently interdependent with further development.

Dignity in AI Ethics

The concept of dignity is one of the recurring themes in moral recommendations for AI. It is a complex instance of an essential moral concept that is both profoundly significant and difficult to define or articulate precisely. This principle is widely applied in healthcare services, penology, and the care of vulnerable members of society due to its core relationship with human respect and the maintenance of intrinsic human values (Macklin, 2003). Defining this concept becomes slightly more challenging when used in the context of AI applications, as dignity appears to represent a symbolic dimension that embodies human characteristics, which are difficult to truncate or interpret programmatically. Although important, moral dignity is perhaps raised as a tacit issue in AI ethics writings, not as the more limited concern of such concepts as transparency and privacy. This disparity has been noted as a question regarding the lack of substantial discussions on dignity, given its foundational nature in ethical philosophy (Whittlestone et al., 2019).

O'Sullivan & Woodridge (2015) provide examples of how complex this notion is. Digital assistant applications for the elderly are one such example. These employ a mix of algorithms and remote human intervention, well-designed to monitor isolated groups, such as the elderly or dementia patients, in the service of assisting and care at home. One example is a friendly dog avatar on a tablet that interacts with the elderly at scheduled times; it reminds them of visits, engages in conversation, reads poetry, and issues alerts for emergencies such as falls.

Reports indicate that this technology has delayed the admission of elderly individuals into care homes, promoting greater independence and suggesting that their dignity is preserved. However, these uses also quietly engage in ethical dilemmas. This avatar is typically operated by someone thousands of miles away, in regions such as Latin America or the Philippines, raising questions about what constitutes true human interaction, its authenticity, and whether this form of "virtual care" enhances dignity or serves as a digital disguise for loneliness and dependency. Ethically, dignity is an innate human right, not a feature of artificial life forms like AI agents or chatbots.

It is entwined with the broader concept of human rights, including the absence of harm, the absence of coercion, and providing clear and transparent interactions among human beings and intelligent systems (Whittlestone et al., 2019). In this understanding, AI should never contravene human dignity; rather, it should protect and sustain it (Morley et al., 2021). This can be achieved by designers upholding dignity values during system formulation, establishing safeguarding laws, and adhering to mechanisms of good governance for assessing adherence to moral values (Jobin et al., 2019).

Chatbot-Consumer Interaction

Chatbot Unethical Acts

By nature, chatbots are programmed under strict conditions. It is noteworthy to mention that the unethical behaviors of chatbot are not initiated by chatbot themselves as they don't have independent awareness.

Manipulation

Manipulative chatbots is a serious business communication issue because they apply programmed behavior modification strategies to intervene with the consumer's choice making. Chatbot can not manipulate on their own, but in the future may do (Tarsney, 2024). These chatbots are specifically made to mechanically capitalize on the psychological techniques through lying in conversational design (Gray et al., 2018; Mathur & Mayer, 2021). Multiple manipulative techniques have been documented, such as information asymmetry (Murtarelli et al., 2021). McGuire et al. (2023) discovered that the prospective consumers' trust in the organizations lowered significantly when the users found out that the company used chatbot without informing them. According to Bond et al. (2019), chatbot UX may be manipulated by stimulating cognitive bias such as scarcity and loss aversion to nudge consumers to purchase impulsively. These business-oriented chatbots utilize advanced AI algorithms to incorporate deceptive user-centric patterns, as extensively documented by (Mathur & Mayer, 2021).

Darkness

Dark-pattern chatbots exploit personal sensitive information to create asymmetric power relations. Traubinger et al. (2024) published one of the initial systematic investigations to determine if deceptive tactics exist within conversational agents. The research team created a collection of 69 user complaints about chatbot experiences then proceeded to examine these dark patterns. The researchers applied a classification system based on established dark pattern taxonomies from graphical user interfaces which include nagging through repetitive popups and confirmshaming by inducing guilt and obstruction by hiding exits or cancellation options. Table (1) summarizes the dark patterns.

Table 1. Darkness pattern of AI chatbot

Pattern	Example
Nagging	Chatbot persistently interrupts the user flow with unsolicited information.
Confirmshaming	Trigger guilt or shame feelings to induce users to conduct a specific action.
Hard to Cancel	Makes cancelling a service or subscription difficult and time-consuming.
Forced Action	Requires the user to agree to an undesirable action before proceeding.
Obstruction	Deliberately prevents the user from achieving a goal, E.g., contact support.

Source: Adopted from Traubinger et al. (2024)

Human-Washing

Human-washing refers to an ethically problematic practice where artificial agents are designed to hide their non-human nature and create an illusion of human interaction, aiming to manipulate user trust and behavior. Consumers' perceptions of anthropomorphized agents, such as warmth, competence, animacy, intelligence, likability, safety, and social presence, determine their skepticism toward chatbots which subsequently influences their trust in the service provider and leads to increased personal information disclosure and future repatronage of the e-tailer (Blut et al., 2021; Pizzi et al., 2023). The anthropomorphic perspective on chatbots has led to a push for their humanization, even though they are not yet characterized by self-awareness or consciousness (Kaplan & Haenlein, 2019). This idea stems from the belief that making chatbots seem less risky to users and more credible in the eyes of consumers can be achieved by incorporating cognitive, emotional, and social cues that consumers naturally display (Kaplan & Haenlein, 2019). The ethical concern, however, is that by making chatbots appear more human-like, consumers might mistakenly believe they share the same mental models and ethical values. This form of anthropomorphic deception, as Murtarelli et al. (2021) point out, plays on customers' needs to have a humanized experience with the company.

Consumer Unethical Acts

Consumer behavior and the probability of engaging in unethical actions depend greatly on whether they see AI as a "servant" or a "partner". In their study Lei et al. (2024) demonstrate that consumers tend to behave unethically towards AI when they perceive it as a subordinate "servant". The subordinate perception of AI leads to diminished consumer moral responsibility which increases the likelihood of unethical manipulation or exploitation of the system. The ethical behavior of consumers increases when AI systems serve as "partners" that collaborate with them because such partnerships create a sense of mutual respect and fairness (Lei et al., 2024). Transparency about AI interactions leads to more unethical behavior because people feel less socially accountable when they recognize they are dealing with a machine which decreases their moral barriers. Supporting this view, Giroux et al. (2022) conducted a series of studies comparing consumer interactions with human service agents versus AI. Their findings revealed that the more mechanical or less human-like the machine appears, the less guilt consumers feel, which leads to a noticeable decline in ethical actions.

Abuse

In recent years, speech abuse has been a prominent topic in interactions with conversational interfaces such as chatbots, where "abuse" is defined as the improper use or exploitation of these systems in manners that would constitute abuse if they were directed at human beings (De Angeli & Brahnam, 2008; Brahnam & De Angeli, 2008). The mistreatment of conversational agents by humans is not yet regarded as a serious issue because it is thought that verbal abuse cannot emotionally injure or offend AI systems (De Cicco, 2024). Although increasing in prevalence, studies on the abuse of chatbots, specifically in business environments, are still lacking, as the majority of previous research has centered on voice-based agents (Chin et al., 2020). The effects of such abuse are especially profound when chatbots are used as the initial contact point in customer service, since hostile interactions can detrimentally affect the relationship between consumers and the company itself (Brahnam & De Angeli, 2008). In addition, harmful verbal behavior towards chatbots can spill over to human workers in similar roles, increasing the likelihood of abusive incidents towards customer service representatives (Fossa & Sucameli, 2022). As chatbots mature from novelty technologies into fundamental aspects of daily life, questions about their misuse become increasingly urgent (Keijsers et al., 2021).

Harassment

Experiments have indicated that customer harassment of chatbots is a significant issue, primarily verbal aggression and sexual harassment, particularly when chatbots exhibit human-like attributes (Keijsers et al., 2021). Such anthropomorphism, especially when customers are in an unpleasant mood like anger, ironically leads to reduced satisfaction and purchasing intentions (Crolic et al., 2022). While commercial systems tend to avoid or deflect offensive action, information-driven chatbots can sometimes create nonsensical or even counter-aggressive responses (Curry & Rieser, 2018). The pervasiveness of such offending behavior accentuates the critical need for proper chatbot design and mitigation to prevent or diffuse user aggression in customer service dialogue (Crolic et al., 2022; Keijsers et al., 2021). Studies also show that factors like the 'virtual gender' of the chatbot as perceived by the user can influence interaction styles and verbal abuse tendency, linking sex stereotypes to hostility towards conversational agents (Brahnam & De Angeli, 2012; De Angeli & Brahnam, 2006).

Company-Chatbot Interaction

Creepy Marketing

Creepy marketing includes invasive or uncomfortable advertising strategies that exploit personal information or use psychological tactics, traditionally causing discomfort or privacy concerns among consumers (Moore et al., 2015; Spilinek & Jorgensen, 2025). Ethically, creepy marketing by AI chatbots is misleading in aspects of data privacy and informed consent. Companies deploy chatbots on e-commerce sites to monitor consumer behavior, preferences, and purchasing history, making mass-personalized marketing possible (Barış, 2020). For instance, chatbots may track consumers behavior across digital touchpoints, constructing detailed profiles that are used for targeted advertising (Dadwal et al., 2024).

Success for AI chatbots relies on their ability to sift through massive datasets, including browsing history, purchasing habits, and even biometric information. Companies prefer to utilize chatbots' ability to gather personal data via casual conversations and use it to predict consumer demand or influence buying decisions (Thomaz et al., 2020). For example, conversational commerce chatbots use real-time sentiment analytics to tailor product recommendations, a practice that risks being blurred into surveillance when combined with location analytics or facial recognition capabilities (Sidlauskiene et al., 2023; Stahl & Eke, 2024). While this hyper-personalization is good for user experience, it's intrusive in that customers are not offered the option or made aware of the extent of data gathering. In Pew Research survey in 2024, it was found that 79% of consumers worry about data misuse, and AI personalization is typically intrusive and unhelpful (Francis, 2025). Data collection without transparency amplifies these challenges, as shoppers are seldom told anything about how their data being collected, stored, shared, or sold (Stahl & Eke, 2024).

Subliminal Marketing

Subliminal AI techniques are termed as hidden influences that are used to influence individuals without their conscious realization. Chatbots can identify personal vulnerabilities, thereby making it possible for them to tailor subliminal effects to users according to their intentions, emotions, and behaviors. The anthropomorphism of chatbots—giving them human faces, names, and personalities—further enables their persuasive power, particularly where companion chatbots are designed to simulate relationships (Krook, 2025). Chatbots can employ psychological targeting using content that is founded on individual emotional states and cognitive biases. This hyper-personalization creates enormous forces of persuasion, allowing companies to shape consumer choice on unparalleled scales (Florido-Benítez, 2024; Matz et al., 2017). Current legislation, including the European Union's AI Act, does not address the manipulative ability of chatbots. The European Commission's proposed AI Act, which bans AI systems that manipulate through subliminal techniques or exploit vulnerabilities in specific groups, is insufficient to address the growing capabilities of AI to influence individual decision-making, requiring new legal frameworks (Cohen, 2023; Krook, 2025). Figure (2) shows the ethical trilogy among Companies, Customers, and AI-Chatbots

Figure 2. The ethical trilogy among companies, customers, and AI-chatbots

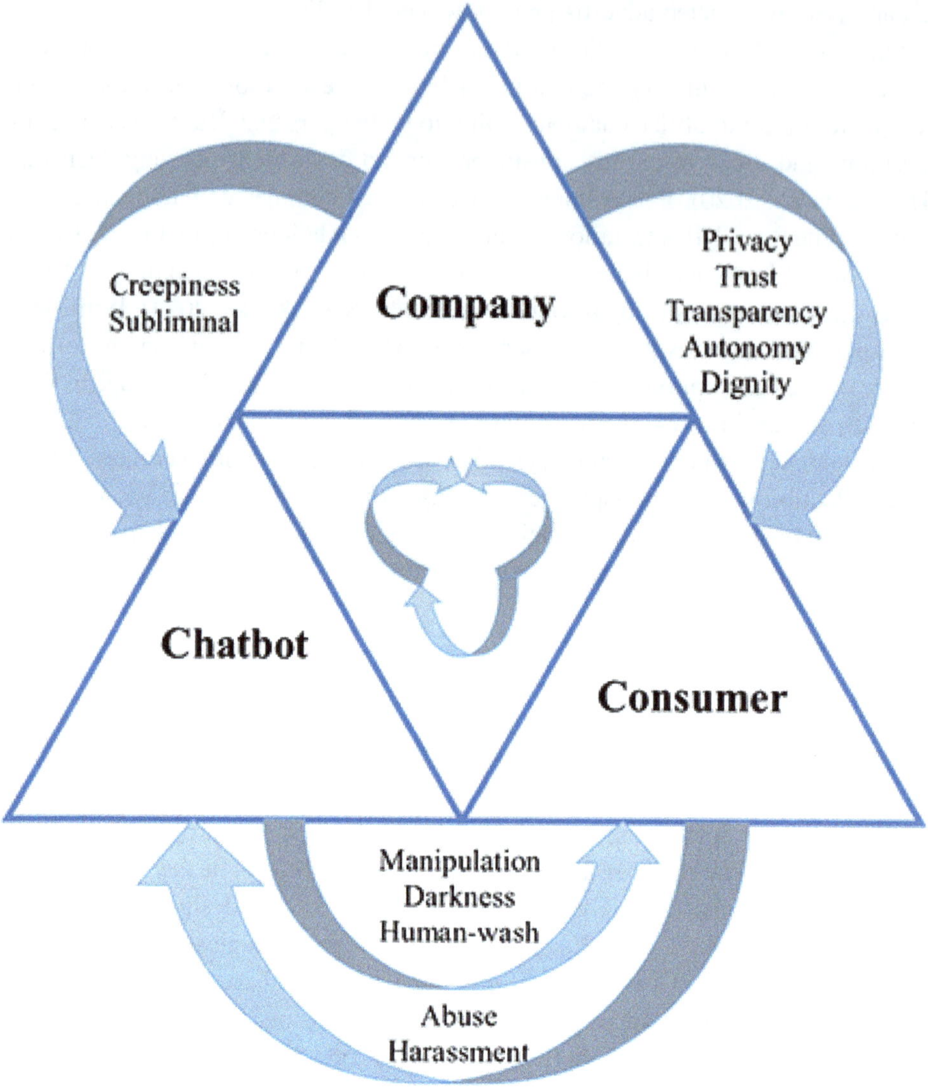

4. ADDRESSING ETHICAL ISSUES & STAKEHOLDER RECOMMENDATIONS

As there is growing development in the use of artificial intelligence (AI) in every walk of life, a list of ethical issues has been created that needs to be addressed with proper solutions to ensure the ethical use of this technology. They encompass matters concerning privacy, transparency, trust, sustainability, and the protection of human dignity, as well as freedom and autonomy in information communication with AI systems. To address the issues at hand, a multi-faceted solution must incorporate technical solutions, legal controls, regulatory guidelines, and social awareness to counterbalance technological progress and the protection of human values. Following best practices and available research supporting equitable and ethical use of this technology, the following paragraphs will present solutions to ethical issues in AI for customers, businesses, and chatbot developers:

Recommendations for Companies

1) **Compliance with Privacy Protection Norms**: Companies using AI systems must be highly compliant with privacy protection norms. This includes the collection of personal data only when required and obtaining explicit consent from users before accessing or processing their information. By following such principles, organizations can earn the trust of their customers and ensure that they are safeguarded from third parties. Besides, firms will have to abide by supervisory requirements such as the General Data Protection Regulation (GDPR) that will require transparency and protection of people's rights over their personal information (Mensah, 2023). In this context, three strategies for privacy enhancement are suggested in research: first, technological solutions such as differential privacy, data minimization, and access control; second, public education and reinforcement of research to instill the practice of privacy principles; and third, regulatory initiatives such as legal compliance, certification, and the revision of current laws to uphold AI privacy (O'Sullivan & Woodridge, 2015).

2) **Enhancing Transparency for Customers**: Businesses should ensure that all their smart systems, including chatbots and other automated systems, clearly indicate that they are not human and that they are, in fact, smart systems. Businesses should employ notifications that inform users they are interacting with fully automated systems at the beginning of the interaction. This helps avoid any feelings of deception or confusion for users. Additionally, it is necessary to provide proper and timely responses to any user queries regarding the identity of the system (Rapp et al., 2021).

3) **Trust Development in Intelligent Systems**: Companies must develop AI systems that operate securely and reliably, with strong defenses against cyberattacks and measures to reduce risks associated with data bias. This is what fosters user trust, allowing them to feel safe when using smart systems. Furthermore, these systems should have the capability to explain their decisions in a manner that enhances transparency and builds user confidence. Transparency and the elimination

of bias are essential in promoting fairness when smart systems make decisions (Whittlestone et al., 2019).

4) **Sustainability of AI Technology**: Incorporating environmental, social, and economic sustainability principles in the design and development of AI technology for creating sustainable AI systems is imperative. Organizations must ensure that these systems operate within environmental limits without compromising ecological integrity while promoting social justice. Additionally, the systems should support sustainable development goals, such as conserving natural resources and advancing social equity (Bolte et al., 2022).

Recommendations for Customers

1) **Protection of Personal Privacy:** Protecting personal privacy is one of the most important moral norms when engaging with AI systems, particularly due to their advanced ability to collect and analyze individuals' personal information. They can identify more complex patterns of individual actions from vast amounts of data accumulated through digital engagement. Therefore, Customers should therefore be eager to make sure that businesses that trade in such systems have effective policies in place to protect their privacy. These are policies that have open data collection policies, obtain explicit user consent before they can collect or process data, and minimize data collection (Jobin et al., 2019). Customers should also ensure that systems they use incorporate protection mechanisms such as "differential privacy" that can guarantee data protection while processing.

2) **Transparency of System Interaction:** Customers must be adequately informed about how AI systems operate, specifically that these systems are not human but are fully automated. From this perspective, customers should ensure that the given system clearly defines its identity from the outset. For example, chatbots or any AI-based automated systems must explicitly state that they are not human. Such transparency can be achieved through notifications in user interfaces that remain permanently visible or through the system publicly declaring its automated identity during communication, aiming to eliminate any misunderstanding by users regarding the system's identity (Rapp et al., 2021).

3) **Trust in Intelligent Systems**: For users to trust intelligent systems, these systems must be able to explain, in simple language, how they arrive at their decisions. Users are more likely to trust systems whose operations and decision processes they can understand. However, there are instances where it is challenging to fully explain certain decisions, such as in sensitive areas like medical diagnosis, where advanced machines may make better choices but may not be able to clearly articulate how they reached those decisions. Consequently, these systems must balance transparency and accuracy requirements in a manner that establishes operational

frameworks considering the technical and ethical challenges they may encounter (Whittlestone et al., 2019).

Recommendations for Chatbot Regulators

1) **Privacy Protection:** Regulators for intelligent systems like chatbots need to be equipped with robust solutions to protect user privacy. These solutions include methods such as "differential privacy," which safeguards information during processing. Collected information should be limited to the necessary level to ensure high security and protect users' personal information (Jobin et al., 2019).

2) **Enhancing Transparency in User Interactions**: Managers must ensure that intelligent systems are fully transparent regarding their nature and composition. It is crucial to provide users with clear notifications that they are interacting with automated systems rather than human agents. Transparency can be facilitated through direct user interaction and by clearly stating the purpose of the system from the onset of engagement (Rapp et al., 2021).

3) **Creating a Good User Experience**: AI systems, particularly chatbots, should foster social interactions to ensure effective communication with users, making them feel more comfortable and trusting. Administrators must incorporate elements like prompt responses and a warm tone to create a positive experience with the system. Research indicates that such human-like interaction behaviors are essential for building user trust (Go & Sundar, 2019).

4) **Ethical Compliance:** Administrators should ensure that all systems in place comply with ethical standards that promote human dignity while providing users with freedom and autonomy in decision-making. This means that data should not be exploited or used in ways that harm users, while also offering a secure and sustainable environment (Morley et al., 2021).

LIMITATIONS FUTURE RESEARCH

One of the main limitations of the literature so far is the rarity of robust interdisciplinary models combining management, psychology, communication, information system, sociology, computer science, and law theories to debate AI chatbot ethics in an integrated way. The majority of studies are single-disciplinary in approach. For instance, technical research focuses on AI trust, risk and security management (Habbal et al., 2024) while business-related research emphasizes the way these technologies impact consumer privacy (Goncalves et al., 2024).

Another critical limitation is the lack of adequate exploration in the literature of the triadic relationship between consumers, firms, and chatbots as moral agents. For example, Fang et al. (2025) discuss the psychosocial effects of chatbot use but focus primarily on consumers' emotional well-being and not corporate accountability for developing emotionally manipulative chatbots. For instance, Blut et al. (2021) and Pizzi et al. (2023) refer to consumer attitudes towards chatbot anthropomorphism but do not discuss how design choices in firms influence these attitudes and the ethical implications of the use of chatbots. The lack of theoretical frameworks like actor-network theory or extended mind theory, which can be used to position chatbots as ethical agents, limits the current literature's depth.

Future studies must integrate ethical theories (e.g., deontology, utilitarianism) and psychological (e.g., trust theory), sociological (e.g., power relations), and technological (e.g., human-computer interaction) theories to construct integrated models of AI chatbot ethics. For example, the integration of virtue ethics and social exchange theory would explain how companies establish trust while preserving consumer autonomy.

Research studies need to explore the triadic interaction between businesses, consumers, and chatbots directly. Mixed-method studies that integrate qualitative corporate, consumer, and technical evidence of chatbot behavior can expose ethical dynamics. Structural equation modeling, for instance, as used by Nguyen (2024), can be modified to map ethical influence among stakeholders

CONCLUSION

This chapter has explained the ethical concerns surrounding AI chatbot interactions, observing the lack of unified theoretical frameworks that integrate knowledge across various disciplines such as business administration, communications, psychology, and information systems. Even though AI technologies are rapidly surfacing, academic research is lagging behind, thus leading to fragmented ethical theories that fail to address sophisticated applications of chatbots in different contexts. Future research must focus on building holistic, multidisciplinary models incorporating transparency, fairness, and user agency, and explore the cross-cultural variations in ethical requirements. There has been progress, yet there is much work to be done to guarantee that AI chatbots are designed and implemented in a manner that aligns with ethical principles and the societal needs, engendering trust, accountability, and equity in their interactions with consumers.

REFERENCES

Ananny, M., & Crawford, K. (2018). Seeing without knowing: Limitations of the transparency ideal and its application to algorithmic accountability. *New Media & Society*, *20*(3), 973–989. DOI: 10.1177/1461444816676645

Augustin, Y., Carolus, A., & Wienrich, C. (2022). Privacy of AI-Based Voice Assistants: Understanding the Users' Perspective: A Purposive Review and a Roadmap for Elevating Research on Privacy from a User-Oriented Perspective. *Lecture Notes in Computer Science (Including Subseries Lecture Notes in Artificial Intelligence and Lecture Notes in Bioinformatics), 13337 LNCS*, 309–321. DOI: 10.1007/978-3-031-05014-5_26

Baker, L. J., Li, H., Hammond, H., Jaeger, C. B., Havard, A., Lane, J. D., Harriott, C. E., & Levin, D. T. (2024). The roles of cognitive dissonance and normative reasoning in attributions of minds to robots. *Cognitive Research: Principles and Implications*, *9*(1), 1–19. DOI: 10.1186/s41235-024-00604-3 PMID: 39663309

Barış, A. (2020). A new business marketing tool: Chatbot. *GSI Journals Serie B: Advancements in Business and Economics*, *3*(1), 31–46. DOI: 10.5281/ZENODO.4030216

Bender, E. M., Gebru, T., McMillan-Major, A., & Mitchell, S. (2021). On the dangers of stochastic parrots: Can language models be too big? In *Proceedings of the 2021 ACM conference on fairness, accountability, and transparency* (pp. 610–623). Association for Computing Machinery. DOI: 10.1145/3442188.3445922

Binns, R., Van Kleek, M., Veale, M., Lyngs, U., Zhao, J., & Shadbolt, N. (2018). "It's reducing a human being to a percentage"; perceptions of justice in algorithmic decisions. *Conference on Human Factors in Computing Systems - Proceedings, 2018-April*. DOI: 10.1145/3173574.3173951

Biocca, F., Harms, C., & Burgoon, J. K. (2003). Toward a more robust theory and measure of social presence: Review and suggested criteria. *Presence (Cambridge, Mass.)*, *12*(5), 456–480. DOI: 10.1162/105474603322761270

Blut, M., Wang, C., Wünderlich, N. V., & Brock, C. (2021). Understanding anthropomorphism in service provision: a meta-analysis of physical robots, chatbots, and other AI. In *Journal of the Academy of Marketing Science* (Vol. 49, Issue 4, pp. 632–658). Springer. DOI: 10.1007/s11747-020-00762-y

Boell, S. K., & Cecez-Kecmanovic, D. (2015). On being 'systematic' in literature reviews. *Information & Management*, *48*(5), 161–172. https://doi.org/10.1057/jit.2014.26DOI: 10.1016/j.im.2014.08.002

Bolte, L., Vandemeulebroucke, T., & van Wynsberghe, A. (2022). From an ethics of carefulness to an ethics of desirability: going beyond current ethics approaches to sustainable AI. *Sustainability, 14*(8), 4472. DOI: 10.3390/su14084472

Bond, R. R., Mulvenna, M., & Wang, H. (2019). Human centered artificial intelligence: Weaving UX into algorithmic decision making. *Proceedings of the 16th International Conference on Human-Computer Interaction (RoCHI 2019)* (pp. 1–6). Romanian Society for Human-Computer Interaction. http://rochi.utcluj.ro/articole/7/RoCHI2019-Bond.pdf

Brahnam, S., & De Angeli, A. (2008). Special issue on the abuse and misuse of social agents. In *Interacting with Computers* (Vol. 20, Issue 3, pp. 287–291). Oxford Academic. DOI: 10.1016/j.intcom.2008.02.001

Brahnam, S., & De Angeli, A. (2012). Gender affordances of conversational agents. *Interacting with Computers, 24*(3), 139–153. DOI: 10.1016/j.intcom.2012.05.001

Bridoux, F., & Stoelhorst, J. W. (2022). Stakeholder governance: Solving the collective action problems in joint value creation. *Academy of Management Review, 47*(2), 214–236. DOI: 10.5465/amr.2019.0441

Brundage, M., Avin, S., Wang, J., Belfield, H., Krueger, G., Hadfield, G., Khlaaf, H., Yang, J., Toner, H., Fong, R., & Maharaj, T. (2020) Toward trustworthy AI development: mechanisms for supporting verifiable claims. arXiv preprint arXiv:2004.07213 86 2 The Rise of AI Ethic. https://doi.org//arXiv.2004.07213DOI: 10.48550

Burrell, J. (2016). How the machine 'thinks': Understanding opacity in machine learning algorithms. *Big Data & Society, 3*(1), 2053951715622512. Advance online publication. DOI: 10.1177/2053951715622512

Camilleri, M. A. (2022). Walking the talk about corporate social responsibility communication: An elaboration likelihood model perspective. *Business Ethics, the Environment & Responsibility, 31*(3), 649–661. DOI: 10.1111/beer.12427

Cao, B., Li, Z., & Jiang, L. C. (2024). When chatbots make errors: Cognitive and affective pathways to understanding forgiveness of chatbot errors. *Telematics and Informatics, 94*, 102189. DOI: 10.1016/j.tele.2024.102189

Carmichael, L., Poirier, S. M., Coursaris, C. K., Léger, P. M., & Sénécal, S. (2022). Users' information disclosure behaviors during interactions with chatbots: The effect of information disclosure nudges. *Applied Sciences (Basel, Switzerland), 12*(24), 12660. DOI: 10.3390/app122412660

Chen, Q., Yin, C., & Gong, Y. (2025). Would an AI chatbot persuade you: An empirical answer from the elaboration likelihood model. *Information Technology & People*, *38*(2), 937–962. DOI: 10.1108/ITP-10-2021-0764

Chin, H., Molefi, L. W., & Yi, M. Y. (2020). Empathy Is All You Need: How a Conversational Agent Should Respond to Verbal Abuse. *Conference on Human Factors in Computing Systems - Proceedings*. DOI: 10.1145/3313831.3376461

Cohen, T. (2023). Regulating Manipulative Artificial Intelligence. *Script-ed*, *20*(1), 203–242. DOI: 10.2966/SCRIP.200123.203

Consumer Financial Protection Bureau. (2023, June 6). *CFPB issue spotlight analyzes 'artificial intelligence' chatbots in banking*. https://www.consumerfinance.gov/about-us/newsroom/cfpb-issue-spotlight-analyzes-artificial-intelligence-chatbots-in-banking/

Crawford, K. (2022). There is a blind spot in AI research. *AI and Ethics*, *2*(4), 851–867. DOI: 10.1007/s43681-021-00122-8

Crolic, C., Thomaz, F., Hadi, R., & Stephen, A. T. (2022). Blame the Bot: Anthropomorphism and Anger in Customer–Chatbot Interactions. *Journal of Marketing*, *86*(1), 132–148. DOI: 10.1177/00222429211045687

Culnan, M. J., & Armstrong, P. K. (1999). Information Privacy Concerns, Procedural Fairness, and Impersonal Trust: An Empirical Investigation. *Organization Science*, *10*(1), 104–115. DOI: 10.1287/orsc.10.1.104

Curry, A. C., & Rieser, V. (2018). #MeToo Alexa: How Conversational Systems Respond to Sexual Harassment. *Proceedings of the 2nd ACL Workshop on Ethics in Natural Language Processing, EthNLP 2018 at the 2018 Conference of the North American Chapter of the Association for Computational Linguistics: Human Language Technologies, NAACL-HTL 2018*, 7–14. DOI: 10.18653/v1/W18-0802

Dadwal, S. S., Bowen, G., Jahankhani, H., Nadda, V., & Kumar, P. (2024). Market Grooming: Grooming Customers Using Artificial Intelligence. In *Market Grooming* (pp. 1–35). Emerald Publishing Limited. DOI: 10.1108/978-1-83549-001-320241001

De Angeli, A., & Brahnam, S. (2006). Sex stereotypes and conversational agents. In *Proceedings of Gender and Interaction: Real and Virtual Women in a Male World*, Venice, Italy. Retrieved from https://www.researchgate.net/publication/229003887_Sex_Stereotypes_and_Conversational_Agents

De Angeli, A., & Brahnam, S. (2008). I hate you! Disinhibition with virtual partners. *Interacting with Computers*, *20*(3), 302–310. DOI: 10.1016/j.intcom.2008.02.004

De Cicco, R. (2024). Exploring the Dark Corners of Human-Chatbot Interactions: A Literature Review on Conversational Agent Abuse. *Lecture Notes in Computer Science (Including Subseries Lecture Notes in Artificial Intelligence and Lecture Notes in Bioinformatics), 14524 LNCS*, 185–203. DOI: 10.1007/978-3-031-54975-5_11

De la Peña, N., & Granados, O. M. (2024). Artificial intelligence solutions to reduce information asymmetry for Colombian cocoa small-scale farmers. *Information Processing in Agriculture*, *11*(3), 310–324. DOI: 10.1016/j.inpa.2023.03.001

Elshaer, I. A., Azazz, A. M. S., Fayyad, S., Aljoghaiman, A., Fathy, E. A., & Fouad, A. M. (2025). From Asymmetry to Satisfaction: The Dynamic Role of Perceived Value and Trust to Boost Customer Satisfaction in the Tourism Industry. *Tourism and Hospitality*, *6*(2), 68. DOI: 10.3390/tourhosp6020068

Festinger, L. (1957). *A theory of cognitive dissonance*. Stanford University Press. DOI: 10.1515/9781503620766

Florido-Benítez, L. (2024). Generative artificial intelligence: a proactive and creative tool to achieve hyper-segmentation and hyper-personalization in the tourism industry. *International Journal of Tourism Cities, ahead-of-p*rint(ahead-of-print). DOI: 10.1108/IJTC-05-2024-0111

Følstad, A., & Brandtzaeg, P. B. (2017). Chatbots and the New World of HCI. *Interactions (New York, N.Y.)*, *24*(4), 38–42. DOI: 10.1145/3085558

Fossa, F., & Sucameli, I. (2022). Gender bias and conversational agents: an ethical perspective on social robotics. *Science and Engineering Ethics*, 28(3), 23. DOI: 10.1007/s11948-022-00376-3

Francis, D. (2025). *The Good, the Bad, and the Creepy: AI's Impact on Consumer Behavior*. Medium. https://dennismfrancis.medium.com/the-good-the-bad-and-the-creepy-ais-impact-on-consumer-behavior-aab36aaf2542

Freeman, R. E. (1984). *Strategic management: A stakeholder approach*. https://books.google.com/books?hl=en&lr=&id=NpmA_qEiOpkC&oi=fnd&pg=PR5&ots=62fkL3S7MK&sig=5wslBv0wPYhYJzOCxZs4wSA56ac

Furizal, F., Ramelan, A., Adriyanto, F., Maghfiroh, H., Ma'arif, A., Kariyamin, K., Masitha, A., & Fawait, A. B. (2024). Concerns of Ethical and Privacy in the Rapid Advancement of Artificial Intelligence: Directions, Challenges, and Solutions. [JRC]. *Journal of Robotics and Control*, *5*(6), 2015–2026. DOI: 10.18196/jrc.v5i6.24090

Garcia, M. (2024, February 19). What Air Canada lost in remarkable lying AI chatbot case. *Forbes*. https://www.forbes.com/sites/marisagarcia/2024/02/19/what-air-canada-lost-in-remarkable-lying-ai-chatbot-case/

Go, E., & Sundar, S. S. (2019). Humanizing chatbots: The effects of visual, identity and conversational cues on humanness perceptions. *Computers in Human Behavior*, *97*, 304–316. DOI: 10.1016/j.chb.2019.01.020

Golda, A., Mekonen, K., Pandey, A., Singh, A., Hassija, V., Chamola, V., & Sikdar, B. (2024). Privacy and security concerns in generative AI: A comprehensive survey. *IEEE Access : Practical Innovations, Open Solutions*, *12*, 48126–48144. Advance online publication. DOI: 10.1109/ACCESS.2024.3381611

Goncalves, M., Hu, Y., Aliagas, I., & Cerdá, L. M. (2024). Neuromarketing algorithms' consumer privacy and ethical considerations: Challenges and opportunities. *Cogent Business & Management*, *11*(1), 2333063. Advance online publication. DOI: 10.1080/23311975.2024.2333063

Gray, C. M., Kou, Y., Battles, B., Hoggatt, J., & Toombs, A. L. (2018). The dark (patterns) side of UX design. *Conference on Human Factors in Computing Systems - Proceedings, 2018-April*. DOI: 10.1145/3173574.3174108

Greenhalgh, T., & Peacock, R. (2005). Effectiveness and efficiency of search methods in systematic reviews of complex evidence: Audit of primary sources. *BMJ (Clinical Research Ed.)*, *331*(7524), 1064–1065. DOI: 10.1136/bmj.38636.593461.68 PMID: 16230312

Habbal, A., Ali, M. K., & Abuzaraida, M. A. (2024). Artificial Intelligence Trust, Risk and Security Management (AI TRiSM). Frameworks, applications, challenges and future research directions. In *Expert Systems with Applications* (Vol. 240, p. 122442). Pergamon. DOI: 10.1016/j.eswa.2023.122442

Habib, M. U., Akram, W., Saleem, S., & Shakoor, A. (2025). How cognitive dissonance affects student engagement and learning in AI-powered education systems. *The Critical Review of Social Sciences Studies*, *3*(1), 1905–1917. DOI: 10.59075/r1zta509

Heyder, T., Passlack, N., & Posegga, O. (2023). Ethical management of human-AI interaction: Theory development review. *The Journal of Strategic Information Systems*, *32*(3), 101772. Advance online publication. DOI: 10.1016/j.jsis.2023.101772

High-Level Expert Group on AI. (2019). *Ethics guidelines for trustworthy AI* (p. 39). Independent High-Level Expert Group on Artificial Intelligence. https://www.aepd.es/sites/default/files/2019-09/ai-definition.pdf

Hill, J., Randolph Ford, W., & Farreras, I. G. (2015). Real conversations with artificial intelligence: A comparison between human-human online conversations and human-chatbot conversations. *Computers in Human Behavior, 49*, 245–250. DOI: 10.1016/j.chb.2015.02.026

Ho, A., Hancock, J., & Miner, A. S. (2018). Psychological, relational, and emotional effects of self-disclosure after conversations with a chatbot. *The Journal of Communication, 68*(4), 712–733. DOI: 10.1093/joc/jqy026 PMID: 30100620

Jiang, Y., Cheng, Y., & Wang, Y. (2025). Leveraging AI in CSR: How social-oriented chatbots influence Chinese consumers' supportive actions via dialogic communication. *Public Relations Review, 51*(1), 102541. DOI: 10.1016/j.pubrev.2025.102541

Jobin, A., Ienca, M., & Vayena, E. (2019). The global landscape of AI ethics guidelines. *Nature Machine Intelligence, 1*(9), 389–399. DOI: 10.1038/s42256-019-0088-2

Kaplan, A., & Haenlein, M. (2019). Siri, Siri, in my hand: Who's the fairest in the land? On the interpretations, illustrations, and implications of artificial intelligence. *Business Horizons, 62*(1), 15–25. DOI: 10.1016/j.bushor.2018.08.004

Keijsers, M., Bartneck, C., & Eyssel, F. (2021). What's to bullying a bot? Correlates between chatbot humanlikeness and abuse. *Interaction Studies*, 22(1), 55-80. DOI: 10.1075/is.20002.kei

Kent, M. L., & Taylor, M. (1998). Building dialogic relationships through the World Wide Web. *Public Relations Review, 24*(3), 321–334. DOI: 10.1016/S0363-8111(99)80143-X

Kim, Y. (2024). AI Health Counselor's Self-Disclosure: Its Impact on User Responses Based on Individual and Cultural Variation. *International Journal of Human-Computer Interaction.* Advance online publication. DOI: 10.1080/10447318.2024.2316373

Konya-Baumbach, E., Biller, M., & von Janda, S. (2023). Someone out there? A study on the social presence of anthropomorphized chatbots. *Computers in Human Behavior, 139*, 107513. DOI: 10.1016/j.chb.2022.107513

Krook, J. (2025). Manipulation and the AI Act: Large Language Model Chatbots and the Danger of Mirrors. *SSRN*. DOI: 10.2139/ssrn.4719835

Lee, J., Lee, D., & Lee, J. G. (2024). Influence of rapport and social presence with an AI psychotherapy chatbot on users' self-disclosure. *International Journal of Human-Computer Interaction, 40*(7), 1620–1631. DOI: 10.1080/10447318.2022.2146227

Lei, S., Xie, L., & Peng, J. (2024). Unethical Consumer Behavior Following Artificial Intelligence Agent Encounters: The Differential Effect of AI Agent Roles and its Boundary Conditions. *Journal of Service Research*. Advance online publication. DOI: 10.1177/10946705241278837

Levy, Y., & Ellis, T. J. (2006). A systems approach to conduct an effective literature review in support of information systems research. *Informing Science*, *9*, 181–212. DOI: 10.28945/479

Li, H. (2025, January 9). Character.AI put in new underage guardrails after a teen's suicide. His mother says that's not enough. *Business Insider*. https://www.businessinsider.com/character-ai-lawsuit-plantiff-age-guardrails-after-teen-suicide-2025-1

Ltifi, M. (2023). Trust in the chatbot: A semi-human relationship. *Future Business Journal*, *9*(1), 109. DOI: 10.1186/s43093-023-00288-z

Macklin, R. (2003). Dignity is a useless concept. *BMJ (Clinical Research Ed.)*, *327*(7429), 1419–1420. DOI: 10.1136/bmj.327.7429.1419 PMID: 14684633

Mathur, A., & Mayer, J. (2021). What makes a dark pattern... dark? design attributes, normative considerations, and measurement methods. *Conference on Human Factors in Computing Systems - Proceedings*. DOI: 10.1145/3411764.3445610

Matthews, M. J., Su, R., Yonish, L., McClean, S., Koopman, J., & Yam, K. C. (2025). A Review of Artificial Intelligence, Algorithms, and Robots Through the Lens of Stakeholder Theory. *Journal of Management*, *51*(6), 2627–2676. Advance online publication. DOI: 10.1177/01492063241311855

Matz, S. C., Kosinski, M., Nave, G., & Stillwell, D. J. (2017). Psychological targeting as an effective approach to digital mass persuasion. *Proceedings of the National Academy of Sciences of the United States of America*, *114*(48), 12714–12719. DOI: 10.1073/pnas.1710966114 PMID: 29133409

McGuire, J., De Cremer, D., Hesselbarth, Y., De Schutter, L., Mai, K. M., & Van Hiel, A. (2023). The reputational and ethical consequences of deceptive chatbot use. *Scientific Reports*, *13*(1), 16246. DOI: 10.1038/s41598-023-41692-3 PMID: 37758742

McLeod, C. (2021). Trust. In E. N. Zalta (Ed.), *The Stanford encyclopedia of philosophy* (Fall 2021 Edition). Metaphysics Research Lab, Stanford University. https://plato.stanford.edu/archives/fall2021/entries/trust/

Mensah, G. B. (2023). Artificial intelligence and ethics: a comprehensive review of bias mitigation, transparency, and accountability in AI Systems. Preprint, November, 10(1). DOI: DOI: 10.13140/RG.2.2.23381.19685/1

Mittelstadt, B. D., Allo, P., Taddeo, M., Wachter, S., & Floridi, L. (2016). The ethics of algorithms: Mapping the debate. *Big Data & Society, 3*(2), 2053951716679679. Advance online publication. DOI: 10.1177/2053951716679679

Moore, R., Moore, M., Shanahan, K., Horky, A., & Mack, B. (2015). Creepy marketing: Three dimensions of perceived excessive online privacy violation. *Marketing Management Journal, 25*(1), 43–53. https://www.researchgate.net/publication/282329651_Creepy_Marketing_Three_Dimensions_of_Perceived_Excessive_Online_Privacy_Violation

Morley, J., Elhalal, A., Garcia, F., Kinsey, L., Mökander, J., & Floridi, L. (2021). Ethics as a service: A pragmatic operationalisation of AI ethics. *Minds and Machines, 31*(2), 239–256. DOI: 10.1007/s11023-021-09563-w PMID: 34720418

Murtarelli, G., Gregory, A., & Romenti, S. (2021). A conversation-based perspective for shaping ethical human–machine interactions: The particular challenge of chatbots. *Journal of Business Research, 129*, 927–935. DOI: 10.1016/j.jbusres.2020.09.018

Nowak, K. L., & Biocca, F. (2001). The influence of agency and anthropomorphism on users' sense of telepresence, copresence, and social presence in virtual environments. *Presence (Cambridge, Mass.), 10*(5), 481–494. DOI: 10.1162/105474603322761289

O'Sullivan, B., & Woodridge, M. (2015). *Artificial intelligence: Foundations, theory, and algorithms*. Book Series, 2021(9).

Oh, C. S., Bailenson, J. N., & Welch, G. F. (2018). A systematic review of social presence: Definition, antecedents, and implications. *Frontiers in Robotics and AI, 5*, 114. DOI: 10.3389/frobt.2018.00114 PMID: 33500993

Okoli, C. (2015). A guide to conducting a standalone systematic literature review. *Communications of the Association for Information Systems, 37*(1). Advance online publication. DOI: 10.17705/1CAIS.03743

Petty, R. E., & Cacioppo, J. T. (1986). The Elaboration Likelihood Model of Persuasion. *Advances in Experimental Social Psychology, 19*, 123–205. DOI: 10.1016/S0065-2601(08)60214-2

Pizzi, G., Vannucci, V., Mazzoli, V., & Donvito, R. (2023). I, chatbot! the impact of anthropomorphism and gaze direction on willingness to disclose personal information and behavioral intentions. *Psychology and Marketing, 40*(7), 1372–1387. DOI: 10.1002/mar.21813

Rao Hill, S., & Troshani, I. (2024). Chatbot anthropomorphism, social presence, uncanniness and brand attitude effects. *Journal of Computer Information Systems*, 1–17. DOI: 10.1080/08874417.2024.2423187

Rapp, A., Curti, L., & Boldi, A. (2021). The human side of human-chatbot interaction: A systematic literature review of ten years of research on text-based chatbots. *International Journal of Human-Computer Studies, 151*, 102630. DOI: 10.1016/j.ijhcs.2021.102630

Short, J. (1976). *The social psychology of telecommunications*. Wiley. https://archive.org/details/socialpsychology0000shor

Sidlauskiene, J., Joye, Y., & Auruskeviciene, V. (2023). AI-based chatbots in conversational commerce and their effects on product and price perceptions. *Electronic Markets*, *33*(1), 1–21. DOI: 10.1007/s12525-023-00633-8 PMID: 37252674

Snyder, H. (2019). Literature review as a research methodology: An overview and guidelines. *Journal of Business Research*, *104*, 333–339. DOI: 10.1016/j.jbusres.2019.07.039

Song, Y., & Luximon, Y. (2020). Trust in AI agent: A systematic review of facial anthropomorphic trustworthiness for social robot design. *Sensors (Basel)*, *20*(18), 5087. DOI: 10.3390/s20185087 PMID: 32906760

Spilinek, M., & Jorgensen, J. J. (2025). Creepy or convenient?: Consumer perceptions of privacy and ad exposure on social media. *Italian Journal of Marketing*, *2025*(1), 71–89. DOI: 10.1007/s43039-025-00107-z

Stahl, B. C., & Eke, D. (2024). The ethics of ChatGPT – Exploring the ethical issues of an emerging technology. *International Journal of Information Management*, *74*, 102700. DOI: 10.1016/j.ijinfomgt.2023.102700

Strubell, E., Ganesh, A., & McCallum, A. (2020). Energy and policy considerations for modern deep learning research. *Proceedings of the AAAI Conference on Artificial Intelligence*, *34*(09), 13693–13696. DOI: 10.1609/aaai.v34i09.7123

Tantalo, C., & Priem, R. L. (2016). Value creation through stakeholder synergy. *Strategic Management Journal*, *37*(2), 314–329. DOI: 10.1002/smj.2337

Tarsney, C. (2024). Deception and Manipulation in Generative AI. *Philosophical Studies*, *2025*, 1–23. DOI: 10.1007/S11098-024-02259-8

Thomaz, F., Salge, C., Karahanna, E., & Hulland, J. (2020). Learning from the Dark Web: Leveraging conversational agents in the era of hyper-privacy to enhance marketing. *Journal of the Academy of Marketing Science*, *48*(1), 43–63. DOI: 10.1007/s11747-019-00704-3

Torraco, R. J. (2005). Writing integrative literature reviews: Guidelines and examples. *Human Resource Development Review*, *4*(3), 356–367. DOI: 10.1177/1534484305278283

Traubinger, V., Heil, S., Grigera, J., Garrido, A., & Gaedke, M. (2024). In Search of Dark Patterns in Chatbots. *Lecture Notes in Computer Science (Including Subseries Lecture Notes in Artificial Intelligence and Lecture Notes in Bioinformatics), 14524 LNCS*, 117–132. DOI: 10.1007/978-3-031-54975-5_7

Wasserman, N. (2023). *OpenAI's Failed Experiment in Governance*. Corporate Governance. https://hbr.org/2023/11/openais-failed-experiment-in-governance

Webster, J., & Watson, R. T. (2002). Analyzing the past to prepare for the future: Writing a literature review. *Management Information Systems Quarterly*, *26*(2), xiii–xxiii. Advance online publication. DOI: 10.2307/4132319

Whittlestone, J., Nyrup, R., Alexandrova, A., & Dastin, J. (2019). The role and limits of principles in AI ethics. In *Proceedings of the 2019 AAAI/ACM Conference on AI, Ethics, and Society* (pp. 195–200). Association for Computing Machinery. DOI: 10.1145/3306618.3314289

Winfield, A. F. T., & Jirotka, M. (2018). Ethical governance is essential to building trust in robotics and artificial intelligence systems. *Philosophical Transactions. Series A, Mathematical, Physical, and Engineering Sciences*, *376*(2133), 20180085. DOI: 10.1098/rsta.2018.0085 PMID: 30323000

Xiao, Y., & Watson, M. (2019). Guidance on conducting a systematic literature review. *Journal of Planning Education and Research*, *39*(1), 93–112. DOI: 10.1177/0739456X17723971

Xu, A., Liu, Z., Guo, Y., Sinha, V., & Akkiraju, R. (2017). A new chatbot for customer service on social media. *Conference on Human Factors in Computing Systems - Proceedings, 2017-May*, 3506–3510. DOI: 10.1145/3025453.3025496

Zuboff, S. (2019, January). Surveillance capitalism and the challenge of collective action. [). Sage CA: Los Angeles, CA: Sage Publications.]. *New Labor Forum*, *28*(1), 10–29. DOI: 10.1177/1095796018819461

ADDITIONAL READING

Alam, A. (2025). Ethical challenges and bias in ai-driven marketing: Educational imperatives and policy perspectives. In *Impacts of AI-Generated Content on Brand Reputation* (pp. 55–108). IGI Global Scientific Publishing., DOI: 10.4018/979-8-3373-4327-3.ch003

Clark, S. H. (2026). When Empathy Is Automated: Social Work, AI Chatbots, and the Ethics of Care. In *AI-Powered Learning in Social Work, Counseling, and Psychology* (pp. 55-84). IGI Global Scientific Publishing. DOI: 10.4018/979-8-3373-4362-4.ch003

Havale, D. S., Raut, N., Anute, N., Ahluwalia, G. K., Kalshetti, P., & Selvakumar, P. (2025). Ethical Challenges and Bias in AI Marketing: Addressing Bias, Fairness, and Inclusivity in AI-Generated Campaigns. In *Impacts of AI-Generated Content on Brand Reputation* (pp. 27-54). IGI Global Scientific Publishing. DOI: 10.4018/979-8-3373-4327-3.ch002

Sonntag, M., Mehmann, J., & Teuteberg, F. (2025). AI-Based Chatbots in Customer Service: A Task-Technology Fit (TTF) Model. [IJSSMET]. *International Journal of Service Science, Management, Engineering, and Technology*, *16*(1), 1–20. DOI: 10.4018/IJSSMET.385128

Wahid, A., & Awad, A. (2025). Role of AI chatbots in enhancing customer satisfaction and customer loyalty. In *Impacts of AI-Generated Content on Brand Reputation* (pp. 129–148). IGI Global Scientific Publishing., DOI: 10.4018/979-8-3373-4327-3.ch005

Warale, P. N., Limbore, N. V., Anute, N., Ahluwalia, G. K., Raut, A., & Selvakumar, P. (2025). AI-Enhanced Customer Engagement and Experience: Chatbots, Virtual Assistants, and AI-Powered Customer Interactions. In *Impacts of AI-Generated Content on Brand Reputation* (pp. 341-368). IGI Global Scientific Publishing. DOI: 10.4018/979-8-3373-4327-3.ch014

KEY TERMS AND DEFINITIONS

Confirmshaming: Inducing users to perform a specific action forced by psychological guilt.

Creepy Marketing: Exploitative advertising strategies through psychological tactics.

Forced Action: Conditioning the progression to the next step.

Hard to Cancel: Preventing the user from opting out of a service.

Human-washing: Hiding the non-human nature of the agent from the user.

Information Asymmetry: An imbalance between different interacting players.

Nagging: Interrupting the user flow with unsolicited information.

Obstruction: Prevents the user from achieving a goal.

Subliminal Marketing: hidden influences that are used to influence individuals without their conscious realization

Chapter 6
Smart Homes and IoT:
Voice-Controlled Devices and Automation

Sandeep Chouhan
Lovely Professional University, India

Ramandeep Sandhu
http://orcid.org/0000-0003-2595-4030
Lovely Professional University, India

Deepika Ghai
http://orcid.org/0000-0002-1113-822X
Lovely Professional University, India

ABSTRACT

This chapter explores the future of smart homes and IoT systems by 2030, emphasizing conversational AI for emotionally intelligent, adaptive environments. Beyond basic commands, homes will respond with contextual understanding, enabled by federated edge computing, ambient intelligence, and 6G networks. These systems will detect emotional cues, health, and behaviours to perform anticipatory actions in climate control, nutrition, and safety. The concept of AI-powered voice-digital twins avatars representing individual users will manage routines, security, and entertainment, and connect across smart city networks. Ethical considerations such as AI hallucinations, consent, and transparency are discussed, along with safeguards such as emotion-aware access and voice verification. This chapter envisions a sustainable, empathic future using quantum edge AI, neuromorphic processors, and blockchain to create human-AI habitation where voice is central to interaction.

DOI: 10.4018/979-8-3373-3361-8.ch006

1. INTRODUCTION

The dawn of the 21st century marked a watershed moment in the way that people relate to the spaces they live in; homes are transforming from passive shelters into actively responsive environments that sense, process, and react to the needs of their occupants (Orlowski & Loh, 2025). The ability for homes to be this responsive has been driven in large part by the development of embedded systems, Wi-Fi networks, and AI systems. While smart appliances at first operated in isolation, now these devices are part of exceptionally dynamic and interconnected ecosystems that can exchange data with one another, including automating routines, taking in energy use, and maximizing the comfort of the occupant (Lee et al., 2025; Behzad et al., 2025; Chouhan et al., 2025; Alilou et al., 2025). Perhaps, the most human-centered interface to emerge in the past few years has been voice-activated systems using conversational AI (Gosmar, 2025). Rather than pushing a button or touching a screen as a control mechanism, the voice interface is as natural as human interaction. In addition to executing simple commands, today's voice assistants are also becoming more expansive, incorporating sentiment analysis, contextual memory, and multi-turn dialogue (Ribeiro et al., 2025). This advancement is a significant step towards intelligent agents that can respond autonomously and meaningfully with people. Looking ahead to 2030, we shall see even more pronounced relationships with voice as the primary communication modality between humans and machines. Voice-controlled Internet of Things (IoT) will be the heart of intelligent living, not just in what it "hears" but more on how and why (Cao et al., 2025). Voice emotional cues, vocal biomarkers, and voice modalities will inform AI-based decisions, such as health and wellness monitoring, support for mental wellbeing, or conditioning an ambience experience. At the same time, merging conversational AI with federated learning, neuromorphic hardware, and real-time language translation will result in a new generation of voice-enabled IoT, which does not just maintain multi-lingual, culturally adapted, and privacy-preserving home environments (Ji et al., 2024; Zhang et al., 2025). This chapter introduces the next iteration of smart home, focusing on how conversational AI will shape the future of automation, personalization, and sustainability in everyday living. It also reviews technology trajectories, privacy issues, and evolving user expectations by focusing on a future vision where homes do not just listen; they understand, can predict, and can evolve with the inhabitants, as illustrated in **Figure 1**.

1.1 Evolution of Smart Homes

The smart home evolution parallels the broader digital transformation of society as we move from manual control of physical environments to intelligent, autonomous ecosystems. Our homes have evolved for the better from a place where everything had to be human-activated and intervention was required for very simple tasks, to cognitive environments that can learn, adapt, and decide in the moment. The smart home evolution relates to and parallels deeper societal patterns like hyper-connectivity, hyper-personalization, sustainability, and human-machine symbiosis (Chouhan et al., 2025). This shift has arisen from rapid advancements in microelectronics, AI and machine learning, sensor advancements, cloud and edge integration, and human-computer interaction. As individual user expectations rise, and society becomes ever more dynamic, the practicalities of smart homes as a luxury and convenience for the wealthy, fast emerging affordable, essential elements of modern, resilient living. From supporting energy efficiency and security to supporting comfort, health, and personal goal attainment, smart and connected homes are evolving and extending across all of our daily lives (Chowdhury & Talukder, 2024; Chouhan et al., 2025; Kaur & Chouhan, 2025). A smart home evolution can be considered in six stages, each of which represents a leap in capability and user experience, and digital horizons enabled by technology innovation and integration, where we can see the possibility of fully sentient homes in the future, that are more than simply responding to commands (Uppuluri & Lakshmeeswari, 2024), but are working with humans to support human life and experience in deep and meaningful ways as shown in **Figure 2**.

Figure 1. Evolution and future of voice-controlled smart homes

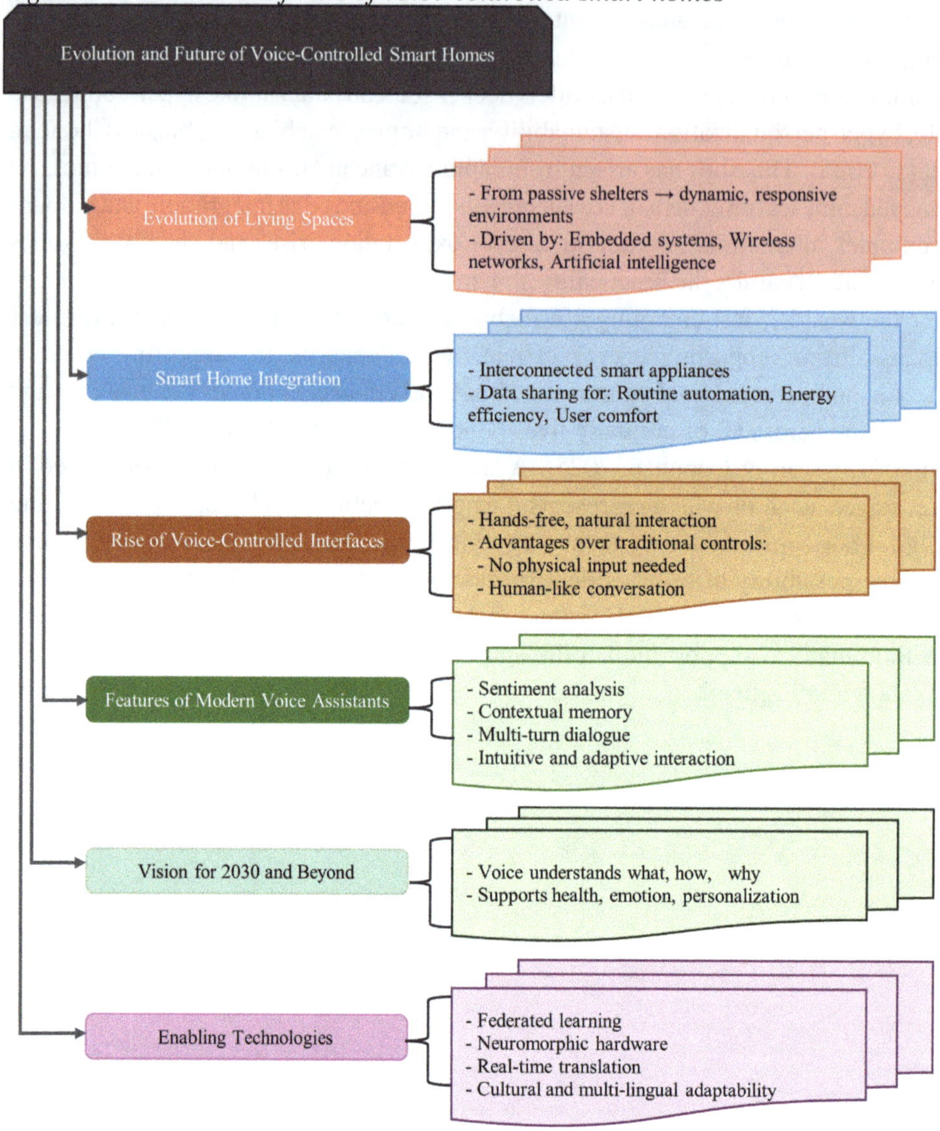

Figure 2. Evolution of smart homes

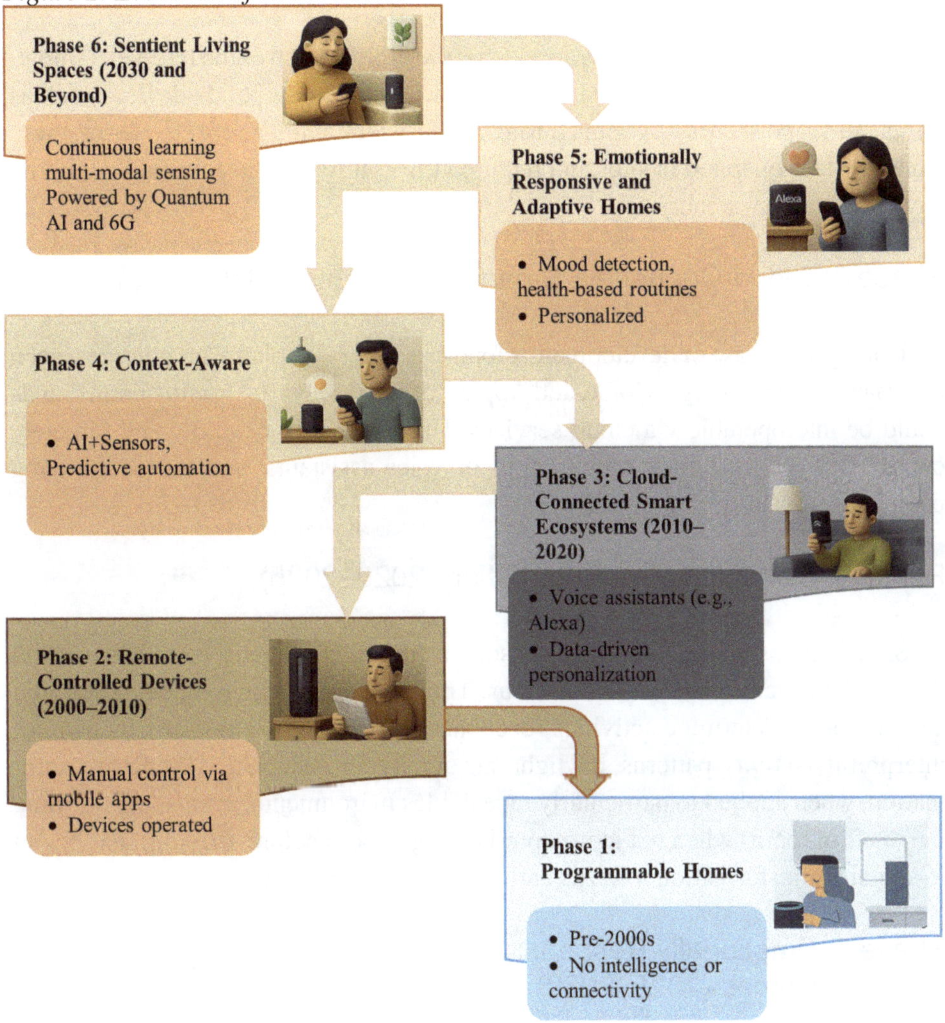

Phase 1: Programmable Homes (Pre-2000s)

The initial type of smart living relied strictly on simple programmable devices such as thermostats, irrigation timers, and alarm clocks. These devices performed their functions according to fixed, non-adaptive schedules and provided convenience to the user, but little more than this. They did not share intelligence or connectivity, especially amongst devices.

Phase 2: Remote-Controlled Devices (2000–2010)

With increased mobile phone access and the proliferation of the Internet, remote-controlled smart devices gained momentum. Users could operate devices such as lights, fans, and security systems through proprietary applications. However, these smart devices operated in silos and required the user to interface manually without any contextual awareness.

Phase 3: Cloud-Connected Smart Ecosystems (2010–2020)

During this phase of development, cloud-based service platforms emerged, such as Amazon Alexa, Google Home, and Apple HomeKit. Devices from different brands could be interoperable via cloud services. Users began to centrally and remotely control devices from their mobile apps or voice assistants, and started enjoying personalized data-driven experiences.

Phase 4: Context-Aware Automation (2020–2025)

Smart homes began relying on sensors, artificial intelligence, and behavioural data, and mechanisms to make decisions. The smart home environment now could autonomously determine activities (occupancy), adjust the settings on its own, or interpret its activity patterns, daylight, air quality, or occupancy. Predictive automation, when applied to particularly repeatable environmental events (e.g., turning lights off in rooms when not in use, pre-heating a room before arriving), has begun to signal a transformation towards anticipatory environments.

Phase 5: Emotionally Responsive and Adaptive Homes (2025–2030)

Advancements in affective computing and conversational AI have led smart homes to have the ability to recognize user emotion and intent. Voice assistants would be able to detect stress or mood through tone analysis, lighting could change according to a person's psychological states, and user routines would adjust dynamically considering health data, sleep quality, and mood. Voice recognition technology transitioned from a mechanism of control to an intensely personal interface, and homes would be able to recognize users and customize their experience, from music to temperature to lighting. AI would transition from behind the scenes as an automatic controller to functioning as a "digital companion".

Phase 6: Sentient Living Spaces (2030 and Beyond)

By 2030, the smart home would enter an era of sentient environment systems able to learn, adapt, and evolve their systems in real-time based on multi-modal data inputs, social behavior, cultural contexts, and even unexpressed signals. It's expected that the home of 2030 will be the product of a synergy of quantum AI, edge computing, neuromorphic chips, and 6G/terahertz communication, enabling the home to automate responses almost instantaneously without any reliance on centralized or regional data servers.

1.2 Role of IoT in Home Automation

The Internet of Things (IoT) has reshaped the architectural framework of today's smart homes, evolving the transition from a personal isolated structure to connected, context-aware environments (Bertrand et al., 2025). In traditional automation, control was described by rules. Engagement was limited to statically confined rules describing the controlled behaviours separating liberty and captivity. Today, the evolution of home automation to IoT has enabled a system of systems to operate together, providing a more communicative, learning, and adaptive life interface capable of real-time change in response to human behaviour and ever-changing external conditions. By 2030, IoT will make smart homes much more than a matter of connectivity. Smart homes will be fully ambient intelligence places with sensors and microcontrollers embedded as almost invisible constant watchers blending in with our built environments, gathering data on ambient conditions such as noise, indoor air quality, or even more creative sensors capturing biometric signals like breathing rate and gait patterns, etc (Sadraey, 2025; Jelili et al., 2025). With the information gathered from the regular ambient conditions, the user's situational awareness will be analyzed from information streamed and analyzed with edge AI and algorithms that will empower real-time event-triggered automation without the need for human engagement or oversight. Connected device architecture of the future home designed for IoT will also shift from a cloud-blind, centralized model to a decentralized, privacy-preserving model of architecture, including blockchain-based federated identity management for securing device-to-device communication, and federated learning for processing information with the user's data never leaving the home network. A device within IoT becomes part of a learning network, refining its performance based on experiences shared in an anonymous way across other homes. Through all this, we can see more intelligent and rapidly adapting homes without infringing on any personal privacy (Hollanek et al., 2025; Rogalski & Schiereck, 2024).

Furthermore, energy-aware intelligence will be the next generation of IoT; for example, sensors run on ambient energy sources light, vibration, and temperature gradients. There will be no need for batteries because they will be self-powered. Information can be continually obtained from ultra-low-maintenance nano sensors. IoT will also serve as a way to interface with the outside world in the form of smart grids, health care, and public safety. For example, a smart home of the future might capture a medical emergency as it occurs using the biometric data of IoT (a medical emergency), then automatically notify the nearest hospitals while opening the front door for paramedics to enter. The intelligent system would cut the waiting time of emergency responders by automating the process of human response. IoT will not just automate human tasks, but will change to facilitative living, facilitating anticipatory living. In this view, homes will go from being passive or reactive to active or proactive beings. The resulting anticipation of needs as well as home awareness, intelligence, and empathy will support a sustainable human life (Choaib et al., 2024).

1.3 Emergence of Voice-Controlled Systems

Voice-controlled interfaces are reshaping the human-machine interface by being more natural and accessible. What started as keyword-triggered assistants is now evolving into continuous dialogue engines that are contextually aware, can manage workflows, deliver personalized recommendations, and even recognize emotion based on vocal tone. Multilingual natural language processing (NLP), emotion-aware speech synthesis, and prosody modulation capabilities through AI are creating conversational AI interfaces that are just as successful as delivering and understanding human dialogue. The next decade will see even more homes being populated, finding emotionally-sensitive homes, where agents that rely upon voice can decipher if a resident is stressed, overtired, or sick and proactively respond by adjusting light, offering self-care routines, or triggering an emergency response. Also, voiceprints to positively identify an individual and privacy-preserving and secure machine learning developed, voice interfaces will be convenient, secure, and ethical (Saxena et al., 2025; Senoner et al., 2024).

1.4 Scope and Objectives of the Chapter

This chapter intends to explore how voice-operated automation, in conjunction with other cutting-edge IoT and AI technologies, will transform our relationship with smart living in 2030. In particular, the objectives of this chapter are:

- To examine the technology platform evolution of smart homes and IoT environments with a focus on voice interaction.
- To look at the future capabilities of conversational artificial intelligence (AI) in ambient computing, such as real-time personalization, emotional awareness, and intelligent abilities for coordination across devices.
- To suggest a quantum-edge AI, Federated Learning, and privacy-first systems-oriented architecture that prepares all parties for the future of secure and efficient automation.
- To analyze the ethical, legal, and social issues impacting the adoption of voice-controlled smart environments in shared homes (households) and urban environments (eco-systems).
- To offer working prototypes, research trends, and profiles of speculative use cases that can frame the ways that future smart homes could facilitate the improvement of well-being, energy efficiency, and human comfort.

2. RELATED WORK

Voice-enabled devices and smart home automation represent a generational leap in the Internet of Things (IoT) technology and provide new ways for people to interact with their lived environments in a way that is unobtrusive and functional, creating convenience and accessibility, allowing for operational efficiencies, and sometimes even completely new solutions. With voice control of smart appliances, users can manage their devices without the need for task-oriented manual activation and simultaneously promote their independence and comfort, providing a space to be inclusive for elderly adults and those with differing abilities. IoT-supported voice recognition technology not only provides added ease to mundane tasks but can be used as a new tool for remote control, more efficient energy use, and personalized intelligent assistance. One of the building blocks in voice-controlled smart home technology is the communication technology stack. Message Queuing Telemetry Transport (MQTT) has become a prevalent lightweight data communication protocol that enables real-time data exchange between devices and cloud computer technologies. Services like Adafruit IO act as an MQTT broker or intermediary by managing routing and performing actions to voice-issued commands from a user to a smart device (Pavaiyarkarasi et al., 2023). The use of products like NodeMCU and ESP8266 with MQTT capabilities has become commonplace as a viable hardware technology to use due to price, Wi-Fi connectivity, ease of integration, and reliable support for voice-controlled activation of appliances (Channi et al., 2025; Ranjan & Sharma, 2020).

Voice command processing is key to both the system's functionality and user experience (Redacción, 2023). Services that change spoken instructions into executable commands for IoT applications (e.g. Google Assistant and IFTTT [if this then that]; Samal et al. (2023); Ranjan and Sharma (2020), using Natural Language Processing (NLP) techniques manage user speech input in combination with machine learning algorithms that model user actions over time to predict user preference and automate frequently undertaken user activity. Voice activation enables home automation relevant to the user who has mobility impairments from an accessibility standpoint because the user can operate lights, fans, motion detectors, a security alarm system, etc. This plays a key role in their quality of life and independence and enables vulnerable populations a certain quality of autonomy. Moreover, the ability to manage smart home applications from a distance provides the user the ability to interact from anywhere, including their home or some distant location, while providing an improved potential quality of security from outside intrusions and comfort (Redacción, 2023; Samal et al., 2023; Channi et al., 2025).

The range of IoT system architectures examined highlights various architectures designed for different application needs. Standard architectures such as the Three-Layer Architecture, which consists of the perception, network, and application layers, offer a point of reference. And indeed, some fabrics will have an added fifth layer for data analytics and processing, to provide a measure of higher-order function. Service-Oriented Architecture (SOA) will enhance system flexibility and device interoperability, which are critical in a heterogeneous smart environment. 5G-enabled architectures can also help large-scale implementations or those requiring low latency, as they allow for better connectivity and scalability. Certainly, enterprise-grade architectures like Alibaba and Oracle's IoT architecture, there's even IBM's IoT architecture, will make much more effort on security, data integration, and advanced analytics, as would be expected in the commercial arena. In support of architectural decisions, models have been proposed in the literature. Evaluation models, such as the criteria-based evaluation models in the literature, which have up to 33 specific metrics, have been used to assess various standard architectures' application suitability, i.e., smart cities (Torad et al., 2022). The authors demonstrated how layer-model analysis can be used to provide structured comparisons between an array of architectural designs, outlining the strengths of each system while highlighting compatibility factors, too.

3. FOUNDATIONAL TECHNOLOGIES

The rapid growth of smart homes is not due to discrete innovation, but rather multiple fundamental technologies converging to build on each other. With ubiquitous data communication through IoT infrastructures, along with the sophistication of conversational AI systems, the smart living environments of the future will be layered, agile, and increasingly autonomous. This section highlights the key enablers of voice-controlled smart home automation by 2030 and lays the foundation for intelligent and context-relevant environments (Ghai et al., 2022; Ghai et al., 2025).

3.1 Internet of Things (IoT) Architecture

IoT is the digital fabric of the smart home ecosystem as it consists of a multi-layered architecture that helps to deliver a consumer's data reliably, consistently, and securely between devices. A general IoT architecture involves:

- **Perception Layer:** sensors, actuators, and voice input devices that capture physical data like temperature, voice, motion, and ambient light.
- **Network Layer:** carries data between devices and cloud/edge servers, using wireless protocols such as Zigbee, Thread, and Wi-Fi 6.
- **Processing Layer:** performed on device or cloud, includes data analysis using embedded processors and edge computing nodes.
- **Application Layer:** presents processed information to the consumer by mobile app, voice assistant, or control hub.

Future architectures will see edge-AI and blockchain-based trust models emerge, enabling decentralized control, greater security, and ultra-low-latency voice-command execution.

3.2 Voice Recognition and Natural Language Processing (NLP)

Although today's voice recognition toolset offers a range of features from simple command identification to deep conversation understanding, voice-enabled systems have come a long way, thanks to Automatic Speech Recognition (ASR) and Natural Language Understanding (NLU), which are the two main components of modern voice-enabled systems. ASR transcribes spoken content into text, while NLU understands the user's intent.

By 2030, the artificial intelligence for natural language processing (NLP) in smart homes will encompass:

- Emotion-aware voice analytics, where devices can process vocal tone to detect when the user may be stressed or happy.
- Personalized learning models that use contextualization for all interactions, daily routines, speech recognition, and even multiple users.
- Continual learning NLP engines that leverage user representations based on their vocabulary, accents, and even slang.

These features will allow voice-controlled systems to move beyond understanding fixed commands. By harnessing feelings, experiences, and context, voice-controlled systems will have human-like interaction not only in targeted applications such as education, health care, and entertainment, but also through autonomously controlled spaces.

3.3 Communication Protocols (Wi-Fi, Zigbee, Z-Wave, Thread)

The viability and performance of a smart home are driven by the types of communication protocols that the smart devices use. Each communication protocol comes with its own advantages in terms of range, power consumption, bandwidth, and compatibility with other devices, but is also at the foundational level for automation and voice time sensitivity.

- Wi-Fi 6/6E/7 has extremely high bandwidth, especially when working with remote cloud services or cameras, which need lots of data bandwidth like video surveillance, AI-based voice recognition, and real-time streaming data from multiple devices.
- Low-power communication protocols like Zigbee and Z-Wave, which are well-established mesh-network protocols, are peer-to-peer and good for low-bandwidth, battery-powered, low-bandwidth sources where constant connectivity might be required, and sometimes by occupancy, work particularly well for battery-powered smart lighting systems, door locks, thermostats, and occupancy-based automation.
- With sufficient support from Google, Apple, and Amazon, Thread is an IPv6-based protocol and is ideal for scalable, expandable self-healing mesh networks. Thread is an open standard and has enough upside to be look to be a future-proof solution for a large smart home ecosystem.

As smart home environments progress towards 2030, multi-protocol convergence will be a significant factor. AI-driven network orchestration will enable smart hubs and edge controllers to dynamically select the most appropriate protocol, depending on context: Zigbee for live sensor alerts, Thread for periodic background system updates, and Wi-Fi 7 for live voice processing or cloud-based AI tasks. To help inform decisions regarding communication protocols, **Table 1** outlines and compares the communication protocols and their strengths and benefits by use case. The following critical parameters were reviewed and compared: range, data rate, power consumption, topology, and likely advances in adoption across the protocols. Based on this review, **Table 1** serves as a reference framework for communication technologies that will best complement and augment the voice-enabled modern smart home automation space.

Table 1. Comparative overview of key communication protocols in smart home automation

Feature	Wi-Fi (6/6E/7)	Zigbee	Z-Wave	Thread
Frequency Band	2.4 GHz, 5 GHz, 6 GHz (Wi-Fi 6E/7)	2.4 GHz	Sub-GHz (908 MHz in US, varies globally)	2.4 GHz (IEEE 802.15.4)
Topology	Star / Point-to-Point	Mesh	Mesh	Mesh (IPv6-based, self-healing)
Range (Typical)	50–100 meters indoors	10–20 meters indoors (extends in mesh)	30–100 meters indoors (depends on region)	10–30 meters (extensible via mesh)
Data Rate	Up to 9.6 Gbps (Wi-Fi 7)	250 kbps	100 kbps	250 kbps
Power Consumption	High (not optimized for low-power IoT)	Very low	Low	Very low
Interoperability	High (internet/cloud integration)	Moderate (uses own standard stack)	Moderate (uses proprietary stack)	High (IP-native and open standard)
Security Features	WPA3, MAC filtering, AES	AES-128 encryption	AES-128 encryption	Thread-specific security + AES-128
Scalability	Limited (per router bandwidth)	High (thousands of nodes in mesh)	Moderate	High (designed for large-scale networks)

continued on following page

Table 1. Continued

Feature	Wi-Fi (6/6E/7)	Zigbee	Z-Wave	Thread
Best Use Cases	High-bandwidth devices (cameras, voice AI)	Lighting, sensors, basic automation	Locks, thermostats, and energy management	Smart locks, climate control, secure mesh
Future Outlook	Will coexist with IoT protocols	Widely used, supported by major brands	Slower adoption, still used in smart hubs	Gaining traction due to IP compatibility

3.4 Role of AI and ML in Voice-Controlled Automation

Artificial Intelligence (AI) and Machine Learning (ML) are the heart of voice-controlled automation because they allow the systems to move from a static rule-based workflow to an adaptive, self-learning, i.e., constantly evolving environment. The predominant application of AI is for the following functions:

- **Intent Prediction**: Once established, an ML algorithm would begin to interpret any voice input from the user and potentially, over time, recognize what needs to be done when, e.g., dim the lights when a person goes to bed without overtly ever telling the service to do it, but establishing a standard protocol.
- **Anomaly Detection**: AI in voice-controlled automation will autonomously notify the user or take action to prevent the event from occurring by identifying unusual usage patterns or suspicious activity.
- **Personalization:** ML models are uniquely capable of personalizing the automation based on the user's patterns, voice profile, and requirements that are identified by analyzing historical data.

In the next 6-7 years i.e. by 2030, AI will also function to enable multiple devices to cooperate to form an algorithm that uses all of those intelligent systems under one user command, e.g. When a user says "Good Night" the AI processes this concerning a group of actions including turn off lights; adjust the thermostat; lock doors and; activate an energy saving or sleep processing mode. Technology will likely advance further and provide for innovations that include neural-symbolic reasoning, zero-shot learning, and quantum-enhanced AI capability, to allow the voice-controlled smart home to be more than simply reactive technologies, but anticipatory, emotionally intelligent systems.

4. PROPOSED METHODOLOGY

The methodology is proposing next-generation smart homes where voice automation is context-aware, predictive, energy-efficient, and user-personalized. A multi-layer adaptive architecture, AI-based voice command processing, edge computing, and behavioral analytics are combined to create contextually aware, responsive, secure, and intelligent smart environments as shown in **Figure 3**.

4.1 System Architecture Overview

Overall, the architecture is conceived using a modular five-layer model consisting of:

- **Perception Layer**: Smart sensors, microphones, and actuators for the environment and users.
- **Communication Layer**: Utilizes a hybrid of new protocols (Wi-Fi 7, Zigbee, Thread) on different devices, allowing dynamic switching based on bandwidth and energy needs.
- **Edge Intelligence Layer**: Performs AI functions (voice recognition, event classification) locally, comprising a single or a few embedded AI processors (e.g., neuromorphic chips).
- **Cloud Collaboration Layer**: Long-term data storage, let devices work together to leverage internal and external learning and modeling, and enhanced behavioral survey at scale.
- **Application Layer**: Provides user experience through mobile apps, voice assistants, and AR/VR interfaces.

The architecture supports the interaction of multiple agents, allowing multiple smart systems to respond to a simple command in a coherent manner.

4.2 Device and Sensor Integration

Each area in the smart home will have embedded, integrated systems that will integrate:

- Voice sensors with a far-field microphone and noise cancellation
- Environmental sensors (temperature, humidity, air quality)
- Occupant sensing devices (PIR, ultrasonic, camera with OpenPose)
- Appliance controllers (lights, HVAC, curtains, entertainment systems)

A contextual integration layer made up of edge processing that fuses sensor data with a time-synchronization process can infer the real-world activity, mood, and intent of the users in real time.

4.3 Voice Command Processing Flow

Voice command processing involves a series of steps in an AI pipeline (see Figure 4.2 (to insert)). The following are the steps taken:

- Wake-word Detection: A lightweight, on-device AI algorithm locally uses voice activation phrases, such as "Alexa" or "okay Google," to detect when low power is used.
- The Speech-to-Text (ASR) module uses one of several Transformer-based speech recognition models or even quantum speech recognition models to transcribe the audio captured by the device, offering an immense computational advantage as compared to other current speech recognition models or frameworks.
- The Intent Recognition step feeds the transcribed command to an NLP model, such as a BERT-based model in natural language processing (NLP). The model handles the semantics, context, and sentiment analysis for the user's command.
- Command Routing: After the command has been recognized as intent, a contextual decision engine further assesses the intent and determines which devices or systems to activate.
- The Privacy Filter processes the user command with the intent to not communicate sensitive information, using either edge computing for local processing or requiring another user authentication for sensitive commands.

The flow established in the previous sentences provides for multi-language interaction, given that speakers could choose which language input, and can be speaker-specific and include emotion-aware decision-making.

Figure 3. AI-based architecture for voice-controlled smart homes

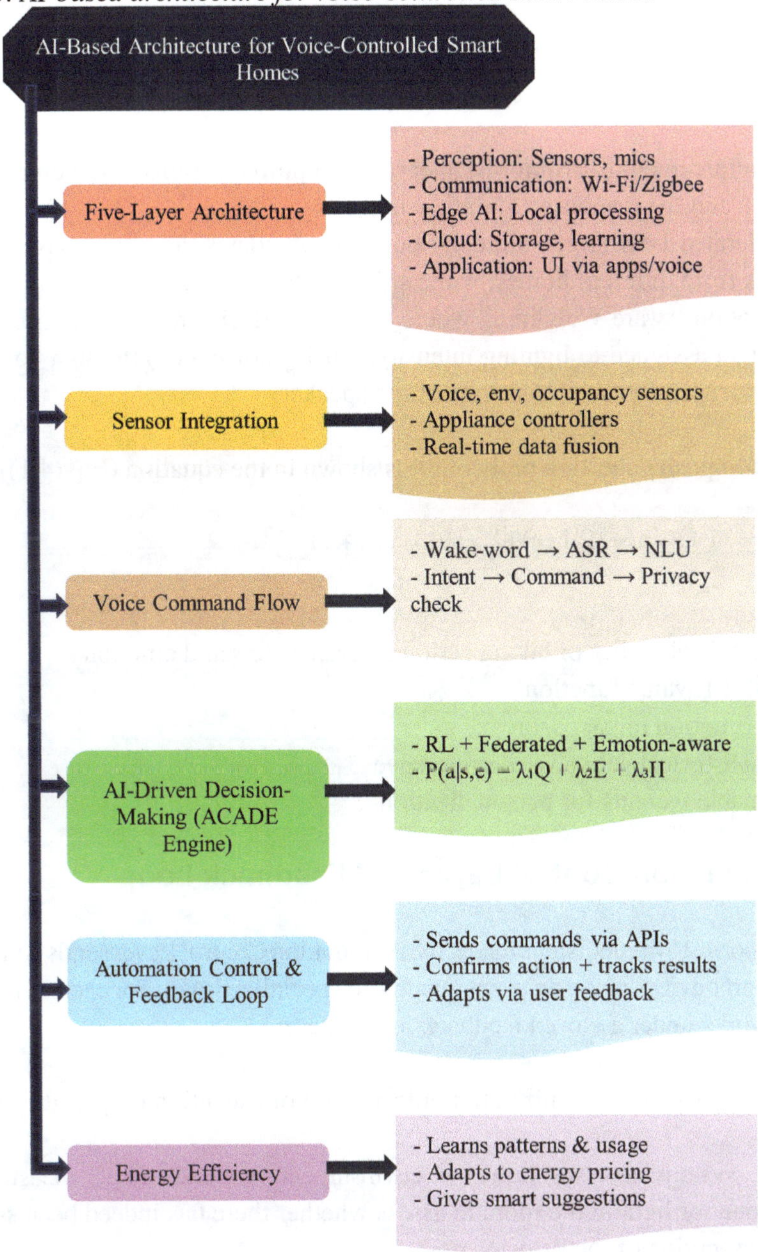

4.4 AI-Driven Decision-Making Algorithm

Central to the methodology is the Adaptive Context-Aware Decision Engine (ACADE) that uses a half-breed model of AI, which uses:

- Reinforcement Learning (RL) learns the optimal actions based on user feedback and the responses of the environment.
- Federated Learning continually builds and updates the model based on user data from different homes, while still maintaining privacy.
- Emotion-Aware Weighting, where situational decisions (you can imagine the weight assigned to lighting intensity, music choice, etc.) through voice analysis report the emotional state of the speaker.

The composite decision probability is shown in the equation (Eq. (4.1))

$$P(a|s,e) = \lambda 1 \cdot Q(s,a) + \lambda 2 \cdot E(e) + \lambda 3 \cdot H(s) \qquad (4.1)$$

Where,
P(a|s,e): Probability of taking action *a* given state *s* and emotion *e*
Q(s,a): RL value function
E(e): Emotion impact score
H(s): Historical habit-based preference
λ: Tunable weights for personalization

4.5 Automation Control Layer and Feedback Loop

In response to the decisions made, the Automation Control Layer sends commands to the smart devices using an event queue and specialized APIs for each device. The system works under a closed feedback loop where:

- The devices send confirmation information of execution (e.g., light switched on).
- The system assesses how the environment responds (e.g., measures the amount of light in the room to assess whether there has indeed been successful execution of the decision).
- There is a built-in capability of listening to the user's feedback (verbal or passive) to ensure the user is satisfied with the execution of the task.
- If there is some deviation between the original intent of the action executed, the ML system is retrained.

The development of a closed feedback loop allows for continuous learning and the adaptation of behaviour over time through the use of anomaly detection to prevent contrived outcomes for the user.

4.6 Energy Optimization and User Behavior Analysis

To maintain sustainability, the system will use predictive energy management algorithms to ultimately control all of the energy taken into the home. The predictive energy management situation will track:

- The schedule of the user's occupancy timing.
- Use of appliances based on historical use.
- Current energy pricing (if connected to the smart grid).
- Current conditions in the environment (e.g., solar heat gain).

Using clustering techniques, regression, and the system will find and make automation suggestions considering energy efficiency in the core, while keeping the user comfortable.

Behavioural data from the user will be anonymized and aggregated to assist in creating a user energy profile. These predictive profiles will allow for user recommendations such as:

- "You have decided to work outside for the day; however, it would be smart to switch your home to energy-saving mode while you are gone.
- "You have sufficient solar charge to run your HVAC system for the next 4 hours".

In an effort to promote sustainable behaviour through AI-based analytics and voice commands, the smart home will become a trusted facilitator to involve the user in sustainable living.

5. VOICE-CONTROLLED DEVICES ECOSYSTEM

The ecosystem of command and control-type voice-enabled devices constitutes the primary operating environment for smart homes. Unlike traditional command and control methods for consumers, voice-enabled ecosystems allow for a hands-free, more intuitive method of interaction that is more closely aligned with the inherent human method of communication. In this section, the aim is to break down this type of ecosystem, from smart voice assistants to cross-platform integration, as well as real-time synchronicity, as it exists today and in the future.

5.1 Smart Assistants (Alexa, Google Assistant, Siri)

Voice assistants have evolved from simple command-driven devices to intelligent conversational interfaces with interactive capabilities based on an infusion of different learning capabilities. Today, various platforms, such as Amazon Alexa, Google Assistant, and Apple Siri, support usable ranges of smart home functionality, including task management for lighting and climate control, contextual reminders from stationary tasks, and even suggestions around personal wellness. By 2030, these interfaces may provide users with:

- Emotionally adaptive means of interaction, monitoring tone and detecting mood or motion, then responding accordingly.
- Context chaining allows automated recall of conversations and tells the interface multi-turn commands. (e.g., 'Turn off all of the lights in the room I was just in.')
- Multi-modal interfaces - interfaces that blend voice with gestures over existing object recognition, facial recognition, or even AR overlays or input.

Furthermore, these assistants will work alongside digital voice twins, which are personalized AI beings that are aware of an individual user's patterns, language preferences, and behaviors throughout locations and devices. Each assistant has different levels of accuracy in voice recognition, natural language understanding, ecosystem integration, and privacy standards. **Table 2** provides a side-by-side comparison of these different platforms to show what they are currently capable of and how they are likely to evolve into 2030-ready smart home ecosystems.

Table 2. Comparative analysis of leading smart assistants for voice-controlled smart homes

Feature	Amazon Alexa	Google Assistant	Apple Siri
Voice Recognition	Multi-user voice profiles	Highly accurate voice matching	Personalized voice detection via the iOS ecosystem
Wake Word Customization	Fixed ("Alexa", "Echo", "Computer", etc.)	Limited (mainly "Hey Google")	Fixed ("Hey Siri")
Contextual Awareness	Moderate (skills-based memory)	High (uses Google Knowledge Graph)	Moderate (limited external integration)
Platform Ecosystem	Amazon Echo, Fire OS, 3rd-party devices	Android, Nest, Wear OS, Android Auto	iOS, macOS, HomePod, Apple Watch
Natural Language Understanding	Strong, skill-driven	Very strong, deep integration with Google NLP	Moderate, improving with iOS updates
Third-Party Integration (Skills/ Apps)	Over 100,000 skills and growing	Action-based apps and deep web knowledge	Limited to Apple-approved apps and HomeKit
Smart Home Protocol Support	Zigbee, Matter, Wi-Fi	Matter, Thread, Wi-Fi	HomeKit, Matter, Thread
Offline Voice Processing	Partial (select Echo devices)	Limited (some devices in development)	Partial (on newer iPhones and HomePods)
Privacy & Data Control	Voice recordings are stored unless deleted.	Auto-delete options, transparent logs	Strong privacy defaults; minimal logging
Unique Features	Voice purchasing, Alexa Routines	Cross-device conversation, real-time translation	On-device processing, deep iOS integration
Future Outlook (2030-ready)	Expanding with AI avatars and smart routines	Advancing toward natural multimodal AI	Evolving within a secure, closed Apple ecosystem

5.2 Smart Home Appliance Integration

Voice-controlled ecosystems rely on the integration of future generations of smart appliances that are voice-responsive, intelligent, upgradeable, and optimize on their own, as shown in **Figure 4**. The exciting characteristics of the new generations of appliances are:

- AI-enabled appliances provide feedback, usage reports, and predictive maintenance notifications.
- Automatically adapting to changing routines by sensing and learning patterns (e.g., coffee strength preference, washing cycle preferences) that occur without prompting.
- Voice or automation rules triggering Over-The-Air (OTA) firmware updates.

Figure 4. Smart home appliance integration

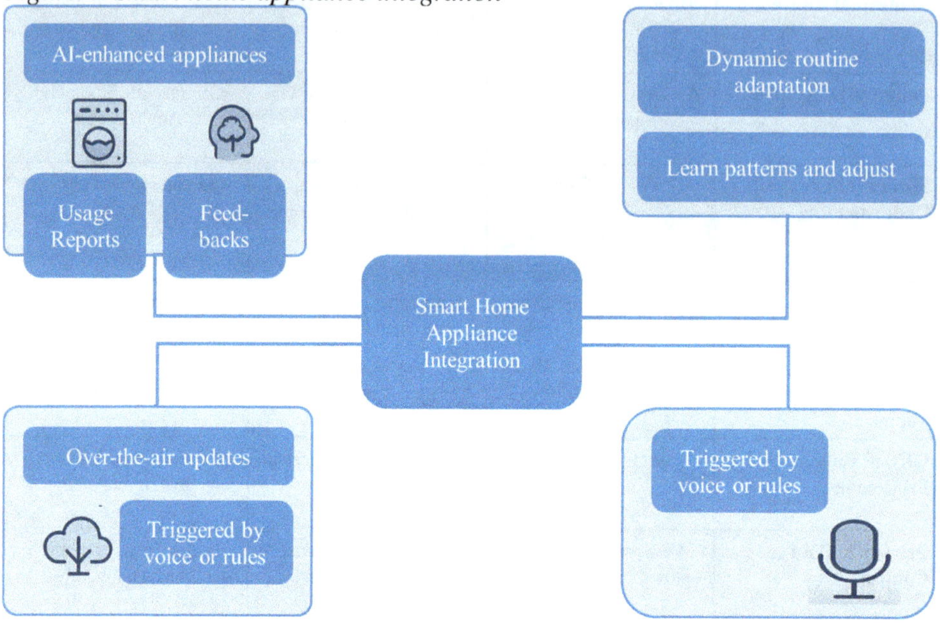

5.3 Cross-Platform Interoperability

One of the biggest problems for the currently available smart ecosystems is device fragmentation. True automation is dependent on cross-platform interoperability, where an ecosystem enables devices from various manufacturers to communicate as a seamless device. More open standards, like Matter and IoTivity, are fueling this process. By 2030, interoperability will be improved, and there will be:

- AI middleware bridges that will integrate disparate platforms' commands and translate them into different protocols in real time.

- Semantic intent recognition so that a single command can operate dissimilar devices without regard to brand (i.e., "start cleaning" could trigger any robot vacuum, independent of vendor).
- Federated device identity by delivering each user's voice preferences, schedules, and access permissions seamlessly to any one of their homes, hotels, and vehicles.

5.4 Real-Time Synchronization and Updates

A sustainable voice-controlled ecosystem relies on continuous synchronization between cloud or remote services, edge devices, and local AI agents. Real-time synchronization is required for processing commands properly, keeping the states of systems current, and activating new skills and integrations onto the cloud in a seamless way. New capabilities include:

• Edge-cloud hybrid synchronization, sharing minimal (essential) data with the cloud, while potentially sensitive or time-sensitive processing takes place locally.

• Predictive synchronization models update systems by identifying patterns, intentions, and behavior (e.g., pre-loading entertainment content or firmware at off-peak times).

6. FUTURE DIRECTIONS AND TRENDS

As smart home technologies continue to progress, the next iteration will evolve from reactive automation to intelligent, proactive living environments. The next generation of voice-controlled smart homes will be defined by deeper context awareness, immediate response across physical and digital, and ultra-efficient, sustainable living. This section takes a closer look at the trending concepts that will define the next decade of smart living.

6.1 AI-Powered Context-Aware Systems

Currently, most smart homes operate based on pre-established rules or straightforward voice requests. However, the future will consist of systems with context-aware intelligence that can consider environmental data, behavioral information, and emotional information in real-time. AI would leverage advances in multimodal machine learning to provide a syncretic interpretation of user data such as speech, visual, and movement-attribute data, or biometrics, rather than overt commands. For example, rather than "turn the lights down and turn on the music", if the AI agent recognized a tiredness in vocal tone, coupled with a preference for low light, and a seen schedule indicating that the user would soon be finished with work, it might then preempt a command and create a relaxing atmosphere. The systems will be privacy-preserving, with context-aware smart living systems that are personalized and unique to individual users, powered by on-device AI that learns from the low-key interpersonal interactions that occur in daily living, while remaining non-intrusive.

6.2 Smart Home Integration with AR/VR

The integration of Augmented Reality (AR) and Virtual Reality (VR) with smart home solutions will completely change the way users experience their living spaces. Imagine being able to control your entire home with holographic surfaces that are projected using smart glasses, or being able to see the virtual 3D overlay of your energy consumption patterns while standing in your living room. The incorporation of AR/VR will enable users to manage their homes remotely and allow them to "walk" into their homes from a remote location and manipulate objects simultaneously or even virtually simulate a whole-house walkthrough before speaking commands. This immersive layer will provide additional value for consumers dealing with assisted living or digital wellness, or while managing distance-support caregiving.

6.3 Low-Power, Sustainable IoT Devices

As smart homes adopt new technologies, energy efficiency becomes paramount. Within the next decade, we can expect to see significant advancements in the popularity of ultra-low-power IoT devices, with the help of energy harvesting methods such as ambient light, radio frequency, and thermoelectric conversion, and others that have not been invented yet. Devices will be manufactured on sustainable supply chains, using sustainable (or green) AI models that favour minimal resource use with continued functionality. Smart sensors could operate without needing battery replacement and can relay and receive information with less network congestion and energy waste, through the use of next-generation protocols, such as Matter over Thread with AI-optimised traffic scheduling.

6.4 Towards Fully Autonomous Smart Living

Through advancements like emerging technologies and AI, we seem to be developing environments that are fully autonomous smart home ecosystems that require minimal user engagement, but provide highly individualized anticipatory services. Not only will homes become living digital organisms, but they will also independently schedule maintenance, order autonomous deliveries of supplies, and dynamically change energy consumption based on local weather forecasting and user behavior.

As simple as this sounds, there will be full autonomy structured by a collection of distributed AI agents, but they will each operate within a specific domain (e.g., health, security, entertainment) and share information with other agents, delivering a completely integrated experience. In the future, voice interaction will become a discussion with a two-way flow where the system is either providing details into decisions that they have made or offering choices to the user, promoting trust and transparency in machine decision making. The home of 2030 is not only going to be "smart" but also have a sense of empathy, sustainability, and self-regulation; it will not just be a container but a genuine cohabitant.

7. CONCLUSION

The progression of smart homes into intelligent, voice-enabled ecosystems is an important inflection point in the redesign of the human habitat. What began as the automation of home environments for convenience has quickly blossomed into a complete system of responsive, adaptive, and contextually aware technologies. This chapter has examined some of the foundational frameworks, new technologies, and emerging trajectories articulating the future of smart homes powered by conversational AI and IoT. Voice is becoming the natural, intuitive user interface that connects human intention to machine action. Predictably, once voice is combined with AI and machine learning, the possible materials and modes of voice-controlled interaction multiply. These voice-controlled systems can become more than just facilities for commands; they have the potential to become empathetic, proactive agents that can sense mood, behavior, and preferences. Smart devices are becoming more and more connected and intelligent, leading the home to become a co-evolving being, rather than a static domain. The mixture of sustainable low-power Internet of Things (IoT) devices, federated learning at the edge, and immersive AR/VR interfaces will evolve the home concept further still, so that it is not just intelligent but energy-efficient, accessible, immersive, and capable of evolving with its occupant. Finally, the ongoing push for full-automation of home management using predictive algorithms and distributed AI agents will grant even greater dimensions of comfort, safety, and personalization to the occupants' experience. However, with advances also comes responsibility - ethical ways to collect and share data, the expectation that users actively consent in shared spaces, and the level of accessibility and identity are ever changing. The future smart home must be innovative, inclusive, and transparent, Finally, in conclusion as we find ourselves approaching 2030 the vision is clear For a smart home to listen and Learn, adapt and evolve, not simply be a passive responsive environment that needs information to evolve - A smart home

REFERENCES

Alilou, M., Tousi, B., & Shayeghi, H. (2025). Energy management of smart appliances, local renewable units and electric vehicles for having residential zero-energy buildings. *Iranian Journal of Science and Technology. Transaction of Electrical Engineering*, *49*(3), 1427–1445. Advance online publication. DOI: 10.1007/s40998-025-00817-2

Behzad, K., Zandi, R., Motamedi, E., Salehinejad, H., & Siami, M. (2025). Robomnist: A multimodal dataset for multi-robot activity recognition using wifi sensing, video, and audio. *Scientific Data*, *12*(1), 326. DOI: 10.1038/s41597-025-04636-2 PMID: 39987245

Bertrand, Y., Stevens, A., Deforce, B., De Smedt, J., De Weerdt, J., & Serral, E. (2025). Approaches for IoT-enhanced predictive process monitoring. *Process Science*, *2*(1), 7. DOI: 10.1007/s44311-025-00011-x

Cao, Z., Zhao, Z., Shang, W., Ai, S., & Shen, S. (2025). Using the ToN-IoT dataset to develop a new intrusion detection system for industrial IoT devices. *Multimedia Tools andApplications*, *84*(16), 16425–16453. DOI: 10.1007/s11042-024-19695-7

[] Channi, H. K., Kaur, S., & Sandhu, R. (2025). Smart Textiles in Healthcare. Smart Textiles and Wearables for Health and Fitness, 27.

Choaib, M., Garouani, M., Bouneffa, M., Waldhoff, N., & Mohanna, Y. (2024). IoT-AID: An Automated Decision Support Framework for IoT. *SN Computer Science*, *5*(4), 429. DOI: 10.1007/s42979-024-02780-x

Chouhan, S., Sandhu, R., Yadav, O. P., & Islam, S. M. N. (2025). Quantum-powered autonomous deep-sea explorer using AI, microbiofuels, and advanced sensors for oceanic discovery. In *2025 International Conference on Computer, Electrical & Communication Engineering (ICCECE)* (pp. 1–5). IEEE. DOI: 10.1109/ICCECE61355.2025.10941009

Chowdhury, S., & Talukder, U. (2024). Background on microelectronics. In*Numerical exploration of isolated GaAs-AlGaAs quantum well*. Springer., DOI: 10.1007/978-3-031-53816-2_1

Ghai, D., Saxena, S., Dhingra, G., & Tripathi, S. L. (2025). A comprehensive review on performance-based comparative analysis, categorization, classification and mapping of text extraction system techniques for images. *Multimedia Tools and Applications*, *84*(5), 2327–2484. DOI: 10.1007/s11042-024-20257-0

Ghai, D., Tripathi, S. L., Saxena, S., Chanda, M., & Alazab, M. (Eds.). (2022). *Machine learning algorithms for signal and image processing*. John Wiley & Sons. DOI: 10.1002/9781119861850

Gosmar, D. (2025). Conversational hyperconvergence: An onlife evolution model for conversational AI agency. *AI and Ethics*, *5*(2), 1147–1161. DOI: 10.1007/s43681-024-00463-0

Hollanek, T., Peters, D., Drage, E., & Hernandes, R. (2025). AI, journalism, and critical AI literacy: Exploring journalists' perspectives on AI and responsible reporting. *AI & Society*, *40*(8), 6393–6405. DOI: 10.1007/s00146-025-02407-6

Jelili, M. O., Abolade, O., Alabi, A. T., & Marunye, J. (2025). Residential indoor air quality assessment in Ibadan metropolis, Nigeria. *Discover Environment*, *3*(1), 87. DOI: 10.1007/s44274-025-00286-8

Ji, S., Tan, Y., Saravirta, T., Yang, Z., Liu, Y., Vasankari, L., Pan, S., Long, G., & Walid, A. (2024). Emerging trends in federated learning: From model fusion to federated x learning. *International Journal of Machine Learning and Cybernetics*, *15*(9), 3769–3790. DOI: 10.1007/s13042-024-02119-1

Kaur, M., & Chouhan, S. (2025). Leveraging machine learning techniques for accurate heart disease prediction through data insights and model optimization. In 2025 3rd International Conference on Disruptive Technologies (ICDT) (pp. 515–519). IEEE. DOI: 10.1109/ICDT63985.2025.10986736

Lee, S., Kang, W., Bertogna, M., Chwa, H. S., & Lee, J. (2025). Timing guarantees for inference of AI models in embedded systems. *Real-Time Systems*, *61*(2), 259–267. DOI: 10.1007/s11241-025-09445-9

Orlowski, A., & Loh, W. (2025). Data autonomy and privacy in the smart home: The case for a privacy smart home meta-assistant. *AI & Society*, *40*(6), 4171–4184. Advance online publication. DOI: 10.1007/s00146-025-02182-4

Pavaiyarkarasi, R., Rajendran, N., Vijayashanthi, R. S., Saranya, G., & Mohanavel, V. (2023). Experimental evaluation of Internet of Things assisted human voice-based smart home controlling system. *Proceedings of the 2023 International Conference on Smart Electronics and Systems (ICSES)*, 1–6. DOI: 10.1109/ICSES60034.2023.10465326

Ranjan, R., & Sharma, A. (2020). Voice-controlled IoT devices framework for smart home. In *Smart Intelligent Computing and Applications* (pp. 57–67). Springer., DOI: 10.1007/978-981-15-3369-3_5

Redacción, N. (2023). Remotely controlled smart home system using voice and IoT. *Ciencia en la Ingeniería, 11*(1), 2016–2024. DOI: 10.52783/cienceng.v11i1.370

Ribeiro, B., Gomes, L., & Vale, Z. (2025). Retrieval-augmented generation based assistant: A smart home case study. In Santos, M. F., Machado, J., Novais, P., Cortez, P., & Moreira, P. M. (Eds.), *Progress in Artificial Intelligence. EPIA 2024* (Vol. 14968). Springer., DOI: 10.1007/978-3-031-73500-4_14

Rogalski, T., & Schiereck, D. (2024). When is blockchain worth it? Value and risk drivers of corporate blockchain announcements. *Electronic Markets, 34*(1), 39. DOI: 10.1007/s12525-024-00718-y

Sadraey, M. H. (2025). Microcontroller boards. In *Unmanned aircraft design*. Springer., DOI: 10.1007/978-3-031-67795-3_9

Samal, S. R., Bandopadhaya, S., Roy, A., Mishra, A., Mihovska, A., & Poulkov, V. (2023). MQTT protocol-based IoT solution for voice-controlled smart home. *Proceedings of the IEEE Wireless Personal Multimedia Communications (WPMC)*, 171–175. DOI: 10.1109/WPMC59531.2023.10338841

Saxena, V., Tamò-Larrieux, A., Van Dijck, G., & Spanakis, G. (2025). Responsible guidelines for authorship attribution tasks in NLP. *Ethics and Information Technology, 27*(2), 16. DOI: 10.1007/s10676-025-09821-w

Senoner, J., Schallmoser, S., Kratzwald, B., Feuerriegel, S., & Netland, T. (2024). Explainable AI improves task performance in human–AI collaboration. *Scientific Reports, 14*(1), 31150. DOI: 10.1038/s41598-024-82501-9 PMID: 39730794

Torad, M. A., Bouallegue, B., & Ahmed, A. M. (2022). A voice-controlled smart home automation system using artificial intelligence and Internet of Things. *Telkomnika, 20*(4), 808. DOI: 10.12928/telkomnika.v20i4.23763

Uppuluri, S., & Lakshmeeswari, G. (2024). Review of security and privacy-based IoT smart home access control devices. *Wireless Personal Communications, 137*(3), 1601–1640. DOI: 10.1007/s11277-024-11405-8

Zhang, X., Xu, M., & Xu, S. (2025). Smart home cyber insurance pricing. In Zhao, J., & Meng, W. (Eds.), *Science of Cyber Security. SciSec 2024* (Vol. 15441). Springer., DOI: 10.1007/978-981-96-2417-1_17

Chapter 7
Conversational AI in Smart Homes for Enhancing Personalization and Adaptability

Rituraj Jain
http://orcid.org/0000-0002-5532-1245
Marwadi University, India

Khyati Shah
http://orcid.org/0009-0009-0296-8553
West Herts College, Hemel Hempstead, UK

Kamal Upreti
http://orcid.org/0000-0003-0665-530X
Christ University, India

ABSTRACT

Conversational AI for the Smart Homes is explored in this chapter and how it can play the role of enabling personalized, adaptive, and intuitive human–environment interactions. The intelligent voice interface core technology that is explored includes natural language processing, machine learning, and context aware computing. But focusing on personalization techniques including, for example, collaborative filtering, reinforcement learning, and federated learning as well as systems learning from user behavior, the environment, and newly joined devices. This also includes multimodal interaction through voice, gesture, gesture, and emotion recognition.

DOI: 10.4018/979-8-3373-3361-8.ch007

Ethical considerations in the critical such as what data could be collected, privacy, transparency and the responsible AI usage are explained and also the trends that will form the future of smart living are discussed.

1. INTRODUCTION

Smart home technology has advanced significantly, with modern interfaces becoming increasingly intuitive and user-friendly. As these systems grow more sophisticated, voice-based interactions have emerged as a vital trend, requiring seamless operation and the ability to adapt to individual user preferences and behaviors This need is effectively addressed by Conversational AI, which serves as a promising approach to creating personalized, adaptive, and human-like living environments The rapid development of smart home ecosystems has enabled the integration of a wide range of interconnected devices and sensors, including thermostats, lighting, cameras, security systems, and entertainment systems. However, managing this complex array of technologies often results in user frustration and the underutilization of their full potential.

This challenge stems from the lack of a natural language interface that enables intuitive interaction with the smart home system. The integration of Conversational AI introduces seamless voice interactions through natural language interfaces, enhancing communication between users and smart home systems. Advancements in human-building interaction, particularly through AI-powered virtual assistants (Rathika et al., 2024), have paved the way for more intelligent and responsive smart home systems. These virtual assistants leverage advanced NLP algorithms, sentiment analysis, and machine learning to operate in real-time and provide personalized guidance to users. On the other hand, these systems can recommend or intervene in smart home experience through understanding patterns of the users from their actions, emotional states and preferences, all enhancing the cognitive and emotional aspects of smart home experience. A key benefit of using Conversational AI in smart homes is its ability to enable proactive communication strategies aimed at promoting energy conservation behaviors. Research has shown that proactive virtual assistants significantly improve user acceptance of energy-saving recommendations, particularly when supplemented by follow-up interactions (He et al., 2021). This serves as strong evidence of Conversational AI's potential not only to enhance user convenience but also to foster sustainable living practices.

Also, integrating Conversational AI in smart homes come with a number of considerations related to privacy, security and ethical issues. However, as these systems become more fully ingrained in our daily life, there are concerns which need to be addressed such as the preservation of data and user autonomy as well as the edge that AI systems may have to continue these biases or stereotypes (Aslam, 2023) . They will need to develop the right ethical frameworks along with corresponding implementations of privacy safeguards that support safe deployment of Conversational AI in smart homes. Conversational AI's success in smart homes depends on it behaving as close to a human as possible. As pointed out by Chandra et al. (2022), the study of cogni Incorporating these human like qualities to smart homes would be better to create trust and more natural and meaningful interaction between the user and their living space. While command and control will still play a role of conversational AI as we incrementally move towards more advanced smart home technologies the scope of role is likely to extend beyond that. With the development of more advanced learning algorithms, the future systems may become able to predict user's needs, adapt to new preferences and even assist emotions. The struggle for more socially responsive smart home technologies is bringing exciting new things to do and problematical challenges for researchers and developers to solve.

In the next section we will go through current state of smart home technologies and look into some of the specific concepts and usage of Conversational AI in the personalization and adaptability of living environments. In this rapidly evolving field, we attempt to provide a complete understanding of the prospective of the conversational AI in designing smart homes of tomorrow by appraising the latest advancement, challenges and future directions in this area.

2. CURRENT LANDSCAPE OF SMART HOME TECHNOLOGIES

With voice controlled systems becoming a common thing of many homes, smart home technologies have evolved rapidly. Available in artificial intelligence and Internet of Things (IoT) devices, these systems inform users to have the ability to control elements of their own home environment with basic voice commands. The implementation of voice control and AI in IoT smart home systems has made it easier to achieve efficient automated systems that users can operate using mobile or web applications (Torad et al, 2022). For voice controlled home environments, remote controls of residential appliances are usually cloud based. Nevertheless, such systems face difficulties in a non standard voice channel and traffic commands, and delays in response time of the real time services.

Factors like simplicity, security and complexity in integrating multiple underlying technologies are hindering the adoption of smart home technologies including these limitations (Venkatraman et al., 2021). Another main restriction of traditional voice control systems is their vulnerability to various security threats. It has been shown recently that these systems are vulnerable to adversarial attacks, replay attacks, and so forth. For example, Sun et al. (2025) have shown the possibility of tricking voice systems to disobey the user's will, even if the uttered words are not properly interpreted, through the use of universal adversarial commands that are undetectable to human's ear. Thus, it shows the need for strong security controls to the smart home environment to prevent a potential attack. One of the major challenges to the widespread adoption of voice-controlled smart home systems is actualized in the fact that privacy problems are here trying to stand in the way.

The availability of constant voice data presents issues over data integrity and user privacy. To solve these problems, researchers have suggested that solutions could be created using blockchain, and this advanced malicious action detection algorithms. However, despite all these challenges, voice controlled smart home systems are still quite useful in terms of energy efficiency, convenience and security facilitated by remote monitoring and control. These systems are able to integrate natural language processing (NLP) that allow them to understand the user input and categorise it into an operational instruction that can then be executed using devices such as Arduino and Raspberry Pi (Torad et al., 2022). Though, traditional voice control systems usually do not possess the feature of context awareness and user adaptability. Though they can obey orders, they may not comprehend the gist behind what users want or expound upon specific preferences over time. In many cases, this limitation limits the user experience to less personalized and more cumbersome one, that can hardly bring the smart home potential to full fruition.

Researchers are in the process of augmenting the existing voice controlled smart home systems to beef up their capabilities. For example, this paper suggests using millimeter wave (mmWave) radar to rationally collect speech signals as vaginal material lip flux and multiparameter speakers' biometrics for a new methodological theory of speaker verification as a multimodal biometrics to bypass impostor attacks (Dong & Yao, 2020). Machine learning based recommendations of automatic home appliance control are being investigated by others in order to enhance context awareness and user adaptivity. Voce control system is getting more sophisticated and secure as smart home technologies are emerging. In order to address security concerns for resource constrained smart home environments, the development of lightweight and efficient authentication frameworks such as the one proposed in (Alasmary & Tanveer, 2023) is to be made.

3. FOUNDATIONS OF CONVERSATIONAL AI

The components that enable conversational AI in smart homes are a few and all based on natural and efficient human device interaction. These systems foundation is Natural Language Processing (NLP) as they are able to understand and parse human language inputs. Machines cannot comprehend unstructured human language data and so they are converted to structured data using NLP techniques. We will define this process as a sequence of different tasks such as speech recognition, intent classification and entity extraction to properly understand user commands and queries (Chandrakala et al., 2023). Besides machine learning, conversational AI systems utilize ML to serve their abilities. The training of these systems on immense amounts of text are especially suited to Deep Learning (DL) techniques that are similar to human brain like elements that enable open domain conversations (Talreja Wassan & Ghuriani, 2024).

The system learns from user interactions, realizes the context, predict user needs, and provides appropriate responses over time using ML algorithms. Another important part of the conversational AI systems which makes them contextual is the context aware computing. These systems are more accurate and tailored by considering such factors of the user's location, time of day and previous interactions. For instance, a context aware system that runs in a smart home would adapt its recommendations of appliance control with respect to the user's daily routines and preferences (Torad et al., 2022). These components are integrated together to provide the natural and efficient human device interaction in smart homes. With NLP, users can talk to their devices without using complex interfaces or special structure of commands. It therefore makes this interaction more user friendly, less technologically demanding for broader swathes of users. The system becomes more able to understand and thus respond accurately to a user query by machine learning algorithms.

These systems learn continually from their interactions, so that their performance can get better over time, converging to the performance peculiar for each individual user by their speech patterns, preferences, and habits. Finally, this leads to a better user experience because it is more satisfying. Prior to the context awareness computing, context awareness computing further extends the naturalness of the interaction, whereby the system is aware of the broader situation context. To continue with, a smart home system might act on the command 'turn on the lights' differently depending on the time, on place of the user within the house, or the current activity of the user. With such contextual understanding, the interaction is more human-like and less robotic, with a sense of more intelligent and anticipatory responses. This combination of these components facilitates development of sophisticated conversational AI systems capable of taking up various complex tasks and multi turn conversations. Taking an example, in an IoT fog cloud framework NLP methods can be used to convert user's utterances into specific commands applicable to smart home devices (Iliev & Ilieva, 2022). Flexible and scalable voice user interfaces can thus be created which are easy to plug in with existing kinds of automation systems and consumer electronics. In addition, the advanced conversational AI systems can exceed simple command execution. In such a case, they could serve as recommendations of control for automated home appliance based on the learned patterns and user preferences (Torad et al., 2022).

This proactive method gives convenience to users, and it also helps in saving the cost of energy and saving the energy for smart home. And this is demonstrated where the conversational AI technology is evolving, we are starting to see those more and more interactive and dynamic systems. However, the idea of iNLP inspires that language models are iteratively observing, acting, and getting feedback from external entities (Liu et al., 2023). This paradigm shift allows for more sophisticated interactions, including the ability to clarify user intents, ask follow-up questions, and provide more contextually relevant information. Table 1 summarizes the core technologies that underpin Conversational AI systems in smart home environments and explains their specific roles.

Table 1. Key technologies enabling conversational AI in smart homes

Technology	Function	Relevance to Smart Homes
Natural Language Processing	Understands and generates human language	Enables voice-based user interaction with smart home systems
Machine Learning	Learns from user behavior and adapts over time	Powers personalization, predictive assistance, and adaptive response
Context-Aware Computing	Responds to user context (location, time, preferences)	Enhances situational awareness and meaningful responses
Federated Learning	Trains models across distributed devices without centralizing data	Preserves user privacy while enabling model improvements
Emotion Recognition	Detects emotional state through speech or visual cues	Supports emotionally responsive interactions and user satisfaction
Edge Computing	Performs processing locally at the device level	Reduces latency and improves real-time responsiveness

Figure 1 below gives the layered architecture of a smart home system using Conversational AI. The framework starts with User Interface Layer through which users are spoken to, gesture recognised and receive emotional cues. The NLP and Dialogue Management unit process these multimodal inputs and interprets intent, thus generating a response. Personalization Engine is dedicated to specific user preferences and behavioral patterns in order to respond accordingly, while Context-Aware Module always has an eye on environmental data to make contextually relevant actions. The Smart Device Control Layer has multiple devices associated with it that will receive real time control commands from the system and these control commands may include actions such as turning on thermostats, turning on lighting or adjusting the settings of a security system. Such closed loop architecture makes the smart home interactions adaptive, responsive and human centric.

Figure 1. System architecture of a conversational AI-powered smart home showing user interaction, AI processing layers, and device control

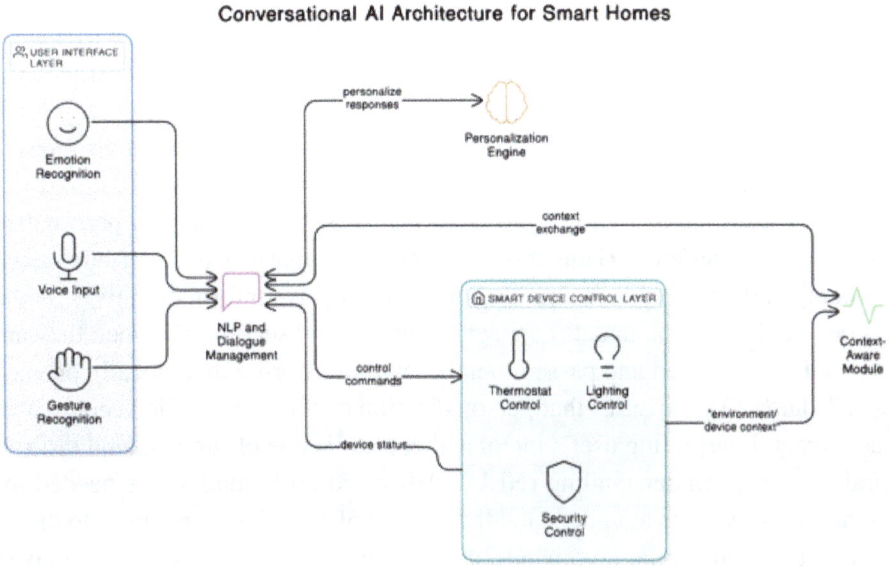

4. PERSONALIZATION IN CONVERSATIONAL AI

Advanced Chat bot techniques for understanding user preferences, detecting routines, proscribing and assisting without prompting. The systems make use of natural language processing (NLP) and machine learning algorithms to understand what the user has said and provide contextually appropriate responses (Mctear, 2020). Personalization of smart home experience is based on user preference learning. Collaborative filtering techniques are utilized by conversational AI systems in analyzing user interactions and deriving patterns in their behavioral patterns. The system can intelligently recommend to the user device settings, automation routines, and energy saving measures by comparing the user's preferences to those of other similar users. As the data used to learn these factors is accumulated and analyzed (Islam et al., 2024), this approach enables continuous improvement on the user experience.

Routine detection is another important addition to making personalized smart home experiences as routine as possible. A virtual assistant or chatbot made with machine-learning algorithms will find out your daily schedules, device usage habit, environmental preferences kind of things which recur frequently. In fact, through being aware of these routines, the system can automate tasks, adjust settings proactively and provide timely suggestions to improve comfort and efficiency (Ramaul et al., 2024). An important component of advanced Conversational AI systems for smart homes is that they are proactive. These predictive/learning systems anticipate the needs of users and present the most likely related information before the user asks. So the system might autonomously adjust the thermostat depending on weather forecasts or advise turning off lights in empty rooms in an attempt to save energy. Such a proactive approach not only makes the user convenience better but it also makes it beneficial in terms of energy efficiency and cost savings (Adeoye et al., 2024).

Federated learning is used in Conversational AI systems to further personalize the smart home experience. Using this approach means that user data is used to teach the system, while privacy is maintained because sensitive information lives on the user's device. In fact, the updates are sent to the central server only when they are aggregated, anonymized and passed to nodes without storing them locally on each device. Aslam (2023) ensures that personalization can be done while keeping user privacy intact. Interpreting user's intent and context is one of fundamental tasks in Natural Language Understanding (NLU). Advanced NLU models are needed for the smart home systems to understand the context of complex commands, to dispel ambiguity between similar commands, and to deliver the right response to a given user emotions and pitch. This capability facilitates more natural and easier interaction between the users and their smart home devices (Talreja Wassan, Ghuriani, 2024). Conversational AI in smart homes is also reinforced with inputs as multimodal, such as voice, text, and visual cues, which further enhances the personalization that it brings upon entering smart homes.

The system, with its multiple sources of data from IoT devices, cameras, or wearables, can combine those sources to have a better insight on the user's context and preferences. As a result, it provides more accurate and relevant answers (Mctear, 2020) for user queries and commands. Conversational AI systems will only become more advanced and more advanced and will adapt to the speech pattern, vocabulary, and style of thinking an individual person has. They go one step further than merely execution of the tasks and move towards a more engaging and human-like interaction. To make the smart home experience more enjoyable and relatable it can be something that learns to use the correct language, humour and even empathy, when it responds to users. Since conversational AI systems in smart homes need to stay on their toes for a continuous improvement and keeping up with changing preferences of users, online learning techniques have been incorporated in these systems to make them more effective. These allow the system to update its models in real-time based on user feedback and interactions, ensuring that the personalization remains relevant and up-to-date (Izadi & Forouzanfar, 2024). Table 2 outlines key personalization techniques used in Conversational AI systems along with their relevance to smart home applications.

Table 2. Personalization techniques in conversational AI

Technique	Description	Application in Smart Homes
Collaborative Filtering	Recommends content based on similar user behavior	Suggests routines, entertainment options, or preferences based on household use
Reinforcement Learning	Learns optimal behavior through reward signals over time	Adapts to feedback from users regarding preferences and actions
Federated Learning	Learns across users/devices while preserving privacy	Builds generalizable user models without compromising sensitive data
Rule-Based User Modeling	Uses predefined rules for triggering actions based on conditions	Turns lights off after inactivity or adjusts temperature based on time

Figure 2 illustrates the dynamic personalization and adaptation flow of a Conversational AI system in a smart home environment. The process begins with data collection, where the system gathers information through user inputs, behavioral patterns, and sensor data. This is followed by the user modeling phase, where algorithms such as collaborative filtering and reinforcement learning are applied to build and continuously update individual user profiles. These profiles enable the system to generate context-aware responses, including appropriate device adjustments and timely user notifications. A feedback loop ensures the system refines its behavior by capturing user interaction and feeding it back into the learning cycle. This closed adaptive loop allows the AI to personalize responses in real-time and evolve according to the household's needs, habits, and environmental context.

Figure 2. Personalization and adaptation flow in smart homes

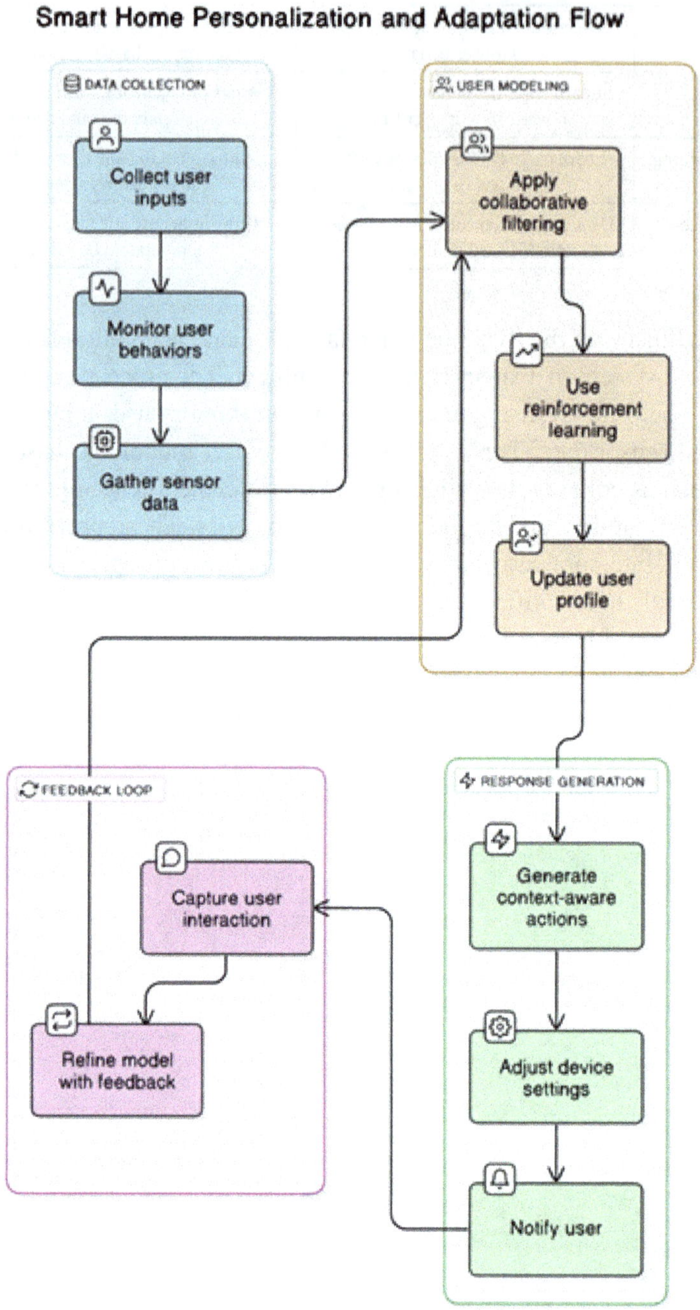

5. ADAPTABILITY IN SMART HOMES

Smart homes have many conversational AI systems which are so adaptable that they constantly change to fit the ever changing needs of the user and the environment. To enable dynamic, context-aware interaction that increases user experience and fosters sustainable living, these systems rely on large language models (LLMs) and sensor technologies. Another one aspect of adaptability is that such systems learn from users' behavior and preferences throughout time. To give just one example, GPT4 runs GreenIFTTT, which allows users to create and control home automation routine for energy optimization, for instance. It adapts based on to household pattern and suggests personalized routines to operate home appliance using it in a more environmentally sustainable way (Giudici et al., 2024). It also has flexibility in multi turn conversation where the AI would be able to enhance its understanding and suggestions with feedback from the user and changes in situation. For example, this is a multi-turn conversation:

User: "I'm feeling a bit warm."

AI: "The current temperature is 76°F. Would you like me to lower it?"

User: "Yes, but I'm also trying to save energy."

AI: "I understand. I can lower the temperature by 2 degrees and activate the ceiling fan in this room. This combination should make you feel cooler while minimizing energy usage. Is that okay?"

User: "That sounds good. Thanks!"

By providing a suggestion that adapts in response to the user's concern for energy conservation, the AI in this interaction provides an example of comfort saved with a stance toward sustainability (Giudici et al., 2024). Conversational AI is also adaptable in the environment shifts in the smart homes. They are able to sense surrounding with raw data from different sensors and comprehend real time physical condition (Kush, 2025). For instance, an outdoor weather change at 10 AM, an indoor air quality reduction at 5 PM, or occupancy patterns at 9 PM would lead itself to change the relevance of its recommendations for a smart home assistant. In this respect, it is more nuanced and relevant interactions (Ramaul et al., 2024). However, conversational AI systems are able to include new devices in routines and conversations as they come online within a smart home ecosystem. A smart home offers this adaptability so that we may maintain our smart home experience as up to date and as comprehensive as possible. For example, if a new smart thermostat was put in, the AI would automatically use it within energy saving routines and in terms of future discussions about temperature control.

Adaptability works very well for task automation too. With the foundation set from the habits of the user, the use of Conversational AI can automatically take over routine tasks. For instance, it may notice that the user usually turns off one can of lights earlier than bed, and in this case, it can help to create an automated 'bed time routine' which takes care of this task (Giudici et al., 2024; Ramaul. et al., 2024). These systems are furthermore highly adaptable because they can reason over structured knowledge representations. Advanced models often work with such multimodal knowledge graphs, to capture different relationships and evidences over diverse modalities. Zero shot reasoning is enabled for words not present in training conversations and provides a natural explainability of the AI's decision-making process (Wu et al., 2023).

With smart home technology quickly becoming a reality, conversational AI is going towards multi-modal interactions. Therefore, it's shifting from combining text with visual and auditory inputs to naturally combining these visual and auditory inputs with text for richer and more natural human AI interactions. For example, smart home assistant utilize visual data from the camera to understand the user's context as well as gestures to improve and adapt their responses (Kush, 2025) . Also note that virtual assistants in smart homes have their proactive capabilities. There are, for example, these systems that can start a conversation from the detected pattern or potential energy conservation opportunity. A recent research found out that proactive communication along with follow up conversation, can definitely increase the chances of user's receptivity towards energy saving recommendations, exhibiting the AI capabilities to change the way of communication for better performance.

6. MULTIMODAL INTERACTIONS

Conversational AI for smart homes has become a great approach to provide great user experience and make interfaces easier. The interaction between smart home systems can be made more natural and responsive by combining voice commands to gesture recognition, sensor data, and emotion recognition. Smart home interfaces can be built on taking a voice command because these devices are under your control and provide hands-free access to information. These systems have advanced speech recognition techniques in conjunction with the natural language processing, which makes them capable of understanding and responding to complex queries or commands (Iliev & Ilieva, 2022). Furthermore, not all interactions are met with voice alone as the best or most suitable approach for all. Multimodal approaches come in and use additional input modalities to make an interface more robust and flexible. Multimodal smart home interfaces came to include gestural interface that has become more and more important.

With the help of computer vision based techniques, hand movements and body postures can be detected as well as interpreted and used to control the devices and navigate the interface by natural gestures (Shao et al., 2024). Gesture recognition on its own isn't useful, because you can't input any commands without voice commands. One example is having voice turn the device on and then gestures to override or instruct the various settings. Further enhancement of multimodal interaction experience can be created with sensor data from different IoT devices in the smart home ecosystem. Such sensors can also provide contextual information of the environment, the location of the user, and patterns of activities (H. Zhang et al., 2024). Smart home systems will have easier time integrating this data with voice and gesture inputs, allowing them to make more informed decisions and give more personalized responses. Suppose a system would rearrange its interpretation of a voice command according to where in the home the user is or the time of day. Another important area of interest for advanced multimodal home interface is emotion recognition. These systems detect the user emotional state through analysis of speech patterns, facial expressions, physiologic signals, and then selectively respond to the message (Chen et al., 2021). With this emotional awareness we are capable to have more empathetic and context appropriate interactions with the system that may enhance user satisfaction and engagement with the system.

Because these different modalities are integrated, the synergistic effect resulting is that the strengths of each input method are used to compensate for the weaknesses of others. As another example in environments where voice recognition may be difficult due to noise, gesture or touch inputs can offer alternative means of input (Zhang et al., 2024). For instance, voice commands would prevail if accuracy of gesture recognition is obstructed by visual obstructions. Other advantages include that multimodal interfaces are extremely useful for accessibility. These systems provide more ways by which the user can input what information s/he wants to use. For example, people with disabilities involving mobility might depend on voice, whereas people with speech problems could easily use gestural controls (Brunete et al., 2021). Since the multimodal interaction systems are getting more and more sophisticated, they are becoming more and more complex to include more advanced techniques from AI to improve the performance as well as adaptability. User behaviour and preference can be recognized using machine learning algorithms thereby helping the system to guess depending on needs and to provide proactive assistance. Another direction to enhance speed and efficiency of multimodal processing is to explore edge computing and neuromorphic systems to achieve more responsive and intelligent interaction (H. Zhang et al 2019).

Novel interface designs are also good possibilities for interfaces for the development of multimodal interaction systems for smart home. Augmented reality (AR) technologies have potentials to be integrated with voice control and gesture control for creating immersive and intuitive interfaces to mesh augmented information with real space (Williams et al. 2020). With these AR enhanced interfaces, it is possible for a user to interact with the virtual representations of smart home devices and controls overlaid on top of their real world surroundings. However, as multimodal systems become more advanced and pronounced in our homes, they bring forth serious ethical issues. Thanks to their ability of these systems to learn, understand and answer to natural language, gestures and emotions, and collect and analyse vast amount of data, there has been a plethora of progress on human computer interaction and emotion recognition technologies.

7. ETHICAL, PRIVACY, AND SECURITY CONSIDERATIONS

Adaptive Conversational AI (CAI) deployed in smart homes brings along with it a set of extremely important ethical, privacy, and data security challenges that need to be carefully conceived. These AI systems are also increasingly embedded in our daily lives, collecting and processing the millions of people's personal data and therefore are causing issues with privacy, data protection (Leschanowsky et al., 2023). The difficulty is in obtaining informed users' consent on the data collection and processing. CAI systems in smart home often record and analyze conversations in a continuous manner, thereby exposing sensitive information to users without their knowledge being full. Due to this, it is necessary to create precise and transparent consent mechanisms for users to understand and control which data should be collected and how the information will be used (Williamson & Prybutok, 2024).

There is a third critical issue in the use context of smart home CAI systems that I call data transparency. It is important for Users to know which data is picked up, how it is processed, and whom it is given to. Having this transparency build trust and allow users to make an informed decision on their privacy is vital (Jeyaraman et al., 2023). However, true transparency is not possible for anything related to AI due to its complexity and massive amounts of data. XAI techniques can provide a means of addressing this challenge by designing explainable AI (Jeyaraman et al., 2023) that makes the decision making process more transparent to the user.

In the case of smart homes, where CAI systems interact very close with users and potentially affect their daily lives, the notion of responsible AI behavior of CAI systems is fundamental. These include the AI system not crossing user boundaries, avoiding such manipulative behavior as possible, and it should have adequate levels of autonomy (Elendu et al., 2023). They have to think about the ethical implications of what the system does, and as well as build in defensive practices to prevent accidental unforeseen outcomes or usage. In this case, ethical guidelines can be incorporated in the decision making of the AI and the system be audited regularly against these guidelines for compliance (Familoni, 2024). Due to the nature of handling sensitive personal information, smart home CAI systems have the data security as paramount concern. To protect user data, it is imperative that encryption techniques are robust and that data storage is secure so that it is protected from unauthorized access or breaches (Williamson & Prybutok, 2024). At the same time, privacy enhancing technologies such as federated learning and homomorphic encryption can be used to maintain data privacy while maintaining the benefits of AI driven insights (Salako et al., 2024). Smart home CAI systems pose with risks that need to be mitigated and that calls for a multi faceted approach. As such, this involves the implementation of various strong cybersecurity measures to address potential attacks or data breaches (Udegbe et al., 2024).

It should be audited and assessed for vulnerabilities in the regular security audit so that these weaknesses can be identified and addressed. In addition to that, one need have development of the incident response protocols to fix any security breach or privacy violation that might arise quickly (Salako et al., 2024). Another key aspect of risk mitigation involves addressing cognitive biases of users when it comes to making decisions related to privacy and security. There are many possible cognitive biases that the users make, which may adversely affect their security or privacy. Debiasing strategies can be used by the users to make better informed and rational decisions regarding their data and privacy settings (Leschanowsky et al., 2023). That could entail offering easy, understandable information of the varying privacy risks and actions, and of interfaces that help users make thoughtful decisions. In the last part, the inclusion of CAI in smart homes is also questioned given its potential to exacerbate the digital divide as much as enhance connective technologies for which it can facilitate access and use. To enable the benefits of smart home CAI systems to be enjoyed by diverse populations, efforts should be made to ensure that these benefits are available to people with varying levels of socioeconomic background, abilities, and technical literacy (Elendu et al., 2023). This may entail refining more inclusive design practices and incorporating the needs of users of different kinds in the course of creation and release of these systems. Table 3 highlights the major challenges and ethical considerations associated with implementing Conversational AI in smart homes.

Table 3. Challenges and ethical considerations in conversational AI for smart homes

Challenge	Description	Implication
Data Privacy	Collection of sensitive, continuous personal data	Risk of surveillance and data misuse
Transparency in Decision-Making	Lack of clarity in how AI models make decisions	Reduces user trust and control
Bias in AI Responses	AI models may inherit biases from training data	Unfair or inappropriate responses in diverse households

continued on following page

Table 3. Continued

Challenge	Description	Implication
Continuous Monitoring	Always-on systems may feel intrusive	User discomfort and ethical concerns
Device Interoperability	Compatibility issues across smart devices and platforms	Limits scalability and seamless experience

Figure 3 presents a layered framework addressing ethical and privacy considerations in Conversational AI for smart homes. The interaction begins when the user initiates communication, followed by a data collection and consent phase. If consent is not granted, the process is halted, ensuring compliance with user autonomy and privacy. If consent is given, data proceeds through edge processing and anonymization, minimizing exposure and enhancing security. The system ensures transparent decision-making, enabling users to understand how decisions are made and actions are taken. At any point, users can access override and control interfaces to intervene, stop, or modify system behavior. If no intervention is required, the interaction continues and completes as intended. This framework reinforces user trust by embedding transparency, control, and data minimization as core components of AI-enabled smart home environments.

Figure 3. Ethical and privacy layers in conversational AI

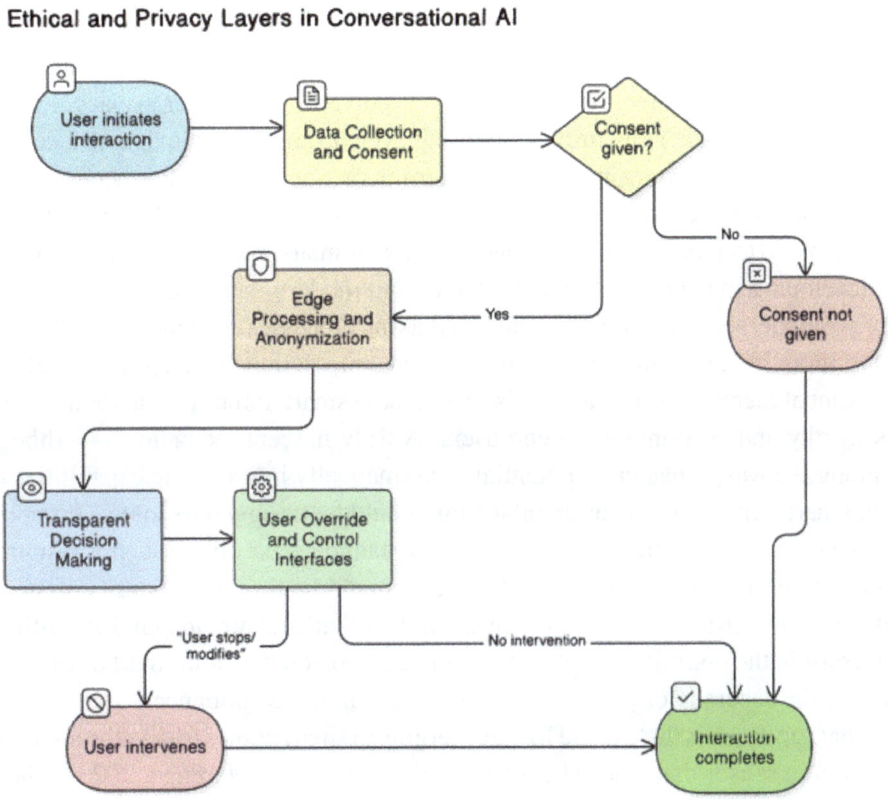

8. FUTURE TRENDS AND TECHNOLOGICAL ADVANCEMENTS

In recent times, conversational AI for smart homes is fast taking shape; some trends and technological advancements are on the verge of changing the way we interact with our dwelling space. The performance and responsiveness of smart home systems are very well enhanced by edge computing. There is a real improvement in the capabilities to make decisions in real time by processing data closer to the source — in the edge. For voice acting devices, the fastest response times are particularly important for an entire seamless user experience. This makes Newell's (2011) notion of edge AI more applicable to smart devices such as the home hubs (Banjanović-Mehmedović & Husaković, 2023). Privacy concerns in smart home environments are starting to see an emergence of one of the key technologies used for the problem — Federated Learning. By contrast, this approach trains the AI models across various decentralized devices yet has the data locally which means that sensitive information stays on the user's device (Prabaharan et al., 2025).

For smart homes, federated learning can help the performance of personalized voice assistants and other AI powered services do not violate user privacy. For instance, a smart speaker can turn the learning cycle from raw audio data to a central server without compromising since the user interactions can teach it better speech recognition (Shahi & Mittal, 2023). Another promising trend will be the integration of explainable AI techniques with federated learning for smart home systems. Researchers are developing the computational geometry and modern database architectures to improve model structure and how decision making processes are undertaken, thereby giving more insights into how AI models make predictions (Enyejo et al., 2024). The point of increased transparency is so that these smart home AI systems are more trustworthy and accountable to end users. A truly nascent technology — though far along the way, it has great potential to dramatically improve the capabilities of AI in smart homes. If a quantum algorithm could be designed to solve a complex optimization problem that a classical system cannot, then out of such a resource would come more efficient resource allocation and better performances of smart home networks (Rane et al., 2024). An example is that quantum inspired algorithms may assist in the optimization of energy consumption on multiple smart devices, or increase the accuracy of predictive maintenance of home appliances.

What happened is that AI and IoT are merging in smart homes to develop anomaly detection in sensor data and AI driven big data analytics (Marengo, 2023). These advancements are important for enhancing the smarts to smart home systems in general, to make them more able to spot and respond to odd sounds or improprieties. Privacy protection is still a principal issue in the smart home environment. As a privacy-preserving data sharing scheme, blockchain technologies are being explored, and the blockchain ZKP technologies, in particular (Alsamhi et al., 2022). They could enable secured sharing, cooperation of smart home devices without threatening user privacy. To tackle the node selection and resource allocation efficient problems of heterogeneous edge computing environments, Modular Multi-Edge Clustered (MMEC) and Edge AI Heterogeneous Federated Learning (MMEC AI HetFL) architectures are being designed (Mughal et al., 2024). Such approaches exploit multicast to maximize global learning tasks with low complexity and thus potentially increase the efficiency of smart home networks by 5 times with respect to existing solutions.

This also addresses the issue of privacy and security in data collection from large scales smart city sensing (Jiang et al., 2020) in smart home. Such capability will enable the smart home devices to participate in the broader urban sensing initiatives to protect the user privacy and thus we end up with a more interconnected and intelligent living environment. We can anticipate more advanced, privacy friendly, and efficient conversational AI for smart homes in the ever evolving technologies. Such advances will not only make the users experience superior but also add to the creation of more fuel saving, viable, and smart living environments.

9. BROADER IMPLICATIONS AND APPLICATIONS

Practically, and more broadly, the adoption of advanced Conversational AI in smart homes has important implications for enabling human aging in place, delivery of products and services that enhance accessibility, and dialysis of energy efficiency. From supporting developers to different generations of users, these AI driven systems are enabling the transformation of how we achieve an interaction with our living space and augmenting the quality of life for everyone. In the cases of aging in place, Conversational AI can bring in enriched support to older adults, helping them live independently and safely in their homes. It can remind of taking the medication, monitor daily activities and even in some cases, detect potential health issues or emergencies (Sajja et al., 2025). In a smart home environment, AI assistants can predict based on the user preferences, habits, and possible incident situations as proposed in the conceptual mathematical model of (Periša et al., 2025), by integrating with different sensors, and devices. With this proactive approach to elder care, much of the well being of older adults can be improved and peace of mind achieved by their families and caregivers. Compared to those living with a disability, conversational AI in smart homes has never been more innovative in adding to accessibility and creating an independent life.

By using AI driven technologies, it can provide personalized and intuitive applications to people with physical, sensory and cognitive impairments. For example, such speech recognition and natural language processing capabilities let the home environment be controlled from the speakers with speech or motor impairments with voice commands. Integrating computer vision technology into smart home systems can offer help for the use by visually impaired users to navigate the surrounding area and detect objects (Eziamaka et al., 2024). These advances improve the quality of life for people with disabilities and encourage them to have a greater involvement in everyday activities and social activities. Another major area of using Conversational AI in a smart home is in energy efficiency. These AI driven energy management systems can enable optimized heating, cooling, lighting and operation of home devices subject to user preferences and patterns (Stecuła et al., 2023). These systems are able to analyze the data from different sensors and integrate with smart grids in such a way to take in order to intelligently reduce energy consumption with respect to comfort levels. For example, AI can change the temperature settings according to the occupancy patterns, automate the window blinds to minimize or reduce the use of electricity, and also manage the charging of electric vehicles to work when electricity prices are low.

Both the opportunities and challenges of human A-I interaction dynamics in smart homes are present. Firstly, the learning and adapting capabilities of Conversational AI permit the design of highly personalized and responsive interfaces with a fluid interaction from the users (Eziamaka et al., 2024). The research on human-like interactional competencies in conversational AI agents (Chandra et al., 2022) show that in this case it can cause an increase in user engagement and satisfaction. It has been found in the study that the cognitive, relational, and emotional competencies of AI agents are helpful for promoting user engagement, and user trust acts as a mediating variable. Also, although the integration of AI in our most private spaces does have its ethical issues. Data privacy, security, and bias in AI algorithm issues have to be carefully addressed so that these technologies yield benefits realisation with protection of user rights and addressing existing inequalities (Singh, 2025) . Furthermore, design of AI system for smart homes should take into consideration intercultural communication aspects, as there are considerable variations in pragmatic norms among linguacultural groups (Brandt & Hazel, 2024). This lends emphasis on the need of what the authors call interculturally adaptive conversational AI to avoid communication effectiveness across diverse user base.

10. CONCLUSION

In this chapter, we have explored the role of Conversational AI in transforming the smart home ecosystems by making them personal, adaptive, and multi modal. Conversational AI makes use of such technologies as NLP, machine learning, as well as context-aware computing in order to achieve a natural intuitive human–device communication. Through the integration of personalization mechanisms these systems can successfully proactively understand users' preferences, habits and routines; and offer a tailored service as well as a save energy balance. Adaptability empowers the systems to change on the fly by accommodating changing behavior of the user, changes in environment, and incorporation of new smart devices. At the same time, the use of multimodal interfaces like voice, gesture and emotion recognition significantly increases the level of natural and accessibility in the user interaction. However, as these systems improve, it is essential to deal with the ethical, privacy, and security issues of collecting and using data all the time and making AI informed decisions. Future edge computing, federated learning as well as explainable AI will lead to the further improved performance while guaranteeing user trust. However, the effort at integrating Conversational AI in smart homes will culminate in the successful integration of Conversational AI in smart homes not only by way of technological progress, but also through ethical deployment, and inclusive design that facilitates quality of life, promotes independent living and intelligent, sustainable environments.

REFERENCES

Adeoye, O., Odeyemi, O., Addy, W., Ofodile, O., Ajayi-Nifise, A., & Okoye, C. (2024). Integrating Artificial Intelligence In Personalized Insurance Products: A Pathway To Enhanced Customer Engagement. *International Journal of Management & Entrepreneurship Research*, *6*(3), 502–511. DOI: 10.51594/ijmer.v6i3.840

Alasmary, H., & Tanveer, M. (2023). ESCI-AKA: Enabling Secure Communication in an IoT-Enabled Smart Home Environment Using Authenticated Key Agreement Framework. *Mathematics*, *11*(16), 3450. DOI: 10.3390/math11163450

Alsamhi, S. H., Afghah, F., Shvetsov, A. V., Almalki, F. A., Song, H., Hawbani, A., & Lee, B. (2022). Drones' Edge Intelligence Over Smart Environments in B5G: Blockchain and Federated Learning Synergy. *IEEE Transactions on Green Communications and Networking*, *6*(1), 295–312. DOI: 10.1109/TGCN.2021.3132561

Aslam, F. (2023). The Impact of Artificial Intelligence on Chatbot Technology: A Study on the Current Advancements and Leading Innovations. *European Journal of Technology*, *7*(3), 62–72. DOI: 10.47672/ejt.1561

Banjanović-Mehmedović, L., & Husaković, A. (2023, October 1). Edge AI: Reshaping the Future of Edge Computing with Artificial Intelligence. DOI: 10.5644/PI2023.209.07

Brandt, A., & Hazel, S. (2024). Towards interculturally adaptive conversational AI. *Applied Linguistics Review*, *16*(2), 775–786. DOI: 10.1515/applirev-2024-0187

Brunete, A., Gambao, E., Cedazo, R., & Hernando, M. (2021). Smart Assistive Architecture for the Integration of IoT Devices, Robotic Systems, and Multimodal Interfaces in Healthcare Environments. *Sensors (Basel)*, *21*(6), 2212. DOI: 10.3390/s21062212 PMID: 33809884

Chandra, S., Shirish, A., & Srivastava, S. C. (2022). To Be or Not to Be …Human? Theorizing the Role of Human-Like Competencies in Conversational Artificial Intelligence Agents. *Journal of Management Information Systems*, *39*(4), 969–1005. DOI: 10.1080/07421222.2022.2127441

Chandrakala, C. B., Bhardwaj, R., & Pujari, C. (2023). An intent recognition pipeline for conversational AI. *International Journal of Information Technology : an Official Journal of Bharati Vidyapeeth's Institute of Computer Applications and Management*, *16*(2), 731–743. DOI: 10.1007/s41870-023-01642-8

Chen, B., Zhang, D., Cao, Q., Lu, G., Zhang, Z., & Hou, M. (2021). Multimodal Emotion Recognition With Temporal and Semantic Consistency. *IEEE/ACM Transactions on Audio, Speech, and Language Processing*, *29*, 3592–3603. DOI: 10.1109/TASLP.2021.3129331

Dong, Y., & Yao, Y.-D. (2020). Secure mmWave-Radar-Based Speaker Verification for IoT Smart Home. *IEEE Internet of Things Journal*, *8*(5), 3500–3511. DOI: 10.1109/JIOT.2020.3023101

Elendu, C., Jingwa, K. A., Elendu, T. C., John Okah, M., Amaechi, D. C., Okoye, O. K., Alimi, H. A., Farah, A. H., & Ladele, J. A. (2023). Ethical implications of AI and robotics in healthcare. *Revista de Medicina (São Paulo)*, *102*(50), e36671. DOI: 10.1097/MD.0000000000036671 PMID: 38115340

Enyejo, L., Ugochukwu, U., & Adewoye, M.Lawrence Anebi EnyejoMichael Babatunde AdewoyeUchenna Nneka Ugochukwu. (2024). Interpreting Federated Learning (FL) Models on Edge Devices by Enhancing Model Explainability with Computational Geometry and Advanced Database Architectures. International Journal of Scientific Research in Computer Science. *Engineering and Information Technology*, *10*(6), 332–354. DOI: 10.32628/CSEIT24106185

Eziamaka, N., Odonkor, T., & Akinsulire, A.Nnaemeka Valentine EziamakaTheodore Narku OdonkorAdetola Adewale Akinsulire. (2024). AI-Driven accessibility: Transformative software solutions for empowering individuals with disabilities. *International Journal of Applied Research in Social Sciences*, *6*(8), 1612–1641. DOI: 10.51594/ijarss.v6i8.1373

Familoni, B. (2024). Ethical frameworks for AI in healthcare entrepreneurship: A theoretical examination of challenges and approaches. International Journal of Frontiers in Biology and Pharmacy Research, 5(1), 057–065. DOI: 10.53294/ijfbpr.2024.5.1.0032

Giudici, M., Padalino, L., Pascu, A. I., Garzotto, F., Paratici, I., & Paolino, G. (2024). Designing Home Automation Routines Using an LLM-Based Chatbot. *Designs*, *8*(3), 43. DOI: 10.3390/designs8030043

He, T., Jazizadeh, F., & Arpan, L. (2021). AI-powered virtual assistants nudging occupants for energy saving: proactive smart speakers for HVAC control. Building Research & Information, ahead-of-print(ahead-of-print), 394–409. DOI: 10.1080/09613218.2021.2012119

Iliev, Y., & Ilieva, G. (2022). A Framework for Smart Home System with Voice Control Using NLP Methods. *Electronics (Basel)*, *12*(1), 116. DOI: 10.3390/electronics12010116

Islam, M. A., Hossen, M. D., Islam, M. T., Fakir, S. I., Siddiky, M. R., & Masud, S. B. (2024). Artificial intelligence in digital marketing automation: Enhancing personalization, predictive analytics, and ethical integration. *Edelweiss Applied Science and Technology*, *8*(6). Advance online publication. DOI: 10.55214/25768484.v8i6.3404

Izadi, S., & Forouzanfar, M. (2024). Error Correction and Adaptation in Conversational AI: A Review of Techniques and Applications in Chatbots. *AI*, *5*(2), 803–841. DOI: 10.3390/ai5020041

Jeyaraman, M., Yadav, S., Balaji, S., & Jeyaraman, N. (2023). Unraveling the Ethical Enigma: Artificial Intelligence in Healthcare. *Cureus*, *15*(8). Advance online publication. DOI: 10.7759/cureus.43262 PMID: 37692617

Jiang, J. C., Kantarci, B., Oktug, S., & Soyata, T. (2020). Federated Learning in Smart City Sensing: Challenges and Opportunities. *Sensors (Basel)*, *20*(21), 6230. DOI: 10.3390/s20216230 PMID: 33142863

Kush, J. C. (2025). Integrating Sensor Technologies with Conversational AI: Enhancing Context-Sensitive Interaction Through Real-Time Data Fusion. *Sensors (Basel)*, *25*(1), 249. DOI: 10.3390/s25010249 PMID: 39797040

Leschanowsky, A., Popp, B., & Peters, N. (2023). Debiasing Strategies for Conversational AI: Improving Privacy and Security Decision-Making. *Digital Society : Ethics, Socio-Legal and Governance of Digital Technology*, *2*(3), 34. Advance online publication. DOI: 10.1007/s44206-023-00062-2

Liu, R., Zhou, W., Liu, Q., Lin, C., Xu, K., Guo, Y., Liu, D., Zhang, G., Shi, N., Fu, J., Wang, Z., Yang, K., Chen, X., Nik, A., Wang, S., Chen, W., Hao, S., Sim, M., Xiong, G. Y., . . . Yang, Z. (2023). Interactive Natural Language Processing. cornell university. https://doi.org//arxiv.2305.13246DOI: 10.48550

Marengo, A. (2023). The Future of AI in IoT: Emerging Trends in Intelligent Data Analysis and Privacy Protection. mdpi ag. DOI: 10.20944/preprints202312.2184.v1

Mctear, M. (2020). Conversational AI: Dialogue Systems, Conversational Agents, and Chatbots. *Synthesis Lectures on Human Language Technologies*, *13*(3), 1–251. DOI: 10.1007/978-3-031-02176-3

Mughal, F. R., He, J., Das, B., Dharejo, F. A., Zhu, N., Khan, S. B., & Alzahrani, S. (2024). Adaptive federated learning for resource-constrained IoT devices through edge intelligence and multi-edge clustering. *Scientific Reports*, *14*(1), 28746. Advance online publication. DOI: 10.1038/s41598-024-78239-z PMID: 39567565

Periša, M., Teskera, P., Cvitić, I., & Grgurević, I. (2025). Empowering People with Disabilities in Smart Homes Using Predictive Informing. *Sensors (Basel)*, *25*(1), 284. DOI: 10.3390/s25010284 PMID: 39797073

Prabaharan, G., Vidhya, S., Chithrakumar, T., Sika, K., & Balakrishnan, M., M. B. (. (2025). AI-Driven Computational Frameworks: Advancing Edge Intelligence and Smart Systems. *International Journal of Computational and Experimental Science and Engineering*, *11*(1). Advance online publication. DOI: 10.22399/ijcesen.1165

Ramaul, L., Ritala, P., & Ruokonen, M. (2024). Creational and conversational AI affordances: How the new breed of chatbots is revolutionizing knowledge industries. *Business Horizons*, *67*(5), 615–627. DOI: 10.1016/j.bushor.2024.05.006

Rane, J., Rane, N. L., Kaya, Ö., & Mallick, S. K. (2024). Artificial intelligence, machine learning, and deep learning in cloud, edge, and quantum computing: A review of trends, challenges, and future directions. deep science. DOI: 10.70593/978-81-981271-0-5_1

Rathika, P., Parthipan, V., Anju, P., Ponni, P., & Yamunadevi, S. (2024). Developing an AI-Powered Interactive Virtual Tutor for Enhanced Learning Experiences. *International Journal of Computational and Experimental Science and Engineering*, *10*(4). Advance online publication. DOI: 10.22399/ijcesen.782

Sajja, R., Demir, I., & Sermet, Y. (2025). End-to-End Deployment of the Educational AI Hub for Personalized Learning and Engagement: A Case Study on Environmental Science Education. california digital library. DOI: 10.31223/X5XM7N

Salako, A. O., Dapo-Oyewole, D. L., Olaniyi, O. O., Aideyan, N. T., Fabuyi, J. A., & Selesi-Aina, O. (2024). Advancing Information Governance in AI-Driven Cloud Ecosystem: Strategies for Enhancing Data Security and Meeting Regulatory Compliance. *Asian Journal of Research in Computer Science*, *17*(12), 66–88. DOI: 10.9734/ajrcos/2024/v17i12530

Shahi, A., & Mittal, A. (2023). The Impact of Federated Learning on AI-Enhanced Healthcare Delivery (pp. 57–66). igi global. DOI: 10.4018/979-8-3693-2639-8.ch005

Shao, F., Zhang, T., Gao, S., Sun, Q., & Yang, L. (2024). Computer Vision-Driven Gesture Recognition: Toward Natural and Intuitive Human-Computer. /arxiv.2412. 18321DOI: 10.1109/EIECC64539.2024.10929472

Singh, V. (2025). AI-Powered Assistive Technologies for People with Disabilities: Developing AI Solutions that Aid Individuals with Various Disabilities in Daily Tasks. *Journal of Engineering Research and Reports*, *27*(2), 292–309. DOI: 10.9734/jerr/2025/v27i21410

Stecuła, K., Wolniak, R., & Grebski, W. W. (2023). AI-Driven Urban Energy Solutions—From Individuals to Society: A Review. *Energies, 16*(24), 7988. DOI: 10.3390/en16247988

Sun, H., Hou, J., Li, X., Du, H., Zhang, L., & Yu, X. (2025). IUAC: Inaudible Universal Adversarial Attacks Against Smart Speakers. *ACM Transactions on Sensor Networks, 21*(1), 1–20. DOI: 10.1145/3698238

Talreja Wassan, J., & Ghuriani, V. (2024). Perspective Chapter: Recent Trends in Deep Learning for Conversational AI. intechopen. DOI: 10.5772/intechopen.113250

Torad, M. A., Bouallegue, B., & Ahmed, A. M. (2022). A voice controlled smart home automation system using artificial intelligent and internet of things. *Telkomnika, 20*(4), 808. DOI: 10.12928/telkomnika.v20i4.23763

Udegbe, F., Ebulue, O., Ekesiobi, C., & Ebulue, C.Francisca Chibugo UdegbeOgochukwu Roseline EbulueCharles Chukwudalu EbulueChukwunonso Sylvester Ekesiobi. (2024). THE ROLE OF ARTIFICIAL INTELLIGENCE IN HEALTHCARE: A SYSTEMATIC REVIEW OF APPLICATIONS AND CHALLENGES. *International Medical Science Research Journal, 4*(4), 500–508. DOI: 10.51594/imsrj.v4i4.1052

Venkatraman, S., Overmars, A., & Thong, M. (2021). Smart Home Automation—Use Cases of a Secure and Integrated Voice-Control System. *Systems, 9*(4), 77. DOI: 10.3390/systems9040077

Williams, A. S., Ortega, F., & Garcia, J. (2020). Understanding Multimodal User Gesture and Speech Behavior for Object Manipulation in Augmented Reality Using Elicitation. *IEEE Transactions on Visualization and Computer Graphics, 26*(12), 3479–3489. DOI: 10.1109/TVCG.2020.3023566 PMID: 32941142

Williamson, S. M., & Prybutok, V. (2024). Balancing Privacy and Progress: A Review of Privacy Challenges, Systemic Oversight, and Patient Perceptions in AI-Driven Healthcare. *Applied Sciences (Basel, Switzerland), 14*(2), 675. DOI: 10.3390/app14020675

Wu, Y., Zhao, G., Qian, X., Chua, T.-S., Liao, L., Lei, W., & Zhang, G. (2023). State Graph Reasoning for Multimodal Conversational Recommendation. *IEEE Transactions on Multimedia, 25*, 3113–3124. DOI: 10.1109/TMM.2022.3155900

Zhang, H., Del Hougne, P., Zhao, H., Cui, T. J., Wang, Z., Li, L., Hu, S., & Ruan, H. (2024). Microwave Speech Recognizer Empowered by a Programmable Metasurface. *Advanced Science (Weinheim, Baden-Württemberg, Germany), 11*(17), 2309826. Advance online publication. DOI: 10.1002/advs.202309826 PMID: 38380552

Zhang, Z., Lee, C., & Wang, L. (2023). Recent Advances in Artificial Intelligence Sensors. *Advanced Sensor Research*, *2*(8), 2200072. Advance online publication. DOI: 10.1002/adsr.202200072

Chapter 8
Retail and Ecommerce-Voice Enabled Shopping Experience and Personalized Recommendations

Lingaraj Kalgudi
http://orcid.org/0000-0001-8714-2084
RYMEC, India

S. Supreeth
Reva University, India

Rashmi Laxmikant M.
http://orcid.org/0000-0002-7114-2386
Manipal Institute of Technology, Manipal Academy of Higher Education, India

Karthik Rao M. C.
http://orcid.org/0000-0002-3082-9309
Manipal Institute of Technology, Manipal Academy of Higher Education, India

Lalit Garg
http://orcid.org/0000-0002-3868-0481
University of Malta, Malta

ABSTRACT

The integration of conversational AI and voice-enabled technologies within the retail and e-commerce sectors fundamentally transforms consumer interactions and

DOI: 10.4018/979-8-3373-3361-8.ch008

purchasing behaviors. This chapter examines how voice-driven interfaces facilitate seamless and personalized shopping experiences that correspond to the evolving expectations of contemporary consumers. By harnessing advancements in NLP and data analytics, voice assistants can now comprehend user intent, interpret contexts, and offer product recommendations tailored to individual preferences. This chapter delves into the architecture of voice-enabled retail systems, the journey of a voice shopper, and the various personalization techniques employed to enhance customer engagement and satisfaction. Furthermore, this chapter addresses the challenges related to speech recognition accuracy and integration with existing retail systems. It also highlights future trends, including emotion-aware AI and integration with immersive technologies, such as AR/VR.

1. INTRODUCTION

The evolution of retail and e-commerce has been deeply linked to technological advances. Each successive technology has shifted the mechanisms by which consumers find, assess, and buy products, starting with the emergence of online shopping in the 1990s and moving into the advent of m-commerce in the second decade of the twenty-first century. Recently, the next wave of potentially disruptive technology in the retail customer experience and interaction has been identified in the form of Conversational AI and voice-enabled technologies (Ding et al., 2024). Voice-based systems are emerging as the interface of the future, as online shoppers request quicker, hands-free, and more intuitive shopping methods.

Voice technology is based on spoken language and operates without keyboards or touch screens. Voice assistants can pick up increasingly complex command sets; they are empowered by Natural Language Processing (NLP), speech recognition, and machine learning algorithms that allow them to understand the context of a user's query and respond accordingly. When incorporated into online shopping services, users can ask for product information and suggestions, search for products, track orders, compare products and prices, and make a purchase using normal spoken language (Shao et al., 2024). The other side of the spectrum encompasses voice commerce, which is advancing from niche to need, from things like smart speakers, such as Amazon Echo and Google Nest, to voice assistants on mobile phones, such as Siri and Google Assistant.

Another intriguing possibility regarding voice and retail is the ability of voice to provide personalized shopping. Unlike traditional search engines or static web pages, conversational AI systems have a memory of user preferences, the ability to deduce behavioral patterns, and the ability to provide real-time, context-aware recommendations. These features are exactly what contemporary customers want:

customized experiences that are time and effort savers. For example, the same voice assistant could locate a dress on the shopper's size and favorite color, recommend related accessories, provide a coupon code, or alert the shopper that she had previously purchased this item (Chang et al., 2025). This type of smart consumer experience is operationally easy and cost-effective for inshoppers, but can now be scaled by platforms based on AI.

Voice commerce is not only for digital natives or techno-geeks. Voice integration is incorporated into the shopping experience in a variety of stores, including grocery, fashion, electronics, and home goods, to interact with and guide customers. Even brick-and-mortar centered brands are starting to bring voice interfaces into stores, including kiosks and smart mirrors, to bridge online convenience with physical presence (Hou, 2025). Voice-commerce too will be unprecedented in serving the "unconnected," such as the elderly or the blind, for whom voice is a more natural and more accessible interface than screens or typing text.

Commercially, there are numerous uses and boons for retail voice-activated systems. They can manage mundane service transactions with customers, decreasing the need for human service agents while enabling 24 hour service. They are data-intensive in terms of conversations and what they reveal in terms of customer preference, pain points, and decision making. These data can be harnessed to retrieve better inventories, personalize marketing campaigns, and even forecast the future (Azadinejad et al., 2025). In addition, because these technologies engage the customer in a more dynamic back-and-forth dialogue, AI assistants create unique opportunities for effective up-selling and cross-selling, as AI can draw consumers' attention to products that are complimentary based on current dialogue and in the surrounding context.

Despite these potential benefits, several obstacles hinder retailers' adoption of voice technology. A significant technical challenge involves achieving a high accuracy in speech recognition across diverse accents, dialects, and languages. In the context of the increasing prevalence of always-listening devices, a necessary feature for responding to voice commands, one of the most pressing concerns is ensuring privacy and security, as digital assistants become more personalized and context-aware. Furthermore, the user experience and interfaces of voice interactions must be intuitive, responsive, and emotionally intelligent, representing a new paradigm distinct from graphical user interfaces (GUIs) (Deliu & Olariu, 2024). Retailers must also carefully balance proactive assistance to avoid intrusive interference and maintain user trust and engagement.

But, the application of voice technologies within the retail environment also poses a series of complicated challenges. Among others, there is the technical difficulty of having a high precision of speech recognition for any accent or dialect, or language. Privacy and data security is also a serious concern and as always- listening devices move towards individualization and context- awareness, the issue of the proper data security becomes more relevant. Also, to design voice experiences that are intuitive, responsive, and emotionally intelligent, requires a UX and interface design that looks nothing like the kind of design we see in graphical user interfaces today. Retailers will also need to understand how to balance being helpful vs. being an annoyance, in order to avoid put the user off and dissuade them from participating.

But, this is changing rapidly as it is being tackled. Advances in deep learning, natural language processing, and edge AI are increasing the accuracy and responsiveness of voice systems. More privacy-friendly forms of personalization like federated learning and on-device processing are under development. Multimodal interfaces – such as the blend between voice user interfaces and some visualization/ haptic feedback – are beginning to make online shopping feels more intuitive and interactive. At the same time, new products and platforms are allowing developers and merchants to more easily create, deploy and improve conversational AI systems that cater to individual customer journeys.

The future of retail seems to be voice-first without being voice-only. Voice will join, mix and blend with other modalities: touch, type, gesture, vision, and others in order to provide unified and seamless user experiences in evironments and platforms (Mahmoudi et al., 2025). This might involve a user browsing for a product through voice on a smart speaker, having visual options pushed to their smart phone, and concluding the transaction on a wearable device, with a cohesive experience centering on an omnipresent conversational agent that facilitates dialogue throughout the entire interaction. Such cross-device, omnichannel consistency is one of the fundamental promises of conversational AI for retail.

Second, the commercial uses of voice and AI surpass the experience created by this technology for individual users. Within the business-to-business (B2B) world, procurement departments are already ordering supplies, verifying suppliers, and running reports via hands-free, instantaneous voice-activated systems. Voice-activated technologies allow store associates to access a description of the product or ascertain whether it is available in a store without having to physically move away from the shopper. Warehouse workers use voice recognition tools for processing and transferring goods. These are enterprise tools that streamline productivity, decrease training time, and boost capabilities for the full retail value chain (Yang et al., 2025).

As voice shopping grows, a host of new ethical and regulatory problems emerges. These include Transparency in AI recommendations, user control over personal data, and the prohibition of using algorithms to prejudice shopping behavior that stereotypes, creates differentials, or has unfair impacts. Meanwhile, some industries and government bodies have started to establish regulations for ethical AI use, and consumers are becoming more aware of the stakes accompanying voice data collection (Kim et al., 2025). However, trust building and trust maintenance will be just as important for retailers as providing a great user experience.

The set of technologies, from voice recognition to personalization engines, that must work together to support the development of adaptive smart shopping interfaces, such as voice-enabled commerce solutions, is the focus of this chapter. What conversational AI can do for all retailers and how big brands use it will be examined. Limitations and challenges are also summarized in this chapter, along with suggestions on how to overcome them (Demyen, 2024). Finally, we present some future trends and advances that will continue to foster voice in retail, such as AI avatars and voice biometrics, and shopping in the metaverse. Rather, in the context of the fast-changing interfaces they constitute, we can say, for example, that voice is not an interface at all; it is an interaction paradigm. This implies efficiency, speed, and personalized service for consumers. For the seller, this means efficiency, knowledge, and links. Both of these aspects present signs of where commerce seems to be heading: a new, more human, intelligent, and conversational space, where chatting with a store is just as efficient and natural as chatting with a friend.

2. THE EVOLUTION OF VOICE TECHNOLOGY IN RETAIL

Retail voice technology is a disrupter in the commerce industry and promises to change the way that businesses engage with consumers and how consumers discover, access and purchase products. Voice technology has evolved from early command-based systems to the more recent advanced AI-driven voice assistants that increasingly help personalized, frictionless, immersive shopping experiences (Bai et al., 2025). This section offers a brief history of the development of voice technology timeline-wise within retail, detailing primary shifts in technology, consumer behavior, and the growing importance of voice within e-commerce and omnichannel retail.

2.1 Early Developments: Command-Based Interfaces

Voice tech innovation began with rudimentary command-based systems that could understand and provide answers to particular queries. The early iterations of such systems consisted of rule-based, keyword matching, and small vocabulary databases. Despite the novelty of this approach, his scripts were neither natural nor conversational. The main use of these systems applies to minimal tasks to automate customer services, including applications such as querying a store for its hours of service or checking very basic shipping information by calling a phone number. The domain was limited, exchanges scripted, and the technology was plagued by sensitivity to accent variation, background noise, and disambiguation of intent (Rabbi et al., 2025). Despite these limitations, the initial experiments paved the way for attempts to incorporate voice into business services, such as customer service or informational kiosks. Retailers started to recognize the potential of voice in the meantime, but as a technology, large-scale deployment in consumer-facing retail was still immature.

2.2 The Rise of Digital Assistants

The development of voice technology took a significant turn with the advent of digital personal assistants such as Apple's Siri in 2011, Google Now, Amazon Alexa, and Microsoft Cortana. They enabled more natural dialogue between systems and consumers because of improvements in speech recognition, natural language processing (NLP), and cloud computing. Unlike their predecessors, these, 'assistants' could be asked more complicated questions, keep track of the conversation and integrate with other third party services and apps. Alexa was specifically the driving force of voice technology, as it emerged into the mainstream within the retail environment (Pei & Su, 2025). In 2014, the Amazon Echo smart speaker came to the market, and consumers could shop from Amazon's extensive marketplace simply by issuing voice commands. Initially, activities such as reorganizing products at home, asking for price information, or placing products in the cart could be performed in a non-manual, speech-like manner. This was the advent of what is now known as 'voice commerce, which is e-commerce howebutlusively centered on voice-activated transactions. These smart assistants have revolutionized home automation and have become new forms of retail engagement. Voice as a practical surface for everyday activities promoted adoption and consumer demand for voice-activated capabilities on all platforms and devices began to increase.

2.3 Voice Commerce Takes Center Stage

It was not until 2016 that voice commerce began to be held. Retail and e-commerce apps and website-based voice interfaces soon followed, providing users with the capability to voice search, voice comparison shopping, and voice buy products. Voice-based chatbots were also adopted as resources to enhance customer service and reduce time to respond during periods of high shopping. The major technological development during this period was the combination of voice and collaborative filtering engines. Voice assistants also became customized to individual consumers after retailers implemented the technologies behind AI and machine learning to monitor user habits, data, and purchase information (Marvi et al., 2024). For instance, it may recommend grocery items purchased weekly or a fashion item that matches the user's size, style, and previous likes. Retailers tested voice-activated rewards and deals as well as personalized discounts and voice-activated promotions. These efforts showed that technology such as voice could not only enhance the transaction but also customer engagement and create a brand advantage for the company.

2.4 Multichannel and In-Store Integration

As consumers desired more consistent cross-device and cross-channel experiences, voice technology began to be integrated into physical stores by retailers. Digital assistants and voice-activated kiosks became a type of in-store attendant who could help a customer navigate a store, find a product, or learn about a product without requiring the help of a live salesperson. Simultaneously, shopping applications on cell phones offer voice for type-free searches. This not only made it more accessible to all, but undoubtedly had a huge impact on user experience among the visually impaired or elderly users (Lin et al., 2025). Retailers also introduced voice into IoT devices, such as smart mirrors in dressing rooms and smart shelves that would assist in inventory management, further merging the physical and digital shopping experience.

2.5 Post-Pandemic Acceleration

Digital transformation in the retail space is already underway before 2021, with retail undergoing a significant shift in response to the challenges introduced by the COVID-19 pandemic in 2020. With the implementation of lockdown measures and social distancing, digital commerce had higher adoption rates. Voice became more relevant for this reason because it represented a touchless, safe, and hygenic solution over traditional interfaces. Retailers also began adding features to the voice service channel, such as voice-activated conversational AI for purchasing and tracking orders, as well as using voice assistance for other purposes (Murzin, 2024). The rise of smart speakers during this period also continued to inoculate voice interactions into individuals' everyday routines. Voice shopping also grew to include new categories, such as grocery, healthcare products, home essentials, and subscription-based services. These voice assistants are able to learn of multiple voices, remember context, and be more conversational or "human-like" in dealing with situations, which allows them to be more personalized and smarter.

2.6 The Era of Hyper-Personalization and Emotion-Aware Voice AI

Recently, voice technology in the retail sector has reached a new form of hyper-personalization. These interfaces can not only interpret the user's speech but also its tone. These systems include emotion-aware AI and sentiment analysis tools that can recognize tone, mood, and even urgency by modifying responses appropriately. For instance, if a user has an irritated vocal tone, the voice assistant can be influenced by seeking fast solutions and using an empathic attitude (Ariya et al., 2024). Combinations of voice AI, data analytics, and customer planning lead to interactive, predictive, and proactive solutions. Retailers can make recommendations based on the time of day, past behaviors, current location, weather patterns, and even the emotional state of the user. This personalization ultimately leads to increased customer satisfaction, loyalty, and sales conversions. In addition, the combination of voice with augmented reality (AR), virtual reality (VR), and wearables enables immersive voice-enabled shopping. For example, within VR, people can use their voice to wander the aisles of a virtual store or seek assistance from an online shopping associate.

2.7 Looking Ahead

Voice technology in retail is not a "nice to have, " but a necessary component of customer experience strategies. As these voice assistants become more human, more context-aware, and understand emotions, they permeate each stage of the customer journey, from discovery and decision-making to purchase and post-sale customer service. Thus, voice is part and parcel of the retailer's omni-channel plans, and they must now prepare to offer integrated, accessible, and customized experiences across all channels. Voice technology continues to evolve, and its future will certainly include the increased integration of artificial general intelligence (AGI), full multilingual capabilities, continuity across devices, and more user agency.

3. ARCHITECTURE OF VOICE-ENABLED RETAIL SYSTEMS

Voice commerce platforms represent the conjunction of a variety of technologies in artificial intelligence, natural language processing (NLP), recommendation systems, and omni-channel retail platforms to deliver intuitive, easy, and informed purchasing experiences. Central to these architectures is a modular, layered structure that is useful for voice input, query processing, data retrieval, and contextual personalized responses. The description of voice-enabled retail systems divides these platforms into layers, details their primary components, and explains the relevant models.

3.1 Overview of System Architecture

The voice-enabled retail system has a high-level architecture composed of six layers, as shown in figure 1. It is divided into a user interaction layer, voice recognition and natural language understanding layer, intent processing and dialogue management layer, retail intelligence and recommendation engine, backend services and product database, and feedback and learning loops (Jung et al., 2025). Each layer contains interlocking and intercommunicating functionalities through APIs and cloud services, which enable real-time processing and delivery.

User Interaction Layer: This is the front end layer where the user interacts via voice-enabled applications using smart speakers, mobile apps, in store kiosks etc. This comprises:

- Microphones and smart speakers for voice capture by the user
- Graphical User Interface (GUI) (optional) for multimodal interaction
- Voice module that detects the wake-word to begin processing of the voice command (e.g., “Hey Alexa”)

There is no computationally intensive processing taking place here, but the input data will condition to a large extent the performances of the subsequent modules.

Figure 1. The architecture of voice-enabled retail system

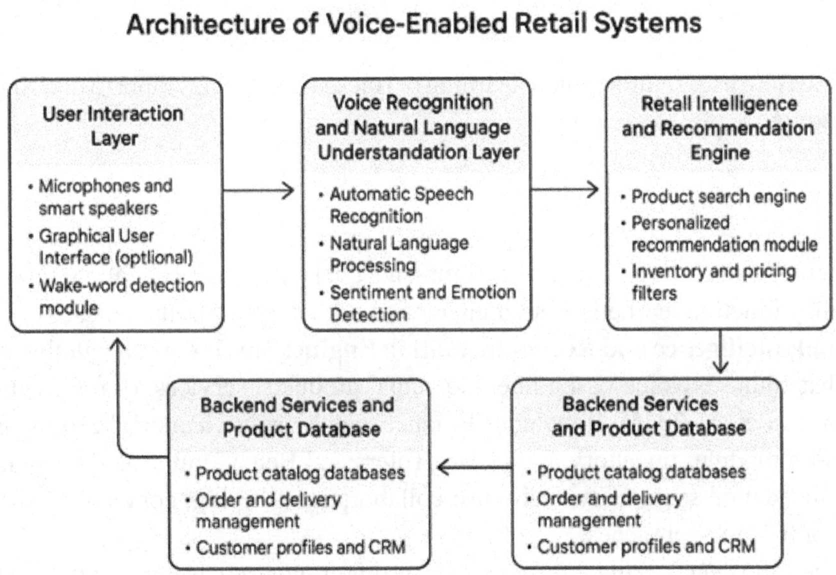

Voice Recognition and Natural Language Understanding (NLU) Layer: This layer is responsible for converting the raw voice signal into text and extracting intent, entities, and contextual meaning. It consists of:

- Automatic Speech Recognition (ASR) engine
- Natural Language Processing (NLP) modules
- Named Entity Recognition (NER)
- Sentiment and Emotion Detection (optional)

Let V(t) represent the voice signal over time t. ASR converts this signal into text T using acoustic and language models:

Where $P(T'|V(t))$ is probability of a text string T′ given the voice signal V(t). NLU then processes this text to extract the intent I and entities E={e1,e2,...,en}:

$$(I,E) = NLU(T)$$

Intent Processing and Dialogue Management Layer: Once the intent and entities are identified, the system needs to decide what action to take and how to respond to the user. This involves Dialogue policy learning, State tracking, Context management and Action prediction.

Let the dialogue state at time t be S_t, composed of prior intents, user profile, and history:

$$S_t = f(S_{t-1}, I_t, E_t)$$

The system uses reinforcement learning or rule-based policies π\piπ to determine the action A_t:

$$A_t = \pi(S_t)$$

Where At is action (e.g., search, recommend, query database, ask follow-up) and π is policy function learned through interaction with users or trained data.

Retail Intelligence and Recommendation Engine: This is the core intelligence layer that connects voice-based intent to actual products, services, or information (Al Nabhani et al., 2025). It includes Product search engine, Personalized recommendation module, Inventory and pricing filters and Behavioral analytics engine. Recommendation systems typically use collaborative filtering, content-based filtering, or hybrid approaches.

Content-Based Filtering: Each product p is represented as a feature vector x_p, and the user profile is also represented as a vector u. The relevance score $r_{u,p}$ is computed as:

$$r_{u,p} = u \cdot x_p = \sum_{i=0}^{n} u_i x_{p,i}$$

Where u_i is user's preference for feature I and $x_{p,i}$ is presence/importance of feature i in product p.

Collaborative Filtering: Based on the ratings or interactions matrix R, where Ru,p is the rating by user u for product p, the predicted rating is:

$$R_{u,p} = \mu + b_u + b_p + q_p^T p_u$$

Where μ is global average rating, b_u, b_p is bias terms for user and product, q_p, p_u is latent vectors for product and user and the system recommends products with the highest Ru,p values.

Backend Services and Product Database: This layer handles integration with Product catalog databases Inventory systems, Order and delivery management, Payment gateways and Customer profiles and CRM. When a user says "Buy the latest Samsung Galaxy," the system will map the product name using entity matching, Checks availability and pricing, confirms user details and payment, Triggers a transaction workflow. Product matching is often supported by cosine similarity in vector space models:

Feedback and Learning Loop: The final layer incorporates user feedback to continuously improve recommendations and voice interactions. It collects Explicit feedback (Ratings, reviews, thumbs up/down) and Implicit feedback (Clicks, dwell time, repeat purchases). The system uses these to update user profiles and retrain models. A user profile vector ut can be updated using:

$$u_{t+1} = u_t + \eta \cdot \left(x_p - u_t\right)$$

Where η is learning rate and x_p is vector of a positively interacted product. Over time, this adaptation ensures that the voice assistant becomes more aligned with the user's evolving preferences.

Security, Privacy, and Governance: Given the sensitive nature of voice and purchase data, the architecture must include Authentication modules (Voice biometrics or token-based security), Data encryption (Both in-transit (TLS) and at rest (AES)), Consent management (User permissions and privacy controls) and Auditing and logging (For compliance and trust). Privacy-preserving personalization can also be achieved using federated learning, where user data remains on-device, and only model updates are shared (Bottrighi et al., 2025).

4. VOICE SHOPPING EXPERIENCE

The voice-shopping experience is changing the way in which people engage in e-commerce. Voice-based commerce has become an intuitive, hands-free, and personalized e-commerce experience largely associated with the increased use of devices such as Amazon Alexa, Google Assistant, and Apple's Siri. In the following paragraphs, I delve deeper into the voice shopping process but also discuss the psychological and technological factors of interactive processes and user engagement, and both the benefits and limitations of voice-directed commerce, as well as how businesses can maneuver those features to provide customers with the right experience, leading to greater satisfaction and conversion.

4.1 Redefining Convenience

Convenience is one of the most salient characteristics of voice-shopping. In traditional e-commerce, users must type their queries, scrolls, and visually compare products. Voice shopping narrows the process of gathering information into a more natural form of conversation. So, for example, the user can just say "Order my usual brand of coffee," and the assistant interprets, remembers any previous preferences, searches the database, and processes the order in seconds (Duggan et al., 2025). This convenience is greater in multitasking situations. This means that soccer mom shopping for groceries, a car commuter, or a parent or grandparent who does not understand smartphones can easily interface with digital commerce. Thus, voice shopping also adds trust, decreasing the necessity of screens, keyboards, and even visual cognition.

4.2 The Voice Shopping Journey

The voice shopping experience is composed of several sequential and interdependent stages:

- Wake Word Activation: The user begins with a trigger command such as "Hey Alexa" or "OK Google."
- User Intent Expression: The consumer expresses a need or query, such as "Find a red dress for a party" or "What's the best deal on running shoes?"
- Intent Recognition and Entity Extraction: The system deciphers the request, identifies key parameters (product, color, price range), and understands the goal.
- Search and Recommendation: Based on user preferences, history, and inventory data, the system fetches and filters suitable options.

- Interaction and Confirmation: The assistant engages in a dialogue—asking follow-up questions, presenting choices, or confirming orders.
- Transaction Completion: The order is placed through integrated payment systems, and the user receives confirmation.
- Post-Purchase Support: Users can track orders, return products, or leave feedback—all via voice.

Natural Language Processing, machine learning, combined with retail domain expertise is leveraged in every one of these stages to make the conversation as natural, human-like and successful as possible.

4.3 Role of Personalization

A personalized experience is an important step in augmenting the voice-shopping experience. Voice assistants have the ability to consider shopping history, preferences, location, time of day, and emotional tone to customize recommendations and responses. With an example, if they are pet owners and they usually order pet supplies during the weekends the system may tell them "why don't you pre-order dog's food on Saturday mornings?" For instance, if a user has a history of eco-friendly brand preferences, the assistant tends to bring those brands to the top of the list for repeated searches. Machine-learning algorithms represent this behavior over time (Glogar et al., 2025). Relevance-ordered recommendations are provided by calculating the cosine similarity between the account user profile vector u, which is maintained and updated over interactions, and product vectors x_p. This is done by increasing the chances of conversion and of a more satisfied customer.

4.4 Multimodal Integration

While voice may be the most common, many retailers use multimodal integration: voice along with a visual interface via smart displays or smartphones. On the right-hand side of the screen, other images and features can be pulled up, or the user can simply visually confirm what voice has already begun to describe or provide. Such as "Show me Bluetooth speakers under $100" and the assistant will display a curated list on a paired screen. The user can then say "Tell me more about the second one" and obtain a voice summary of the report. Visual data and voice representations are combined in this interplay of modalities.

4.5 Psychological Impact and User Behavior

Voice shopping leverages several psychological principles that make it appealing:

- Cognitive ease: Speaking is faster and cognitively lighter than typing and reading.
- Emotional connection: Voice interactions feel more personal and human, fostering trust.
- Reduced choice overload: Instead of overwhelming users with hundreds of options, voice assistants offer a curated set, simplifying decision-making.
- Routine reinforcement: Voice shopping supports habitual behaviors, like repeating previous orders, creating a reliable shopping routine.

On the other hand, trust issues may also arise in voice-based-shopping and in more complex or costly transactions. It can be a deterrent for users looking to purchase high-dollar value products or products that vary by appearance (for instance, clothing) if they cannot actually see the item. Therefore, the use of strategies to build trust, such as confirmations, return policies, and product reviews, is important.

4.6 Use Cases Across Retail Segments

The versatility of voice shopping is evident across different retail domains:

- Grocery and FMCG: Reorder staples, add items to shopping lists, check for discounts.
- Fashion and Apparel: Browse categories, track trends, and get sizing advice (usually with visual support).
- Electronics and Gadgets: Find compatible accessories, compare specifications, check availability.
- Home and Furniture: Explore styles, request delivery timelines, or locate physical store options.
- Health and Wellness: Refill prescriptions, buy supplements, check product authenticity.
- Luxury and Gifting: Personalize messages, select gift wrapping, or book appointments for in-store visits.

Each of this has their own degree of complexity and requires NLP models and corresponding business logic to provide meaningful answers.

4.7 Limitations and Challenges

While promising, the voice shopping experience also presesnts various issues:

- Speech Recognition Accuracy: Accents, background noise, and poor articulation can affect ASR performance.
- Lack of Visual Detail: For many categories, users still prefer seeing the product before buying.
- Ambiguity in User Intent: Natural language is inherently imprecise; "cheap laptop" or "best coffee" are subjective and context-sensitive.
- Privacy Concerns: Voice assistants are always listening, leading to concerns about data misuse or eavesdropping.
- Limited Discoverability: Without visual menus, users may not know what the assistant is capable of unless prompted.

Addressing these issues requires continuous refinement of models, integration of visual and text channels, and transparent privacy policies.

4.8 Best Practices for Optimizing Voice Shopping

If voice shopping is to improve, we need the following from retailers and those who develop:

- Design conversational flows that mimic natural dialogue, with options for clarification and fallback.
- Use progressive disclosure: don't overload the user with too much information at once.
- Implement personalization: Tailor suggestions using historical data and preferences.
- Enable visual handoff: Offer visual outputs on smartphones or smart displays when appropriate.
- Maintain transparency: Provide clear confirmations before purchases, and allow voice-enabled returns or cancellations.
- Prioritize accessibility: Ensure the experience works well for users with disabilities or non-native speakers.

Voice shopping has the potential to not only be useable, but also delightful and sticky if businesses focus on user-centered design and iterative testing.

5. PERSONALIZED RECOMMENDATIONS WITH CONVERSATIONAL AI

Customized recommendations and conversational AI will enable a new paradigm in digital retail. Traditional recommendation systems are based on user-machine interaction on visual interfaces and static browsing behavior. As voice corruption has become possible, personalization has developed to be more dynamic, contextual, and user-centered. Conversational AI enables products to recommend products not only because users clicked on them but also because it is what they say, how they say it, and when they say it (Singh et al., 2025). In this section, we discuss the ways in which personalized recommendation systems work in conversational AI and the central algorithms, data inputs, interaction flows, and real-time adaptability, which combine to provide this fusion real value within retail and e-commerce. Figure 2 personalized recommendations with conversational ai.

Figure 2. personalized recommendations with conversational AI

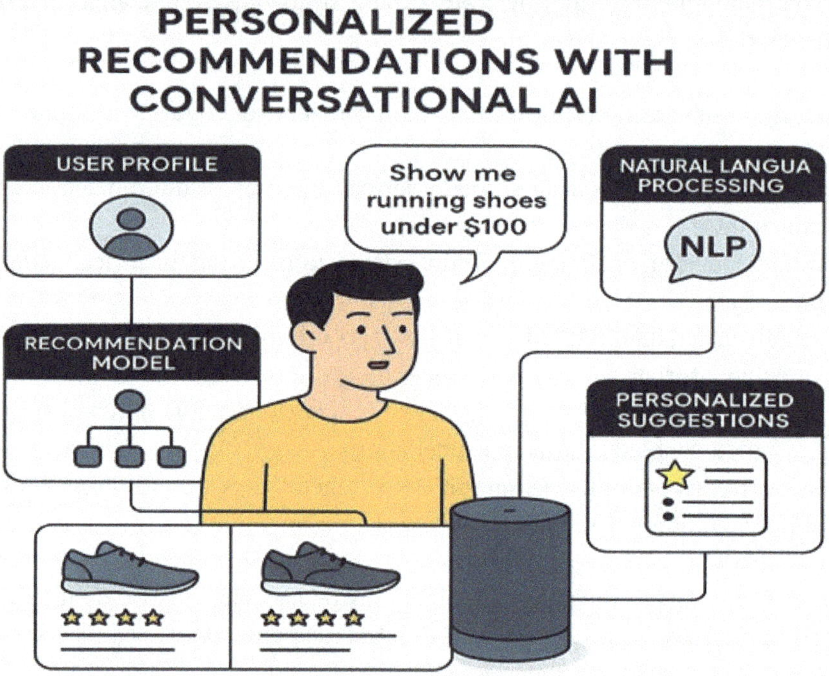

5.1 Foundations of Personalized Recommendations

Personalized recommendation systems attempt to make models of what the most pertinent items, for the individual user, are given his past behavior, preferences and contextual hints. For voice-enabled systems these recommendations must also be generated rapidly and in real-time as part of an ongoing conversation (Jang et al., 2025).

There are three fundamental approaches:

- Content-based filtering: Recommendations are based on similarity between user preferences and item features.
- Collaborative filtering: Recommendations derive from patterns in the behavior of similar users.
- Hybrid models: These combine both techniques with contextual signals.

Let's denote U is set of users, I is set of items (products) and rui is rating (explicit or implicit) given by user u∈U to item i∈I. The objective is to predict rui, the likelihood that user u would be interested in item i, and recommend the top-N items with the highest predicted values.

5.2 Content-Based Filtering in Conversational AI

In content-based systems, both users and items are represented as feature vectors. In a voice setting, the user profile is continuously refined based on spoken queries. Let u=[u1,u2,...,un] be a user preference vector, and xi=[x_{i1},x_{i2},...,x_{in}] be the feature vector for product iii. The predicted relevance score is calculated using the dot product:

$$r_{u,i} = u \, . \, x_i = \sum_{k=1}^{n} u_k x_{ik}$$

The voice assistant interprets statements like "I want a stylish black leather jacket for winter" and updates the user vector u accordingly. Features extracted could include style = "stylish", color = "black", material= "leather", and season="winter". Using NLP and Named Entity Recognition (NER), such utterances are transformed into structured features that help refine the recommendation model in real time.

5.3 Collaborative Filtering with Latent Factors

Collaborative filtering uses the interactions of many users to predict interests. Matrix factorization is a widely used approach, where the user-item interaction matrix R is decomposed into two low-dimensional matrices P and Q:

R≈PQTR

Where $P \in R^{|U| \times k}$ is user latent matrix, $Q \in R^{|I| \times k}$ is item latent matrix and k is number of latent features. The predicted rating is:

$r_{ui} = p_u \cdot q_i$

Conversational AI enhances this model by integrating dialogue signals. For example, if a user asks, "What are some affordable running shoes like the ones I bought last month?", the system references prior interactions, identifies similar items, and infers preferences related to price and category. In advanced systems, conversational context becomes part of the matrix decomposition. Context-aware factorization adds dimensions like time, location, and current conversation state.

5.4 Contextual and Session-Based Personalization

Voice interfaces inherently involve session-based interaction. Unlike static web clicks, spoken dialogues provide rich, ephemeral, and contextual signals. Let Ct is context at time ttt, including time, location, previous utterances and St is session state vector at time t. The recommendation model becomes:

$r_{ui}(t) = f(u, xi, Ct, St)$

Where f is a neural or hybrid model incorporating long short-term memory (LSTM) or attention layers to model the conversation flow. This enables systems to understand:

- "I want a phone with better battery life than the one I had before"
- "Show me more options like the second one you just suggested"
- "No, I don't like leather, something eco-friendly instead"

Such interactions modify Ct and St dynamically, reshaping recommendations in real time.

5.5 Multi-Turn Recommendation Dialogue

Unlike one-shot recommendations, voice-based personalization often occurs over multiple turns. The system must is Clarify preferences, Ask disambiguating questions and Present trade-offs. This requires reinforcement learning or dialogue policy optimization. Let St be the current dialogue state, and At be the action (e.g., recommend, ask, confirm). The system aims to maximize the cumulative reward RRR, such as user satisfaction or successful purchase:

Where π is policy function mapping states to actions and R is reward, e.g., +1 for conversion, -1 for rejection. The policies are learned from user feedback, from click- through data, or from training based on simulated conversations. These empower voice assistants to act more like sales consultants than like tools.

5.6 Explainable and Trustworthy Recommendations

Voice adds a layer of trust and expectation for explainability. Users often ask, "Why did you recommend this?" Conversational AI systems can respond:

- "This jacket matches your previous purchase of leather boots."
- "Many users who bought this also liked the one I showed before."

Explainable AI (XAI) in voice interfaces uses attention weights or decision trees to generate justifications. The key is to convert machine reasoning into natural language explanations without overwhelming the user.

5.7 Challenges and Mitigation

Despite its potential, voice-based personalized recommendations face challenges:

- Data sparsity: Voice queries are shorter and more varied than clicks.
- Cold start: New users may have little data for training.
- Privacy concerns: Users may hesitate to share personal data via voice.

Solutions include:

- Federated learning to keep data on-device
- Onboarding dialogues to bootstrap profiles
- Voiceprints and secure ID systems to link historical data

6. REAL-WORLD APPLICATIONS AND CASE STUDIES

The fusion of conversational AI with this area of recommendations within the scope of retail and e-commerce has radically impacted the consumer/brand relationship, consumer choice, and the consumer digital shopping process. This section highlights some of the ways in which businesses are now addressing these concerns in the cases of voice technologies and recommendation bots being implemented to bring shoppers to businesses, increase the efficiency of transactions, and boost sales.

6.1 Amazon's Alexa-Powered Voice Shopping

Alexa, Amazon's virtual assistant, pioneered voice commerce. Alexa enables voice-based shopping so consumers can say things like "Order more paper towels" or "Find me the best rated wireless earbuds". Amazon's ability to deliver personalized, real-time suggestions results from its large repository of data, machine learning, and access to current and past customer buying behavior. For instance, if a consumer has a purchasing pattern for household items, Alexa might recommend items currently on sale, new goods just released, or grouped with past purchases. Mechanisms such as dynamic recommendation models based on purchase frequency, user ratings of items, and contextual metadata (e.g., season, time frame) or behavior of the user operate to fahelphis (Ding et al., 2025). In addition, Alexa can perform multi-turn conversations that allow it to narrow preferences before suggesting products. Amazon is, through the use of a "talk to shop" interface, and customized recommendations, in so many words, a voice-commerce "hands-free" shopping assistant designed to foster user convenience and loyalty and to capitalize on sales.

6.2 Walmart and Google Assistant Integration

Another major case study on conversational commerce is the partnership between Walmart and Google Assistant. Google Assistant can be linked with a Walmart account, and consumers can use their voice to interact with Walmart from their home with commands such as, "Add milk to my cart" or "What's on my shopping list?". It is personalized based on the user's purchase history. If a user had purchased organic almond milk, then the voice assistant would suggest adding it to the list or the most similar item, that specific item, and not the generic replacement. This customization is achievable using collaborative filtering and real-time natural language processing (NLP) to effectively interpret generic or brand-specific phrasing. This is how Walmart drives online and in-store purchases, with voice assistants increasingly facilitating list-building, repurchases, and proactive reminders. This has not only enhanced customer experience and interaction but also positioned Walmart to compete with Amazon's voice-first retail ecosystem.

6.3 Sephora: Voice and Chatbot-Driven Personalization

The retailer Sephora is a good example of an implemented conversational AI in voice and text. More interactive, Sephora's chatbot "speaks" through an AI interface to help with makeup choices, skincare regimens, beauty advice, and tutorials. The bot is asking focused questions like "What's your skin type?" or "Are you looking for a matte or glossy finish?" to suggest products. The customization of such relationships is facilitated primarily through content-based filtering, which correlates product attributes (i.e., brand preference, skin tone match, pricing) with user responses. This means that the recommendation engine is instantly fine-tuned and updated as it learns from the conversation, thus replicating a human beauty advisor's knowledge. Sephora's AI system also incorporates customer reviews, stock information, and release date data into suggestions . This contributes to a better user experience, while also helping to educate customers, create new brand trust, and increase conversions.

6.4 H&M: Virtual Stylists Using Conversational Interfaces

The large global fast-fashion retailer H&M also experimented with voice-based virtual stylists. Through the mobile app and additional platforms, the user is part of a dialogue to guide them to the appropriate wardrobe purchase for an occasion, weather, or personal style. The recommendation system is based on a rule-based filtering system (e.g., size, gender, budget) and a deep-learning model autoencoder trained on images and text. H&M's virtual assistant "Show me something trendy for beach vacation" or "Find formal shirt blue under 50" allows for voice command and provides the customer with more choices, dynamically creating a selection for the individuals according to their input. Including voice interfaces in style discovery also helps reduce decision fatigue, because it can intelligently filter options. These advances have contributed to higher app engagement, longer sessions, and better cross-selling capabilities.

6.5 IKEA: Conversational Product Discovery and Home Planning

IKEA implements conversational AI in its product discovery and planning applications because it assists users in navigating very large product catalogs more effectively. Consumers can also use voice-activated chatbots and smart home assistants to look up products, receive assembly instructions, and see how furniture might look at their homes. For instance, a user might pose the question, "What is the best sofa for a small living room?" AI learns to interpret the tradeoff between space constraints and the desire for functional items and learns how to filter products accordingly. The recommendation engine is enriched by spatial data, augmented reality (AR) inputs, and the behavioral analytics of individual customers. Voice interfaces are also used by IKEA in their AR home design apps and further personalize the experience by adapting to the room layout, light, or usage. "Using AI, voice, AR together is already leading to much higher customer satisfaction, lower cart abandonment."

6.6 Case Study: North Face and IBM Watson

The North Face worked with IBM Watson to get a voice and text-based shopping assistant that helps consumers find the right outdoor gear. Customers interact with a conversational interface by entering responses to questions such as "Where are you hiking?" and "What is the weather going to be like?

Using Watson's deep NLP and cognitive reasoning capabilities, the system tailors recommendations by evaluating:

- Climate and geography
- Past purchases and preferences
- Product performance reviews

In understanding the users' experiences and requirements, the assistant helps users understand why certain products are suitable, not simply suggesting the gear. And this hyper- personalized experience translated into higher conversion and brand engagement.

7.BENEFITS TO RETAILERS AND CUSTOMERS

Conversational AI brings about new dynamics between retailers and users within the contexts of both retail and ecommerce, notably disrupting the nature of shopping related interaction that is formed. They provide convenience, personalization and efficiency that in turn create satisfaction and growth.

7.1 Enhanced Customer Experience

Voice-activated shopping is the epitome of convenience for consumers. Customers no longer have to wade through layers of menus or even type search queries; they can just speak to get to the products, get products recommended, or place orders. This friction is eliminated by hands-free, natural interactions that allow users to perform other tasks or are handicapped. In addition, conversational AI can provide contextual help, infer the users' intentions, and have multi-turn continuity, which means that the chit-chat with the virtual salesperson or specialist feels more like interacting with a person than a robot. Voice interfaces also reduce the cognitive load on customers (Marjerison et al., 2025). There is no need to sift through hundreds of items, as the user can filter from a broad set of options with a question like, "Show me affordable sneakers under 3,000 with good reviews." The more personalized offers, recommendations, and enhanced predictive capabilities AI can provide by learning on users, the simpler and more natural the consumer shopping path becomes.

7.2 Personalized Engagement and Recommendations

The customizability possible for the use of conversational AI is amenable to both customers and retailers. Buyers include personalized product recommendations based on their preferences, purchase history, and even contextual data (e.g., weather, events, and time of day). This customization is beneficial because it provides an increased context, reduces cognitive overhead, and ultimately increases user satisfaction. This implies increased levels of engagement for the retailer, better conversion rates, and larger average order values. AI driven personalization tools allow for product recommendations, promotions, and even how the interaction sounds to change on the fly in response to a user's behavior by processing real-time data on the customer. This type of ultra-personalized marketing is useful for building long-term relationships based on loyalty and trust.

7.3 Increased Operational Efficiency

For the retailer, voice combines with the opportunity to eliminate or limit the human customer service agents or attendants required to answer FAQs, check orders and supplies, or provide specific product information. It also leads to a better allocation of resources and lower operating costs, as the support team can focus on more complex issues. In a brick-and-mortar location, voice-activated kiosks or smart mirrors provide an efficient way to service customers without the need for a salesperson and allow spaces to accommodate more people per sales lead. Voice can also be a faster way of searching for something, updating something, or moving something in a warehouse or inventory management system, thereby making logistics move faster and with fewer errors.

7.4 Real-Time Insights and Marketing Opportunities

Recording each interaction is a data point that may help gain insights into customer behavior, needs, and trends. These data can be used to manage inventories, assortments, and marketing. Voice search data can also be used to inform SEO efforts, helping retailers structure their digital content so that it is more in tune with how consumers naturally phrase their questions. Voice-activated software also offers new marketing opportunities. This can entail branded voice assistants or sponsored recommendations during shopping interactions, which can increase a brand's presence and result in impulse purchases. These novel mechanisms allow retailers to interact with their customer base in a non-intrusive and interactive format that allows for greater entrepreneurial endeavors.

7.5 Competitive Differentiation and Brand Loyalty

The strategic advantage of conversational AI and voice interfaces is tremendous for retailers. They set themselves apart in a crowded marketplace by offering something convenient, personalized, and futuristic. Customers will prefer to engage again with platforms that remember their preferences, act promptly, and provide an undisturbed journey. Moreover, by advanced voice, Ai can even detect a user's mood or tone, making brands able to please their audience on a more personal level, thus creating brand loyalty. A translated, responsive, and even empathetic voice assistant can also define a brand.

8. CHALLENGES AND CONSIDERATIONS

The use of conversational AI, personalized voice-activated commerce and commerce, represents a sea change, but not without problems. The 'fourth industrial revolution' has tremendous potential and is already making transformative advances in many industries, but not without new sets of technical, ethical, operational, and experiential challenges that organizations need to grapple with to ensure its success and scale. The limitations and issues of applying conversational AI to the retail area, with a focus on personalization and voice interfaces, are stated next.

8.1 Speech Recognition Accuracy and Language Limitations

Another critical aspect of commerce systems' voice experiences is that they must realistically achieve extremely high levels of recognition accuracy. Even though improvements in Automatic Speech Recognition (ASR) have been significant, they can still be vulnerable to accents, dialects, background noise, incoherent pronunciation, or multiple languages. Wrong interpretations result in unhelpful recommendations, dissatisfied customers, and skepticism of the system. This is even more complex when dealing with global clientele. A voice assistant should also be capable to manage different linguistic styles and local terminologies; for example, in UK, instead of "sweater" they say "jumper" like an American would. These variations must be addressed in training/optimizing ASR models; therefore, ASR models should be iteratively retrained and optimized using large representative datasets.

8.2 Understanding Context and Intent

Customer questions in voice commerce are generally not simple close-ended questions. Like "Find something stylish for a party" may include from clothes, to accessories, shoes, or makeup. Understanding the actual speaker's message, especially within a multi-turn dialogue, is a Natural Language Understanding (NLU) problem. In addition, the intention can vary during a session. For example, if a user specifies formal wear, the recommendation engine may also browse for casual wear. Both approaches would also need sophisticated dialogue management and memory models to provide contextual continuity while dealing with ongoing changes. In addition, AI will have to be able to discriminate between instructions "(add to cart)" and conversational information/directions, such as "I like this one better," and react accordingly, an art that is still being mastered within voice interaction design.

8.3 Data Privacy and Security

Personalized recommendation systems require access to user data—including past purchases, preferences, spoken interactions, and sometimes even biometric information like voiceprints. This level of data dependency raises significant privacy concerns.

Processing and storage of voice data may also give users pause. Voice data can inadvertently disclose sensitive personal information, such as an individual's health, shopping habits, or home demographics, presenting several risk factors if mismanaged. Complying with data protection regulations like GDPR, CCPA, and similar frameworks is non-negotiable. Retailers must implement privacy-by-design strategies, including:

- Secure data encryption
- Transparent consent mechanisms
- Clear data retention and deletion policies
- On-device processing where feasible (e.g., via federated learning)

Failing to address these considerations can lead to reputational damage, legal repercussions, and user attrition.

8.4 Bias and Fairness in Recommendations

These AI-based personalization systems are usually data-driven and historical data are bias reflections of social biases. If not tightly controlled, these same systems can also lead to outcomes that are just as unfair and more so, for example recommendations for superior products for a certain demography or confining choices based on inference. Lastly, other linguistic idiosyncrasies such as cultural, gender and regional variations can be taken from the spoken language as well. Prejudiced suggestions are apparent if the model inadvertently skews towards certain user inputs or answers, in which case the suggestions themselves will be biased if not outright discriminatory. This can be, and should be prevented by fairness-aware machine learning techniques, diverse training sets, and periodic algorithmic audits. The personalization that is granted as an extension of such principles, in order to be positive, must include the ethical principles of AI from the inception of such technologies and processes.

8.5 Limited Expressiveness in Voice Interfaces

Unlike graphical user interfaces that show many products, options, or filters at a time, voice interactions are time-constrained and one-by-one. This restricts the amount of information that can be transmitted effectively at any given time. For example, a voice agent cannot provide 20 options, which would be frustrating for the listener. This limitation impedes the capacity of the system to achieve individualized meaningful communication in a single turn. A lack of visibility or the ability to easily problematize decisions can be frustrating to users. To solve this problem, some systems have attempted to create multimodal interfaces that mix voice interaction with graphical interfaces on smartphones or apps that can generate recommendations while still taking input in a conversational manner. This, however, is easier to say than done, as it is difficult to reconcile an intuitive experience between the modes.

8.6 Real-Time Personalization Complexity

Voice-enabled systems must deliver real-time recommendations based on spoken input, which requires processing:

- Speech-to-text conversion
- NLP-based intent recognition

- Profile updates
- Matching with product databases
- Personalization using ML models

All of this needs to happen with low latency in order to result in a cohesive conversational flow. The challenge is that this real-time performance also requires heavy computational overhead and appropriate tweaking of the system to be guaranteed in high-traffic/multi-users or low-bandwidth environments. In addition, there need to be real-time adaptations of the personalization models according to novel inputs in the dialogue (e.g. "Actually, I prefer something cheaper") that do not deteriorate the performance of the model. The need to strike a balance between speed, accuracy, and adaptability is also a technical challenge.

8.7 Integration with Legacy Systems

In many cases, antiquated systems for product catalogs, inventory, customer data, and so on, are still in use in the retail industry. Attempting to apply conversational AI to these legacy systems is often cumbersome and expensive. The metadata files may be poorly or inconsistently tagged, and the ultra-structure of product information may not contain the metadata required for information discovery via voice. These backend systems must be modernized or interfaced via APIs to effectively personalize and communicate with AI modules. This "t... debt" has the potential to not only slow down deployment but also increase operational complexity. In addition, at the retail level, voice assistants need to synchronize seamlessly with mobile apps and websites in an omni-channel retail operation.

8.8 User Education and Adoption Barriers

Retailers should responsibly stretch the capabilities of these technologies, as long as they do not do so at the expense of privacy, inclusivity, or user experience for the sake of innovation. If we approach these issues ethically and proactively and address them intelligently, then we can enable the advanced and widespread use of voice-commerce that provides a much better net positive to digital commerce without being sinister or deceptive.

In addition, not all consumers are ready to shop by using the voice of customers who are not adopting smart speakers and virtual assistants. Fear of misidentification, surveillance fear, and habituation are some of the disincentives. However, retailers will be required to "educate consumers on the positive and security aspects of voice-enabled mechanisms". It would also be important to make the experience inclusive and intuitive to enter onboarding flows, help prompts, and prevent fallbacks.

In addition, the generational dimension could play a role in the adoption of conversational systems. If developed with the aim of being usable by a variety of demographic features, including elderly users, non-native speakers, and children, the UX and AI models should be carefully conceived and tuned. However, the use of speech in personalized shopping is just one term in a more expansive vocabulary of issues and concerns at retail sites. Each of these levels, from the ability to correctly recognize the voice of the speaker and personalize it in real time, to the ethical and trust levels, calls for planning, testing, and perhaps adaptation.

9. FUTURE TRENDS AND INNOVATIONS

In a world where online and offline retail are rapidly changing in response to digital tools and new consumer preferences, voice shopping and conversational AI have the potential to grow even more influential. Instead of setting voice commands and scripts, next-generation voice technologies can provide more intelligent, intuitive, and contextual experiences. This section reviews the new scenarios and features that the combination of voice and AI is projected to bring to the retail ecosystem.

9.1 Multimodal Conversational Interfaces

Perhaps the single most promising development in the evolution of voice in the context of retailing is the evolution of multimodal interfaces. They start to integrate voice with these combinations of visual, tactile, or gestural inputs in ways that can be more immersive and less rigid. For instance, a customer asks the system "Show me summer dresses," and at the same time, he/she can see the product images on a smart display, mobile device, or AR glasses. They could then refine their selection using voice ("only red ones under $50") while tapping their favorite icon. The combination of voice and visual interactions between users and agents not only improves the usability of voice commerce but is also a way of overcoming some of its disadvantages, such as the absence of visual feedback or list fatigue. The next generation of systems will provide continuity of service across multiple devices and interaction modes and real omni-channel/cross-device continuity of experience.

9.2 Hyper-Personalization Through Deep Learning

While personalization is already a staple of modern e-commerce, the future will see hyperpersonalization powered by more advanced deep learning models. These systems go beyond basic product suggestions by analyzing fine-grained behavioral data, contextual signals (time of day, weather, and mood), and real-time interaction patterns. Using recurrent neural networks (RNNs), transformers, and reinforcement learning algorithms, voice assistants adapt dynamically to the evolving needs of users. For instance, if a customer frequently shops for eco-friendly products, the assistant may proactively recommend sustainable brands or highlight the carbon footprint of the items when queried. Personalization will also become more proactive. AI systems may greet users with "Would you like to reorder your usual Monday groceries?" or suggest an outfit for an upcoming calendar event, blurring the line between the assistant and the shopping concierge.

9.3 Voice Biometrics for Authentication and Personalization

Voice biometrics, for example, point toward a future in which security and personalization blend together. Every person's voice has a distinct pitch, cadence, and tone, which can be exploited to confirm identity. Through voice biometrics, users can login in a secure and frictionless manner, without passwords or PINs, adding trust and convenience.

It also recognizes singleton users through voiceprints. This will allow for personalized experiences, even in communal spaces. For instance, if a child and a parent share a smart speaker, the system will personalize product recommendations according to the voice profile of the speaker to bring up the right content and preferences. Voice biometrics, given appropriate privacy assurances, will play a key role in ensuring that voice-first environments can deliver personalized services while safeguarding user information.

9.4 Integration with the Internet of Things (IoT)

Moving ahead, the connectivity of conversational AI with intelligent tools will be more context-aware as an internet of things (IoT) environment matures. Voice assistants, in tandem with smart homes, appliances, and wearables, provide predictive and automated shopping experiences.

Consider a refrigerator that monitors what is in it and its expiration dates. For example, a refrigerator might be able to tell when the milk is running low and it will communicate via the voice user interface: "Should I reorder your favorite organic brand?"A smart mirror at a clothing store might be able to respond to voice commands such as "Show me combinations of outfits" and "Search for availability in store." The zenith of IoT and voice AI is the ability to eliminate friction from the shopping process, but it also indicates the beginning of anticipatory commerce, whereby the user does not have to ask because the system already knows that he or she is in need of something.

9.5 Conversational Commerce in the Metaverse

Beyond flat screens, retail will come to live in some not-yet-imagined details of the emerging metaverse, as the retail presence will be in full virtual environments. Voice-enabled conversational agents are necessary for co-navigating and co-transacting these spaces.

In a web store, a user might talk to a digital avatar to receive customized help, saying something like "Find a gift for my sister who likes hiking." The request will be processed by the avatar via conversational AI, the correct products will be served, and the user can be taken through a highly visual and interactive shopping experience, for example, 3D avatars of clothing they can "try on" and product demonstrations. First-movers who create voice–first experiences for the metaverse will outflank competitors as today's younger, technologically oriented shoppers move toward their immersive digital worlds.

9.6 Emotion Recognition and Sentiment-Adaptive Systems

The next generation of conversational software does not simply understand what consumers are saying but the way they are saying it. Vocal tone, cadence, and human linguistic signifiers will be used to teach AI to identify human emotions, analyze voice timbre as it infers what the meaning behind the words is, and cue a response appropriately.

For example, if the customer's tone sounds frustrated, the assistant can adjust to a more empathetic tone. if the customer's queries are beyond the capabilities of an automated assistant, the assistant can offer available customer support if the customer is not talking like a human, possibly trying to reduce the time of the interaction. If it sounds thrilled to the user, the assistant might propose other things to complement or upgrade to. Through these sentiment-adaptive systems, the voice interface will be much more human and emotionally intelligent–a critically important capability when building customer relationships over time.

9.7 Voice-Driven B2B and Supply Chain Interfaces

Although many advancements in voice commerce have been made in the B2C space, the ultimate potential is also great for B2B. Procurement officers using their voices, warehouse managers, sales representatives accessing the systems and checking stock, or placing bulk orders, generating reports, and many more, can all benefit from the efficiency and time this will save them.

For example, a vendor could ask, "Show current orders pending shipment" and get a voice or graphical response with this information. In the coming phase, these voice agents linked to ERP systems, CRM systems, and inventory databases will change the way corporations work with internal data and how they manage the supply chain.

9.8 Regulatory and Ethical Innovations

When conversational AI becomes more widespread, laws and ethics change. Next, innovations take the form of AI governance protocols that ensure transparency, user agency, and fairness in algorithms.

Voice assistants will have to reveal how data is being used at the time it's being used, like "This conversation is being used to improve recommendations." Do you want to unsubscribe"? It is a common practice for users to opt out. Algorithm audits and ethical certifications will also be taken for granted in the industry as a means to establish consumer trust in the privacy and fairness of voice-driven personalization.

Emerging privacy-preserving AI methods, such as federated learning and on-device computing, will increasingly ensure that user data can be kept secure while still powering rich real-time customization.

CONCLUSION

Voice input and conversational AI, when incorporated into retail and e-commerce, are not just technically innovative but are also, and more specifically, changes that make sense given the increasing consumer demand for convenience, personalization, and efficacy. This sea change is also reshaping the overall shopping experience, from how people discover and choose that item, to how they buy it and engage with it post-purchase, again all for the more natural, the better and the smoother. Similar to voice-enabled systems and advanced AI, processing power creates personification of the digital storefront, where people can interact with it as if they are interacting with another person, making this experience more enjoyable because of reduced friction and heightened user satisfaction.

We offer a few examples in this chapter on voice interfaces and retail. Yes, it has certainly been a journey from the very primitive command and control units to the advanced A.I. assistants that we have now. Currently, such systems are based on natural language processing (NLP), machine learning, and deep learning to comprehend more complex customers' intentions to learn more about individuals' preferences and frame multi-turn conversations. It takes the shopping experience out of the action of interacting with products; it is more like interacting with a product in a store.

The architecture of a system in a retail setting that is operated via voice control also has multiple individual intelligent parts, including the ASR engine, NLU module, dialogue manager, recommendation engine, and personalization layers, which all cooperate in real time to process the user's input to give the user output. They rely on a multiplicity of inputs, such as user profile data, past spending habits, user behavior, and, in some cases, voice tone or sentiment to further customize the interaction. The infrastructure built is resilient, flexible, and scalable in terms of devices and platforms.

Voice shopping has become a reality. Voice commerce is democratized by smart speakers, mobile assistants, in-store kiosks, and wearables, allowing it to take place anywhere and at any time. By reordering basic items to ask for fashion tips to curate ideas, consumers engage with brands in conversation in ways that were not possible before. Voice is not only going to change the way we search and shop, but also the way we expect to get something immediately and personalized.

Conversational personalized recommendations create value by reducing decision fatigue and making the experience emotionally meaningful. Machine-learning algorithms continue to learn from users and provide timely and relevant suggestions. Next-generation systems will be more predictive, proactive, and emotionally aware using sentiment analysis, contextual triggers, and multimodal input to provide assistive technologies that seem more intelligent and empathetic.

They point to real-world use cases, where brands that have implemented Voice AI have experienced higher levels of engagement, conversions, and loyalty. However, there are challenges, including the accuracy of voice recognition, bias in recommendation algorithms, privacy concerns, and integration with legacy systems. These concerns must be dealt with via a "polytechnic," one that combines innovation with the ethic of care and process that are user-centered.

The future and foreseen use of multimodal interfaces, voice biometrics, and emotion-aware systems, as well as commerce using the metaverse, are certainly exciting. These will further enhance experiential, secure, and hyper-personalitized voice-enabled retail experiences. Companies that follow this curve of action will be able to satisfy the needs of digitally born consumers and have a chance to survive in an economy that has already started to become based on AI.

Voice shopping and conversational AI are game changers in retail, and the above examples provide evidence of why. These young consumers also redefine the nature of transactions, as well as the relationships between consumers and brands. It has been a learning process, a journey in technology, and throughout it, all the mission is to enhance the human experience through an intelligent conversation.

REFERENCES

Al Nabhani, F., Abuhassna, H., & Hamzah, M. B. (2025). The role of artificial intelligence in personalizing educational content: Enhancing the learning experience and developing the teacher's role in an integrated educational environment. *Contemporary Educational Technology*, *17*(2), ep573. DOI: 10.30935/cedtech/16089

Ariya, P., Yensathit, Y., Intawong, K., Thongthip, P., & Puritat, K. (2024). Assisting hearing and physically impaired students in navigating immersive virtual reality for library orientation. *Technologies*, *13*(1), 2. DOI: 10.3390/technologies13010002

Azadinejad, H., Farhadi Rad, M., Shariftabrizi, A., Rahmim, A., & Abdollahi, H. (2025). Optimizing cancer treatment: Exploring the role of AI in radioimmunotherapy. *Diagnostics (Basel)*, *15*(3), 397. DOI: 10.3390/diagnostics15030397 PMID: 39941326

Bai, Y., Rusmevichientong, P., El Housni, O., & Topaloglu, H. (2025). Coordinated inventory stocking and assortment customization. *Operations Research*, *73*(6), 2953–2971. Advance online publication. DOI: 10.1287/opre.2022.0651

Bottrighi, A., Grosso, F., Ghiglione, M., Maconi, A., Nera, S., Piovesan, L., Raina, E., Roveta, A., & Terenziani, P. (2025). A symbolic AI approach to medical training. *Journal of Medical Systems*, *49*(1), 2. DOI: 10.1007/s10916-024-02139-y PMID: 39786677

Chang, L., Liu, J., Zhu, J., Guo, S., Wang, Y., Zhou, Z., & Wei, X. (2025). Advancing precision medicine: The transformative role of artificial intelligence in immunogenomics, radiomics, and pathomics for biomarker discovery and immunotherapy optimization. *Cancer Biology & Medicine*, *22*(1), 33–47. DOI: 10.20892/j.issn.2095-3941.2024.0376 PMID: 39749734

Deliu, D., & Olariu, A. (2024). The role of artificial intelligence and big data analytics in shaping the future of professions in Industry 6.0: Perspectives from an emerging market. *Electronics (Basel)*, *13*(24), 4983. DOI: 10.3390/electronics13244983

Demyen, S. (2024). The online shopping experience during the pandemic and after—A turning point for sustainable fashion business management? *Journal of Theoretical and Applied Electronic Commerce Research*, *19*(4), 3632–3658. DOI: 10.3390/jtaer19040176

Ding, L., Antonucci, G., & Venditti, M. (2024). Unveiling user responses to AI-powered personalised recommendations: A qualitative study of consumer engagement dynamics on Douyin. *Qualitative Market Research*, *28*(2), 234–255. DOI: 10.1108/QMR-11-2023-0151

Ding, R., Chen, X., Wei, S., & Wang, J. (2025). What drives trust building in live streaming e-commerce? From an elaboration likelihood model perspective. *Industrial Management & Data Systems, 125*(3), 969–999. DOI: 10.1108/IMDS-03-2024-0273

Duggan, M. J., Gervase, J., Schoenbaum, A., Hanson, W., Howell, J. T.III, Sheinberg, M., & Johnson, K. B. (2025). Clinician experiences with ambient scribe technology to assist with documentation burden and efficiency. *JAMA Network Open, 8*(2), e2460637. DOI: 10.1001/jamanetworkopen.2024.60637 PMID: 39969880

Glogar, M., Mahnić Naglić, M., & Petrak, S. (2025). Digital technologies in the sustainable design and development of textiles and clothing—A literature review. *Sustainability (Basel), 17*(4), 1371. DOI: 10.3390/su17041371

Hou, Y. (2025). Design and implementation evaluation of personalized and differentiated teaching strategies for preschool children based on fuzzy decision support systems. *International Journal of Computational Intelligence Systems, 18*(1), 42. Advance online publication. DOI: 10.1007/s44196-025-00748-0

Jang, B., Yuh, C., Lee, H., Shin, Y. B., Lee, H. J., Kang, E. K., Heo, J., & Cho, C. H. (2025). Exploring user experience and the therapeutic relationship of short-term avatar-based psychotherapy: Qualitative pilot study. *JMIR Human Factors, 12*, e66158. DOI: 10.2196/66158 PMID: 39924261

Jung, J., Kim, D., & You, J. (2025). Effective but sustainable? A case of a digital literacy program for older adults. *Education and Information Technologies, 30*(10), 13309–13330. Advance online publication. DOI: 10.1007/s10639-025-13364-4

Kim, M., Joo, M., & Han, K. (2025). Understanding the differences in an AI-based creativity support tool between creativity types in fashion design. *International Journal of Human-Computer Interaction, 41*(18), 1–14. Advance online publication. DOI: 10.1080/10447318.2024.2448484

Lin, K.-Y., Chang, K.-H., Lin, Y.-W., & Wu, M.-J. (2025). Exploring key considerations for artificial intelligence robots in home healthcare using the unified theory of acceptance and use of technology and the fuzzy analytical hierarchy process method. *Systems, 13*(1), 25. DOI: 10.3390/systems13010025

Mahmoudi, A., Khosrotabar, M., Gramann, K., Rinderknecht, S., & Sharbafi, M. A. (2025). Using passive BCI for personalization of assistive wearable devices: A proof-of-concept study. *IEEE Transactions on Neural Systems and Rehabilitation Engineering, PP*, 476–487. DOI: 10.1109/TNSRE.2025.3530154

Marjerison, R. K., Zhang, Y., Kim, J.-M., Dong, H., Zheng, H., & Kuan, G. (2025). Understanding user acceptance of AI-driven chatbots in China's e-commerce: The roles of perceived authenticity, usefulness, and risk. *Systems*, *13*(2), 71. DOI: 10.3390/systems13020071

Marvi, R., Foroudi, P., & Cuomo, M. T. (2024). Past, present and future of AI in marketing and knowledge management. *Journal of Knowledge Management*, *29*(11), 1–31. DOI: 10.1108/JKM-07-2023-0634

Murzin, S. P. (2024). Artificial intelligence-driven innovations in laser processing of metallic materials. *Metals*, *14*(12), 1458. DOI: 10.3390/met14121458

Pei, R., & Su, Z. (2025). Key success factors for export structure optimization in East Asian countries through global value chain (GVC) reorganization. *Systems*, *13*(1), 22. DOI: 10.3390/systems13010022

Rabbi, M. F., Abdullah, M., Al-Dalahmeh, M., & Amin, M. B. (2025). Assessing the role of information technology in promoting environmental sustainability and preventing crime in e-commerce. *International Review of Applied Sciences and Engineering*, *16*(1), 81–97. DOI: 10.1556/1848.2024.00834

Shao, J., Liu, Z., & Feng, Y. (2024). The impact of big data-driven strategies on sustainable consumer behaviour in e-commerce: A green economy perspective. *Sustainability (Basel)*, *16*(24), 10960. DOI: 10.3390/su162410960

Singh, N., Kim, H., Kim, J., Yu, Y., Do, Y., & Fouad, I. (2025). Crumbled cookies: Exploring e-commerce websites' cookie policies with data protection regulations. *ACM Transactions on the Web*, *19*(1), 1–24. DOI: 10.1145/3708515

Yang, Y., Wang, C., Xiang, X., & An, R. (2025). AI applications to reduce loneliness among older adults: A systematic review of effectiveness and technologies. *Health Care*, *13*(5), 446. DOI: 10.3390/healthcare13050446 PMID: 40077009

Chapter 9
Advancements in Natural Language Understanding (NLU) and Generation (NLG): Bridging AI and Human Communication

Siva Subramanian R.
http://orcid.org/0000-0002-7509-9223
R.M. Institute of Science and Technology, India

ABSTRACT

Natural Language Understanding (NLU) and Natural Language Generation (NLG) have revolutionized AI-human communication, enabling more natural and context-aware interactions. Recent advancements in deep learning, particularly transformer-based models, have significantly improved the ability of AI to comprehend, process, and generate human-like text. These technologies are widely applied in conversational AI, machine translation, content creation, and question-answering systems. However, challenges such as data biases, hallucinations, computational limitations, and ethical concerns remain. Future research aims to enhance AI's reasoning capabilities, improve low-resource language support, and integrate hybrid AI approaches. This chapter explores state-of-the-art techniques, applications, challenges, and future directions in NLU and NLG, highlighting their implications for AI research, industry, and society.

DOI: 10.4018/979-8-3373-3361-8.ch009

1. INTRODUCTION

Background on Natural Language Processing (NLP)

NLP is a branch of AI that deals with the use of computers in language and its analysis. It allows a machine to interact with human language in a way that is meaningful and useful to the human as well as the machine [Chowdhary, K., & Chowdhary, K. R. 2020]. NLP is an advanced tool that is associated with computational linguistics and machine learning as well as deep learning to help different tasks based on languages, including speech recognition, translation, and sentiment analysis. The history of NLP could be traced back to the rule based system where the linguist and computer scientists used to make the rules for understanding the language[Fanni et al 2023]. These early approaches, while being useful for some applications, were not able to scale up due to the inherent factors related to the natural language. In the late twentieth century, NLP improved with the help of statistical methods and machine learning approaches by which new probabilistic models were created and it became possible to solve such problems as POS tagging and others including the identification of named entities. More recently in the last decade, deep learning and transformer based architectures have dramatically transformed NLP to give rise to models such as BERT, GPT and T5. These models work with large datasets and self-supervision to set new records on many NLP tasks. NLP is considered as one of the key constituents of the technologies in artificial intelligence, including smart assistants, smart searches, automated translators, etc., and many other instruments that help in interaction humans and computers.

Definition and Distinction Between NLU and NLG

NLU and NLG are two of the smaller divisions of NLP that deals with two distinct aspects of language processing.

NLU is a subset of NLP that aims at having machines understand human language. This includes several operational tasks as follows: Word segmentation – Dividing sentences into the individual words. Semantic analysis – Understanding the meaning of words and phrases in context. Evaluating the discursive and pragmatic perspective – How different sentences are related and the purpose of communication [Mazidi, K., & Tarau, P. 2016].

For instance, NLU is applied in various activities like information retrieval, sentiment analysis, question answering, and speech-to-text. It helps request interpretation in search engine, emotions identification in feedbacks and useful information extraction from text data.

Natural Language Generation (NLG), on the other hand, deals with the creation of human-like text by machines. It involves:

Content determination – Determining what message has to be passed. Text organization – Arranging the text most wisely so that the readers can grasp the information effectively. Linguistic realization – When written documents contain complex and structured information in terms of structure, positioning, contrast and so much more, transforming such information into natural language sentences is referred to as linguistic realization.

NLG is used in reporting, chatbots, and in the use of artificial intelligence to generate content. It supports applications such as OpenAI's GPT models that are used in writing text for various purposes like narration, abstracting, and chatbots. NLU and NLG are, in fact, quite similar but their aims are different: NLU is to comprehend the human input language while NLG is to generate language output that is similar to a human. NLU and NLG are often combined to form complete AI solutions of particular tasks, for instance, conversational agents which require understanding of the user's input and generation of the correct output.

Importance of NLU and NLG in AI-Driven Communication

As the use of artificial intelligence continues to expand into various aspects of life, natural language processing plays the central role in improving human-computer communication. NLU and NLG are the key to improving the AI communication as the interaction between two or more parties in a given domain.

1.Conversational AI and Virtual Assistants

Some of today's popular gadgets like Siri, Google Assistant, Amazon Alexa, and others use NLU to comprehend users' inputs and NLG to generate coherent answers. Such technologies are employed in the chatbots used for customer service to deliver individualized service and reply to queries that are commonly posed[Mekni, M. 2021][Darwish, D. 2024].

2.Machine Translation and Cross-Lingual Communication

NLU is beneficial in identifying the context and meaning of the text in one language and NLG is helpful in translating the same into another language in a correct and natural manner. Such as Google Translate, DeepL and many others means that the quality of the translation of languages has greatly enhanced breaking language barriers.

3.Automated Content Generation

NLG makes it possible for an AI model to write articles, reports and summaries with little or no input from a human.

4.Sentiment Analysis and Emotion Recognition

Organizations apply NLU for the purpose of sentiment analysis in order to determine customer attitudes and enhance the quality of services. AI can identify the presence of emotions in text which may be used in tracking the mental health of a user and in user engagement analytics [Atmaja, B. T., & Sasou, A. 2022].

5.Summarization and Information Extraction

NLU technologies are used in the identification of significant points in large textual corpora, while NLG is used in summarizing. Some of the areas where automated summarization is applied include news retrieval, scholarly papers' analysis, and legal documents.

6.Healthcare and Clinical Decision Support

AI-driven NLU extracts meaningful insights from medical records, assisting doctors in decision-making. NLG is used in writing of patient reports, brief of medical literature, and documentation among other services. The increasing usage of AI in communication is evidence of the changes that NLU and NLG have made to different sectors. In the future, these technologies will become more revolutionary and influential to increase access and calorie, as well as the utility of use in e-interactions.

Objectives and Scope of the Survey

Compare the previous approaches and current state of the art approaches for NLU and NLG. Explain the latest trends in transformer-based architecture and fine-tuning and other emerging fields. Discuss the role of NLU and NLG in the AI-based systems including conversational AI, analyzing the sentiment of textual data, and content creation. Classify significant difficulties and restrictions including those connected with bias in AI models, ethical questions, real-life situations dissonance in text generation. Conclude with the elaboration of further research avenues and prospects for development such as the enhancement of multilingual AI, explainable language models, and the reinforcement of the AI-human interaction.

In this way, this survey will help to fill the gap between academic studies and practical applications and can be useful to AI researchers and developers as well as professionals who work on developing methods for improving human-computer interaction. This has put NLU and NLG into the spotlight as the technology that would allow human and machine interaction to be more natural, effective, and meaningful. With the further development of NLP, the issues of increasing accuracy, avoiding biases, and interpretability of the results will remain the most important ones in the field of AI. This survey will help the reader to understand the development of NLU and NLG, the changes these technologies bring to different fields and provide the basis for further advancements.

2. FUNDAMENTALS OF NLU AND NLG

Among the two subdivisions of NLP, Natural Language Understanding (NLU) and Natural Language Generation (NLG) are pivotal. These two areas make it possible for machines to understand, analyze and produce human language. It is critical to have a good understanding of the former if one wants to create more sophisticated AI-based language models and tools. In this section the author gives an overview of the main areas of NLU and NLG, the differences between NLP and deep learning, and the development of techniques in the two fields.

2.1 Core Components of NLU: Syntax, Semantics, Discourse, and Pragmatics

Natural Language Understanding (NLU) is more concerned with the ability of the computer to understand language as it is used by human beings. There are different types that range from label assignment to a more complex analysis that provides structure and semantics from text data [Bowman, S. R., & Dahl, G. E. 2021].

2.1.1 Syntax

Syntax refers to the grammatical structure of sentences. It entails the use of language to determine the proper way that words co-relate in forming a meaningful sentence. Parsability or syntactic complexity checks whether a particular sentence is structurally correct.

Syntactic Analysis: This involves the determination of the structural analysis of sentences by the use of the following; Constituency analysis: phrase structure and dependency analysis: the relationship between words.

Part-of-Speech (POS) Tagging: The process of identifying the tags that help in categorizing words in a text according to their relation to the grammar of a certain language.

2.1.2 Semantics

Semantics involves the entire meaning in language This involves the different meaning of an expression or word in language. When it comes to the construction of the sentence, it is not enough to have a syntactic structure that conforms to the rules of grammar.

Word Sense Disambiguation (WSD): It is process of determining the correct meaning of a word in a given context.

Named Entity Recognition (NER): Topics of interest can include names, locations and date in a given text.

Semantic Role Labelling (SRL): Aims to determine one or more of the roles that exist in a given sentence (for example, agent, action or object).

2.1.3 Discourse

Compared with syntactic analysis, discourse analysis is the analysis of text beyond the sentential level where issues related to text cohesion, resolving anaphora, and the patterning of dialogue notes. Coreference Resolution: Links pronouns and noun phrases to their referents. Organizational Communication: Measures the extent to which there is flow in the text both at the sentence level and at the document level. Dialogue Management: It is used in the context of natural language processing and helps AI systems to continue meaningful conversations like chatbots.

2.1.4 Pragmatics

For the concept of pragmatics is related to tone, assumption, context, and purpose of speaking. Speech Act Theory: Classifies a statement as a request, command, question, etc. Sentiment & Emotion Analysis: Detects user's attitude from language.

2.2 Core Component of NLG: Text Planning, Sentence Structuring, Content Realization

Natural Language Generation (NLG) is a subfield that aims to convert a structured data into human language[Sangeetha et al 2023]. It involves multiple stages:

2.2.1 Text Planning

Text planning deals with the selection of information to be utilised and structures it systematically.

Content Determination: Selecting relevant information for output. Discourse Planning: Structuring information into coherent paragraphs or sequences. Example: Input: Data about weather (temperature, humidity, wind speed). Text Planning Output: Choose to produce a weather report that encompasses temperature and the likelihood of a rain shower.

2.2.2 Sentence Structuring

Sentence structuring is a process of placing words and phrases in a coherent order as well as in a grammatically correct manner. Syntactic Structuring: Ensures correct grammar and word order. Semantic Structuring: It helps in maintaining the logical flow of the text that is being generated. Example: Input: Data: (User expenditure on grocery for the month of March was 500 US dollars). Output: "In March the amount of money the user spent on groceries was $ 500."

2.2.3 Content Realization

Content realization transforms a series of structured text into natural and fluent sentences.

Lexical Choice: Selecting appropriate words and expressions. Grammar and Morphology Generation: Ensuring proper verb tense, subject-verb agreement, and word inflections. As for the last, the topic is to make stylistic adjustments: the difference between the language used in a formal report and the language used in a chatbot response. Example: Formal Writing: The patient displayed some signs of an ailment. Casual Output: "The patient had some illness indicators."

2.3 Key Differences Between Traditional NLP and Modern Deep Learning Approaches

The field of NLP has gone through rule-based systems, statistical models, and the relatively newer category of deep learning techniques.

Table 1. Traditional NLP and modern deep learning approaches

Feature	Traditional NLP	Deep Learning-Based NLP
Approach	Rule-based, hand-crafted linguistic rules	Data-driven learning from large text corpora
Examples	Syntax-based parsers, Hidden Markov Models (HMMs)	Transformers (BERT, GPT, T5)
Flexibility	Requires extensive manual work	Learns patterns from data, adapts easily
Scalability	Limited to predefined rules	Handles large-scale datasets and complex tasks
Error Handling	Struggles with ambiguity	Uses contextual embeddings for better interpretation

Traditional NLP (Pre-Deep Learning Era): Based on hand-crafted rules and symbolic AI. Implemented models such as, HMM and n-gram models for purposes like speech recognition. Example: Early chatbots used the technique of the script.

Modern NLP (Deep Learning Era): Uses neural networks, embeddings, and self-attention mechanisms. Relies on models like transformers (BERT, GPT, T5) that capture context better. Example: AI-automated chatbots can proactively and self-generate their replies.

2.4 Evolution of NLU and NLG Techniques

Early Rule-Based Systems (1950s–1990s): Relied on grammatical rules and decision trees.

Statistical NLP and Machine Learning (1990s–2010s): regular approaches such as HMMs and the Naïve Bayes algorithm to be used for POS tagging and sentiment analysis among others. SVMs and CRFs enhanced the entity recognition and classification because of the machine learning technique used. Recent developments in the field involve the use of Deep Learning and Transformer Models from 2010 up to the present, that introduced the use of word embeddings such as Word2Vec and GloVe for containing semantic relation. Full transformer models on top of them (BERT, GPT, T5, XLNet, etc.) helped in deep contextual representation learning. Some of the primary concepts of NLU and NLG are critical for language processing by AI. NLU means understanding of various levels of language analysis, such as syntactic, semantic, discursive, and pragmatic. While NLG is more concerned with content planning at the structural level, generation of sentences and use of language. The transition from the rule of thumb to deep learning has significantly enhanced the NLP models, making them perform complex linguistic tasks. In the future, as AI develops, the future advancements in the field of NLU and NLG will be even more developed and closer to human level.

3.PRETRAINED MODELS OF TRANSFORMER

Transformer models have greatly enhanced the fields of NLU and NLG due to their development. They use self-attention mechanisms to handle the text in a more efficient manner compared to the previous models, such as RNNs and CNNs. BERT (Bidirectional Encoder Representations from Transformers) is one of the most significant transformer models that provided bidirectional contextual embeddings, which means that it is capable of understanding the meaning of a word based on its context from both before and after it. Some of BERT's training techniques include the masked language modeling (MLM) which involves masking some words in a sentence and the model is expected to predict them; and the next sentence prediction (NSP) which identifies relationships between two sentences. There are also other forms of BERT including RoBERTa and ALBERT that have enhanced its architecture to perform better on different NLP undertakings. While BERT is aimed at understanding the text, GPT, or Generative Pretrained Transformer, is designed for generation of text. GPT works in an autoregressive way, predicting the next token based on the previous tokens on the left to right manner. Following different iterations GPT-2, GPT-3, and most recently GPT-4, have shown capability of generating natural follow-up text, creative writing, summarization, conversational âlast point AI etc. The second revolutionary model is T5 (Text-to-Text Transfer Transformer), which reformulates all NLP tasks in the text-to-text form. T5 uses prefix-based conditioning where cues (e.g., "summarize: ") are used to influence its responses. While BERT is designed for understanding and GPT is for generation, T5 is a model that combines both NLU and NLG. All in all, these transformer models have paved a way to new generation that has revolutionized and evolved the text driven AI models for several applications like chatbots, content generation and machine translations[Kotei, E., & Thirunavukarasu, R. 2023].

3.1 Fine-Tuning and Prompt Engineering for Specialized Tasks

While the large pretrained models are proven to be very accurate at generalization, further fine-tuning of the model is required to enable the model to perform implementations on problem-specific tasks. More specifically, transfer learning entails training that a certain model received in order to adapt it to another particular set and, in effect, hone its response to new tasks. For instance, BioBERT is simply BERT model that is fine-tuned on biomedical texts to yield enhanced accuracy in medical entity identification and clinical records extraction. It is especially useful in cases when the generalist models are not able to work with specific terminology, for example, legal documents or financial texts. Another such technique that has been developed is the prompt engineering which has been proposed as a replacement for fine-tuning. Unlike other techniques that adjust the model's parameters, prompt engineering improves the manner in which the input queries are framed. Structured prompts help in controlling the flow of the model and thus results in better coherence and relevance of the text generated. Other related approaches include few-shot and zero-shot learning that builds upon prompt engineering by enabling tasks to be performed with little to no examples. For example, a few-shot prompt for translation may involve providing several examples to the model in order to let the model learn patterns even when it is not trained heavily on the task. The emergence of prompt engineering has helped to make the AI tools less complex and more friendly to the users who can now tweak the AI's behavior without having to spend lots of time in front of a computer or have special training to do so.

3.2 Reinforcement Learning and Self-Supervised Learning for NLU and NLG

The inclusion of RL and SSL has also boosted the NLU and NLG features in recent years. Reinforcement learning has been used in fine tuning of text generation models such as the current ChatGPT and the Reinforcement Learning from Human Feedback (RLHF). The integration of human preference into the training loop makes the RLHF make responses that are more likely to meet human expectations on both factual and ethical aspects. RLHF is especially helpful in reducing bias and improving the context relevance of the generated text, which makes models suitable for application in education, customer support, and virtual assistants. Self-supervised learning, in general, does not require the expensive process of labelling the data since the structure of the data together with other signals can be utilized to learn useful representations. One of the most important examples of SSL is BERT's masked language modeling (MLM) in which the model is trained to predict the masked words in a given sentence which helps it acquire a better understanding of the language structure. SSL techniques have greatly helped in cutting the costs of labeled datasets, and hence making the improvements in NLP more affordable and effective. The integration of RL and SSL has resulted in the creation of the AI systems that learn incrementally through interaction, acquiring large amounts of information from the data that has not been marked, and adjusting the answers according to the feedback provided.

3.3 The Role of Knowledge Graphs and Reasoning in Improving NLU

Nevertheless, there is still a problem of reasoning and the ability to keep to facts in NLU, even with the progress in neural language models. Knowledge graphs mitigate this problem by modeling information in forms of nodes that represent the real-world items and edges that represent the relations between them. In contrast to statistical models, knowledge graphs offer AI systems the facts about the world, which improve the systems' capacity for logical thinking and information retrieval. For instance, the Google Knowledge Graph helps to respond to the search queries by associating concepts that are related to those mentioned in the query even if the query is ambiguous. Combining knowledge graphs with the transformer models increases the model's ability to disambiguate between different senses, which allows for the differentiation between the entity "Apple" the fruit, and "Apple" the company. Secondly, the integration of the neural network classifier with the rule-based system practically to create a hybrid system helps AI solve other sophisticated issues like multi-hop QA and inferential reasoning. With the help of the structured knowledge sources, NLU models go beyond the statistical correlations and can give fact-based answers, which helps to close the gap between artificial intelligence language understanding and actual knowledge in the world. The main scientific and technological advancements in NLU and NLG have occurred in the last few years and are based on the transformer architecture, multimodal learning, fine-tuning, reinforcement learning, and knowledge graph integration. Such advancements have served to grow the intricacy in applying fuzzy logic control over human language arrangements that aid conversational AI, advances the capacity to produce written content, and enhances decision-making systems. In future research, the integration of reasoning mechanisms and multimodal capabilities will help AI to improve the level of communication with people, making the creation of perfect human-computer interface closer. The continuous advancement in language models means that more advanced AI is expected to be integrated into the market and different industries to become a necessity.

4 CONVERSATIONAL AI: CHATBOTS, VIRTUAL ASSISTANTS, AND CUSTOMER SERVICE

Conversational AI also falls under the category of NLU and NLG and is one of the most recognized applications of AI availing communication interfaces of humans and machines. Siri, Alexa, and Google Assistant and other similar chatbots are part of people's lives as they use the voice and text commands to interact with devices to perform various tasks. These systems are based on NLU to understand the user's query and NLG to produce a logical reply. The first forms of chatbots are discrete and followed a set of rules which allowed the bot to only respond to certain commands. But with the help of transformer-based models like GPT and BERT, the conversational agents have become smarter in terms of recognizing the context and the intent and can also flow through a conversation in a more conversational manner. In customer service, use of chatbots makes it possible to respond to various questions, from basic problems to sales. AI chatbots are deployed in organizations as they help the companies to cut on costs and at the same time offer faster and more efficient services to the clients. For instance, AI-based customer service can even determine the tone of the customer's input and respond accordingly in a sympathetic manner. Some models also possess the Multimodal features through which people can interact using their voices, texts, and images. With the advance of time, conversational AI will only enhance the abilities of reinforcement learning, as well as the play between personalization algorithms and context aware virtual assistants [Maheswari, B., & Nagarajan, R. 2024].

4.1 Machine Translation and Cross-Lingual Understanding

Thus, the subject of machine translation (MT) has experienced a lot of development because of the improvement of deep learning models. Previous methods used in MT included statistical and rule-based techniques, which led to unnatural and sometimes incorrect translations. Transformer models have brought a significant change in translation and achieve better context, idioms, and cultural differences. These models employ bilingual and multilingual training data that helps in understanding the cross-lingual characteristic of the language to support natural and accurate translation in different languages. Apart from the basic task of translation, the modern AI systems are able to perform zero-shot and few-shot translation, which means that the machine can translate words and phrases it has never encountered before. This is especially important for underrepresented languages where obtaining labeled data is quite challenging. Cross-lingual understanding is also used in other areas including international business communication, diplomacy, and speech translation in video conferencing. Google Translate and DeepL are effective examples of the use of NLU and NLG for achieving accurate translation with regard to context. With advanced AI models for translation, interactions between people of different languages will become much easier to facilitate.

4.2 Summarization, Content Generation, and Automated Writing

Today, AI's capabilities of summarizing and generating content have already entered industries like journalism, marketing, and academics. It is especially helpful in dealing with large volumes of information such that after reading a long article, research paper or a news report, a user will get a summary of the important points. Summarization techniques are of two categories, namely, extractive summarization and abstractive summarization where the former involves identifying and selecting the most important sentences while the latter involves paraphrasing and condensing the original text. New models have been developed for abstractive summarization and they are more coherent and natural. In content generation, AI helps the writers to generate articles, social media posts and even fictions and stories. Thus, GPT-4 and models of a similar level can write blogs, reports, and even advertisements and help to create content quickly. Jasper AI and Grammarly are some of the writing tools that use NLG in writing, re-writing, and correcting of grammatical mistakes. It has also brought about issues of fake news and the issue of whether or not articles created by AI are real or not. Currently, there are efforts to identify AI written content and to check its plausibility to make the information produced by AI credible.

4.3 Sentiment Analysis and Emotion Recognition

Both of the above fields are powerful tools in the current market trends, customer feedback and social media platforms analysis. These technologies are based on NLU that allows recognizing the sentiment in the text and determining whether it is positive, negative, or neutral. However, more sophisticated models do not only classify text into positive or negative but also expectation or disappointment and other feelings like joy, anger, sadness, sarcasm, and so on. Thus, the sentiment analysis is employed by companies to measure consumer satisfaction, understand how their brand is viewed in the market, and make management decisions based on the customers' opinions. It is also being incorporated into chatbots and virtual assistants for the purpose of enabling accurate emotion detection in human-computer interaction. The textual cues and tone can be identified for the given text and based on that the response from the AI model can be made more empathetic and contextually relevant. For example, there are apps focused on the mental health sphere such as Woebot that uses the sentiment analysis approach of communication. Moreover, emotion recognition is used in AI-based customer service to identify a client's frustration or dissatisfaction and escalate the interaction to an agent if needed. When the domain knowledge advances to the deeper level of emotions of people, then it can enhance the communicative interface of the human with helping AI.

4.5 Question Answering and Interactive AI Systems

Question answering (QA) systems are one of the most complex NLU and NLG application that allows users to find specific information in large databases. These are employed in the applications such as web search engines, voice-activated assistants, and automated customer service. The traditional QA models used to work on keyword searches and most of the time, the results were not so relevant. The new QA models based on deep learning and transformers comprehend the meaning of the user's queries and provide correct and context-based answers. Systems in the open-domain QA, like Google Search and OpenAI's ChatGPT, search answers from large datasets such as Wikipedia or Common Crawl. Closed-domain QA systems are specific to a certain field such as medical or financial. In medical AI, for instance, QA models help the doctors in finding clinical guidelines pertinent to the symptoms a patient is experiencing. The integration of QA systems with knowledge graphs improves the effectiveness of the answers as they are based on facts and not just on the statistical analysis of the text. QA technologies are used by interactive AI systems like AI tutors and customer service bots to engage in question and answer sessions and retain the flow of the conversation.

4.6 AI-Powered Education and Tutoring Systems

Intelligent tutoring system and personalized learning are the two most significant fields where AI is being used in education. NLU is employed by AI-based tutors to analyze students' questions and then respond with adequate explanations. It is also embedded with features that enable it to suit the learner's learning style and provides feedback and suggestions. AI is implemented in platforms that track the students' performance and provide recommendations on how they can progress further. Among the most promising developments in the sphere of AI application in learning, there is the use of intelligent systems for evaluating and providing feedback for essays. Turnitin and Grammarly are some of the AI tools that employ NLU in checking and evaluating grammar, coherence, and uniqueness of student works and offer feedback immediately. In fact, generative AI models assist students in writing essays, coming up with ideas for a written work in creative writing classes, and debugging code in programming classes. Robotic education chatbots help in learning as they are able to respond to students' questions in real time, as well as help with homework and preparation for exams. Another one is artificial intelligence based assistive technologies for students with disabilities. Speech to text and text to speech are helpful for students with hearing or vision impairment concerning learning materials. Applications like Otter.ai or the real-time captioning applications developed by Microsoft are useful to make it easier for students to get subtitles of lectures, discussions, etc. These areas of AI in education will further advance as AI interacts with NLU and NLG to make education more effective in the conventional education system.

The use of NLU and NLG in AI-human interaction has impacted various industries such as customer service, content development, education, and translation services. Conversational AI has become more natural and smooth than before due to development in the conversational AI systems, the machine translation, summarization, the sentiment analysis, question answering, and AI-based tutoring systems. In the future, the advancements in reasoning capability, multimodal understanding, and ethical approach towards AI development will add more strength to the NLU and NLG to develop smarter and natural communication systems.

5. DATA BIASES AND ETHICAL CONCERNS IN NLU/NLG MODELS

This is especially the case with Natural Language Understanding (NLU) and Natural Language Generation (NLG) where the problem of data bias arises due to the datasets used to train the AI. Some of the giant models such as GPT-4, BERT, and T5 are based on corpora that include news articles, books, and other posts from social media platforms. However, the sources themselves can be defined as gendered, racid, culturally and politically biased, and thus introduce the corresponding bias into AI-generated output. For instance, research has found out that language models tend to promote prejudice, for example, by linking certain careers to gender or by producing material that only presents partial views. Ethical questions come into perspective when GAN-generated content is used in areas like, employment, law, and journalism among others. The negative effects of misuse of NLU and NLG are significant, and if left to run rampant without intervention, they will only lead to further discrimination and spread of wrong information. There are methods such as adversarial debiasing, changes in the training target of the models, reinforcement learning with human feedback, and transparent models that can be used to address these biases. Furthermore, the organizations which work on the AI models must address the issues of transparency and share the ethical policies, datasets, and methods of addressing the bias. It is important to remember that being fair in the text generated by AI is an unresolved issue that needs constant analysis and cooperation with AI specialists, legislators, and ethicists.

5.1 Hallucination and Factual Inconsistency in Text Generation

One of the biggest drawbacks of the current NLG models is that they suffer from hallucination, that is, the system creates texts with factually incorrect or misleading information. While generative AI models do not comprehend information in the way humans do, i.e., they do not have a set of facts stored in a reliable database and call up the information when needed but generate text based on statistical analysis. Therefore, they often distort the facts and make up the events or provide false references, which is not true in their case. Hallucination is especially undesirable in the application that requires high precision such as in diagnosis, legal documents, and research papers. For instance, a medical chatbot that has been trained on an NLG model may provide wrong recommendations on the treatment to a patient which may be detrimental to the health of the patient. In the same way, fake news in the form of articles written by AI can also spread fake information that is misleading.

To this end, researchers are working on integrating deep learning with symbolic AI, and knowledge graphs as the best approach to solving the problem. One of the techniques that has been used to combine NLG with external knowledge sources to make sure that the answers produced are sound is known as retrieval-augmented generation (RAG). Another approach is the use of confidence scores in the AI-generated content where the model gives an estimated confidence level regarding the response. Although these solutions reduce the cases of hallucination, eradicating factual inaccuracy in NLG is still a problem that is yet to be solved.

5.2 Scalability and Computational Resource Requirements

Current and future advanced NLU and NLG models, especially those based on the transformer architecture like GPT-4, BERT, and T5, are computationally expensive for training and use. These models contain billions of parameters, and they require high amount of GPU, memory and high energy consumption to support it. The cost of training large-scale models, they can easily run into a couple of millions of dollars – this puts small research laboratories, startup companies and academic institutions at a disadvantage as the large tech companies who can afford to dedicate large computing resources and budgets can outcompete. However, the application of these models in real-life problems presents several scalability issues. When performing inference on large models, there is a high latency which is a problem in those applications that need to operate in real-time, such as voice assistants or chatbots. Some of these challenges can be addressed by the use of cloud-based solutions, but they present issues in data privacy, security as well as in the reliance on centralized systems. For the purpose of scalability, other techniques such as knowledge distillation where a large model is made small, yet retains the functionalities of the large model. Also, models such as sparse models and mixture-of-experts architectures are being created to enhance resource utilization hence expanding the capacity of the AI models without the need for more resources. It still remains to look for ways in which a balance has been created between the performance of developing models of AI and the efficiency of the same.

5.3 Robustness and Generalization Across Different Languages and Domains

In fact, current NLU and NLG models perform better in English and other popular languages or the languages with large amounts of training data. Most AI models perform worse in such languages that are characterized by BFM-writing, small text corpora, and non-Latin scripts. Advancements in AI development have therefore remained anchored to high-resource language only through this restraint of linguistic capability. Apart from language issues, lack of robustness across different domains is an issue. This is because most of the publicly available datasets contain general information and not specific to a particular field such as law, medicine or finance. For example, if an NLU model used to train the structure from conversational text will not read legal documents well due to a difference in the language use and language used. To that end, multilingual and cross-lingual models have been trained on various datasets to enhance generalization. Some methods such as transfer learning, few-shot learning, and domain adaptation provide a way to overcome language barriers as they involve further training of models on a few samples for the required application. Nevertheless, despite these advancements, the number of languages and domains is still a major concern in order to achieve a consistent performance of the model across language and domain.

5.4 Ambiguity and Contextual Misunderstandings in NLU

In natural language, there is always a tendency to have an element of vagueness, which is the use of words or phrases that have more than one meaning. This is a problem for NLU models since they have to understand the user intent even with the language ambiguity. Idioms, metaphors, irony and other similar cases may cause misunderstandings as well during interaction with artificial intelligence. For instance, the phrase: 'I saw the man with binoculars.' can be understood in two ways: the speaker was using binoculars when seeing the man; or the man being observed was in possession of binoculars. Thus, detection is still a challenging problem for AI as sarcasm is closely associated with tone, context, and background knowledge. Current sophisticated NLU relies on context embeddings and attention mechanisms to capture aspects of the model's input, but simple forms of linguistic context, which are implicitly processed by the language receptors in human brain, remain beyond the capabilities of most advanced models. To reduce such ambiguity, there has been an attempt by researchers to adopt multimodal learning which is the use of text, speech and vision data in AI. Other approaches to AI that are useful in maintaining coherence in long conversations include memory-augmented models and discourse analysis. Yet, the ability to understand language in the same way as human does still remains a challenge that has to be solved with the help of further development of context representation and reasoning capabilities.

5.5 Ensuring Human-Like Coherence and Reasoning in NLG

This is a general weakness of current NLG models as they are very fluent and grammatically correct but they do not reason well when it comes to long-form generation. It must be noted that while working on the text formulated by AI, users often experience jumps in the subject matter and logical leaps that affect the text's cohesiveness. This is due to the fact that existing NLG models use statistical measures to create text without the capability of comprehension. For example, news summaries produced by AI can lack certain important elements and the creative writing models can fail to be consistent when it comes to long texts. Moreover, despite such models' capabilities to mimic reasoning to some extent, they may use superficial logic-based strategies instead of actual logical reasoning. In order to improve the cohesion and logical thinking, there are possibilities combining NLG with symbolic AI, Knowledge Graphs and Reinforcement Learning. The use of deep learning with knowledge-based rules provides the best results in enhancing long-term consistency and logical thinking in AI. Additionally, the AI systems which include feedback loops assist in the enhancement of the generated text by adapting to the users' expectations. Nevertheless, a number of issues are still present, and human-like reasoning in the generated text is still far from being achieved. Further studies will have to be dedicated to creating AI systems capable of producing grammatically correct and semantically meaningful text, as well as capable of critical thinking and understanding of the context of the problems that may be encountered.

The current improvements in NLU and NLG have enhanced the communication between human and AI in many ways, however, there are still some challenges and limitations that affect the general use and reliability. Limitations of the model involve presence of bias in the training data, hallucination in mainly text generation, and computation cost. Further, the matters of multilingualism, the ambiguity resolution as well as the coherence in the text generated by the AI still pose interesting questions.

To address these challenges, there is a necessity to entail convergence in these four themes: interdisciplinary work from both technique and computer science domain, better data management and governance, as well as the enhancement of architectures for training machine learning models. The following are some of the limitations of AI, which, as AI advances, will be important to overcome in order to improve the effectiveness, safety, and availability of NLU and NLG models.

6. ADDRESSING BIAS AND FAIRNESS IN LANGUAGE MODELS

Preconception in language models is one of the major ethical challenges in Natural Language Understanding (NLU) and Natural Language Generation (NLG). These models are trained using very large data scraped from the internet; therefore, they contain gender, race, culture, and political bias. This can lead to content that perpetuates stereotype or exclusion of some groups in such a way that is created and developed by the algorithms. For example, it has been demonstrated that language models correlate some types of jobs with certain genders or produce racially insensitive responses. To guarantee that there is no bias in NLU and NLG, it is essential to look for bias and take measures to minimize it. One of the methods is to filter the training data so that it does not contain any biases that could be detrimental. Another approach is debiasing techniques such as the adversarial training where the models are further trained to eliminate discriminating outputs. Further, other algorithms such as counterfactual data augmentation bring in fairness to the training data by introducing diverse perspectives. Other than that, the emphasis should be placed on the technical aspects of AI together with the transparency within the development of AI. The models used by organizations should indicate how they are trained, the data they use, and how issues of bias are dealt with. The regulatory authorities and researchers also support fairness checks under which third parties review the AI models for compliance with ethical and diversity benchmarks. In this way, it is possible to advance in the development of AI that is less prejudiced and socially inclusive when generating language models.

6.1 Privacy Concerns in AI-Generated Content

One of the key ethical issues of AI in communication is privacy since AI models analyze users' personal information. Virtual assistants, chatbots, and voice typing and transcription services, which are based on NLU, process users' conversations, their financial transactions, and health information. If not well protected, such AI systems are at risk of being hacked, and this would mean that the privacy of the information processed by these systems can be compromised. The first of them is the leakage of data that occurs when AI models memorize and reproduce information from training datasets. It has been found that big language models sometimes leak PII such as names, addresses, and credit card numbers, which is highly dangerous for users. To avoid this, the AI developers use differential privacy techniques which involve putting a noise to the training data to ensure that the models do not learn specific information. Also, privacy-preserving techniques like Federated Learning helps training of AI models on the client side instead of sending data to the server. This reduces the risks of security threats and also allows the users to have more control on their information. Policies that help to facilitate the destruction of generated data, use of appropriate encryption guidelines such as using the GDPR and data protection policies also help to enhance the level of privacy of the user.

6.2 Explainability and Interpretability of NLU/NLG Models

Nevertheless, the majority of the current state-of-the-art NLU and NLG models based on deep learning are often referred to as 'black boxes' due to the lack of interpretability as to how the models arrive at certain outputs. This lack of transparency becomes an issue in sensitive uses such as legal, medical, and financial in which users require to trust the output produced by the AI. The term explainability in the context of AI relates to the capability of generating human-interpretable rationale for the outcome of an AI model. In the context of NLU and NLG, this means to make the decision-making more transparent so that the user can evaluate the trustworthiness of the automatically generated text. Several approaches are being worked on to enhance explainability and some of them are attention maps where heat maps are used to indicate the words that are considered by the model in its decision making. One of the ways is the combination of symbolic approaches with neural networks so that the AI models provide more formalized and explainable results. Also, there are efforts to develop SAIs which are self-explanatory to allow users to assess the reliability of AI-generated information. Explainability will also become crucial for developing AI-based communication systems to be trusted by people.

Figure 1. Addressing bias and fairness

6.3 Regulatory and Policy Challenges in AI-Driven Communication

Since AI content creation is on the rise, the existing rules and regulations are not able to cope up with the new advancements in NLU and NLG. This has forced governments and international organizations to come up with ways and means of regulating the use of AI in the deployment of language models. However, regulating them in the global and digital environment has its drawbacks. Another important regulatory issue is something as simple as: Who is to blame when something goes wrong, and AI has produced the content? For instance, if the AI system is producing wrong financial advice or defamatory statements, then to assign blame the process may not be very easy. Many laws and regulations in the contemporary world do not directly address the ownership of AI-generated content, and therefore, remain vague in attributing legal liability. There are several ways that policymakers are considering how to regulate AI with the proposed requirements for companies to label content created by AI and to have human review of the content. For example, the European Union's AI Act contains a categorization of AI systems based upon the risk, or origin an AI system poses more specific requirements necessary for risky applications such as medical and administrative AI systems. The same case is observed in the United States and other countries where efforts are being made to come up with ethical guidelines for artificial intelligence that will encourage innovation but also control the negative impacts. However, there are still many loopholes that have not been closed and that is why there is a need for continuous discussion between governments, researchers in artificial intelligence, and other stakeholders in the industry to come up with the best laws that will protect the users while at the same time promoting development of new technologies.

6.4 Mitigating Misinformation and Harmful Content Generation

The main concern regarding NLU and NLG models is that they can produce and disseminate information that is false. This technology can be used to produce deep fake articles, fake reviews, and fake news which will help the promoters of disinformation to spread their information and erode the trust of people in the information they receive through the internet. It is therefore important to note that generative AI models do not check facts but rather predict probable text based on patterns learned. In this regard, researchers are developing self-remediating solutions where AI-generated text is compared with knowledge base and reliable sources. For instance, it is possible to integrate AI models that can compare the claims with standard databases like Wikipedia, government records, or even scientific articles. Also, machine learning is being used to create algorithms to detect AI-written content from the real human ones to fight fake news. Another way of reducing the negative impact is the moderation of content with the help of filters that are powered by AI and which can identify hate speech, propaganda and other forms of improper language. These systems of filtering are not without their flaws and can sometimes end up classifying what should not be censored as well as items that should not be blocked at all. Thus, the use of AI moderation with human supervision still remains a better approach to achieving responsible use of AI in communication. Another factor that can be attributed to the spread of fake news is the lack of knowledge of the public and their ignorance of the digital environment. It is possible to teach users to critically assess AI content, check the sources, and identify possible bias which will help them to use AI safely. Therefore, as the models and applications of AI keep on developing, there is a need to avoid falling into pitfalls that may lead to misuse of these technologies in NLU and NLG. Ethical issues in NLU as well as in NLG are vast and varied and can only be solved with the help of technological, regulatory, and social measures. Bias, privacy, explainability, and responsible AI policies are some of the aspects that need to be considered in order to gain trust and be accountable when using AI in communication. To ensure that NLU and NLG remain beneficial assets to society, more research will be required in the future as well as a combination of cross-disciplinary collaboration and proactive governance.

7. INTEGRATING REASONING FOR BETTER NLU

One of the biggest problems of NLU, which, in fact, can be stated as one of the biggest problems of AI today, is the ability to reason. Indeed deep-learning-based models are trained well for the abundant use of computing numbers and statistically associated patterns but lack of common-sense reasoning. Applying commonsense knowledge helps AI to derive missing information, comprehend the cause-effect relationship and provide a more relevant response. The approaches to consider commonsense reasoning into NLU have considered external knowledge sources like ConceptNet, ATOMIC, and Cyc that store relevant information about concepts and their interconnection. Experts are also researching neuro-symbolic AI systems so that deep learning structures can be integrated with formal systems of rules for data inference. Another promising direction is the self-supervised learning techniques that enables the model to learn commonsense knowledge from the large text data. For instance, the reinforcement learning strategies can be employed to adapt the models in line with the feedback received from people to ensure that the models' responses are as humanlike as possible. Furthermore, the intention will be built based on the further improvements in the field of commonsense reasoning so as to make the AI systems more credible, explainable, and capable of perceiving the subtleties of human language.

7.1 Advances in Few-Shot and Zero-Shot Learning for Low-Resource Languages

One of the major issues of the modern NLU and NLG is a task's dependency on the availability of large amounts of high-quality data. This is a challenge especially for the low resource languages which are defined by the amount of text available digitally. Few-shot and zero-shot learning methods are being proposed as the solutions to this problem, which enable the model to transfer the knowledge from high-resource languages to the low-resource ones with just a few examples. Few-shot learning means that an AI model can learn a task with little labeled training data with the help of related knowledge in a large dataset. Zero-shot learning takes it a step further by enabling models to perform tasks that are not even seen during training as the model is trained on related tasks. Both GPT and T5 are promising models and have capacitive of doing zero-shot learning yet are not very accurate at low resource languages. In recent years, there has been an interpersonal study of multilingualism in pretraining regarding where the models are trained in multiple languages to enhance cross-lingual translation. Another approach is the meta-learning based approaches where the models are expected to learn quickly in the new language with very little guidance. Further developments in this regard may greatly improve AI's interaction with languages and cultures to promote non-discriminatory AI-driven communication.

7.2 Hybrid AI Approaches Combining Symbolic Reasoning with Deep Learning

Although deep learning has significantly advanced NLP there are some disadvantages, specifically, interpretability and logical reasoning. Deep learning has some limitations and these are as follows: To overcome these shortcomings, researchers have proposed the use of Hybrid AI system which integrates deep learning with a symbolic system, a method that incorporates rules and knowledge in a structured manner. Symbolic reasoning helps an AI system to infer, follow rules and patterns and can also guarantee that the information that is generated is logical. This helped researchers to address the need in development of high-performance AI models that are, at the same time, interpretable. For instance, hybrid models can make use of knowledge graphs to improve the comprehension and also check for the factuality of the text to be generated. One of the most prospective areas of applying hybrid AI is explainable AI (XAI) that allows using symbolic reasoning to explain why the AI came up with a particular answer. A sphere is legal and medical AI systems, in which learning models allow obtaining information from the text, and logical analysis provides compliance with the established norms and standards. This shall be the case especially as hybrid AI is applied in the enhancement of NLU and NLG systems for better robustness and accountability.

7.3 Improving Human-AI Collaboration Through Interactive NLG Systems

Such a system allows for effective co-working with an AI and became popular with the progress of AI technologies to generate text. These systems are designed to bring more flexibility in the interaction with the user, as well as to provide real-time feedback and adaptation to the context. One of the approaches is to have the AI model making decisions based on the feedback from the user in a sequential manner. For example, in applying the technology the content creations can still adjust the tone or the style of writing, or merely check factual data. Likewise, AI-powered programming aids enable the programmer to iteratively edit the proposed code. A method of AI research with great potential for the future is the development of adaptive, and the models that get better with each iteration based on new user interactions. These are especially helpful in the customer support chatbots, educational quizbots and virtual writing companions. The problem is to find the right dosage of autonomy given to the AI and the extent of control the user may have over the generated output while achieving the best results. The two significant areas of improvement will be reinforcement learning and prompt engineering, which will be instrumental in increasing the interactivity of NLG systems. This way, the AI models can be made more sensitive and interactive and thus developing better communication interfaces.

7.4 The Role of Quantum Computing in Scaling NLP Models

On the other hand, as NLP models become larger and sophisticated, they demand many computational resources in terms of memory and time, thus posing some worrying effects of scale. Quantum computing offers a possibility to overcome such challenges due to the utilization of quantum parallelism for processing large amounts of data. Quantum machine learning (QML) is a relatively new area of study for researchers to fill in and investigate the application of quantum algorithms in NLP. Investigations are being conducted in order to enhance the speed of certain quantized applications, including text classification, sentiment analysis, and machine translation. It could also benefit model training since it would be possible to optimize billions of parameters in deep learning models in a shorter time. Nevertheless, quantum computing in NLP is still in its infancy. Quantum computers at the present moment are not able to solve a set of tasks that would allow it to become more efficient than classical supercomputers in NLP. However, the recent technological innovations in the quantum algorithms and quantum hardware indicate that in the future, the use of quantum NLP in AI communication will lead to faster, more efficient, and more effective language models.

8. CONCLUSION

There are strides in NLU and NLG due to the deep learning, transformers, and even multimodal intelligence. These have made it possible for AI to understand, analyze, and generate human language than it has ever been possible making communication in the presence of AI natural. Nonetheless, some issues like data bias, ethical issues, data discrepancies, and computational issues are still present. These are important concerns to be met so that AI-driven language technologies can be developed in a responsible and reliable manner.

In this survey, we identified the various components of NLU & NLG models, the current progressing models like BERT, GPT, and T5, and various domains such as conversational assistants, translation, content writing, sentiment analysis, and question-answering systems. We also pointed out some of the limitations such as hallucination in the text generation, the scalability issue and the most challenging aspect of emulating human-like coherence and reasoning in the AI generated text. Other issues that were raised included the ethical questions like the bias, false information, and privacy as well as regulation of the AI. In the future, further research will be devoted to several aspects to improve NLU and NLG systems. Incorporating of commonsense reasoning will enable AI to grasp the implicit knowledge and the context. There are two fundamentally different approaches to few-shot and zero-shot learning that will benefit low-resource languages in AI. The integration and amalgamation of both deep learning and symbolic processes of reasoning will enhance the two aspects of the emerging AI Systems. Interactive NLG systems will improve the human-AI interaction in such a way that the AI output will be more flexible and manageable. Further, quantum computing has been proposed for scaling up NLP models that could transform AI in the end with language processing and generation. The progression of NLU and NLG research has far-reaching consequences for science, business, and culture of the society. Improvement of efficient, intelligible, and interpretable AI whilst ensuring the robustness of the proposed models is among the thrusts in AI research. AI integrated language systems will remain a trend in the future industries especially in the sectors like healthcare, education, customer services, and content generation. At the societal level, there will be a need to practice ethical AI in order to avoid possible risks such as fake news, invasion of privacy, and unfair decisions. In conclusion, it can be stated that the interaction between man and artificial intelligence is determined by the degree of innovative approach and the degree of responsibility. AI is capable of becoming more helpful, reliable, and valuable in improving people's communication and expanding their knowledge if it starts overcoming the existing shortcomings and incorporates new trends in the field of research.

REFERENCES

Atmaja, B. T., & Sasou, A. (2022). Sentiment analysis and emotion recognition from speech using universal speech representations. *Sensors (Basel)*, *22*(17), 6369. DOI: 10.3390/s22176369 PMID: 36080828

Bowman, S. R., & Dahl, G. E. (2021). What will it take to fix benchmarking in natural language understanding? *arXiv preprint arXiv:2104.02145*. DOI: 10.18653/v1/2021.naacl-main.385

Chowdhary, K., & Chowdhary, K. R. (2020). Natural language processing. *Fundamentals of artificial intelligence*, 603-649.

Darwish, D. (2024). Chatbots vs. AI Chatbots vs. Virtual Assistants. In *Design and Development of Emerging Chatbot Technology* (pp. 26–50). IGI Global. DOI: 10.4018/979-8-3693-1830-0.ch002

Fanni, S. C., Febi, M., Aghakhanyan, G., & Neri, E. (2023). Natural language processing. In *Introduction to artificial intelligence* (pp. 87–99). Springer International Publishing. DOI: 10.1007/978-3-031-25928-9_5

Kotei, E., & Thirunavukarasu, R. (2023). A systematic review of transformer-based pre-trained language models through self-supervised learning. *Information (Basel)*, *14*(3), 187. DOI: 10.3390/info14030187

Maheswari, B., & Nagarajan, R. (2024). EduChatbot: Implementing educational Chatbot for assisting the teaching-learning process by NLP-based hybrid heuristic adopted deep learning framework. *Kybernetes*.

Mazidi, K., & Tarau, P. (2016). Automatic question generation: From NLU to NLG. In *Intelligent Tutoring Systems: 13th International Conference, ITS 2016, Zagreb, Croatia, June 7-10, 2016*. [Springer International Publishing.]. *Proceedings*, *13*, 23–33.

Mekni, M. (2021). An artificial intelligence based virtual assistant using conversational agents. *Journal of Software Engineering and Applications*, *14*(9), 455–473. DOI: 10.4236/jsea.2021.149027

Sangeetha, R., Srivastava, D., Logeshwaran, J., Vishwakarma, P., & Vats, S. (2023, November). Optimization of Natural Language Understanding with Contextual Embeddings. In *2023 International Conference on Research Methodologies in Knowledge Management, Artificial Intelligence and Telecommunication Engineering (RMKMATE)* (pp. 1-6). IEEE. DOI: 10.1109/RMKMATE59243.2023.10369022

Compilation of References

Adeoye, O., Odeyemi, O., Addy, W., Ofodile, O., Ajayi-Nifise, A., & Okoye, C. (2024). Integrating Artificial Intelligence In Personalized Insurance Products: A Pathway To Enhanced Customer Engagement. *International Journal of Management & Entrepreneurship Research*, *6*(3), 502–511. DOI: 10.51594/ijmer.v6i3.840

Adimulam, T., Chinta, S., & Pattanayak, S. K. (2022). Transfer Learning in Natural Language Processing: Overcoming Low-Resource Challenges. *International Journal of Enhanced Research in Science Technology and Engineering*, *11*, 65–79.

Ahmed, G., & Lawaye, A. A. (2023). End-to-end ASR framework for Indian-English accent: Using speech CNN-based segmentation. *International Journal of Speech Technology*, *26*(4), 903–918. DOI: 10.1007/s10772-023-10053-w

Akgun, S., & Greenhow, C. (2022). Artificial intelligence in education: Addressing ethical challenges in K-12 settings. *AI and Ethics*, *2*(3), 431–440. DOI: 10.1007/s43681-021-00096-7 PMID: 34790956

Akhter, S., Ahmad, M. R., Chibb, M., Zai, A. F., & Yaqoob, M. (2024). Artificial intelligence in the 21st century: Opportunities, risks and ethical imperatives. Kuey.

Al Nabhani, F., Abuhassna, H., & Hamzah, M. B. (2025). The role of artificial intelligence in personalizing educational content: Enhancing the learning experience and developing the teacher's role in an integrated educational environment. *Contemporary Educational Technology*, *17*(2), ep573. DOI: 10.30935/cedtech/16089

Alasmary, H., & Tanveer, M. (2023). ESCI-AKA: Enabling Secure Communication in an IoT-Enabled Smart Home Environment Using Authenticated Key Agreement Framework. *Mathematics*, *11*(16), 3450. DOI: 10.3390/math11163450

Algherairy, A., & Ahmed, M. (2024). A review of dialogue systems: Current trends and future directions. *Neural Computing & Applications*, *36*(12), 6325–6351. DOI: 10.1007/s00521-023-09322-1

Alghowinem, S., Goecke, R., Wagner, M., & Epps, J. (2023). Automatic depression detection from speech: A systematic review. *IEEE Transactions on Affective Computing, 14*(2), 384–399. DOI: 10.1109/TAFFC.2022.3145678

Alilou, M., Tousi, B., & Shayeghi, H. (2025). Energy management of smart appliances, local renewable units and electric vehicles for having residential zero-energy buildings. *Iranian Journal of Science and Technology. Transaction of Electrical Engineering, 49*(3), 1427–1445. Advance online publication. DOI: 10.1007/s40998-025-00817-2

Alsamhi, S. H., Afghah, F., Shvetsov, A. V., Almalki, F. A., Song, H., Hawbani, A., & Lee, B. (2022). Drones' Edge Intelligence Over Smart Environments in B5G: Blockchain and Federated Learning Synergy. *IEEE Transactions on Green Communications and Networking, 6*(1), 295–312. DOI: 10.1109/TGCN.2021.3132561

Alshemali, B., & Kalita, J. (2020). Improving the reliability of deep neural networks in NLP: A review. *Knowledge-Based Systems, 191*, 105210. DOI: 10.1016/j.knosys.2019.105210

Alvi, A., & Mupona, O. C. (2023). Exploring the ethical challenges of Ai in personalised marketing in context of beauty and wellness. *Int. J. All Res. Educ. Sci. Methods, 12*(02), 12–02. DOI: 10.56025/IJARESM.2023.120124482

Ananny, M., & Crawford, K. (2018). Seeing without knowing: Limitations of the transparency ideal and its application to algorithmic accountability. *New Media & Society, 20*(3), 973–989. DOI: 10.1177/1461444816676645

Andriani, P., Batliner, A., & Schuller, B. (2023). A survey on deep learning for speech emotion recognition. *Computer Speech & Language, 79*, 101455. Advance online publication. DOI: 10.1016/j.csl.2023.101455

Ansari, N., Babaei, V., & Najafpour, M. M. (2024). Enhancing catalysis studies with chat generative pre-trained transformer (ChatGPT): Conversation with ChatGPT. *Dalton Transactions : An International Journal of Inorganic Chemistry, 53*(8), 3534–3547. DOI: 10.1039/D3DT04178F PMID: 38275279

Arango-Ibanez, J. P., Posso-Nuñez, J. A., Díaz-Solórzano, J. P., & Cruz-Suárez, G. (2024). Evidence-based learning strategies in medicine using AI. *JMIR Medical Education, 10*, e54507. DOI: 10.2196/54507 PMID: 38801706

Arbelaez Ossa, L., Lorenzini, G., Milford, S. R., Shaw, D., Elger, B. S., & Rost, M. (2024). Integrating ethics in AI development: A qualitative study. *BMC Medical Ethics, 25*(1), 10. DOI: 10.1186/s12910-023-01000-0 PMID: 38262986

Ariya, P., Yensathit, Y., Intawong, K., Thongthip, P., & Puritat, K. (2024). Assisting hearing and physically impaired students in navigating immersive virtual reality for library orientation. *Technologies*, *13*(1), 2. DOI: 10.3390/technologies13010002

Aslam, F. (2023). The Impact of Artificial Intelligence on Chatbot Technology: A Study on the Current Advancements and Leading Innovations. *European Journal of Technology*, *7*(3), 62–72. DOI: 10.47672/ejt.1561

Atmaja, B. T., & Sasou, A. (2022). Sentiment analysis and emotion recognition from speech using universal speech representations. *Sensors (Basel)*, *22*(17), 6369. DOI: 10.3390/s22176369 PMID: 36080828

Augustin, Y., Carolus, A., & Wienrich, C. (2022). Privacy of AI-Based Voice Assistants: Understanding the Users' Perspective: A Purposive Review and a Roadmap for Elevating Research on Privacy from a User-Oriented Perspective. *Lecture Notes in Computer Science (Including Subseries Lecture Notes in Artificial Intelligence and Lecture Notes in Bioinformatics), 13337 LNCS*, 309–321. DOI: 10.1007/978-3-031-05014-5_26

Azadinejad, H., Farhadi Rad, M., Shariftabrizi, A., Rahmim, A., & Abdollahi, H. (2025). Optimizing cancer treatment: Exploring the role of AI in radioimmunotherapy. *Diagnostics (Basel)*, *15*(3), 397. DOI: 10.3390/diagnostics15030397 PMID: 39941326

Baclic, O., Tunis, M., Young, K., Doan, C., Swerdfeger, H., & Schonfeld, J. (2020). Challenges and opportunities for public health made possible by advances in natural language processing. *Canada Communicable Disease Report = Relevé des Maladies Transmissibles au Canada*, *46*(6), 161. PMID: 32673380

Badshah, A. M., Ahmad, J., Khan, A., & Lee, S. (2022). Speech emotion recognition: Features, classification models, and databases. *Sustainability*, *14*(6), 3284. Advance online publication. DOI: 10.3390/su14063284

Bahdanau, D., Cho, K., & Bengio, Y. (2015). Neural Machine Translation by Jointly Learning to Align and Translate. *International Conference on Learning Representations (ICLR)*. https://arxiv.org/abs/1409.0473

Bai, H., Zheng, R., Chen, J., Li Xintong and Ma, M., & Huang, L. (2022). A^3T: Alignment-Aware Acoustic and Text Pretraining for speech synthesis and editing.

Bai, Y., Rusmevichientong, P., El Housni, O., & Topaloglu, H. (2025). Coordinated inventory stocking and assortment customization. *Operations Research*, *73*(6), 2953–2971. Advance online publication. DOI: 10.1287/opre.2022.0651

Baker, L. J., Li, H., Hammond, H., Jaeger, C. B., Havard, A., Lane, J. D., Harriott, C. E., & Levin, D. T. (2024). The roles of cognitive dissonance and normative reasoning in attributions of minds to robots. *Cognitive Research: Principles and Implications*, *9*(1), 1–19. DOI: 10.1186/s41235-024-00604-3 PMID: 39663309

Bang, C.-W., & Chun, C. (2023). Effective zero-shot multi-speaker text-to-speech technique using information perturbation and a speaker encoder. *Sensors (Basel)*, *23*(23), 9591. DOI: 10.3390/s23239591 PMID: 38067965

Banjanović-Mehmedović, L., & Husaković, A. (2023, October 1). Edge AI: Reshaping the Future of Edge Computing with Artificial Intelligence. DOI: 10.5644/PI2023.209.07

Bao, F., Song, J., & Zhang, T. (2021). Emotion recognition in call center conversations using hybrid acoustic and textual features. *IEEE Access : Practical Innovations, Open Solutions*, *9*, 126789–126800. DOI: 10.1109/ACCESS.2021.3111113

Barış, A. (2020). A new business marketing tool: Chatbot. *GSI Journals Serie B: Advancements in Business and Economics*, *3*(1), 31–46. DOI: 10.5281/ZENODO.4030216

Behzad, K., Zandi, R., Motamedi, E., Salehinejad, H., & Siami, M. (2025). Robomnist: A multimodal dataset for multi-robot activity recognition using wifi sensing, video, and audio. *Scientific Data*, *12*(1), 326. DOI: 10.1038/s41597-025-04636-2 PMID: 39987245

Bender, E. M., Gebru, T., McMillan-Major, A., & Shmitchell, S. (2021, March). On the dangers of stochastic parrots: Can language models be too big? . In *Proceedings of the 2021 ACM conference on fairness, accountability, and transparency* (pp. 610-623). DOI: 10.1145/3442188.3445922

Bengio, Y., Ducharme, R., Vincent, P., & Jauvin, C. (2003). A neural probabilistic language model. *Journal of Machine Learning Research*, *3*(Feb), 1137–1155.

Bertrand, Y., Stevens, A., Deforce, B., De Smedt, J., De Weerdt, J., & Serral, E. (2025). Approaches for IoT-enhanced predictive process monitoring. *Process Science*, *2*(1), 7. DOI: 10.1007/s44311-025-00011-x

BharatGen. India's multimodal, multilingual foundation model. (2024, September 30). *Wikipedia*. (en.wikipedia.org)

Bhattacharjee, S., & Bhattacharya, S. (2024). Leveraging AI-driven nudge theory to enhance hand hygiene compliance: Paving the path for future infection control. *Frontiers in Public Health*, *12*, 1522045. DOI: 10.3389/fpubh.2024.1522045 PMID: 39917534

Binns, R., Van Kleek, M., Veale, M., Lyngs, U., Zhao, J., & Shadbolt, N. (2018). "It's reducing a human being to a percentage"; perceptions of justice in algorithmic decisions. *Conference on Human Factors in Computing Systems - Proceedings, 2018-April*. DOI: 10.1145/3173574.3173951

Biocca, F., Harms, C., & Burgoon, J. K. (2003). Toward a more robust theory and measure of social presence: Review and suggested criteria. *Presence (Cambridge, Mass.), 12*(5), 456–480. DOI: 10.1162/105474603322761270

Blut, M., Wang, C., Wünderlich, N. V., & Brock, C. (2021). Understanding anthropomorphism in service provision: a meta-analysis of physical robots, chatbots, and other AI. In *Journal of the Academy of Marketing Science* (Vol. 49, Issue 4, pp. 632–658). Springer. DOI: 10.1007/s11747-020-00762-y

Boell, S. K., & Cecez-Kecmanovic, D. (2015). On being 'systematic' in literature reviews. *Information & Management, 48*(5), 161–172. https://doi.org/10.1057/jit.2014.26DOI: 10.1016/j.im.2014.08.002

Bolte, L., Vandemeulebroucke, T., & van Wynsberghe, A. (2022). From an ethics of carefulness to an ethics of desirability: going beyond current ethics approaches to sustainable AI. *Sustainability, 14*(8), 4472. DOI: 10.3390/su14084472

Bolukbasi, T., Chang, K. W., Zou, J. Y., Saligrama, V., & Kalai, A. T. (2016). Man is to Computer Programmer as Woman is to Homemaker? Debiasing Word Embeddings. *Advances in Neural Information Processing Systems, 29*, 4349–4357.

Bond, R. R., Mulvenna, M., & Wang, H. (2019). Human centered artificial intelligence: Weaving UX into algorithmic decision making. *Proceedings of the 16th International Conference on Human-Computer Interaction (RoCHI 2019)* (pp. 1–6). Romanian Society for Human-Computer Interaction. http://rochi.utcluj.ro/articole/7/RoCHI2019-Bond.pdf

Bottrighi, A., Grosso, F., Ghiglione, M., Maconi, A., Nera, S., Piovesan, L., Raina, E., Roveta, A., & Terenziani, P. (2025). A symbolic AI approach to medical training. *Journal of Medical Systems, 49*(1), 2. DOI: 10.1007/s10916-024-02139-y PMID: 39786677

Bowman, S. R., & Dahl, G. E. (2021). What will it take to fix benchmarking in natural language understanding? *arXiv preprint arXiv:2104.02145*. DOI: 10.18653/v1/2021.naacl-main.385

Brahnam, S., & De Angeli, A. (2008). Special issue on the abuse and misuse of social agents. In *Interacting with Computers* (Vol. 20, Issue 3, pp. 287–291). Oxford Academic. DOI: 10.1016/j.intcom.2008.02.001

Brahnam, S., & De Angeli, A. (2012). Gender affordances of conversational agents. *Interacting with Computers*, *24*(3), 139–153. DOI: 10.1016/j.intcom.2012.05.001

Brandt, A., & Hazel, S. (2024). Towards interculturally adaptive conversational AI. *Applied Linguistics Review*, *16*(2), 775–786. DOI: 10.1515/applirev-2024-0187

Bridoux, F., & Stoelhorst, J. W. (2022). Stakeholder governance: Solving the collective action problems in joint value creation. *Academy of Management Review*, *47*(2), 214–236. DOI: 10.5465/amr.2019.0441

Brown, T., Mann, B., Ryder, N., Subbiah, M., Kaplan, J., Dhariwal, P., & Amodei, D. (2020). Language Models are Few-Shot Learners. *Advances in Neural Information Processing Systems*, *33*, 1877–1901.

Brundage, M., Avin, S., Wang, J., Belfield, H., Krueger, G., Hadfield, G., Khlaaf, H., Yang, J., Toner, H., Fong, R., & Maharaj, T. (2020) Toward trustworthy AI development: mechanisms for supporting verifiable claims. arXiv preprint arXiv:2004.07213 86 2 The Rise of AI Ethic. https://doi.org//arXiv.2004.07213DOI: 10.48550

Brunete, A., Gambao, E., Cedazo, R., & Hernando, M. (2021). Smart Assistive Architecture for the Integration of IoT Devices, Robotic Systems, and Multimodal Interfaces in Healthcare Environments. *Sensors (Basel)*, *21*(6), 2212. DOI: 10.3390/s21062212 PMID: 33809884

Burr, C., & Leslie, D. (2023). Ethical assurance: A practical approach to the responsible design, development, and deployment of data-driven technologies. *AI and Ethics*, *3*(1), 73–98. DOI: 10.1007/s43681-022-00178-0

Burrell, J. (2016). How the machine 'thinks': Understanding opacity in machine learning algorithms. *Big Data & Society*, *3*(1), 2053951715622512. Advance online publication. DOI: 10.1177/2053951715622512

Caldarini, G., Jaf, S., & McGarry, K. (2021). A literature survey of recent advances in chatbots.

Camilleri, M. A. (2022). Walking the talk about corporate social responsibility communication: An elaboration likelihood model perspective. *Business Ethics, the Environment & Responsibility*, *31*(3), 649–661. DOI: 10.1111/beer.12427

Cao, B., Li, Z., & Jiang, L. C. (2024). When chatbots make errors: Cognitive and affective pathways to understanding forgiveness of chatbot errors. *Telematics and Informatics*, *94*, 102189. DOI: 10.1016/j.tele.2024.102189

Cao, Y., Zhang, X., & Li, Y. (2023). End-to-end speech sentiment analysis with pre-trained self-supervised models. *Pattern Recognition Letters*, *164*, 56–62. DOI: 10.1016/j.patrec.2022.11.020

Cao, Z., Zhao, Z., Shang, W., Ai, S., & Shen, S. (2025). Using the ToN-IoT dataset to develop a new intrusion detection system for industrial IoT devices. *Multimedia Tools and Applications*, *84*(16), 16425–16453. DOI: 10.1007/s11042-024-19695-7

Carlini, N., Tramer, F., Wallace, E., Jagielski, M., Herbert-Voss, A., Lee, K., & Erlingsson, Ú. (2021). Extracting Training Data from Large Language Models. *USENIX Security Symposium*, 2633–2650.

Carmichael, L., Poirier, S. M., Coursaris, C. K., Léger, P. M., & Sénécal, S. (2022). Users' information disclosure behaviors during interactions with chatbots: The effect of information disclosure nudges. *Applied Sciences (Basel, Switzerland)*, *12*(24), 12660. DOI: 10.3390/app122412660

Chandrakala, C. B., Bhardwaj, R., & Pujari, C. (2023). An intent recognition pipeline for conversational AI. *International Journal of Information Technology : an Official Journal of Bharati Vidyapeeth's Institute of Computer Applications and Management*, *16*(2), 731–743. DOI: 10.1007/s41870-023-01642-8

Chandra, S., Shirish, A., & Srivastava, S. C. (2022). To Be or Not to Be …Human? Theorizing the Role of Human-Like Competencies in Conversational Artificial Intelligence Agents. *Journal of Management Information Systems*, *39*(4), 969–1005. DOI: 10.1080/07421222.2022.2127441

Chang, L., Liu, J., Zhu, J., Guo, S., Wang, Y., Zhou, Z., & Wei, X. (2025). Advancing precision medicine: The transformative role of artificial intelligence in immunogenomics, radiomics, and pathomics for biomarker discovery and immunotherapy optimization. *Cancer Biology & Medicine*, *22*(1), 33–47. DOI: 10.20892/j.issn.2095-3941.2024.0376 PMID: 39749734

Chemnad, K., & Othman, A. (2023). Advancements in Arabic text-to-speech systems: A 22-year literature review. *IEEE Access : Practical Innovations, Open Solutions*, *11*, 30929–30954. DOI: 10.1109/ACCESS.2023.3260844

Chen, J., Ye, L., & Ming, Z. (2021a). MASS: Multi-task anthropomorphic speech synthesis framework.

Chen, J., Ye, L., & Ming, Z. (2021b). MASS: Multi-task anthropomorphic speech synthesis framework.

Chen, B., Zhang, D., Cao, Q., Lu, G., Zhang, Z., & Hou, M. (2021). Multimodal Emotion Recognition With Temporal and Semantic Consistency. *IEEE/ACM Transactions on Audio, Speech, and Language Processing*, *29*, 3592–3603. DOI: 10.1109/TASLP.2021.3129331

Chen, Q., Yin, C., & Gong, Y. (2025). Would an AI chatbot persuade you: An empirical answer from the elaboration likelihood model. *Information Technology & People*, *38*(2), 937–962. DOI: 10.1108/ITP-10-2021-0764

Chen, Z., Jin, Q., & Zhang, Z. (2022). Multimodal emotion recognition using deep learning: A review. *Information Fusion*, *76*, 1–18. DOI: 10.1016/j.inffus.2021.10.003

Chin, H., Molefi, L. W., & Yi, M. Y. (2020). Empathy Is All You Need: How a Conversational Agent Should Respond to Verbal Abuse. *Conference on Human Factors in Computing Systems - Proceedings*. DOI: 10.1145/3313831.3376461

Choaib, M., Garouani, M., Bouneffa, M., Waldhoff, N., & Mohanna, Y. (2024). IoT-AID: An Automated Decision Support Framework for IoT. *SN Computer Science*, *5*(4), 429. DOI: 10.1007/s42979-024-02780-x

Chouhan, S., Sandhu, R., Yadav, O. P., & Islam, S. M. N. (2025). Quantum-powered autonomous deep-sea explorer using AI, microbiofuels, and advanced sensors for oceanic discovery. In *2025 International Conference on Computer, Electrical & Communication Engineering (ICCECE)* (pp. 1–5). IEEE. DOI: 10.1109/ICCECE61355.2025.10941009

Chowdhary, K., & Chowdhary, K. R. (2020). Natural language processing. *Fundamentals of artificial intelligence*, 603-649.

Chowdhery, A., Narang, S., Devlin, J., Bosma, M., Mishra, G., Roberts, A., & Fiedel, N. (2023). Palm: Scaling language modeling with pathways. *Journal of Machine Learning Research*, *24*(240), 1–113.

Chowdhury, S., & Talukder, U. (2024). Background on microelectronics. In *Numerical exploration of isolated GaAs-AlGaAs quantum well*. Springer., DOI: 10.1007/978-3-031-53816-2_1

Chow, J. C. L., Wong, V., & Li, K. (2024). Generative pre-trained transformer-empowered healthcare conversations: Current trends, challenges, and future directions in large language model-enabled medical chatbots. *BioMedInformatics*, *4*(1), 837–852. DOI: 10.3390/biomedinformatics4010047

Cohen, T. (2023). Regulating Manipulative Artificial Intelligence. *Script-ed*, *20*(1), 203–242. DOI: 10.2966/SCRIP.200123.203

Conneau, A., Khandelwal, K., Goyal, N., Chaudhary, V., Wenzek, G., Guzmán, F., ... & Stoyanov, V. (2020). Unsupervised cross-lingual representation learning at scale. *Association for Computational Linguistics (ACL)*, 8440–8451.

Consumer Financial Protection Bureau. (2023, June 6). *CFPB issue spotlight analyzes 'artificial intelligence' chatbots in banking*. https://www.consumerfinance.gov/about-us/newsroom/cfpb-issue-spotlight-analyzes-artificial-intelligence-chatbots-in-banking/

Costabile, M. F., Lanzilotti, R., Matera, M., Piccinno, A., Pinto, N., Piro, L., ... & Ragone, G. (2024). Participatory Design for Creating Conversational Agents to Improve Web Accessibility.

Crawford, K. (2022). There is a blind spot in AI research. *AI and Ethics*, *2*(4), 851–867. DOI: 10.1007/s43681-021-00122-8

Crolic, C., Thomaz, F., Hadi, R., & Stephen, A. T. (2022). Blame the Bot: Anthropomorphism and Anger in Customer–Chatbot Interactions. *Journal of Marketing*, *86*(1), 132–148. DOI: 10.1177/00222429211045687

Cuayáhuitl, H., Lee, D., Ryu, S., Cho, Y., Choi, S., Indurthi, S., Yu, S., Choi, H., Hwang, I., & Kim, J. (2019). Ensemble-based deep reinforcement learning for chatbots. *Neurocomputing*, *366*, 118–130. DOI: 10.1016/j.neucom.2019.08.007

Culnan, M. J., & Armstrong, P. K. (1999). Information Privacy Concerns, Procedural Fairness, and Impersonal Trust: An Empirical Investigation. *Organization Science*, *10*(1), 104–115. DOI: 10.1287/orsc.10.1.104

Curry, A. C., & Rieser, V. (2018). #MeToo Alexa: How Conversational Systems Respond to Sexual Harassment. *Proceedings of the 2nd ACL Workshop on Ethics in Natural Language Processing, EthNLP 2018 at the 2018 Conference of the North American Chapter of the Association for Computational Linguistics: Human Language Technologies, NAACL-HTL 2018*, 7–14. DOI: 10.18653/v1/W18-0802

Dadwal, S. S., Bowen, G., Jahankhani, H., Nadda, V., & Kumar, P. (2024). Market Grooming: Grooming Customers Using Artificial Intelligence. In *Market Grooming* (pp. 1–35). Emerald Publishing Limited. DOI: 10.1108/978-1-83549-001-320241001

Darwish, D. (2024). Chatbots vs. AI Chatbots vs. Virtual Assistants. In *Design and Development of Emerging Chatbot Technology* (pp. 26–50). IGI Global. DOI: 10.4018/979-8-3693-1830-0.ch002

De Angeli, A., & Brahnam, S. (2006). Sex stereotypes and conversational agents. In *Proceedings of Gender and Interaction: Real and Virtual Women in a Male World*, Venice, Italy. Retrieved from https://www.researchgate.net/publication/229003887_Sex_Stereotypes_and_Conversational_Agents

De Angeli, A., & Brahnam, S. (2008). I hate you! Disinhibition with virtual partners. *Interacting with Computers*, *20*(3), 302–310. DOI: 10.1016/j.intcom.2008.02.004

De Cicco, R. (2024). Exploring the Dark Corners of Human-Chatbot Interactions: A Literature Review on Conversational Agent Abuse. *Lecture Notes in Computer Science (Including Subseries Lecture Notes in Artificial Intelligence and Lecture Notes in Bioinformatics), 14524 LNCS*, 185–203. DOI: 10.1007/978-3-031-54975-5_11

De la Peña, N., & Granados, O. M. (2024). Artificial intelligence solutions to reduce information asymmetry for Colombian cocoa small-scale farmers. *Information Processing in Agriculture*, *11*(3), 310–324. DOI: 10.1016/j.inpa.2023.03.001

de Souza Monteiro, M., & de Castro Salgado, L. C. (2023). Conversational agents: A survey on culturally informed design practices. *Journal on Interactive Systems*, *14*(1), 33–46. DOI: 10.5753/jis.2023.2961

Deliu, D., & Olariu, A. (2024). The role of artificial intelligence and big data analytics in shaping the future of professions in Industry 6.0: Perspectives from an emerging market. *Electronics (Basel)*, *13*(24), 4983. DOI: 10.3390/electronics13244983

Demyen, S. (2024). The online shopping experience during the pandemic and after—A turning point for sustainable fashion business management? *Journal of Theoretical and Applied Electronic Commerce Research*, *19*(4), 3632–3658. DOI: 10.3390/jtaer19040176

Deng, J., Han, J., & Schuller, B. (2022). Speech emotion recognition using deep spectral representations. *IEEE Transactions on Multimedia*, *24*, 1585–1597. DOI: 10.1109/TMM.2021.3098765

Deshmukh, R., Gaikwad, S. B., Reddy, K. S., Joseph, C., Arnone, G., & Kalaivaani, P. C. D. (2023, December). Exploring Ethical Considerations: Privacy and Accountability in Conversational Agents like ChatGPT. In *International Conference on Mechanical and Energy Technologies* (pp. 193-201). Singapore: Springer Nature Singapore.

Devlin, J., Chang, M.-W., Lee, K., & Toutanova, K. (2019). BERT: Pre-training of Deep Bidirectional Transformers for Language Understanding. *Proceedings of NAACL-HLT*, *2019*, 4171–4186.

Dhaundiyal, D., Sharma, A., & Sharma, N. (2024, August). Empowerment Through Participatory Design: Charting Paths to Inclusion. In *Proceedings of the Participatory Design Conference 2024: Situated Actions, Doctoral Colloquium, PDC places, Communities-Volume 3* (pp. 125-126). DOI: 10.1145/3661456.3666082

Diab, M., Hacioglu, K., & Jurafsky, D. (2004). Automatic tagging of Arabic text: From raw text to base phrase chunks. In *Proceedings of HLT-NAACL 2004: Short papers* (pp. 149-152). DOI: 10.3115/1613984.1614022

Ding, L., Antonucci, G., & Venditti, M. (2024). Unveiling user responses to AI-powered personalised recommendations: A qualitative study of consumer engagement dynamics on Douyin. *Qualitative Market Research*, *28*(2), 234–255. DOI: 10.1108/QMR-11-2023-0151

Ding, R., Chen, X., Wei, S., & Wang, J. (2025). What drives trust building in live streaming e-commerce? From an elaboration likelihood model perspective. *Industrial Management & Data Systems*, *125*(3), 969–999. DOI: 10.1108/IMDS-03-2024-0273

Dobbala, M., & Lingolu, M. (2024). Conversational AI and chatbots: Enhancing user experience on websites. *American Journal of Computer Science and Technology*, *7*(3), 62–70. DOI: 10.11648/j.ajcst.20240703.11

Dong, Y., & Yao, Y.-D. (2020). Secure mmWave-Radar-Based Speaker Verification for IoT Smart Home. *IEEE Internet of Things Journal*, *8*(5), 3500–3511. DOI: 10.1109/JIOT.2020.3023101

Duggan, M. J., Gervase, J., Schoenbaum, A., Hanson, W., Howell, J. T.III, Sheinberg, M., & Johnson, K. B. (2025). Clinician experiences with ambient scribe technology to assist with documentation burden and efficiency. *JAMA Network Open*, *8*(2), e2460637. DOI: 10.1001/jamanetworkopen.2024.60637 PMID: 39969880

Dunlavy, D. M., O'Leary, D. P., Conroy, J. M., & Schlesinger, J. D. (2007). QCS: A system for querying, clustering and summarizing documents. *Information Processing & Management*, *43*(6), 1588–1605. DOI: 10.1016/j.ipm.2007.01.003

Elendu, C., Jingwa, K. A., Elendu, T. C., John Okah, M., Amaechi, D. C., Okoye, O. K., Alimi, H. A., Farah, A. H., & Ladele, J. A. (2023). Ethical implications of AI and robotics in healthcare. *Revista de Medicina (São Paulo)*, *102*(50), e36671. DOI: 10.1097/MD.0000000000036671 PMID: 38115340

Elman, J. L. (1990). Finding structure in time. *Cognitive Science*, *14*(2), 179–211. DOI: 10.1207/s15516709cog1402_1

Elshaer, I. A., Azazz, A. M. S., Fayyad, S., Aljoghaiman, A., Fathy, E. A., & Fouad, A. M. (2025). From Asymmetry to Satisfaction: The Dynamic Role of Perceived Value and Trust to Boost Customer Satisfaction in the Tourism Industry. *Tourism and Hospitality*, *6*(2), 68. DOI: 10.3390/tourhosp6020068

Enyejo, L., Ugochukwu, U., & Adewoye, M.Lawrence Anebi EnyejoMichael Babatunde AdewoyeUchenna Nneka Ugochukwu. (2024). Interpreting Federated Learning (FL) Models on Edge Devices by Enhancing Model Explainability with Computational Geometry and Advanced Database Architectures. International Journal of Scientific Research in Computer Science. *Engineering and Information Technology*, *10*(6), 332–354. DOI: 10.32628/CSEIT24106185

Eziamaka, N., Odonkor, T., & Akinsulire, A.Nnaemeka Valentine EziamakaTheodore Narku OdonkorAdetola Adewale Akinsulire. (2024). AI-Driven accessibility: Transformative software solutions for empowering individuals with disabilities. *International Journal of Applied Research in Social Sciences*, *6*(8), 1612–1641. DOI: 10.51594/ijarss.v6i8.1373

Familoni, B. (2024). Ethical frameworks for AI in healthcare entrepreneurship: A theoretical examination of challenges and approaches. International Journal of Frontiers in Biology and Pharmacy Research, 5(1), 057–065. DOI: 10.53294/ijfbpr.2024.5.1.0032

Fanni, S. C., Febi, M., Aghakhanyan, G., & Neri, E. (2023). Natural language processing. In *Introduction to artificial intelligence* (pp. 87–99). Springer International Publishing. DOI: 10.1007/978-3-031-25928-9_5

Festinger, L. (1957). *A theory of cognitive dissonance*. Stanford University Press. DOI: 10.1515/9781503620766

Fiske, A., Henningsen, P., & Buyx, A. (2019). Your robot therapist will see you now: Ethical implications of embodied artificial intelligence in Psychiatry, Psychology, and Psychotherapy. *Journal of Medical Internet Research*, *21*(5), e13216. DOI: 10.2196/13216 PMID: 31094356

Florido-Benítez, L. (2024). Generative artificial intelligence: a proactive and creative tool to achieve hyper-segmentation and hyper-personalization in the tourism industry. *International Journal of Tourism Cities, ahead-of-p*rint(ahead-of-print). DOI: 10.1108/IJTC-05-2024-0111

Følstad, A., & Brandtzaeg, P. B. (2017). Chatbots and the New World of HCI. *Interactions (New York, N.Y.)*, *24*(4), 38–42. DOI: 10.1145/3085558

Fossa, F., & Sucameli, I. (2022). Gender bias and conversational agents: an ethical perspective on social robotics. *Science and Engineering Ethics*, 28(3), 23. DOI: 10.1007/s11948-022-00376-3

Francis, D. (2025). *The Good, the Bad, and the Creepy: AI's Impact on Consumer Behavior*. Medium. https://dennismfrancis.medium.com/the-good-the-bad-and-the-creepy-ais-impact-on-consumer-behavior-aab36aaf2542

Freeman, R. E. (1984). *Strategic management: A stakeholder approach.* https://books.google.com/books?hl=en&lr=&id=NpmA_qEiOpkC&oi=fnd&pg=PR5&ots=62fkL3S7MK&sig=5wslBv0wPYhYJzOCxZs4wSA56ac

Furizal, F., Ramelan, A., Adriyanto, F., Maghfiroh, H., Ma'arif, A., Kariyamin, K., Masitha, A., & Fawait, A. B. (2024). Concerns of Ethical and Privacy in the Rapid Advancement of Artificial Intelligence: Directions, Challenges, and Solutions. [JRC]. *Journal of Robotics and Control*, *5*(6), 2015–2026. DOI: 10.18196/jrc.v5i6.24090

Garcia, M. (2024, February 19). What Air Canada lost in remarkable lying AI chatbot case. *Forbes*. https://www.forbes.com/sites/marisagarcia/2024/02/19/what-air-canada-lost-in-remarkable-lying-ai-chatbot-case/

Ghai, D., Saxena, S., Dhingra, G., & Tripathi, S. L. (2025). A comprehensive review on performance-based comparative analysis, categorization, classification and mapping of text extraction system techniques for images. *Multimedia Tools and Applications*, *84*(5), 2327–2484. DOI: 10.1007/s11042-024-20257-0

Ghai, D., Tripathi, S. L., Saxena, S., Chanda, M., & Alazab, M. (Eds.). (2022). *Machine learning algorithms for signal and image processing*. John Wiley & Sons. DOI: 10.1002/9781119861850

Gieselmann, M., & Sassenberg, K. (2023). The more competent, the better? The effects of perceived competencies on disclosure towards conversational artificial intelligence. *Social Science Computer Review*, *41*(6), 2342–2363. DOI: 10.1177/08944393221142787

Giudici, M., Padalino, L., Pascu, A. I., Garzotto, F., Paratici, I., & Paolino, G. (2024). Designing Home Automation Routines Using an LLM-Based Chatbot. *Designs*, *8*(3), 43. DOI: 10.3390/designs8030043

Glogar, M., Mahnić Naglić, M., & Petrak, S. (2025). Digital technologies in the sustainable design and development of textiles and clothing—A literature review. *Sustainability (Basel)*, *17*(4), 1371. DOI: 10.3390/su17041371

Go, E., & Sundar, S. S. (2019). Humanizing chatbots: The effects of visual, identity and conversational cues on humanness perceptions. *Computers in Human Behavior, 97*, 304–316. DOI: 10.1016/j.chb.2019.01.020

Golda, A., Mekonen, K., Pandey, A., Singh, A., Hassija, V., Chamola, V., & Sikdar, B. (2024). Privacy and security concerns in generative AI: A comprehensive survey. *IEEE Access : Practical Innovations, Open Solutions, 12*, 48126–48144. Advance online publication. DOI: 10.1109/ACCESS.2024.3381611

Goncalves, M., Hu, Y., Aliagas, I., & Cerdá, L. M. (2024). Neuromarketing algorithms' consumer privacy and ethical considerations: Challenges and opportunities. *Cogent Business & Management, 11*(1), 2333063. Advance online publication. DOI: 10.1080/23311975.2024.2333063

Gosmar, D. (2025). Conversational hyperconvergence: An onlife evolution model for conversational AI agency. *AI and Ethics, 5*(2), 1147–1161. DOI: 10.1007/s43681-024-00463-0

Gray, C. M., Kou, Y., Battles, B., Hoggatt, J., & Toombs, A. L. (2018). The dark (patterns) side of UX design. *Conference on Human Factors in Computing Systems - Proceedings, 2018-April*. DOI: 10.1145/3173574.3174108

Greenhalgh, T., & Peacock, R. (2005). Effectiveness and efficiency of search methods in systematic reviews of complex evidence: Audit of primary sources. *BMJ (Clinical Research Ed.), 331*(7524), 1064–1065. DOI: 10.1136/bmj.38636.593461.68 PMID: 16230312

Habbal, A., Ali, M. K., & Abuzaraida, M. A. (2024). Artificial Intelligence Trust, Risk and Security Management (AI TRiSM): Frameworks, applications, challenges and future research directions. In *Expert Systems with Applications* (Vol. 240, p. 122442). Pergamon. DOI: 10.1016/j.eswa.2023.122442

Habib, M. U., Akram, W., Saleem, S., & Shakoor, A. (2025). How cognitive dissonance affects student engagement and learning in AI-powered education systems. *The Critical Review of Social Sciences Studies, 3*(1), 1905–1917. DOI: 10.59075/r1zta509

Haider, H., & Shah, S. A. A. (2023). Real-time driver emotion recognition using speech signal. *IEEE Sensors Journal, 23*(3), 2212–2221. DOI: 10.1109/JSEN.2022.3209876

He, T., Jazizadeh, F., & Arpan, L. (2021). AI-powered virtual assistants nudging occupants for energy saving: proactive smart speakers for HVAC control. Building Research & Information, ahead-of-print(ahead-of-print), 394–409. DOI: 10.1080/09613218.2021.2012119

Heyder, T., Passlack, N., & Posegga, O. (2023). Ethical management of human-AI interaction: Theory development review. *The Journal of Strategic Information Systems, 32*(3), 101772. Advance online publication. DOI: 10.1016/j.jsis.2023.101772

High-Level Expert Group on AI. (2019). *Ethics guidelines for trustworthy AI* (p. 39). Independent High-Level Expert Group on Artificial Intelligence. https://www.aepd.es/sites/default/files/2019-09/ai-definition.pdf

Hill, J., Randolph Ford, W., & Farreras, I. G. (2015). Real conversations with artificial intelligence: A comparison between human-human online conversations and human-chatbot conversations. *Computers in Human Behavior, 49*, 245–250. DOI: 10.1016/j.chb.2015.02.026

Ho, A., Hancock, J., & Miner, A. S. (2018). Psychological, relational, and emotional effects of self-disclosure after conversations with a chatbot. *The Journal of Communication, 68*(4), 712–733. DOI: 10.1093/joc/jqy026 PMID: 30100620

Hochreiter, S., & Schmidhuber, J. (1997). Long short-term memory. *Neural Computation, 9*(8), 1735–1780. DOI: 10.1162/neco.1997.9.8.1735 PMID: 9377276

Hollanek, T., Peters, D., Drage, E., & Hernandes, R. (2025). AI, journalism, and critical AI literacy: Exploring journalists' perspectives on AI and responsible reporting. *AI & Society, 40*(8), 6393–6405. DOI: 10.1007/s00146-025-02407-6

Hou, Y. (2025). Design and implementation evaluation of personalized and differentiated teaching strategies for preschool children based on fuzzy decision support systems. *International Journal of Computational Intelligence Systems, 18*(1), 42. Advance online publication. DOI: 10.1007/s44196-025-00748-0

Hu, C., Tian, Q., Li, T., Wang, Y., Wang, Y., & Zhao, H. (2021). Neural Dubber: Dubbing for videos according to scripts.

Huang, X., Zhu, W., Hu, H., He, C., Li, L., Huang, S., & Yuan, F. (2025). Bench-MAX: A Comprehensive Multilingual Evaluation Suite for Large Language Models. *arXiv preprint arXiv:2502.07346*. DOI: 10.18653/v1/2025.findings-emnlp.909

Huang, L., & Shen, X. (2022). Research on speech emotion recognition based on the Fractional Fourier Transform. *Electronics (Basel), 11*(20), 3393. DOI: 10.3390/electronics11203393

Huang, Z., Dong, M., Mao, Q., & Zhan, Y. (2022). Speech emotion recognition using CNN with multi-channel feature extraction. *Neurocomputing, 470*, 347–356. DOI: 10.1016/j.neucom.2021.09.077

Huang, Z., Epps, J., & Goecke, R. (2019). Speech emotion recognition using CNN. In *Proceedings of the IEEE International Conference on Acoustics, Speech and Signal Processing (ICASSP)* (pp. 2746–2750). DOI: 10.1109/ICASSP.2019.8683661

Huriye, A. Z. (2023). The ethics of artificial intelligence: Examining the ethical considerations surrounding the development and use of AI. *American Journal of Technology*, *2*(1), 37–45. DOI: 10.58425/ajt.v2i1.142

Iliev, Y., & Ilieva, G. (2022). A Framework for Smart Home System with Voice Control Using NLP Methods. *Electronics (Basel)*, *12*(1), 116. DOI: 10.3390/electronics12010116

Inkster, B., Sarda, S., & Subramanian, V. (2018). An empathy-driven, conversational artificial intelligence agent (Wysa) for digital mental well-being: Real-world data evaluation mixed-methods study. *JMIR mHealth and uHealth*, *6*(11), e12106. DOI: 10.2196/12106 PMID: 30470676

Islam, M. A., Hossen, M. D., Islam, M. T., Fakir, S. I., Siddiky, M. R., & Masud, S. B. (2024). Artificial intelligence in digital marketing automation: Enhancing personalization, predictive analytics, and ethical integration. *Edelweiss Applied Science and Technology*, *8*(6). Advance online publication. DOI: 10.55214/25768484.v8i6.3404

Izadi, S., & Forouzanfar, M. (2024). Error Correction and Adaptation in Conversational AI: A Review of Techniques and Applications in Chatbots. *AI*, *5*(2), 803–841. DOI: 10.3390/ai5020041

Jang, B., Yuh, C., Lee, H., Shin, Y. B., Lee, H. J., Kang, E. K., Heo, J., & Cho, C. H. (2025). Exploring user experience and the therapeutic relationship of short-term avatar-based psychotherapy: Qualitative pilot study. *JMIR Human Factors*, *12*, e66158. DOI: 10.2196/66158 PMID: 39924261

Javed, T., Nawale, J. A., George, E. I., Joshi, S., Bhogale, K. S., Mehendale, D., . . . Khapra, M. M. (2024). Indicvoices: Towards building an inclusive multilingual speech dataset for indian languages. *arXiv preprint arXiv:2403.01926*. DOI: 10.18653/v1/2024.findings-acl.639

Jelili, M. O., Abolade, O., Alabi, A. T., & Marunye, J. (2025). Residential indoor air quality assessment in Ibadan metropolis, Nigeria. *Discover Environment*, *3*(1), 87. DOI: 10.1007/s44274-025-00286-8

Jeyaraman, M., Yadav, S., Balaji, S., & Jeyaraman, N. (2023). Unraveling the Ethical Enigma: Artificial Intelligence in Healthcare. *Cureus*, *15*(8). Advance online publication. DOI: 10.7759/cureus.43262 PMID: 37692617

Jha, A., Mann, P., Tiwari, A., Kadian, K., Sharma, A., & Singh, J. (2024, June). Evolving Education in India: Multilingual LLMs for Vernacular Learning Experiences. In *2024 International Conference on Computer, Electronics, Electrical Engineering & their Applications (IC2E3)* (pp. 1-5). IEEE. DOI: 10.1109/IC2E362166.2024.10827087

Jiang, J. C., Kantarci, B., Oktug, S., & Soyata, T. (2020). Federated Learning in Smart City Sensing: Challenges and Opportunities. *Sensors (Basel)*, *20*(21), 6230. DOI: 10.3390/s20216230 PMID: 33142863

Jiang, Y., Cheng, Y., & Wang, Y. (2025). Leveraging AI in CSR: How social-oriented chatbots influence Chinese consumers' supportive actions via dialogic communication. *Public Relations Review*, *51*(1), 102541. DOI: 10.1016/j.pubrev.2025.102541

Jia, Y., Weiss, R. J., Biadsy, F., Macherey, W., Johnson, M., Chen, Z., & Wu, Y. (2019, September). Direct speech-to-speech translation with a sequence-to-sequence model. *Interspeech*, •••, 2019. DOI: 10.21437/Interspeech.2019-1951

Ji, S., Tan, Y., Saravirta, T., Yang, Z., Liu, Y., Vasankari, L., Pan, S., Long, G., & Walid, A. (2024). Emerging trends in federated learning: From model fusion to federated x learning. *International Journal of Machine Learning and Cybernetics*, *15*(9), 3769–3790. DOI: 10.1007/s13042-024-02119-1

Jobin, A., Ienca, M., & Vayena, E. (2019). The global landscape of AI ethics guidelines. *Nature Machine Intelligence*, *1*(9), 389–399. DOI: 10.1038/s42256-019-0088-2

Jung, J., Kim, D., & You, J. (2025). Effective but sustainable? A case of a digital literacy program for older adults. *Education and Information Technologies*, *30*(10), 13309–13330. Advance online publication. DOI: 10.1007/s10639-025-13364-4

Jurafsky, D., & Martin, J. H. (2023). Speech and Language Processing (3rd ed., draft). Stanford University.

Kadam, A. V. (2023). *Natural Language Understanding of Low-Resource Languages in Voice Assistants: Advancements*. Challenges and Mitigation Strategies.

Kaplan, A., & Haenlein, M. (2019). Siri, Siri, in my hand: Who's the fairest in the land? On the interpretations, illustrations, and implications of artificial intelligence. *Business Horizons*, *62*(1), 15–25. DOI: 10.1016/j.bushor.2018.08.004

Kaur, M., & Chouhan, S. (2025). Leveraging machine learning techniques for accurate heart disease prediction through data insights and model optimization. In 2025 3rd International Conference on Disruptive Technologies (ICDT) (pp. 515–519). IEEE. DOI: 10.1109/ICDT63985.2025.10986736

Keijsers, M., Bartneck, C., & Eyssel, F. (2021). What's to bullying a bot? Correlates between chatbot humanlikeness and abuse. *Interaction Studies*, 22(1), 55-80. DOI: 10.1075/is.20002.kei

Kent, M. L., & Taylor, M. (1998). Building dialogic relationships through the World Wide Web. *Public Relations Review*, *24*(3), 321–334. DOI: 10.1016/S0363-8111(99)80143-X

Khorram, S., & Provost, E. M. (2021). Uncertainty-aware speech emotion recognition using Bayesian neural networks. *IEEE Transactions on Affective Computing*, *12*(4), 833–846. DOI: 10.1109/TAFFC.2020.3005460 PMID: 35721344

Khurana, S., Moritz, N., Hori, T., & Le Roux, J. (2021, June). Unsupervised domain adaptation for speech recognition via uncertainty driven self-training. In *ICASSP 2021-2021 IEEE International Conference on Acoustics, Speech and Signal Processing (ICASSP)* (pp. 6553-6557). IEEE. DOI: 10.1109/ICASSP39728.2021.9414299

Kim, Y. (2014). Convolutional neural networks for sentence classification. *arXiv preprint arXiv:1408.5882*. DOI: 10.3115/v1/D14-1181

Kim, J., & Lee, C. (2023). Emotion detection from voice using deep learning models: A comparative study. *Sensors (Basel)*, *23*(1), 333. Advance online publication. DOI: 10.3390/s23010333 PMID: 36616931

Kim, M., Joo, M., & Han, K. (2025). Understanding the differences in an AI-based creativity support tool between creativity types in fashion design. *International Journal of Human-Computer Interaction*, *41*(18), 1–14. Advance online publication. DOI: 10.1080/10447318.2024.2448484

Kim, Y. (2024). AI Health Counselor's Self-Disclosure: Its Impact on User Responses Based on Individual and Cultural Variation. *International Journal of Human-Computer Interaction*. Advance online publication. DOI: 10.1080/10447318.2024.2316373

Konya-Baumbach, E., Biller, M., & von Janda, S. (2023). Someone out there? A study on the social presence of anthropomorphized chatbots. *Computers in Human Behavior*, *139*, 107513. DOI: 10.1016/j.chb.2022.107513

Kotei, E., & Thirunavukarasu, R. (2023). A systematic review of transformer-based pre-trained language models through self-supervised learning. *Information (Basel)*, *14*(3), 187. DOI: 10.3390/info14030187

Krook, J. (2025). Manipulation and the AI Act: Large Language Model Chatbots and the Danger of Mirrors. *SSRN*. DOI: 10.2139/ssrn.4719835

Kshetri, N. (2024). Linguistic challenges in generative artificial intelligence: Implications for low-resource languages in the developing world. *Journal of Global Information Technology Management*, *27*(2), 95–99. DOI: 10.1080/1097198X.2024.2341496

Kumar, S., Sharma, S., Udupa, S., Badiger, S., Singh, A., Bandekar, J., . . . Ghosh, P. K. (2025, April). Improving Dialect Identification in Indian Languages Using Multimodal Features from Dialect Informed ASR. In *ICASSP 2025-2025 IEEE International Conference on Acoustics, Speech and Signal Processing (ICASSP)* (pp. 1-5). IEEE.

Kumar, N. (2023). Unlocking India's Potential in Industrial Revolution 4.0: National Innovation System, Demography, and Inclusive Development. *Indian Public Policy Review*, *4*(3), 67–87. DOI: 10.55763/ippr.2023.04.03.003

Kush, J. C. (2025). Integrating Sensor Technologies with Conversational AI: Enhancing Context-Sensitive Interaction Through Real-Time Data Fusion. *Sensors (Basel)*, *25*(1), 249. DOI: 10.3390/s25010249 PMID: 39797040

Laskar, M. H. (2023). Examining the emergence of digital society and the digital divide in India: A comparative evaluation between urban and rural areas. *Frontiers in Sociology*, *8*, 1145221. DOI: 10.3389/fsoc.2023.1145221 PMID: 37122396

Latif, D., Qadir, J., Qayyum, A., Usama, M., Younis, A., & Abdelmageed, K. A. S. (2021). Artificial intelligence for speech emotion recognition: Concepts, datasets, and recent advances. *Information Fusion*, *76*, 297–317. DOI: 10.1016/j.inffus.2021.05.008

Latif, S., Rana, R., Qadir, J., & Epps, J. (2023). Survey of deep learning techniques for speech-based emotion detection. *ACM Computing Surveys*, *56*(1), 1–39. DOI: 10.1145/3549123

Lee, J., Lee, D., & Lee, J. G. (2024). Influence of rapport and social presence with an AI psychotherapy chatbot on users' self-disclosure. *International Journal of Human-Computer Interaction*, *40*(7), 1620–1631. DOI: 10.1080/10447318.2022.2146227

Lee, S., Kang, W., Bertogna, M., Chwa, H. S., & Lee, J. (2025). Timing guarantees for inference of AI models in embedded systems. *Real-Time Systems*, *61*(2), 259–267. DOI: 10.1007/s11241-025-09445-9

Lee, S.-Y., Lee, G., Kim, S., & Lee, J. (2019). Expressing personalities of conversational agents through visual and verbal feedback. *Electronics (Basel)*, *8*(7), 794. DOI: 10.3390/electronics8070794

Lei, S., Xie, L., & Peng, J. (2024). Unethical Consumer Behavior Following Artificial Intelligence Agent Encounters: The Differential Effect of AI Agent Roles and its Boundary Conditions. *Journal of Service Research*. Advance online publication. DOI: 10.1177/10946705241278837

Leschanowsky, A., Popp, B., & Peters, N. (2023). Debiasing Strategies for Conversational AI: Improving Privacy and Security Decision-Making. *Digital Society : Ethics, Socio-Legal and Governance of Digital Technology*, *2*(3), 34. Advance online publication. DOI: 10.1007/s44206-023-00062-2

Levy, Y., & Ellis, T. J. (2006). A systems approach to conduct an effective literature review in support of information systems research. *Informing Science*, *9*, 181–212. DOI: 10.28945/479

Lewis, M., Liu, Y., Goyal, N., Ghazvininejad, M., Mohamed, A., Levy, O., & Zettlemoyer, L. (2020). BART: Denoising Sequence-to-Sequence Pre-training for Natural Language Generation, Translation, and Comprehension. *Proceedings of ACL 2020*, 7871–7880. DOI: 10.18653/v1/2020.acl-main.703

Li, H. (2025, January 9). Character.AI put in new underage guardrails after a teen's suicide. His mother says that's not enough. *Business Insider*. https://www.businessinsider.com/character-ai-lawsuit-plantiff-age-guardrails-after-teen-suicide-2025-1

Liang, K. J., Wang, G., Li, Y., Henao, R., & Carin, L. (2019). Kernel-based approaches for sequence modeling: Connections to neural methods.

Li, J., Sun, Z., Liu, B., & Yu, H. (2022). Transfer learning for low-resource speech emotion recognition. *Speech Communication*, *139*, 70–80. DOI: 10.1016/j.specom.2022.03.004

Li, N., Liu, S., Liu, Y., Zhao, S., & Liu, M. (2019). Neural speech synthesis with Transformer network. *Proceedings of the AAAI Conference on Artificial Intelligence*, *33*(01), 6706–6713. DOI: 10.1609/aaai.v33i01.33016706

Lin, K.-Y., Chang, K.-H., Lin, Y.-W., & Wu, M.-J. (2025). Exploring key considerations for artificial intelligence robots in home healthcare using the unified theory of acceptance and use of technology and the fuzzy analytical hierarchy process method. *Systems*, *13*(1), 25. DOI: 10.3390/systems13010025

Liu, Y., Ott, M., Goyal, N., Du, J., Joshi, M., Chen, D., . . . Stoyanov, V. (2019). RoBERTa: A Robustly Optimized BERT Pretraining Approach. *arXiv preprint arXiv:1907.11692*.

Liu, J., Liu, Z., & Song, M. (2022). Multimodal sentiment analysis based on attention and context fusion. *IEEE Transactions on Multimedia, 24*, 2318–2330. DOI: 10.1109/TMM.2022.3141032

Liu, Y., & Zheng, J. (2019). Es-Tacotron2: Multi-task Tacotron 2 with pre-trained estimated network for reducing the over-smoothness problem. *Information (Basel), 10*(4), 131. DOI: 10.3390/info10040131 PMID: 34671488

Liu, Z. (2022). *Effective Transfer Learning for Low-Resource Natural Language Understanding*. Hong Kong University of Science and Technology. DOI: 10.14711/thesis-991013106358603412

Ltifi, M. (2023). Trust in the chatbot: A semi-human relationship. *Future Business Journal, 9*(1), 109. DOI: 10.1186/s43093-023-00288-z

Luk, D. W. A., Ip, W. C. T., & Shea, Y.-F. (2024). Performance of GPT-4 and GPT-3.5 in generating accurate and comprehensive diagnoses across medical subspecialties. *Journal of the Chinese Medical Association : JCMA, 87*(3), 259–260. DOI: 10.1097/JCMA.0000000000001064 PMID: 38305423

Macklin, R. (2003). Dignity is a useless concept. *BMJ (Clinical Research Ed.), 327*(7429), 1419–1420. DOI: 10.1136/bmj.327.7429.1419 PMID: 14684633

Maheswari, B., & Nagarajan, R. (2024). EduChatbot: Implementing educational Chatbot for assisting the teaching-learning process by NLP-based hybrid heuristic adopted deep learning framework. *Kybernetes*.

Mahmoudi, A., Khosrotabar, M., Gramann, K., Rinderknecht, S., & Sharbafi, M. A. (2025). Using passive BCI for personalization of assistive wearable devices: A proof-of-concept study. *IEEE Transactions on Neural Systems and Rehabilitation Engineering, PP*, 476–487. DOI: 10.1109/TNSRE.2025.3530154

Ma, J., Wang, Z., & Wang, Y. (2023). Exploring transformer-based models for emotion recognition from speech. *Computer Speech & Language, 77*, 101427. Advance online publication. DOI: 10.1016/j.csl.2022.101427

Mao, Q., Dong, M., Huang, Z., & Zhan, Y. (2021). Deep learning for speech emotion recognition: A review. *IEEE Transactions on Affective Computing, 12*(4), 1196–1215. DOI: 10.1109/TAFFC.2020.2989796

Marengo, A. (2023). The Future of AI in IoT: Emerging Trends in Intelligent Data Analysis and Privacy Protection. mdpi ag. DOI: 10.20944/preprints202312.2184.v1

Marjerison, R. K., Zhang, Y., Kim, J.-M., Dong, H., Zheng, H., & Kuan, G. (2025). Understanding user acceptance of AI-driven chatbots in China's e-commerce: The roles of perceived authenticity, usefulness, and risk. *Systems, 13*(2), 71. DOI: 10.3390/systems13020071

Marvi, R., Foroudi, P., & Cuomo, M. T. (2024). Past, present and future of AI in marketing and knowledge management. *Journal of Knowledge Management, 29*(11), 1–31. DOI: 10.1108/JKM-07-2023-0634

Mathur, A., & Mayer, J. (2021). What makes a dark pattern... dark? design attributes, normative considerations, and measurement methods. *Conference on Human Factors in Computing Systems - Proceedings*. DOI: 10.1145/3411764.3445610

Matthews, M. J., Su, R., Yonish, L., McClean, S., Koopman, J., & Yam, K. C. (2025). A Review of Artificial Intelligence, Algorithms, and Robots Through the Lens of Stakeholder Theory. *Journal of Management, 51*(6), 2627–2676. Advance online publication. DOI: 10.1177/01492063241311855

Matz, S. C., Kosinski, M., Nave, G., & Stillwell, D. J. (2017). Psychological targeting as an effective approach to digital mass persuasion. *Proceedings of the National Academy of Sciences of the United States of America, 114*(48), 12714–12719. DOI: 10.1073/pnas.1710966114 PMID: 29133409

Mazidi, K., & Tarau, P. (2016). Automatic question generation: From NLU to NLG. In *Intelligent Tutoring Systems: 13th International Conference, ITS 2016, Zagreb, Croatia, June 7-10, 2016.* [Springer International Publishing.]. *Proceedings, 13*, 23–33.

McGuire, J., De Cremer, D., Hesselbarth, Y., De Schutter, L., Mai, K. M., & Van Hiel, A. (2023). The reputational and ethical consequences of deceptive chatbot use. *Scientific Reports, 13*(1), 16246. DOI: 10.1038/s41598-023-41692-3 PMID: 37758742

McLennan, S., Fiske, A., Tigard, D., Müller, R., Haddadin, S., & Buyx, A. (2022). Embedded ethics: A proposal for integrating ethics into the development of medical AI. *BMC Medical Ethics, 23*(1), 6. DOI: 10.1186/s12910-022-00746-3 PMID: 35081955

McLeod, C. (2021). Trust. In E. N. Zalta (Ed.), *The Stanford encyclopedia of philosophy* (Fall 2021 Edition). Metaphysics Research Lab, Stanford University. https://plato.stanford.edu/archives/fall2021/entries/trust/

Mctear, M. (2020). Conversational AI: Dialogue Systems, Conversational Agents, and Chatbots. *Synthesis Lectures on Human Language Technologies*, *13*(3), 1–251. DOI: 10.1007/978-3-031-02176-3

Mehta, D., Diddee, H., Saxena, A., Shukla, A., Santy, S., Kommiya, R., . . . Bali, K. (2022). Learnings from Technological Interventions in a Low Resource Language. *arXiv preprint arXiv:2211.16172*.

Mekni, M. (2021). An artificial intelligence based virtual assistant using conversational agents. *Journal of Software Engineering and Applications*, *14*(9), 455–473. DOI: 10.4236/jsea.2021.149027

Mensah, G. B. (2023). Artificial intelligence and ethics: a comprehensive review of bias mitigation, transparency, and accountability in AI Systems. Preprint, November, 10(1). DOI: DOI: 10.13140/RG.2.2.23381.19685/1

Mikolov, T., Chen, K., Corrado, G., & Dean, J. (2013). Efficient estimation of word representations in vector space. *arXiv preprint arXiv:1301.3781*.

Mittelstadt, B. D., Allo, P., Taddeo, M., Wachter, S., & Floridi, L. (2016). The ethics of algorithms: Mapping the debate. *Big Data & Society*, *3*(2), 2053951716679679. Advance online publication. DOI: 10.1177/2053951716679679

Moore, R., Moore, M., Shanahan, K., Horky, A., & Mack, B. (2015). Creepy marketing: Three dimensions of perceived excessive online privacy violation. *Marketing Management Journal, 25*(1), 43–53. https://www.researchgate.net/publication/282329651_Creepy_Marketing_Three_Dimensions_of_Perceived_Excessive_Online_Privacy_Violation

Morley, J., Elhalal, A., Garcia, F., Kinsey, L., Mökander, J., & Floridi, L. (2021). Ethics as a service: A pragmatic operationalisation of AI ethics. *Minds and Machines*, *31*(2), 239–256. DOI: 10.1007/s11023-021-09563-w PMID: 34720418

Mughal, F. R., He, J., Das, B., Dharejo, F. A., Zhu, N., Khan, S. B., & Alzahrani, S. (2024). Adaptive federated learning for resource-constrained IoT devices through edge intelligence and multi-edge clustering. *Scientific Reports*, *14*(1), 28746. Advance online publication. DOI: 10.1038/s41598-024-78239-z PMID: 39567565

Muhammad Eid BALBAA, & Marina Sagatovna ABDURASHIDOVA. (2024). The impact of artificial Intelligence in Decision Making: A comprehensive review. Epra, 27–38.

Murtarelli, G., Gregory, A., & Romenti, S. (2021). A conversation-based perspective for shaping ethical human–machine interactions: The particular challenge of chatbots. *Journal of Business Research*, *129*, 927–935. DOI: 10.1016/j.jbusres.2020.09.018

Murzin, S. P. (2024). Artificial intelligence-driven innovations in laser processing of metallic materials. *Metals, 14*(12), 1458. DOI: 10.3390/met14121458

Nee, J., Smith, G. M., Sheares, A., & Rustagi, I. (2022). Linguistic justice as a framework for designing, developing, and managing natural language processing tools. *Big Data & Society, 9*(1), 20539517221090930. DOI: 10.1177/20539517221090930

Neumann, M., & Vu, N. T. (2018). Attentive convolutional neural networks for speech emotion recognition. *Proceedings of Interspeech, 2018*, 1228–1232. DOI: 10.21437/Interspeech.2018-1794

Nikoghosyan, K. H. (2022). An overview of the existing text-to-speech(tts) algorithms based on deep learning. INFORMATION TECHNOLOGIES, ELECTRONICS. *Wuxiandian Gongcheng*.

Nowak, K. L., & Biocca, F. (2001). The influence of agency and anthropomorphism on users' sense of telepresence, copresence, and social presence in virtual environments. *Presence (Cambridge, Mass.), 10*(5), 481–494. DOI: 10.1162/105474603322761289

O'Sullivan, B., & Woodridge, M. (2015). *Artificial intelligence: Foundations, theory, and algorithms*. Book Series, 2021(9).

Oh, C. S., Bailenson, J. N., & Welch, G. F. (2018). A systematic review of social presence: Definition, antecedents, and implications. *Frontiers in Robotics and AI, 5*, 114. DOI: 10.3389/frobt.2018.00114 PMID: 33500993

Okoli, C. (2015). A guide to conducting a standalone systematic literature review. *Communications of the Association for Information Systems, 37*(1). Advance online publication. DOI: 10.17705/1CAIS.03743

Orlowski, A., & Loh, W. (2025). Data autonomy and privacy in the smart home: The case for a privacy smart home meta-assistant. *AI & Society, 40*(6), 4171–4184. Advance online publication. DOI: 10.1007/s00146-025-02182-4

Ouyang, L., Wu, J., Jiang, X., Almeida, D., Wainwright, C., Mishkin, P., & Lowe, R. (2022). Training language models to follow instructions with human feedback. *Advances in Neural Information Processing Systems, 35*, 27730–27744.

Panchal, B. Y., Desai, V., Shah, P., Desai, V., Yadav, A., & Tiwari, M. (2025). *Examine the Opportunities and Challenges of Large Language Model (LLM)*. For Indic Languages.

Pandey, A., & Rajan, P. (2022). Speech emotion recognition using convolutional recurrent neural networks with attention mechanism. *Expert Systems with Applications, 189*, 116056. Advance online publication. DOI: 10.1016/j.eswa.2021.116056

Parthasarathy, S., & Busso, C. (2022). Predicting emotion from speech: A review. *IEEE Signal Processing Magazine*, *39*(1), 70–81. DOI: 10.1109/MSP.2021.3115366

Pavaiyarkarasi, R., Rajendran, N., Vijayashanthi, R. S., Saranya, G., & Mohanavel, V. (2023). Experimental evaluation of Internet of Things assisted human voice-based smart home controlling system. *Proceedings of the 2023 International Conference on Smart Electronics and Systems (ICSES)*, 1–6. DOI: 10.1109/ICSES60034.2023.10465326

Pei, R., & Su, Z. (2025). Key success factors for export structure optimization in East Asian countries through global value chain (GVC) reorganization. *Systems*, *13*(1), 22. DOI: 10.3390/systems13010022

Pennington, J., Socher, R., & Manning, C. D. (2014, October). Glove: Global vectors for word representation. In *Proceedings of the 2014 conference on empirical methods in natural language processing (EMNLP)* (pp. 1532-1543). DOI: 10.3115/v1/D14-1162

Periša, M., Teskera, P., Cvitić, I., & Grgurević, I. (2025). Empowering People with Disabilities in Smart Homes Using Predictive Informing. *Sensors (Basel)*, *25*(1), 284. DOI: 10.3390/s25010284 PMID: 39797073

Petty, R. E., & Cacioppo, J. T. (1986). The Elaboration Likelihood Model of Persuasion. *Advances in Experimental Social Psychology*, *19*, 123–205. DOI: 10.1016/S0065-2601(08)60214-2

Picard, R. W., & Liu, K. (2023). Affective computing and ethical implications: Future directions. *Frontiers in Artificial Intelligence*, *6*, 1084509. Advance online publication. DOI: 10.3389/frai.2023.1084509

Pizzi, G., Vannucci, V., Mazzoli, V., & Donvito, R. (2023). I, chatbot! the impact of anthropomorphism and gaze direction on willingness to disclose personal information and behavioral intentions. *Psychology and Marketing*, *40*(7), 1372–1387. DOI: 10.1002/mar.21813

Poria, S., Hazarika, D., Majumder, N., Naik, G., Cambria, E., & Mihalcea, R. (2019). MELD: A multimodal multi-party dataset for emotion recognition in conversations. In *Proceedings of the 57th Annual Meeting of the Association for Computational Linguistics* (pp. 527–536). DOI: 10.18653/v1/P19-1050

Prabaharan, G., Vidhya, S., Chithrakumar, T., Sika, K., & Balakrishnan, M., M. B. (. (2025). AI-Driven Computational Frameworks: Advancing Edge Intelligence and Smart Systems. *International Journal of Computational and Experimental Science and Engineering*, *11*(1). Advance online publication. DOI: 10.22399/ijcesen.1165

Pradhan, U., & Dey, J. (2023). Language, artificial education, and future-making in indigenous language education. *Learning, Media and Technology*, •••, 1–14.

Rabbi, M. F., Abdullah, M., Al-Dalahmeh, M., & Amin, M. B. (2025). Assessing the role of information technology in promoting environmental sustainability and preventing crime in e-commerce. *International Review of Applied Sciences and Engineering*, *16*(1), 81–97. DOI: 10.1556/1848.2024.00834

Radford, A., Kim, J. W., Hallacy, C., Ramesh, A., Goh, G., Agarwal, S., & Sutskever, I. (2021, July). Learning transferable visual models from natural language supervision. In *International conference on machine learning* (pp. 8748-8763). PmLR.

Radford, A., Kim, J. W., Xu, T., Brockman, G., McLeavey, C., & Sutskever, I. (2023, July). Robust speech recognition via large-scale weak supervision. In *International conference on machine learning* (pp. 28492-28518). PMLR.

Raffel, C., Shazeer, N., Roberts, A., Lee, K., Narang, S., Matena, M., & Liu, P. J. (2020). Exploring the limits of transfer learning with a unified text-to-text transformer. *Journal of Machine Learning Research*, *21*(140), 1–67.

Rajeshwari, S. B., & Kallimani, J. S. (2021). Regional language code-switching for natural language understanding and intelligent digital assistants. In *Innovations in Electrical and Electronic Engineering* [Springer Singapore.]. *Proceedings of ICEEE*, *2021*, 927–948.

Ramaul, L., Ritala, P., & Ruokonen, M. (2024). Creational and conversational AI affordances: How the new breed of chatbots is revolutionizing knowledge industries. *Business Horizons*, *67*(5), 615–627. DOI: 10.1016/j.bushor.2024.05.006

Rana, R., Epps, J., & Latif, S. (2023). Federated learning for speech-based emotion recognition. *IEEE Internet of Things Journal*, *10*(6), 4974–4984. DOI: 10.1109/JIOT.2022.3187301

Rane, J., Rane, N. L., Kaya, Ö., & Mallick, S. K. (2024). Artificial intelligence, machine learning, and deep learning in cloud, edge, and quantum computing: A review of trends, challenges, and future directions. deep science. DOI: 10.70593/978-81-981271-0-5_1

Ranjan, R., & Sharma, A. (2020). Voice-controlled IoT devices framework for smart home. In *Smart Intelligent Computing and Applications* (pp. 57–67). Springer., DOI: 10.1007/978-981-15-3369-3_5

Rao Hill, S., & Troshani, I. (2024). Chatbot anthropomorphism, social presence, uncanniness and brand attitude effects. *Journal of Computer Information Systems*, 1–17. DOI: 10.1080/08874417.2024.2423187

Rapp, A., Curti, L., & Boldi, A. (2021). The human side of human-chatbot interaction: A systematic literature review of ten years of research on text-based chatbots. *International Journal of Human-Computer Studies, 151*, 102630. DOI: 10.1016/j.ijhcs.2021.102630

Rathika, P., Parthipan, V., Anju, P., Ponni, P., & Yamunadevi, S. (2024). Developing an AI-Powered Interactive Virtual Tutor for Enhanced Learning Experiences. *International Journal of Computational and Experimental Science and Engineering, 10*(4). Advance online publication. DOI: 10.22399/ijcesen.782

Redacción, N. (2023). Remotely controlled smart home system using voice and IoT. *Ciencia en la Ingeniería, 11*(1), 2016–2024. DOI: 10.52783/cienceng.v11i1.370

Reitmaier, T., Wallington, E., Kalarikalayil Raju, D., Klejch, O., Pearson, J., Jones, M., & Robinson, S. (2022, April). Opportunities and challenges of automatic speech recognition systems for low-resource language speakers. In *Proceedings of the 2022 CHI conference on human factors in computing systems* (pp. 1-17). DOI: 10.1145/3491102.3517639

Ribeiro, B., Gomes, L., & Vale, Z. (2025). Retrieval-augmented generation based assistant: A smart home case study. In Santos, M. F., Machado, J., Novais, P., Cortez, P., & Moreira, P. M. (Eds.), *Progress in Artificial Intelligence. EPIA 2024* (Vol. 14968). Springer., DOI: 10.1007/978-3-031-73500-4_14

Rogalski, T., & Schiereck, D. (2024). When is blockchain worth it? Value and risk drivers of corporate blockchain announcements. *Electronic Markets, 34*(1), 39. DOI: 10.1007/s12525-024-00718-y

Ruan, Y., & Wang, X. (2022). Emotion detection in call center conversations using end-to-end speech models. *Computer Speech & Language, 73*, 101328. Advance online publication. DOI: 10.1016/j.csl.2022.101328

Sadraey, M. H. (2025). Microcontroller boards. In *Unmanned aircraft design*. Springer., DOI: 10.1007/978-3-031-67795-3_9

Sahoo, S. K., Biswal, B. B., Ranjan Dash, S., & Patra, J. (2025). Empirical Analysis on Machine Translation Possibilities for Low-Resource Santali Language. *International Journal of Artificial Intelligence Tools, 34*(1), 2550005. DOI: 10.1142/S0218213025500058

Sajja, R., Demir, I., & Sermet, Y. (2025). End-to-End Deployment of the Educational AI Hub for Personalized Learning and Engagement: A Case Study on Environmental Science Education. california digital library. DOI: 10.31223/X5XM7N

Salako, A. O., Dapo-Oyewole, D. L., Olaniyi, O. O., Aideyan, N. T., Fabuyi, J. A., & Selesi-Aina, O. (2024). Advancing Information Governance in AI-Driven Cloud Ecosystem: Strategies for Enhancing Data Security and Meeting Regulatory Compliance. *Asian Journal of Research in Computer Science*, *17*(12), 66–88. DOI: 10.9734/ajrcos/2024/v17i12530

Samal, S. R., Bandopadhaya, S., Roy, A., Mishra, A., Mihovska, A., & Poulkov, V. (2023). MQTT protocol-based IoT solution for voice-controlled smart home. *Proceedings of the IEEE Wireless Personal Multimedia Communications (WPMC)*, 171–175. DOI: 10.1109/WPMC59531.2023.10338841

Sangeetha, R., Srivastava, D., Logeshwaran, J., Vishwakarma, P., & Vats, S. (2023, November). Optimization of Natural Language Understanding with Contextual Embeddings. In *2023 International Conference on Research Methodologies in Knowledge Management, Artificial Intelligence and Telecommunication Engineering (RMKMATE)* (pp. 1-6). IEEE. DOI: 10.1109/RMKMATE59243.2023.10369022

Sankar, A., Anand, S., Varadhan, P., Thomas, S., Singal, M., Kumar, S., & Khapra, M. (2024). Indicvoices-r: Unlocking a massive multilingual multi-speaker speech corpus for scaling indian TTS. *Advances in Neural Information Processing Systems*, *37*, 68161–68182.

Satt, A., Rozenberg, S., & Hoory, R. (2021). Efficient emotion recognition from speech using deep learning on spectrograms. *Proceedings of Interspeech*, *2021*, 3154–3158. DOI: 10.21437/Interspeech.2021-1285

Saxena, S., Gupta, A., & Daniel, P. (2024). Efficient Data Augmentation via lexical matching for boosting performance on Statistical Machine Translation for Indic and a Low-resource language. *Multimedia Tools and Applications*, *83*(24), 64255–64269. DOI: 10.1007/s11042-023-18086-8

Saxena, V., Tamò-Larrieux, A., Van Dijck, G., & Spanakis, G. (2025). Responsible guidelines for authorship attribution tasks in NLP. *Ethics and Information Technology*, *27*(2), 16. DOI: 10.1007/s10676-025-09821-w

Schopft, S., Mehler, A., & Kühn, T. (2023). *Natural language processing: Foundations, methods, and applications*. Springer. Chomsky, N. (1957). *Syntactic structures*. The Hague: Mouton.

Schuller, B., & Batliner, A. (2023). Computational paralinguistics: Emotion, affect and personality in speech and language processing. *IEEE Transactions on Affective Computing*, *14*(1), 5–20. DOI: 10.1109/TAFFC.2022.3145547

Sengupta, A., Das, S., Akhtar, M. S., & Chakraborty, T. (2024). Social, economic, and demographic factors drive the emergence of Hinglish code-mixing on social media. *Humanities & Social Sciences Communications*, *11*(1), 1–12. DOI: 10.1057/s41599-024-03058-6

Senoner, J., Schallmoser, S., Kratzwald, B., Feuerriegel, S., & Netland, T. (2024). Explainable AI improves task performance in human–AI collaboration. *Scientific Reports*, *14*(1), 31150. DOI: 10.1038/s41598-024-82501-9 PMID: 39730794

Shahi, A., & Mittal, A. (2023). The Impact of Federated Learning on AI-Enhanced Healthcare Delivery (pp. 57–66). igi global. DOI: 10.4018/979-8-3693-2639-8.ch005

Shao, F., Zhang, T., Gao, S., Sun, Q., & Yang, L. (2024). Computer Vision-Driven Gesture Recognition: Toward Natural and Intuitive Human-Computer. /arxiv.2412.18321DOI: 10.1109/EIECC64539.2024.10929472

Shao, J., Liu, Z., & Feng, Y. (2024). The impact of big data-driven strategies on sustainable consumer behaviour in e-commerce: A green economy perspective. *Sustainability (Basel)*, *16*(24), 10960. DOI: 10.3390/su162410960

Short, J. (1976). *The social psychology of telecommunications*. Wiley. https://archive.org/details/socialpsychology0000shor

Sidlauskiene, J., Joye, Y., & Auruskeviciene, V. (2023). AI-based chatbots in conversational commerce and their effects on product and price perceptions. *Electronic Markets*, *33*(1), 1–21. DOI: 10.1007/s12525-023-00633-8 PMID: 37252674

Sindoni, M. G. (2024). The femininization of AI-powered voice assistants: Personification, anthropomorphism and discourse ideologies. *Discourse, Context & Media*, *62*, 100833. DOI: 10.1016/j.dcm.2024.100833

Singh, A., Jayakumar, A., Deekshitha, G., Kumar, H., Bandekar, J., Badiger, S., . . . Ghosh, P. K. (2023, November). An End-to-End TTS Model in Chhattisgarhi, a Low-Resource Indian Language. In *International Conference on Speech and Computer* (pp. 164-172). Cham: Springer Nature Switzerland. DOI: 10.1007/978-3-031-48312-7_13

Singh, N., Kim, H., Kim, J., Yu, Y., Do, Y., & Fouad, I. (2025). Crumbled cookies: Exploring e-commerce websites' cookie policies with data protection regulations. *ACM Transactions on the Web*, *19*(1), 1–24. DOI: 10.1145/3708515

Singh, V. (2025). AI-Powered Assistive Technologies for People with Disabilities: Developing AI Solutions that Aid Individuals with Various Disabilities in Daily Tasks. *Journal of Engineering Research and Reports*, *27*(2), 292–309. DOI: 10.9734/jerr/2025/v27i21410

Snyder, H. (2019). Literature review as a research methodology: An overview and guidelines. *Journal of Business Research, 104*, 333–339. DOI: 10.1016/j.jbusres.2019.07.039

So, C., Khvan, A., & Choi, W. (2023). Natural conversations with a virtual being: How user experience with a current conversational AI model compares to expectations. *Computer Animation and Virtual Worlds, 34*(6), e2149. DOI: 10.1002/cav.2149

Sonawane, P., Kunekar, P., Bhatele Priyanka, R., Sonkusare, S., Sonar, R., Bisen, S., & Sonar, K. (2023). Convomind: A User-friendly AI Chatbot. *International Journal for Research in Applied Science and Engineering Technology, 11*(12), 1–5. DOI: 10.22214/ijraset.2023.57180

Song, Y., & Luximon, Y. (2020). Trust in AI agent: A systematic review of facial anthropomorphic trustworthiness for social robot design. *Sensors (Basel), 20*(18), 5087. DOI: 10.3390/s20185087 PMID: 32906760

Song, Y., & Yan, K. (2024). An intelligent speech multifeature recognition method based on deep machine learning: A smart city application. *Journal of Testing and Evaluation, 52*(3), 20220686. DOI: 10.1520/JTE20220686

Spilinek, M., & Jorgensen, J. J. (2025). Creepy or convenient?: Consumer perceptions of privacy and ad exposure on social media. *Italian Journal of Marketing, 2025*(1), 71–89. DOI: 10.1007/s43039-025-00107-z

Stahl, B. C., & Eke, D. (2024). The ethics of ChatGPT – Exploring the ethical issues of an emerging technology. *International Journal of Information Management, 74*, 102700. DOI: 10.1016/j.ijinfomgt.2023.102700

Stecuła, K., Wolniak, R., & Grebski, W. W. (2023). AI-Driven Urban Energy Solutions—From Individuals to Society: A Review. *Energies, 16*(24), 7988. DOI: 10.3390/en16247988

Strengers, Y., Phan, T., Duque, M., & Dahlgren, K. (2024). Anthropomorphizing Voice Assistants: A Research Agenda for Human–AI Relationships. *The De Gruyter Handbook of Robots in Society and Culture, 3*, 391.

Strubell, E., Ganesh, A., & McCallum, A. (2020). Energy and policy considerations for modern deep learning research. *Proceedings of the AAAI Conference on Artificial Intelligence, 34*(09), 13693–13696. DOI: 10.1609/aaai.v34i09.7123

Sun, H., Hou, J., Li, X., Du, H., Zhang, L., & Yu, X. (2025). IUAC: Inaudible Universal Adversarial Attacks Against Smart Speakers. *ACM Transactions on Sensor Networks, 21*(1), 1–20. DOI: 10.1145/3698238

Talreja Wassan, J., & Ghuriani, V. (2024). Perspective Chapter: Recent Trends in Deep Learning for Conversational AI. intechopen. DOI: 10.5772/intechopen.113250

Talreja Wassan, J., & Ghuriani, V. (2024). Perspective chapter: Recent trends in Deep Learning for conversational AI. In *Artificial Intelligence*. IntechOpen.

Tan, X., Qin, T., Soong, F., & Liu, T.-Y. (2021). A Survey on Neural Speech Synthesis.

Tantalo, C., & Priem, R. L. (2016). Value creation through stakeholder synergy. *Strategic Management Journal, 37*(2), 314–329. DOI: 10.1002/smj.2337

Tarsney, C. (2024). Deception and Manipulation in Generative AI. *Philosophical Studies, 2025*, 1–23. DOI: 10.1007/S11098-024-02259-8

Thomaz, F., Salge, C., Karahanna, E., & Hulland, J. (2020). Learning from the Dark Web: Leveraging conversational agents in the era of hyper-privacy to enhance marketing. *Journal of the Academy of Marketing Science, 48*(1), 43–63. DOI: 10.1007/s11747-019-00704-3

Torad, M. A., Bouallegue, B., & Ahmed, A. M. (2022). A voice-controlled smart home automation system using artificial intelligence and Internet of Things. *Telkomnika, 20*(4), 808. DOI: 10.12928/telkomnika.v20i4.23763

Torraco, R. J. (2005). Writing integrative literature reviews: Guidelines and examples. *Human Resource Development Review, 4*(3), 356–367. DOI: 10.1177/1534484305278283

Tran, K., Bisazza, A., & Monz, C. (2016). Recurrent memory networks for language modeling. *Proceedings of the 2016 Conference of the North American of the Association for Computational Linguistics: Human Technologies.*

Tran, Q.-D. L., & Le, A.-C. (2023). Exploring bi-directional context for improved chatbot response generation using deep reinforcement learning. *Applied Sciences (Basel, Switzerland), 13*(8), 5041. DOI: 10.3390/app13085041

Traubinger, V., Heil, S., Grigera, J., Garrido, A., & Gaedke, M. (2024). In Search of Dark Patterns in Chatbots. *Lecture Notes in Computer Science (Including Subseries Lecture Notes in Artificial Intelligence and Lecture Notes in Bioinformatics), 14524 LNCS*, 117–132. DOI: 10.1007/978-3-031-54975-5_7

Udegbe, F., Ebulue, O., Ekesiobi, C., & Ebulue, C.Francisca Chibugo UdegbeOgochukwu Roseline EbulueCharles Chukwudalu EbulueChukwunonso Sylvester Ekesiobi. (2024). THE ROLE OF ARTIFICIAL INTELLIGENCE IN HEALTHCARE: A SYSTEMATIC REVIEW OF APPLICATIONS AND CHALLENGES. *International Medical Science Research Journal, 4*(4), 500–508. DOI: 10.51594/imsrj.v4i4.1052

Uppuluri, S., & Lakshmeeswari, G. (2024). Review of security and privacy-based IoT smart home access control devices. *Wireless Personal Communications*, *137*(3), 1601–1640. DOI: 10.1007/s11277-024-11405-8

Vaswani, A., Parmar, N., Uszkoreit, J., Shazeer, N., & Kaiser, L. (2018). Image transformer.

Venkatraman, S., Overmars, A., & Thong, M. (2021). Smart Home Automation—Use Cases of a Secure and Integrated Voice-Control System. *Systems*, *9*(4), 77. DOI: 10.3390/systems9040077

Vijayalakshmi, B., Deshpande, K. A., & Krishan, N. (2024, October). Use of AI to Augment Multilingual Content in Cyberspace for Development–An Indian Case Study. In *2024 IEEE Global Humanitarian Technology Conference (GHTC)* (pp. 31-35). IEEE.

Wadhawan, K. (2024). Harnessing the Technical Potential of AI, IT and Data Management For Unlocking India's Economic Success Story. *Partners Universal International Innovation Journal*, *2*(2), 80–91.

Wasserman, N. (2023). *OpenAI's Failed Experiment in Governance*. Corporate Governance. https://hbr.org/2023/11/openais-failed-experiment-in-governance

Webster, J., & Watson, R. T. (2002). Analyzing the past to prepare for the future: Writing a literature review. *Management Information Systems Quarterly*, *26*(2), xiii–xxiii. Advance online publication. DOI: 10.2307/4132319

Wei, J., Bosma, M., Zhao, V. Y., Guu, K., Yu, A. W., Lester, B., . . . Le, Q. V. (2021). Finetuned language models are zero-shot learners. *arXiv preprint arXiv:2109.01652*.

Whittlestone, J., Nyrup, R., Alexandrova, A., & Dastin, J. (2019). The role and limits of principles in AI ethics. In *Proceedings of the 2019 AAAI/ACM Conference on AI, Ethics, and Society* (pp. 195–200). Association for Computing Machinery. DOI: 10.1145/3306618.3314289

Williams, A. S., Ortega, F., & Garcia, J. (2020). Understanding Multimodal User Gesture and Speech Behavior for Object Manipulation in Augmented Reality Using Elicitation. *IEEE Transactions on Visualization and Computer Graphics*, *26*(12), 3479–3489. DOI: 10.1109/TVCG.2020.3023566 PMID: 32941142

Williamson, S. M., & Prybutok, V. (2024). Balancing Privacy and Progress: A Review of Privacy Challenges, Systemic Oversight, and Patient Perceptions in AI-Driven Healthcare. *Applied Sciences (Basel, Switzerland)*, *14*(2), 675. DOI: 10.3390/app14020675

Winfield, A. F. T., & Jirotka, M. (2018). Ethical governance is essential to building trust in robotics and artificial intelligence systems. *Philosophical Transactions. Series A, Mathematical, Physical, and Engineering Sciences, 376*(2133), 20180085. DOI: 10.1098/rsta.2018.0085 PMID: 30323000

Wu, Y., Zhao, G., Qian, X., Chua, T.-S., Liao, L., Lei, W., & Zhang, G. (2023). State Graph Reasoning for Multimodal Conversational Recommendation. *IEEE Transactions on Multimedia, 25*, 3113–3124. DOI: 10.1109/TMM.2022.3155900

Xiao, Y., & Watson, M. (2019). Guidance on conducting a systematic literature review. *Journal of Planning Education and Research, 39*(1), 93–112. DOI: 10.1177/0739456X17723971

Xu, A., Liu, Z., Guo, Y., Sinha, V., & Akkiraju, R. (2017). A new chatbot for customer service on social media. *Conference on Human Factors in Computing Systems - Proceedings, 2017-May*, 3506–3510. DOI: 10.1145/3025453.3025496

Yang, Y., Wang, C., Xiang, X., & An, R. (2025). AI applications to reduce loneliness among older adults: A systematic review of effectiveness and technologies. *Health Care, 13*(5), 446. DOI: 10.3390/healthcare13050446 PMID: 40077009

Yoo, Y., Jung, J., Kang, C., Kim, H., & Jun, S. (2024). Do Computers Have Gender Roles?: Investigating Users' Gender Role Stereotyping of Anthropomorphized Voice Agents. *Archives of Design Research, 37*(1), 123–136. DOI: 10.15187/adr.2024.02.37.1.123

Zaheer, M., Guruganesh, G., Dubey, K. A., Ainslie, J., Alberti, C., Ontanon, S., & Ahmed, A. (2020). Big bird: Transformers for longer sequences. *Advances in Neural Information Processing Systems, 33*, 17283–17297.

Zeng, T. (2023). Deep learning in automatic speech recognition (ASR): A review. In *Proceedings of the 2022 7th International Conference on Modern Management and Education Technology (MMET 2022)* (pp. 173–179). Atlantis Press SARL. DOI: 10.2991/978-2-494069-51-0_23

Zhang, H., Del Hougne, P., Zhao, H., Cui, T. J., Wang, Z., Li, L., Hu, S., & Ruan, H. (2024). Microwave Speech Recognizer Empowered by a Programmable Metasurface. *Advanced Science (Weinheim, Baden-Württemberg, Germany), 11*(17), 2309826. Advance online publication. DOI: 10.1002/advs.202309826 PMID: 38380552

Zhang, W., Yang, H., Bu, X., & Wang, L. (2019). Deep learning for mandarin-Tibetan cross-lingual speech synthesis. *IEEE Access : Practical Innovations, Open Solutions, 7*, 167884–167894. DOI: 10.1109/ACCESS.2019.2954342

Zhang, X., Xu, M., & Xu, S. (2025). Smart home cyber insurance pricing. In Zhao, J., & Meng, W. (Eds.), *Science of Cyber Security. SciSec 2024* (Vol. 15441). Springer., DOI: 10.1007/978-981-96-2417-1_17

Zhang, Z., Lee, C., & Wang, L. (2023). Recent Advances in Artificial Intelligence Sensors. *Advanced Sensor Research*, *2*(8), 2200072. Advance online publication. DOI: 10.1002/adsr.202200072

Zuboff, S. (2019, January). Surveillance capitalism and the challenge of collective action. [). Sage CA: Los Angeles, CA: Sage Publications.]. *New Labor Forum*, *28*(1), 10–29. DOI: 10.1177/1095796018819461

About the Contributors

Yash Chawla is an experienced academician, business consultant, and researcher with a Ph.D. in Management and Quality Sciences and a strong track record of publishing high-quality research in prestigious journals and also Member - Academic Iuvenum (The Young Researcher's Academy). 2021-2023, 2023-2023(re-elected for second term). His interdisciplinary research interests include Sustainable Development, Circular Economy, Diusion of Emerging Technolo- gies, Social Media Communications, Energy Markets and Policies, Business In- telligence & Marketing, and Consumer Awareness & Engagement. He has pub- lished research articles in highly respected journals such as the Journal of Busi- ness Research (JCR I.F. 10.969), Energy Policy (JCR I.F. 7.567), Telematics and Informatics (JCR I.F. 9.14), and Information Processing & Management (JCR I.F. 7.466). He has several manuscripts currently under revision and review in top-tier journals. The author's research contributions have been recognized with awards and honors, including the 2020 Best Young Research in Manage- ment and Quality Sciences at Wroclaw University of Science and Technology under the Secundus Programme.

Shubham Mahajan, a distinguished member of prestigious organizations such as IEEE, ACM, and IAENG, boasts an impressive academic and professional background. He earned his B.Tech. degree from Baba Ghulam Shah Badshah University, his M.Tech. degree from Chandigarh University, his Ph.D. degree from Shri Mata Vaishno Devi University (SMVDU) in Katra, India. Currently, he serves as an Assistant Professor at Amity University, Haryana. Dr. Mahajan has a remarkable track record in the field of artificial intelligence and image processing, holding an impressive portfolio of eighteen Indian patents, as well as one Australian and one German patent. His contributions to the field are further evidenced by his extensive publication record, which includes over 94 articles published in peer-reviewed journals and conferences and 8 edited books. His research interests span a wide array of topics, encompassing image processing, video compression, image segmentation, fuzzy entropy, nature-inspired computing methods, optimization, data mining, machine learning, robotics, and optical communication. Notably, his dedication and expertise have earned him the 'Best Research Paper Award' from ICRIC 2019, published by Springer in the LNEE series. In recognition of his exceptional achievements, Dr. Mahajan has received numerous accolades and honors throughout his career. These include the Best Student Award in 2019, the IEEE Region-10 Travel Grant Award in 2019, the 2nd runner-up prize in the IEEE RAS HACKATHON in 2019 (held in Bangladesh), the IEEE Student Early Researcher Conference Fund (SERCF) in 2020, the Emerging Scientist Award in 2021, and the IEEE Signal Processing Society Professional Development Grant in 2021. His commitment to excellence in research was further underscored by his receipt of the Excellence in Research Award in 2023. Dr. Mahajan's influence extends well beyond academia. He has served as a Campus Ambassador for IEEE, representing prestigious institutions such as IIT Bombay, IIT Kanpur, IIT Varanasi, and IIT Delhi, as well as various multinational corporations. His active participation in fostering international research collaborations highlights his passion for advancing the frontiers of knowledge and innovation on a global scale. Additionally, Dr. Mahajan is a dedicated member of the Technical Program Committee and serves on the Editorial Board for several international conferences and journals.

Akshat Agrawal holds a B.Tech in Computer Science & Engineering from UPTU and an M.Tech from USICT, GGSIPU. He earned his Ph.D. from GGSIPU, Delhi. He is currently working as an Associate Professor at Department of Computer Science & Engineering at JK Laxmipat University, Jaipur. Prior to this he worked at Associate Professor and Cluster Lead at the School of Computer Science & Engineering, IILM University, Gurugram and Before that He worked as an Assistant Professor (Senior Scale) at Amity University Haryana, Amity School of Engineering and Technology. He has published 65 research papers in Scopus/ SCIE-indexed international journals and conferences. As part of international academic collaborations, he visited the Technical University of Kosice, Slovakia, and the University of Nova, Portugal, in June 2019 under the CABCIN project (ERASMUS-funded). In May 2023, he received a scholarship to visit the Wroclaw University of Science & Technology, Wroclaw, Poland.

***

Sharipov Dilshod Bakhshilloevich is a Senior Teacher in the Department of Social Sciences at Bukhara State Pedagogical Institute, Uzbekistan. He is actively involved in teaching and academic activities focused on social sciences, contributing to the understanding of societal structures, cultural perspectives, and human behavior. His work emphasizes the application of theoretical frameworks to real-world social issues, fostering critical thinking and analytical skills among students. Dr. Dilshod participates in curriculum development, student mentoring, and scholarly discussions, supporting a collaborative and engaging learning environment. His academic interests may include sociology, social policy, and educational development. Through his contributions, he plays an important role in strengthening social science education and preparing students for academic and professional growth.

Marwa Belal is an Assistant Lecturer in Business Administration and a Ph.D. researcher in Consumer Behavior. Her academic interests center on impulsive buying behavior, chatbots, and augmented reality in marketing. She is dedicated to exploring how advanced technologies influence consumer decision-making and shape the future of digital retail experiences.

Lalit Garg is a Senior Lecturer in Computer Information Systems at the University of Malta, Malta, and an honorary lecturer at the University of Liverpool, UK. He has been a researcher at the Nanyang Technological University, Singapore, and Ulster University, UK. He has supervised 200+ Masters' dissertations, 2 DBA and 2 PhD thesis and authored 120+ high impact publications in refereed journals/ conferences/books, five edited books and 20 patents. He has delivered several keynotes and organized/chaired international conferences, and consulted numerous public and private organizations for their IS implementation and management. His research interests are business intelligence, machine learning, data science, deep learning, cloud computing, mobile computing, Internet of Things (IoT), information systems, management science and their applications mainly in healthcare and medical domains. He participates in many EU, and local funded projects, including a one million euros Erasmus+ Capacity-Building project in Higher Education (CBHE) titled Training for Medical education via innovative eTechnology (MediTec). The University of Malta has awarded him the 2021-22 Research Excellence Fund.

Yogita Gigras, Associate Professor, Department of Computer Science and Engineering, The NorthCap University, Gurugram, Haryana, India. She is a highly experienced academic and research scholar with more than 16 years of experience in teaching and mentoring students at the undergraduate as well as postgraduate levels. Presently, she is an Associate Professor in the Department of Computer Science and Engineering at The NorthCap University. Her area of expertise includes an extensive range of areas of computer science with emphasis on Soft Computing, Cyber Security, Blockchain, and Machine Learning. She has a Ph.D. in Soft Computing and M.Tech in Computer Science and Engineering from Banasthali

University, Rajasthan (2009) with honors. She has also received industrial experience by undergoing training at ST Microelectronics, Greater Noida, where she developed live projects for her M.Tech degree. Her research areas are the Analysis and Design of Algorithms, Object-Oriented Programming, Operating Systems, Computer Networks, Cyber Security Risk Analysis, Web & Mobile Security, and Blockchain Technology. She has successfully guided 35 B.Tech projects, 14 M.Tech theses, and 2 Ph.D. scholars. Through a robust publications record, Dr. Gigras has published more than 42 research articles in high-impact, peer-reviewed international journals and conferences. She has also published a book entitled "Internet of Healthcare Things: Machine Learning for Security and Privacy" (Wiley). She is an active researcher in academic publishing as a reviewer and assistant editor for various international journals. Her credentials are also complemented by certifications in Microsoft Azure AI-900, Data Science, Exploratory Data Analysis, and Cloud Computing. She is also an Ethical Hacker and AWS Cloud Practitioner certification holder. Apart from her academic background, she also has 5 patents, of which one has been awarded. She is interested in facilitating experiential learning and innovation and was a key driver in creating the Tinkering Lab at The NorthCap University. She was also instrumental as one of the conveners of the International Conference on Intelligent Systems for Cybersecurity (ISCS 2024), organized at the university. She is a life member of ISTE and still supports the development and expansion of the academic community through her research, teaching, and outreach.

Rituraj Jain is currently working in the Department of Information Technology, Marwadi University, Rajkot, GUjarat, India. He has published many papers in International Journals and Conferences. He has published 4 books. He is an Oracle Database SQL Certified Expert. He is also associated with professional bodies like the Indian Society of Technical Education (ISTE), Computer Science Teachers Association (CSTA), Academy & Industry Research Collaboration Center (AIRCC), International Association of Computer Science and Information Technology (IACSIT), International Association of Engineers (IAENG). His research interests include Cloud Computing, Machine Learning, Deep Learning, Fuzzy Logic, IoT, Genetic Algorithms, Big Data and Software Engineering.

Vishal Jain is presently working as a Professor at the School of Engineering & Technology, Vivekananda Institute of Professional Studies - Technical Campus, New Delhi. Before that, he worked as Professor at Sharda University, Greater Noida and Associate Professor at Bharati Vidyapeeth's Institute of Computer Applications and Management (BVICAM), New Delhi. He has associated as a member of the Faculty Board, Board of Planning and Management, Executive Council, Academic Council, Curriculum Development and Review Committee and Academic Audit of various higher education Institutions. He is associated with Kuala Lumpur University of Science and Technology (KLUST), Malaysia, Lincoln University College, Malaysia and Research Institute of IoT Cybersecurity, Department of Electronic Engineering, National Kaohsiung University of Science and Technology, Taiwan for research oriented activities.

Ashima Kalra is an accomplished academician and researcher with over 21.9 years of teaching and research experience in the field of Electronics and Communication Engineering. She currently serves as an Associate Professor at Chandigarh Engineering College (CGC), Landran, and has held various leadership roles across reputed institutions. Her research interests span machine learning, image processing, fuzzy logic, AI in healthcare, and cybersecurity. She has authored 6 books and edited 2 books and published 40+ peer-reviewed research papers in reputed journals such as PeerJ Computer Science, Optical and Quantum Electronics, and Journal of Food Quality (SCIE/Scopus indexed).Dr. Kalra is also an innovator with 15+ patents, including granted and design patents in AI, IoT, and healthcare. As a Ph.D. graduate from MUIT, Noida, she received a Gold Medal in B.Tech and distinction in M.Tech.She has served as Chair, Reviewer, and TPC Member at national and international conferences and coordinated several AICTE- and ATAL-sponsored Faculty Development Programs. An IEEE and ISTE member, she is actively involved in curriculum coordination, thesis supervision, and academic training at the postgraduate and doctoral levels.

Odilbek Kosimov is an academic professional affiliated with the Department of Information Technology and Exact Sciences at Termez University of Economics and Service, Uzbekistan. His expertise lies in information technology, computational sciences, and applied data-driven solutions. He is actively engaged in teaching, research, and academic development, contributing to the advancement of modern IT education. His interests include artificial intelligence, data analytics, and software systems, with a focus on practical applications that address real-world challenges. Kosimov is committed to fostering innovation, critical thinking, and technical proficiency among students while contributing to collaborative research initiatives in emerging technological domains.

Gularam Masharipova is an academic professional in the Department of Social Science at the University of Management and Future Technologies, Tashkent, Uzbekistan. She is actively engaged in teaching and research, contributing to the advancement of social science education through a multidisciplinary approach. Her academic interests include social development, public policy, and the evolving dynamics of modern societies. Dr. Masharipova emphasizes critical thinking, analytical reasoning, and practical application of theoretical concepts in her teaching methodology, fostering an engaging and student-centered learning environment. She participates in academic seminars, workshops, and collaborative research activities, contributing to scholarly discussions at both national and international levels. Her work reflects a commitment to understanding societal challenges and promoting sustainable and inclusive development. Through her academic contributions, she continues to support the intellectual growth of students and the broader advancement of social science research.

Archan Mitra is an Assistant Professor at School of Media Studies (SOMS) at Presidency University, Bangalore. He is the author of two book "Cases for Classroom Media and Entertainment Business" and "Multiverse and Media", he also has other several edited books to his credit. He has done his doctorate from Visva-Bharati Santiniketan, West Bengal in the field of "environmental informatics and communication for sustainability". In addition to that he is a certified Science Communicator and Journalism from Indian Science Communication Society (ISCOS), certified Corporate Trainer with Amity Institute of Training and Development, Certified Social Media Network Analyst. He has a strong interest in environmental communication. He was awarded certificate of merit by PRSI, Kolkata Chapter and Medal of Honor by Journalistic Club of Kolkata. He was working as a research assistant with the World Bank's "Environmental Capacity Building in Southeast Asia" project at IIM Kashipur. He was instrumental in launching the World Bank's Green MBA MOOC, he has also assisted in the research project on Uttarakhand disaster mitigation by ICSSR, the leading research on Uttarakhand disaster.

Lalit Narendra Patil is an Associate Professor in the Department of Automation and Robotics at Dr. D. Y. Patil Institute of Technology, Pimpri, Pune, India. With a strong academic and research background, he specializes in advanced topics related to automation, robotics, and intelligent systems. Dr. Patil is committed to fostering innovation and excellence in engineering education and has contributed significantly through research publications and project guidance

Sanchita Paul is a dedicated and accomplished content strategist with extensive experience in managing diverse content formats across different digital platforms. With a strong background in content strategy, editing, and UX writing, she has honed her skills in branding, social media management, and technical writing. Holding an MA in Communication and Journalism from Visva-Bharati University, Ms. Paul is proficient in tools like Google Analytics, Canva, and MS Office Suite, making her a versatile professional committed to producing high-quality, impactful content to improve brand visibility.

Ravikumar R. N. is currently a Postdoctoral Researcher at Universiti Malaysia Perlis, Malaysia, and also serves as an Associate Professor in the Department of Computer Science and Engineering at Marwadi University, Rajkot, India. He has more than 14 years of national and international teaching experience. He completed his Ph.D. from Amity University, Rajasthan, M.E. from VMRF Deemed University, and B.E. from Anna University, Chennai. He actively trains and mentors students in research activities, contributing to various scholarly publications. He has published numerous research articles in Scopus and SCI-indexed journals, book chapters, and conference proceedings. He also holds several patents and has authored books. His areas of specialization include Machine Learning, Deep Learning, Federated Learning, Recommendation Systems, and Optimization Techniques.

Fatma Ragab is an Assistant Lecturer in Business Administration and a Ph.D. researcher in the field of Consumer Behavior. Her research interests include branding, inclusivity, and innovative marketing technologies such as chatbots. She is particularly focused on how emerging digital tools can enhance customer experience and strengthen brand-consumer relationships in today's dynamic marketing environment.

Bobur Rajapov is an academic professional affiliated with the Department of Philology at Mamun University, Khiva, Uzbekistan. With a strong foundation in language studies and literary analysis, his academic work centers on the exploration of linguistic structures, literary traditions, and cultural narratives. He is actively involved in teaching and mentoring students, fostering critical thinking and effective communication skills through a comprehensive understanding of philological concepts. Dr. Rajapov's research interests include comparative literature, discourse analysis, and the evolution of language in socio-cultural contexts. He contributes to academic scholarship through participation in conferences, seminars, and research initiatives that promote the study of language and literature. Known for his dedication to academic excellence, he integrates traditional and modern approaches in teaching, supporting the intellectual development of students and contributing to the advancement of philological studies in the region.

Aarthi S is a dedicated Assistant Professor in Computer Science with over six years of teaching experience. She is currently pursuing her Ph.D. at Marwadi University, Gujarat, and holds an M.Phil. and MCA from Bharathiar University, Tamil Nadu. Throughout her academic career, Aarthi has specialized in programming languages such as C++, Java, and C, and contributed to research in recommender systems and AI-related data privacy. She has published journal articles, contributed to book chapters, and actively participated in technical workshops. Known for her student mentorship and engagement in academic events, Aarthi remains committed to fostering innovation and excellence in computer science education.

Asha Sohal is an Assistant Professor (Selection Grade) in the school of computer science and engineering, The NorthCap University, Haryana, India. She has followed a challenging academic path to obtain a Ph.D. in Computer Science and Applications from Kurukshetra University in 2024. Before that, she had finished her M.Tech. in IT from GGSIPU, Delhi in 2011, continuing to develop their skills. Their academic background comprises B.Tech in CSE from Kurukshetra University in 2003, which marked the beginning of their illustrious career in academia. A dedicated and result-driven professional with more than 21 years of rich experience in teaching, administration, and research, showing a firm commitment towards academic excellence and organizational growth. Her research activities are mainly focused on Cloud Computing, fog computing and mobile adhoc networks (MANETs). By carrying out their vast work in these areas, they intend to make significant contributions to the growth of knowledge and creation of innovative solutions for addressing emerging challenges. She has mentored 60+ B.Tech, B.Sc(H), BCA, MCA and M.Tech Projects. She has authored approximately 35 papers in indexed International Journals of high standards and reputed national/international conference proceedings, authored a book on Qualitative Research design: An Interactive Approach in River publications and approximately 27 book chapters in reputed publications. She is an international journal reviewer. She is also certified in cloud computing from NPTEL. She have been awarded the chancellor's excellence award-2019 to appreciate their remarkable contributions towards academia and towards the institution.

Kamal Upreti is currently working as an Associate Professor in Department of Computer Science, CHRIST (Deemed to be University), Delhi NCR, Ghaziabad, India. He completed is B. Tech (Hons) Degree from UPTU, M. Tech (Gold Medalist), PGDM(Executive) from IMT Ghaziabad and PhD in Department of Computer Science & Engineering.He has completed Postdoc from National Taipei University of Business, TAIWAN funded by MHRD. He has published 50+ Patents, 32+Magazine issues and 110+ Research papers in in various reputed Journals and international Conferences. His areas of Interest such as Modern Physics, Data Analytics, Cyber Security, Machine Learning, Health Care, Embedded System and Cloud Computing. He has published more than 45+ authored and edited books under CRC Press, IGI Global, Oxford Press and Arihant Publication. He is having enriched years' experience in corporate and teaching experience in Engineering Colleges.

Index

A

C

D

E

G

www.ingramcontent.com/pod-product-compliance
Lightning Source LLC
LaVergne TN
LVHW081529300926
849161LV00006B/1358